WITHDRAWN
UTSA LIBRARIES

YOUTH IN THE ROMAN EMPIRE

Modern society has a negative view of youth as a period of storm and stress, but at the same time cherishes the idea of eternal youth. How does this compare with ancient Roman society? Did a phase of youth exist there with its own characteristics? How was youth appreciated? This book studies the lives and the image of youngsters (around fifteen to twenty-five years of age) in the Latin West and the Greek East in the Roman period. Boys and girls of all social classes come to the fore; their lives, public and private, are sketched with the help of a range of textual and documentary sources, while the authors also employ the results of recent neuropsychological research. The result is a highly readable and wide-ranging account of how the crucial transition between childhood and adulthood operated in the Roman world.

CHRISTIAN LAES is Associate Professor of Latin and Ancient History at the Free University of Brussels and at the University of Antwerp. He has published five monographs and over fifty international contributions on social history, especially the human life course in Roman antiquity. Childhood, youth, old age, marriage, and sexuality – as well as disability – are the main focuses of his scholarly work. His book *Children in the Roman Empire* was published by Cambridge in 2011.

JOHAN STRUBBE was formerly Senior Lecturer in the Department of Ancient History at the University of Leiden. In his research he has focused on the Greek epigraphy of Asia Minor, and has published many articles on social and economic subjects; he has also published two corpora of Greek inscriptions. His second long-standing interest is in children and youth in ancient society on which he has published several articles, for example on consolation decrees for youngsters and on public offices held by young people.

To Emiel Eyben (1942–2013)
Qui post tantum onus, multos crebrosque labores
Nunc silet et tacito contentus sede quiescit.
(CIL VIII 2401; CLE 573)

YOUTH IN THE ROMAN EMPIRE

The young and the restless years?

CHRISTIAN LAES
JOHAN STRUBBE

CAMBRIDGE
UNIVERSITY PRESS

University Printing House, Cambridge CB2 8BS, United Kingdom

Published in the United States of America by Cambridge University Press, New York

Cambridge University Press is part of the University of Cambridge.

It furthers the University's mission by disseminating knowledge in the pursuit of education, learning, and research at the highest international levels of excellence.

www.cambridge.org
Information on this title: www.cambridge.org/9781107048881

Original Dutch edition © Christian Laes, Johan Strubbe, and Davidsfonds Uitgeverij NV 2008
Originally entitled *Jeugd in het Romeinse Rijk: Jonge jaren, wilde haren?*

This English translation © Cambridge University Press 2014

This publication is in copyright. Subject to statutory exception and to the provisions of relevant collective licensing agreements, no reproduction of any part may take place without the written permission of Cambridge University Press.

First published 2008
This English edition 2014

Printed in the United Kingdom by Clays, St Ives plc

A catalogue record for this publication is available from the British Library

Library of Congress Cataloguing in Publication data
Laes, Christian.
[Jeugd in het Romeinse Rijk. English]
Youth in the Roman empire : the young and the restless years? / Christian Laes,
Johan Strubbe.
 pages cm
Originally entitled Jeugd in het Romeinse Rijk. First published: Leuven : Davidsfonds, 2008.
Includes bibliographical references and index.
ISBN 978-1-107-04888-1 (alk. paper)
1. Youth – Rome – History. 2. Youth – Rome – Social conditions. 3. Rome – History – Empire, 30 BC – AD 284   I. Strubbe, J. H. M. II. Title.
DG91.L3313 2014
937'.06083–dc23
2013048048

ISBN 978-1-107-04888-1 Hardback

Cambridge University Press has no responsibility for the persistence or accuracy of URLs for external or third-party internet websites referred to in this publication, and does not guarantee that any content on such websites is, or will remain, accurate or appropriate.

Library
University of Texas
at San Antonio

Contents

List of illustrations		*page* viii
List of tables		ix
Preface		xi
List of abbreviations		xv

1	Questioning the concept of youth	1
	1.1 A problem of definition	1
	1.2 Mead in Samoa	3
	1.3 Ariès, Shorter, and Stone: in search of change in history	7
	1.4 Philosophers, psychologists, and sociologists on the invention of youth	11
	1.5 Ancient history and the controversy over youth: Eyben versus Pleket and Kleijwegt	14
	1.6 New challenges for ancient historians	20

2	Minority, majority: youth, divisions of the human life cycle, and Roman law	23
	2.1 Youth and the division of the life cycle	23
	2.2 Roman law	30
	2.3 Ages in practice	37

3	Terminology and characteristics of youth	41
	3.1 Terminology	41
	3.2 Characteristics of youths and adolescents	42

4	Rites of passage	49
	4.1 In the Greek East	49
	4.2 In Rome and the Latin West	55

5	Youth and ancient medicine	61
	5.1 Medical observations concerning young people: similarities and differences	61

v

	5.2	Sickness in teenagers: some examples	65
	5.3	Excursus: Aristotle on puberty	68

6 Youth and education: the rhetor and 'university' — 70

	6.1	The schooling system in the Roman Empire	70
	6.2	Higher education in the Greek East	72
	6.3	Higher education in Rome and the Latin West	79
	6.4	Instruction provided by the rhetor	86
	6.5	Students' lives at 'university'	92
	6.6	The instruction of girls	99
	6.7	Excursus: Ovid's education	102

7 Associations of adolescent youths — 104

	7.1	Greek ephebes	104
	7.2	Excursus: the honorary decree for Menas of Sestus	120
	7.3	Roman *iuvenes*	122
	7.4	Concluding remarks	133

8 Youthful behaviour — 136

	8.1	'Restlessness'	136
	8.2	Conflict	149
	8.3	Excursus: letter of Marcus Cicero Jr	162

9 Youths in public office — 164

	9.1	Youths in central government: senators and equestrians	164
	9.2	Youths in municipal office	169
	9.3	Concluding remarks	181

10 Occupational training — 184

	10.1	Physicians and jurists in East and West	184
	10.2	Other occupations	191
	10.3	Excursus: the schooling of the physician Galen	195

11 Marriage — 197

	11.1	Roman marriage as an institution	197
	11.2	Age at first marriage	199
	11.3	Wedding ceremonies	201
	11.4	What did it mean to contract a marriage?	206
	11.5	Marriage as the end of youth for boys?	209
	11.6	Girls and marriage: a history of submission?	210

12	Youth and Christianity: continuity or change?		215
	12.1	Early Christians: a young church?	216
	12.2	Young office-holders within the church	218
	12.3	Young people and sexuality	221
	12.4	Excursus: a real-life case of early Christian youth: the *Vita Severi*	225
13	Conclusion		228

Bibliography 233
Index 249

Illustrations

2.1	Sarcophagus of the four seasons, third century AD. Capitoline Museum, Palace of the Conservators, Rome.	*page* 25
3.1	Bronze honorary statue of a runner from Cyme, late first century BC. Archaeological Museum, Izmir.	45
7.1	The Ephebe of Tralleis, late first century BC. Archaeological Museum, Istanbul.	105
8.1	Antinous, Archaeological Museum, Delphi.	142
8.2	Marcus Tullius Cicero, Capitoline Museum, Rome.	156
11.1	Mummy mask of Aphrodite, daughter of Didas, from Hawara, Fayum, *c.* AD 50–70. British Museum, London.	211
13.1	Fresco from Herculaneum (*c.* AD 70). National Archaeological Museum, Naples.	229

Tables

2.1	The division of the human life cycle into four stages	*page* 25
2.2	The division of the life cycle into five stages (Varro)	26
2.3	The division of the human life cycle into seven stages (Ps.-Hippocrates)	27
2.4	The division of the human life cycle into seven stages (Pollux)	27
12.1	The ecclesiastical career (mid-fourth century)	220

Preface

In 2007 it was *The Young Roman*'s thirtieth birthday. Back in 1977 the Leuven scholar Emiel Eyben published his monumental work *De jonge Romein volgens de literaire bronnen der periode c. 200 v. Chr. tot c. 500 n. Chr.* (The Young Roman according to the Literary Sources from the Period c. 200 BC–AD 500) with the Royal Academy of Belgium. This impressive volume of about 700 pages set the basis for a series of other books. In 1987, Eyben published a concise version for a larger Dutch reading public: *De onstuimigen. Jeugd en (on)deugd in het oude Rome* (The Restless. Youth and Virtue/Vice in Ancient Rome). In 1993 the English edition, *Restless Youth in Ancient Rome* (Routledge), brought him international fame. Eyben is also the author of an abundant stream of scholarly and more popular articles on 'his' subject, the Roman adolescent. His wide-ranging scholarship and his fine sense for every single Greek or Latin text which could offer even the tiniest clue enabled him to sketch a *Gesamtbild* of Roman youthful life. It is hard to think of any subject that is not discussed in Eyben's oeuvre: the Roman view of youth (life stages, juridical and medical or biological demarcations of puberty, explanations of the stormy crisis of adolescents' life), the daily whereabouts of the young Roman (his recreational life, youth as a military or a political force), his way of thinking (perception of study, rhetoric, philosophy, and even youthful poetry), his affective life (love, friendship, idols, parents, and religion). Basically, in Eyben's view the Romans perceived adolescence as a separate period of human life with its own characteristics, and Roman adolescents were much comparable to modern adolescents.

Eyben's work did not remain without criticism. It was generally objected that his picture of the Roman adolescent was overly biased by psychological approaches from the stormy sixties of the twentieth century. Eyben's young Romans look like hippies in toga: pacifists or impetuous rebels, pubescents with rosy cheeks and clammy hands, vexed by generational conflicts and *Sturm und Drang*. Eyben's picture of the Roman youth was also criticised from a methodological point of view, mainly by scholars from Leiden (The Netherlands). Marc Kleijwegt, who followed in the path of his supervisor Harry Pleket, submitted the concept of adolescence to a critical historical analysis in a comparative perspective. In his book bearing the telling title *Ancient Youth. The Ambiguity of Youth and the Absence of Adolescence*, published in 1991, he focused on epigraphic sources more than on literary texts. Kleijwegt argued that the concept of adolescence, which is basically psychologically coloured, was unknown to the Romans. Young Romans quite early in their lives took on political or occupational responsibilities; they were expected to act as adults and conformed to adult society from an early age. Since Kleijwegt's book, there has been a remarkable silence on the subject of youth as far as Roman antiquity is concerned.[1] The question as to whether these two apparently opposite views may be reconciled is still an open one. In this book we attempt to evaluate these views; by using a broad combination of all kinds of sources (literary, epigraphic and many others) we try to avoid the rather one-sided approaches of Eyben and Kleijwegt.

The book focuses on youth in the Roman Empire, boys as well as girls, roughly from their mid-teens to their mid-twenties. We study the Greek East from the Hellenistic period (approximately 300 BC) to late antiquity, and the Latin West, including the capital of Rome, from the late Republic (c. 200 BC) to the end of the Empire (approximately AD 500). In an earlier book on Roman children Laes has argued that it is indeed justified to treat such a long period of time over such a vast geographical area as a whole.[2] The basic questions we ask about youth in the Roman Empire are the following. Do juridical texts and social practice allow us to use the concept of youth for Roman antiquity? If this is indeed the case, which age groups are involved? Are there any differences between social classes, between boys and girls? We will also try to sketch the rich and very diverse lives of Roman youngsters, using specific cases. Did they undergo specific ceremonies or rites of passage? How did ancient doctors view them? What forms of higher education did they attend? Did there exist associations or groups of youths? Were youths involved in politics and did they take up their responsibility early by holding important offices? At what age did they start to work? Was there anything like a youthful recreational life? Did marriage bring about

---

[1] Exceptions are the volumes edited by Levi and Schmitt 1996 and the article by the Spanish scholar Bancalari Molina 1998, which does not offer much new. Contributions which explicitly discuss Eyben's approach include Christes 1998 and Vatai 2004.
[2] Laes 2006a: 264–7 and 2011: 2–6.

the end of youth? Did Christianity cause changes in expectations about young people's behaviour?

This book can be read on two levels. For the general reader with a broad cultural and historical interest, the book offers an overall picture of the lives of Roman boys and girls. This picture is based on literary sources, inscriptions and papyri and takes into account new findings and scholarly literature up to 2009 (see below). Indeed, new papyri, new archaeological evidence and above all new inscriptions emerge every year and constantly broaden our knowledge of antiquity. Many subjects will be familiar to the Roman social historian, but the general topics from social history are here applied to the young in particular. For the ancient historian, the book not only offers a *status quaestionis* of the problem of youth, but also new approaches and new views on many subjects. New views are based on a thorough and scholarly study of the ancient sources, which is rather technical (e.g. Chapters 7 and 9), but is conveniently summarised for the general reader in the concluding remarks. New approaches are based on sociology, psychology, anthropology, and modern literary science, which generate new insights and induce the historian to ask new questions. The specialist historian will thus recognise the use of new tendencies in research: attention is paid to the formation of groups of peers, interaction, and conflicts with the elder, feasts, ceremonies, and other cultural practices which enabled young people to experience their own youth subculture, or even different styles of being young.[3]

This book is a slightly adapted version of the Dutch book, *Jeugd in het Romeinse Rijk. Jonge jaren, wilde haren?*, published in 2008 by the two authors with Davidsfonds, Leuven. The manuscript of the English version was completed in 2009. Only a few very important studies published after 2009 have been incorporated in the present book. All translations of the sources are our own, unless indicated. With respect to inscriptions and papyri, we do not give a complete bibliography but refer only to standard editions and recent or easily accessible re-editions. Square brackets are used in translations to indicate that text has been restored; round brackets indicate editorial additions.

We are grateful to our editor at Cambridge University Press, Dr Michael Sharp, not only for accepting our book but also for correcting the English of the first five chapters. For the other chapters, we gratefully acknowledge corrections by Stephen Windross. Both the University of Antwerp and the

---

[3] On these tendencies, see Krausman Ben-Amos 2004.

Universitaire Stichting generously funded costs involved in the revision of the English.

Thanks are also due to the anonymous readers, both from Cambridge University Press and Universitaire Stichting, for their valuable suggestions.

The original book was dedicated to Emiel Eyben on the occasion of his 65th birthday in 2007. Both authors wish to rededicate the present book to Eyben, in memory of his warm character and passionate scholarship. Sadly, Emiel Eyben did not live to see the publication of this book. He passed away on 11 September 2013.

Abbreviations

The abbreviations of editions of sources are in line with the standard publications named below, in which the reader will find bibliographical data for all the editions used.

Greek inscriptions: *Supplementum Epigraphicum Graecum. Consolidated Index for Volumes* XXXVI–XLV *(1986–1995)* (*SEG*) (ed. J. H. M. Strubbe; Amsterdam, 1999), pp. 677–88 and subsequent volumes of *SEG*.

Latin inscriptions: *L'Année Épigraphique* (*AnÉp*) (2004) (Paris, 2007) pp. 699–705 and the *Epigraphische Datenbank Frankfurt* (*EDCS*) (http://www.manfredclauss.de).

Papyri: *Checklist of Editions of Greek, Latin, Demotic and Coptic Papyri, Ostraca and Tablets* (eds. J. F. Oates *et al.*; Oakville, Conn., 2001) (http://scriptorium.lib.duke.edu/papyrus/texts/clist.html).

NON-LITERARY SOURCES

AnÉp	*L'Année Épigraphique*
BGU	*Aegyptische Urkunden aus den Königlichen* (later *Staatlichen*) *Museen zu Berlin, Griechische Urkunden*
Boubon	*Boubon. The Inscriptions and Archaeological Remains. A Survey 2004–2006* (C. Kokkinia)
CIL	*Corpus Inscriptionum Latinarum*
CIRB	*Corpus Inscriptionum Regni Bosporani* (V. V. Struve etc.)
CLE	*Carmina Latina Epigraphica* (F. Bücheler)
Cod. Iust.	*Codex Iustinianus*
Cod. Theod.	*Codex Theodosianus*
Dig.	*Digesta*
EAOR II–III	*Epigrafia anfiteatrale dell'Occidente Romano* II (G. L. Gregori), III (M. Buonocore)
EDCS	*Epigraphische Datenbank Frankfurt*

ERRioja	*Epigrafía Romana de la Rioja* (U. Espinoza)
FD	*Fouilles de Delphes*
Gaius, Inst.	*Gaius, Institutiones*
GG	*Griechische Grabgedichte* (W. Peek)
GV	*Griechische Vers-Inschriften* (W. Peek)
I. Beroia	*Epigraphes Kato Makedonias* 1. *Epigraphes Beroias* (L. Gounaropoulou and M. Hatzopoulos)
I. Bubon	*Die Inschriften von Bubon (Nordlykien)* (F. Schindler)
I. Ephesos	*Die Inschriften von Ephesos* (H. Wankel, R. Merkelbach etc.)
I. Hadrianoi	*Die Inschriften von Hadrianoi und Hadrianeia* (E. Schwertheim)
I. Heraclea Pontica	*The Inscriptions of Heraclea Pontica* (L. Jonnes)
I. Iasos	*Die Inschriften von Iasos* (W. Blümel)
I. Kaunos	*Die Inschriften von Kaunos* (Chr. Marek)
I. Klaudiupolis	*Die Inschriften von Klaudiupolis* (F. Becker-Bertau)
I. Metropolis I	*Die Inschriften von Metropolis I* (B. Dreyer and H. Engelmann)
I. Pergamon	*Die Inschriften von Pergamon* (M. Fraenkel)
I. Perge	*Die Inschriften von Perge* (S. Şahin)
I. Priene	*Die Inschriften von Priene* (F. Hiller von Gaertringen)
I. Prusa	*Die Inschriften von Prusa ad Olympum* (Th. Corsten)
I. Sestos	*Die Inschriften von Sestos und der thrakischen Chersones* (J. Krauss)
I. Smyrna	*Die Inschriften von Smyrna* (G. Petzl)
I. Stratonikeia	*Die Inschriften von Stratonikeia* (M. Şahin)
IDRE	*Inscriptiones Daciae Romanae. Inscriptions de la Dacie Romaine. Inscriptions externes concernant l'histoire de la Dacie (1er s. – IIIe s.)* (C. Petolescu)
IG	*Inscriptiones Graecae*
IGBulg	*Inscriptiones Graecae in Bulgaria repertae* (G. Mihailov)
IGR	*Inscriptiones Graecae ad res Romanas pertinentes*
IGUR	*Inscriptiones Graecae Urbis Romae* (L. Moretti)
ILJug	*Inscriptiones Latinae quae in Iugoslavia inter annos* MCMXL *et* MCMLX *repertae et editae sunt* (A. and J. Šašel)
ILN III	*Inscriptions latines de Narbonnaise* III. *Aix-en-Provence* (J. Gascou)

List of abbreviations

ILTun	*Inscriptions latines de la Tunisie* (A. Merlin)
InscrIt	*Inscriptiones Italiae*
Inst. Iust.	*Institutiones Iustinianae*
IRC IV	*Inscriptions romaines de Catalogne* IV. *Barcino* (G. Fabre etc.)
IulCarnicum	*Iulium Carnicum (Zuglio)* (P. M. Moro)
LBW	*Voyage archéologique* ... (Ph. Le Bas and W. H. Waddington)
MAMA	*Monumenta Asiae Minoris Antiqua*
Michel	*Recueil d'inscriptions grecques* (Ch. Michel)
Nov.	*Novellae*
P. Alex. Giss.	*Papyri variae Alexandrinae et Gissenses*
P. Giss.	*Griechische Papyri im Museum des oberhessischen Geschichtsvereins zu Giessen*
P. Hamb.	*Griechische Papyrusurkunden der Hamburger Staats- und Universitätsbibliothek*
P. Laur.	*Dai papyri della Biblioteca Medicea Laurenziana*
P. Lond.	*Greek Papyri in the British Museum*
P. Mich.	*Michigan Papyri*
P. Mil. Vogl.	*Papiri della R. Università di Milano*
P. Oxy.	*The Oxyrhynchus Papyri*
P. Tebt.	*The Tebtunis Papyri*
RHP I	*Die römischen Hilfstruppen in Pannonien während der Prinzipatszeit* I. *Die Inschriften* (B. Lőrincz)
RIB I	*The Roman Inscriptions of Britain* I. *Inscriptions on Stone* (R. G. Collingwood and R. P. Wright)
SB	*Sammelbuch griechischer Urkunden aus Aegypten*
SEG	*Supplementum Epigraphicum Graecum*
SGO	*Steinepigramme aus dem griechischen Osten* (R. Merkelbach and J. Stauber)
Syll.³	*Sylloge Inscriptionum Graecarum (3rd edn)* (W. Dittenberger)
TAM	*Tituli Asiae Minoris*
Tit. Ulp.	*Tituli Ulpiani*
ZaCarnuntum	*Zivilinschriften aus Carnuntum* (E. Vorbeck)

LITERARY WORKS

1 Corinthians	1st Epistle to the Corinthians (Paul)
1 Peter	1st Epistle of Peter

1 Thessalonians	1st Epistle to the Thessalonians (Paul)
1 Timothy	1st Epistle to Timothy (Paul)
Ps.-Acro, *Schol. in Hor. Serm.*	*Scholia in Horatium. Sermones*
Aetius, *Plac.*	*Placita*
Alexander of Aphrodisias, *Problem.*	*Problemata*
Ambrose, *De Abr.*	*De Abraham*
Anth. Pal.	*Anthologia Palatina*
Apuleius, *Apol.*	*Apologia*
Met.	*Metamorphoses*
Aristotle, *De gen. anim.*	*De generatione animalium*
Hist. anim.	*Historia animalium*
Rhet.	*Rhetorica*
Arnobius, *Adv. nat.*	*Adversus nationes*
Athanasius, *Vita Anton.*	*Vita Antonii*
Augustine, *Conf.*	*Confessiones*
De civ. Dei	*De civitate Dei*
Epist.	*Epistulae*
Ausonius, *Epitaph.*	*Epitaphia*
B. Ber.	Babylonian Talmud, *tract. Berachot*
Cassius Dio, *Hist. Rom.*	*Historia Romana*
Cassius Felix, *De med.*	*De medicina*
Celsus, *De med.*	*De medicina*
Censorinus, *De die nat.*	*De die natali*
Cicero, *Ad Att.*	*Epistulae ad Atticum*
Ad fam.	*Epistulae ad familiares*
Brut.	*Brutus*
De off.	*De officiis*
De orat.	*De oratore*
De senect.	*De senectute*
Phil.	*Philippicae*
Pro Cael.	*Pro Caelio*
Pro Sest.	*Pro Sestio*
Top.	*Topica*
Tusc. disp.	*Tusculanae disputationes*
Clement of Rome, *Epist. ad Corinth.*	*Epistulae ad Corinthios*
Cyprian, *Epist.*	*Epistulae*

List of abbreviations

Ps.-Cyprian, *De sing. cler.*	*De singularitate clericorum*
Demosthenes, *Or.*	*Orationes*
Diogenes Laertius, *Vitae philos.*	*Vitae philosophorum*
Eumenius, *Pro inst. scholis*	*Pro instaurandis scholis oratio* (Panegyrici Latini IX)
Eunapius, *Vitae sophist.*	*Vitae sophistarum*
Euripides, *Ph.*	*Phoenissae*
Eusebius, *Hist. eccles.*	*Historia ecclesiastica*
Festus, *De signif. verb.*	*De significatione verborum* (ed. Lindsay)
Florus, *Epit.*	*Epitome*
Fronto, *Eloq.*	*Ad M. Antoninum de eloquentia liber* (ed. van den Hout)
Galatians	Epistle to the Galatians (Paul)
Galen (ed. Kühn),	
Comm. in Hipp. Aph.	*In Hippocratis Aphorismos commentarii*
Comm. in Hipp. Epid.	*In Hippocratis Epidemiarum librum* VI *commentarii*
Comm. in Hipp. Hum.	*In Hippocratis de Humoribus librum commentarii*
De comp.	*De compositione medicamentorum per genera*
De diff.	*De differentia pulsuum*
De loc. aff.	*De locis affectis*
De meth. med.	*De methodo medendi*
De opt. med. cogn.	*De optimo medico cognoscendo*
De ord. libr.	*De ordine librorum suorum*
De praen.	*De praenotione ad Epigenem*
De prob.	*De probis pravisque alimentorum sucis*
De san. tuenda	*De sanitate tuenda*
De sem.	*De semine*
De temp.	*De temperamentis*
De usu part.	*De usu partium*
Gellius, *Noctes Att.*	*Noctes Atticae*
Georgius of Eleusis, *Vita Theod. Sic.*	*Vita Theodori Siceotae*
Gregory of Nazianzus, *Carm.*	*Carmina*
Or.	*Orationes*
Heraclitus (ed. Diels)	
Hippocrates (ed. Littré), *Aph.*	*Aphorismi*

De affect. int.   *De affectionibus interioribus*
De morb.   *De morbis*
De virg. morb.   *De virginum morbis*
Ps.-Hippocrates, *De hebd.*   *De hebdomadibus*
Homer, *Il.*   *Iliad*
Horace, *Ars poet.*   *Ars poetica*
Ignatius, *Epist. ad Magn.*   *Epistula ad Magnesios*
Isidore of Seville, *Diff.*   *Differentiae*
    Lib. num.   *Liber numerorum*
    Orig.   *Origines*
Jerome, *Adv. Rufinum*   *Apologia adversus Rufinum*
    Comm. in Isaiam   *Commentarii in Isaiam libri* XII
John Chrysostom, *De sacerd.*   *De sacerdotio*
Juvenal, *Sat.*   *Saturae*
Libanius, *Epist.*   *Epistulae*
    Or.   *Orationes*
Livy, *Ab Urbe cond.*   *Ab Urbe condita*
Lucian, *Somn.*   *Somnium*
Lucretius, *De rer. nat.*   *De rerum natura*
Luke   Gospel according to Luke
Macrobius, *Saturn.*   *Saturnalia*
    Comm. Somn. Scip.   *Commentarii in Somnium Scipionis*
Martial, *Epigr.*   *Epigrammata*
Nonius Marcellus,   *De compendiosa doctrina*
    De comp. doctr.
Olympiodorus of   (apud Photium, *Bibl.* p. 60 B)
    Thebes, fr. 28
Oribasius (ed. Raeder),   *Collectionum medicarum reliquiae*
    Coll. med. rel.
    Lib. inc.   *Liber incertus*
Origen, *Contra Cels.*   *Contra Celsum*
Ovid, *Ars amat.*   *Ars amatoria*
    Fasti   *Fasti*
    Tristia   *Tristia*
Pauline of Nola, *Carm.*   *Carmina*
Paulus, *Sent.*   *Sententiae*
Pausanias, *Perieg.*   *Periegesis*
Persius Flaccus, *Sat.*   *Saturae*
    Schol. ad Pers.   *Scholia ad Persium*

Petronius, *Satyr.*	*Satyrica*
Philippians	Epistle to the Philippians (Paul)
Philo, *Cher.*	*Cherubim*
De opif. mundi	*De opificio mundi*
In Gen.	*In Genesim*
Jos.	*Joseph*
Leg. alleg.	*Legum allegoriae*
Philostratus, *Vita Apoll.*	*Vita Apollonii*
Vitae sophist.	*Vitae sophistarum*
Photius, *Bibl.*	*Bibliotheca*
PL	*Patrologia Latina*
Plautus, *Curc.*	*Curculio*
Pseud.	*Pseudolus*
Pliny (the Younger), *Epist.*	*Epistulae*
Pliny the Elder, *Nat. hist.*	*Naturalis historia*
Plutarch, *Cleom.*	*Cleomenes*
De E apud Delph.	*De E apud Delphos*
De mul. virt.	*De mulierum virtutibus*
Mor.	*Moralia*
Numa	*Numa*
Praec. coniug.	*Praecepta coniugalia*
Quaest. conv.	*Quaestiones convivales*
Ps.-Plutarch, *De lib. educ.*	*De liberis educandis*
Pollux, *Onom.*	*Onomasticon*
Polycarpus, *Epist. ad Philipp.*	*Epistula ad Philippenses*
Propertius, *Eleg.*	*Elegiae*
Ptolemy, *Tetr.*	*Tetrabiblos*
Quintilian, *Inst. or.*	*Institutio oratoria*
Ps.-Quintilian, *Decl.*	*Declamationes*
R. Benedicti	*Regula Benedicti*
Sallust, *Cat.*	*Catiline*
Seneca, *Ad Helv.*	*Ad Helviam*
De ben.	*De beneficiis*
De clem.	*De clementia*
De const. sap.	*De constantia sapientis*
Epist. mor.	*Epistulae morales*
Seneca the Elder (Rhetor), *Contr.*	*Controversiae*
Suas.	*Suasoriae*

Servius, *Comm. Aen.*	*Commentarii in Vergilii Aeneidos libros*
Comm. Ecl.	*Commentarii in Vergilii Bucolica*
SHA	*Scriptores Historiae Augustae*
Siricius, *Epist.*	*Epistulae* (Migne, *PL* 13)
Solon (*Fragmenta* ed. Diehl)	
Sophocles, *Ter.*	*Tereus* (*Fragmenta* ed. Radt; ed. Nauck)
Soranus, *Gyn.*	*Gynaecia*
Statius, *Silv.*	*Silvae*
Strabo, *Geogr.*	*Geographica*
Suetonius, *Aug.*	*Augustus*
Cal.	*Caligula*
De gramm.	*De grammaticis*
De rhet.	*De rhetoribus*
Jul.	*Julius*
Nero	*Nero*
Otho	*Otho*
Vesp.	*Vespasianus*
Tacitus, *Ann.*	*Annales*
Dial. de orat.	*Dialogus de oratoribus*
Terence, *Andria*	*Andria*
Tertullian, *De an.*	*De anima*
Test. Porcelli	*Testamentum Porcelli*
Thucydides, *Hist.*	*Historiae*
Titus	Epistle to Titus (Paul)
Valerius Maximus, *Fact. et dict. mem.*	*Facta et dicta memorabilia*
Varro, *De ling. Lat.*	*De lingua Latina*
Men.	*Menippearum fragmenta* (ed. Bücheler; ed. Cèbe)
Vita Marci Aur.	*Vita Marci Aurelii Antonini* (*SHA* by Julius Capitolinus)
Vita Melaniae	
Zacharias Scholasticus, *Vita Sev.*	*Vita Severi* (ed. Kügener)
Zosimus, *Epist.*	*Epistulae* (Migne, *PL* 20)

CHAPTER I

Questioning the concept of youth

1.1 A problem of definition

> We are living in a period of considerable indignation and concern about our young people. If we believe the media, there is little right with today's youth: they drink too much, they overindulge in sex and violence, they hang around the streets and disturb the neighbourhood, they are irresponsible in taking risks and not thinking about the future, they have no concern for other people and are only interested in their own gain, they are self-indulgent and lazy, and are obsessed by the internet. In education there is a culture of 'a pass is good enough' – and these malingerers then have the nerve to go on strike!

These are the opening words of a lecture delivered in 2008 by P. M. Westenberg, Professor of Developmental and Educational Psychology at Leiden University in the Netherlands. The lecture was on 'The Youth of Today!' Westenberg and his team at the Leiden Brain and Development Lab have studied the cognitive and psychological development of adolescents. Their research has demonstrated that the brain is not fully developed at the end of childhood: the brain continues to mature up to the age of twenty or even twenty-four. The different parts of the brain do not develop synchronously: development runs roughly speaking from the bottom up and from back to front. The frontal parts are the last in line. Since particular parts of the brain support specific functions, the cognitive and psychosocial behaviour of adolescents seems to be influenced by the continuous development of the brain. Adolescence is thus not limited to puberty. These new insights explain in part the age-old confusion about young people: are they mature or not? In some ways yes, and in others no. Westenberg throws historical light on the subject: 'For centuries, adolescents have been put in a bad light because of their impulsive, restless and immoral behaviour. This was the case in Egypt four thousand years ago, and it is no different now.'[1]

Neuropsychological research informs us about human behaviour and human reactions – patterns we all share in a certain sense across the borders of time and culture, by the very fact that we are all human beings. When these statements are applied at the level of society, one practises sociobiology. Yet the relation between historians and sociobiologists has never been a happy one. If one wishes to examine love over a period of many centuries employing sociobiological theories and axioms, one is prone to be seduced by history of a very *longue durée*, inevitably coming to the conclusion that people from the past in many cases reacted 'just like us'. A radical application of sociobiological premises is found in Linda Pollock's original book *Forgotten Children. Parent–Child Relations from 1500 to 1900*. It seems as if humans are programmed into feelings of attachment in the course of bringing up children, since the survival of the species is dependent on this. So it comes as no surprise to read that Pollock in her study of autobiographical documents from over a period of more than 400 years concludes that parents and educators have always loved their children and have always done their utmost to secure their best chances of survival.

In the conclusion of this book, we will again turn our attention to the question as to whether it is advisable to exclude the results of sociobiological research from sociocultural studies. Suffice it to mention here that historians are not so much interested in general biological patterns as in the ways people and societies in the past shaped those patterns.[2] In the case of pubescents or adolescents, did people in the past recognise their typical youthful behaviour? Did they use specific terms to denote these youngsters and their way of life? Did they have laws or social customs to protect this particular phase of life? Was this life stage a problem at all? This last question in particular became increasingly important and urgent in the first half of the twentieth century. The immediate cause of the renewed attention brought to bear on youth was the findings of a young American anthropologist on the beautiful Polynesian island of Samoa in the South Pacific. This anthropological description came at exactly the right moment and was so skilfully reported in the media and popularised that no true intellectual could afford simply to pass over the question.

---

[1] Westenberg 2008. For more information on the neuropsychological research on adolescence at Leiden University, especially by the Brain and Development Lab (part of the Leiden Institute for Brain and Cognition), see www.libc-leiden.nl or http://brainanddevelopmentlab.nl; see also Chapter 8.1.
[2] For an example from the field of ancient history, see Evenepoel and Van Houdt 1997.

1.2 Mead in Samoa

The American anthropologist Margaret Mead (1901–78) performed her fieldwork on Samoa during 1925–6. She wrote about social life on this island in her best-selling book *Coming of Age in Samoa*, which first appeared in 1928 and which describes many remarkable findings concerning upbringing in this remote part of the world. Readers were struck by the very different attitude towards children and education. While people in Samoa celebrated the birth of a baby, birthdays and age awareness were hardly important in later life. Children at the age of five or six were entrusted with caring for the toddlers in the community. In no way did children form a segregated and protected group: adults frequently behaved brutally towards children who did not belong to their own families. There were very few significant choices to be made by young people. While boys had to choose between a limited number of professions, namely those of fisherman, hunter or builder of huts, girls had to look to their honour and good reputation in order to become marriageable and wanted wives.

Family life in Samoa did not resemble the western nuclear family at all. Concepts such as maternal love or gratitude towards a parent hardly existed. Children often moved into other families – they certainly did not stay with their biological parents during the entire period of their youth. Age groups were important for socialisation and entertainment. In such groups, the division between boys and girls was very strict. First encounters and sexual experiences between boys and girls were regulated according to fixed traditions and rituals.

The lack of privacy, as western people understand it, was striking. Owing to the circular construction of the huts, which had only one living space, the people of Samoa were hardly ever alone. Moreover, daily conversation did not pay much attention to the inner psychological motivations which led people to perform specific deeds. However, the so-called *nusu*-attitude served to compensate for this lack of privacy. At every single moment a person could refuse to do something. He was not expected to give a reason for his refusal, nor was it customary to ask about this. This was the way in which people were somehow protected against others constantly looking at them or interfering with their psyche.

Mead marvelled at the open and unrestrained attitude of the Samoans towards sexuality. Children were confronted with it at an early age. The lack of privacy caused them to view adults' sexual acts. First menstruation was a subject openly discussed. Masturbation occurred in groups and homosexual acts were tolerated as a kind of boyish game.

There were hardly ever conflicts over education as so often arise in western society. When education became a problem in one particular family, the young person was simply transferred to another family. Moreover, alliances between peers were never binding: tensions were resolved simply by moving into another group. Mead mentions conflicts which arose at the mission school: yet neither there did conflicts ever escalate. Parents considered sending their children to the mission school to be a very normal event (they could also simply send them to another family), and the children were not troubled by tensions at school since they were simply transferred to another family in the case of difficulties. Generational conflicts were most rare: the elders' advice was appreciated. Old men continued to contribute to Samoan society, just as older women continued doing jobs in the household.

Based on her description of Samoan society, Mead came to far-reaching conclusions. It seemed to her that the unspoiled society of New Guinea was in many respects happier than western society. There were hardly any frictions or tensions and no neuroses as in the modern world. Life was much more casual, without passion or hate, war or ambition. Life was slower: upbringing and education were gradual processes. Precocious children were not particularly appreciated, nor was precocity encouraged. There was no distinction between work and play: children both worked and played and often learned their trade while playing. Samoan children were never confronted with difficult and distressing choices, whether relating to religion or sexuality or group membership (there was no intermingling between girls' and boys' gender groups). Moreover, children were not exposed to the ambiguities of divisive hypocrisy (Mead was drawing attention both to the United States of her lifetime – which preached equality in the Declaration of Independence while practising racism – and the Christian churches – which suffered from the contradiction between ideals and everyday reality). Some evident truths of western societies were simply non-existent in Samoa. The individual had no importance. For this reason, there was no 'specialised' parenthood, whereby parents transmitted their personality to their children; rather there was a plurality of educators, thought of as aunts or uncles. Friendship was considered to be a category (the fact of having good contacts with people from the same age or sex group) rather than a special feeling. Birth, sex, and death were considered natural things: children were often confronted with these phenomena, and the confrontation was not regarded as traumatising.

Mead's main conclusion was that the *Sturm und Drang* period of youth in western Europe and the United States was not at all caused by physiological factors. On the contrary, it was a product of western culture and the role imposed on young people in that society. In all this western education played a major role. In her final remarks, Mead displayed her own paedagogical concerns. It was no longer possible to return western people back to a 'primitive' society and a life without difficult choices. The major task of both parents and educators now consisted of teaching children how to make choices: 'Children must be taught how to think, not what to think.'[3]

Mead's description of an untouched, peaceful and stress-free society beside the white beaches of the South Pacific resonated with a large audience of readers in American society, then troubled by the economic crisis of the nineteen-twenties. With her first book, the young anthropologist became a leading figure in her branch of scholarship and a media personality whose theories were eagerly adopted by paedagogues and psychologists. *Coming of Age in Samoa* has been a classic for students of anthropology for decades, and was considered to provide definitive proof of the theses of Mead's supervisor Franz Boas (1858–1942), who had stated that nurture dominates nature and that human behaviour and social customs were by and large culturally determined.

Mead's picture of Samoan society turned out to be a dream, a dream from which Mead was possibly awoken at the end of her life. According to the testimonies of her personal friends, she met the anthropologist Derek Freeman at this time. He informed her of his discoveries about Samoan society. The results of his research were devastating for Mead's theses, and the personal allegations were not to be dismissed easily: Mead's fieldwork was characterised as careless and inaccurate, and she was accused of prejudice and generalisation in her conclusions, even of academic fraud in order to confirm the cultural-deterministic theories of her supervisor Boas.[4] Freeman published his findings five years after Mead's death. The reactions of the anthropological establishment were violent. In 1983 the American Anthropological Association accepted a motion in which it was stated that Freeman's work was 'unscholarly, irresponsible and deceptive'. It seemed as if the mere thought that the image of the 'noble and untouched savage' needed adjustment was unbearable to cultural relativists.[5]

One can hardly claim that Freeman's direct attack came from a suspect source. Freeman had become fascinated by Samoan culture shortly after the publication of *Coming of Age in Samoa*. He became a regular visitor to the

---

[3] Mead 1928: 240–54 (quote on p. 253).   [4] Freeman 1983: 281–93.
[5] Meanwhile, anthropologists have partly acknowledged the existence of errors in Mead's work. Kleijwegt 1991: 7 mentions some modest anthropological defences of Mead, which turned out to be unconvincing.

island, learned the language and got to know the culture; he even became a full member of Samoan society, in which he was politically active. His deep acquaintance with Samoa led him to conclusions which were remarkably contrary to Mead's results. He sharply criticised the methodological shortcomings of her research: she spent only ten weeks learning the language and had to rely on interpreters. During her short stay on the island she never lived with the inhabitants, as she stayed with an American family. She often conducted her research using interviews, the results of which she never checked. Moreover, she was not always aware of the customs or peculiarities of Samoan culture: on her trips she was often accompanied by two Samoan girls who told her stories about sexual encounters and games with their peers. It turned out that an open conversation about sexuality was very unusual in Samoa: teasingly lying about such matters was considered a national sport. In an interview in 1987 one of the girls acknowledged that they had indeed both lied about their first promiscuous sexual experiences. It should not come as a surprise that Freeman's conclusions were radically opposite to Mead's views. Samoa was not at all a paradise of sexual liberty. The inhabitants stuck to a rather strict sexual moral code, emphasising the girls' virginity. Freeman's analysis of the composition of households revealed that the nuclear family was by far the best represented, and that children were in no way arbitrarily exchanged. Samoan society was quite brutal and violent: physical punishment of children was a rather frequent phenomenon.

As was to be expected, Freeman's attack was in turn nuanced. The findings of Raymond Firth and the Ritchie brothers on the Polynesian isle of Tikopia largely confirmed Mead's views. Moreover, these anthropologists found education and upbringing to be secured by the broader social environment, a smooth transition from childhood to adulthood and labour, and rites of passage which strongly emphasised adult status, not the specificity of the youthful stage of life. In the end, it is hardly possible to deny the significant differences between western and Polynesian views of youth.[6]

*****

One could question the relevance of an anthropological discussion of Samoan society to an ancient historian's inquiry into youth in the Roman Empire. Indeed, through its preference for wealth and conspicuous consumption, Roman society seems much closer to contemporary society than

---

[6] Kleijwegt 1991: 7–11 succinctly summarises Firth's and the Ritchies' theories.

to the habits of a remote nation in the South Pacific. However, the Mead case can be instructive for ancient historians for two reasons. Firstly, Mead's mistakes are a reminder of the dangers of theoretical prejudice (the obstinate defence of a theory, even if all proof runs counter to it). Her faults can serve as a warning against projecting a view from the present and the erroneous conclusions which are then based on it. If even a direct form of investigation like the interview proves to be unreliable (this being due not to cheating but rather to forms of self-representation or language games in a certain culture), so much more caution should an ancient historian exercise when confronted with seemingly personal information in literary sources embedded in fashions of composition and rhetorical conventions. Nor should one view Samoan society as a paradise of sexual liberty simply because Samoans exhibited sexual acts which seem strange or libertine from our western point of view. On the contrary, they too had rules and standards, although these norms were quite different from our own.

Secondly, Mead's opinions were accepted by such a large audience of scholars that the refusal to take part in a dialogue would suggest an almost unworldly aloofness. We should at least be prepared to face the possibility that youth is not a cross-cultural and self-evident phenomenon, and that some societies did not in a certain sense recognise youth. This counts for Roman society too.

1.3 Ariès, Shorter, and Stone: in search of change in history

L'enfant et la vie familiale sous l'Ancien Régime by Philippe Ariès first appeared in 1960 and was to become a milestone in the historiography of childhood and youth in earlier centuries. Ariès' main thesis is well known: in the past, childhood and youth were hardly ever appreciated as specific phases of life with their own identity.[7] Childhood was a short period characterised by physical weakness and dependence. Immediately after this stage of life, children were thrown into adult life. There was no period of youth with an adolescent crisis or a search for identity. The sensibility of childhood and youth (Ariès uses the somewhat ambiguous term *le sentiment de l'enfance*) is a modern invention. This gradual invention is to be situated in the seventeenth and eighteenth centuries, beginning with the upper class, but spreading to a larger part of the population as well in the nineteenth century.

---

[7] 'The past' Ariès refers to is the Middle Ages, mainly in France and England. In the foreword to the third edition (1973, p. ii) he admits that things might have been different in antiquity.

It would take us too long to set out all Ariès' arguments in the present book. He tries to prove the absence of a specific phase of childhood or youth in divisions of the human life span, in arts and in clothing. Play and games were also approached very differently in the Middle Ages: they were not specifically oriented towards children. Dolls were adult figures. Adults and children often played together, especially in communal participation in seasonal festivities. As far as bodily matters and sexuality are concerned, there was a remarkable indifference, contrary to the fearful attention towards childish innocence and concerns for the moral integrity of adolescents in modern times. On the other hand, Ariès describes the harsh disciplinary approach towards children in schools as a product of the invention of childhood. In schools and colleges of the Early Modern period youngsters were placed in quarantine, as it were, segregated from society. Finally, the rise of the bourgeois family in the eighteenth century and the new ideals of privacy and intimacy were factors that contributed to the valuing of children and youths. Evidently, some of Ariès' theses have been revised and corrected by historical research of the past forty-five years. But it has to be admitted that some critics have made oversimplified judgements about Ariès. Prevailing opinion alleges that, according to him, people in the past, before the invention of childhood, did not care for their children. This is at the very least an incomplete rendering of his thesis. Ariès has always stressed that the nuclear family was by no means the exclusive focus of love and affection in the Middle Ages. Love and care could be found in the broad social context of, for instance, the village community.[8] So, according to Ariès, love and care also existed in the medieval family, but it was not an essential part of it, as it is at least expected to be in our society.

What methodological objections could be made against Ariès' 'discoveries'? Of course, he approaches the past from quite a narrow point of view. The past is, as it were, evaluated against a twentieth-century concept of childhood. When practices or concepts do not match contemporary ideas, they are branded as *absence du sentiment de l'enfance*. Consequently, Ariès sticks to a very linear approach to history, presupposing a progressive evolution towards the present. Meanwhile, refined methodological approaches towards history have taught that it is possible for historians who are imprisoned in their own age to free themselves from extremely relativist opinions.[9] Furthermore, the metaphor of 'discovery' is in fact an infelicitous one. It is much safer to assume that people in the past also had

---

[8] In the 1973 edition Ariès defends himself against this unjustified critique on pp. ii–iii.
[9] Wilson 1980: 147–9.

their *sentiment d'enfance* (even if it were quite different from ours) and that changes in mentality (affective, rational or moral changes) develop only very gradually in different periods and in different places (geographical and/or social).[10] Moreover, the remarkable underestimation of the Middle Ages is symptomatic of Ariès' work. Many studies have shown Ariès' picture of medieval times not to be in keeping with reality. Theoretical and reflective treatises from the Middle Ages did pay attention to the specificity of children. The daily life of small toddlers did happen in the family – it was the family that took care of babies' development in terms of early nutrition, first steps or hygiene. Apprentice boys were mostly older than Ariès believed them to be. Sending children away from their homes at an early age was not a widespread practice. Disciplinary measures were certainly not an invention of the Modern period: the beating of children with a rod by the schoolmaster is frequently mentioned in medieval literature.[11] Ariès' neglect of demographic evidence and the numbers it can provide for life expectancy, mortality rates, etc. is distressing. Moreover, he paid but little attention to early childhood, the period before seven years of age, most probably because he presumed that such children were mainly left to fend for themselves. However, psychology has pointed to the crucial importance of this phase of life for further human development. First contacts with adults, the discovery of love or rejection, the development of the motor system and intelligence, are fields one should bear in mind when sketching a balanced view of children, regardless of the period of time or society. Paradoxically enough, Ariès somehow stuck to the traditional picture of children's clothing, school and games, despite his broad view and attention to unconventional sources.[12] Finally, Ariès' use of iconographical sources is debatable. One can justifiably ask oneself how far the appearance of child portraits in Renaissance art points to changing attitudes in society. Other factors might have played a role: Renaissance artists deeply admired art from antiquity, they had better technical possibilities at their disposal, ideas on art had changed. Until the fourteenth century art had been basically religious and symbolic. One should therefore question whether the lack of realistic or everyday scenes in paintings reflects a lack of interest in these aspects of life.[13]

---

[10] See Flandrin 1964: 329; Wilson 1980: 142–3; Kleijwegt 1991: 17–18. Ariès himself has confessed to this weakness in his work: Ariès 1973: vii–ix.
[11] Wilson 1980: 140–3; Kleijwegt 1991: 18–19 and Becchi and Julia 1998: 23–4 on Ariès' misconception of the Middle Ages and an ample bibliography on childhood in this period of history. The standard work by Orme 2001 strongly opposes Ariès' view of the Middle Ages.
[12] Flandrin 1964: 322–3; Becchi and Julia 1998: 20.
[13] Flandrin 1964: 328; Wilson 1980: 145–6; Strubbe 1982: 50–1; Becchi and Julia 1998: 24–5.

Despite these critiques, one can say that Ariès' work has stood the test of time: childhood and youth are no longer considered as suprahistorical givens but as phenomena which are closely linked with cultural customs and change in a particular society.

*****

Even more ambitious and proof of an even bigger intellectual force is the monumental *The Family, Sex and Marriage in England 1500–1800* by Lawrence Stone (1977), a massive book of more than 800 pages and about 1,300 footnotes. The manner of its composition and presentation, the size and nature of its subject, as well as the author's academic reputation, all contributed to the interest with which the book was received, not least through attracting a large audience of readers. Much more than Ariès, Stone directs his attention to the lower middle class and the poorer sector of the population. He has an eye for social diversity and changes through time, and sketches a truly brilliant picture of daily life in England in the period under study. Generally speaking, he sees a shift from the extended patriarchal familial model, operative until about 1600 after having been the predominant model in Europe for at least a millennium, via a smaller family with strict patriarchal power, to the 'modern' nuclear family unit, in which affection, privacy, exclusivity in the choice of a partner, love, and understanding between spouses and children were cherished as important values. The patriarchal family model came into being around 1540, reached its zenith in the Puritan period of 1580–1640, only to die out around about 1700. Stone dates the beginning of the nuclear family to about 1640, and it became the dominant model only after 1800. Stone carefully shuns naive belief in progress and emphasises that the history of family life actually progresses at different speeds, depending on social class and cultural diversity. As explanatory factors for the rise of the modern nuclear family he points to what he calls the typical Anglo-Saxon sense of individualism, fed by Protestantism and philosophical currents.

Edward Shorter's *The Making of the Modern Family (18th–20th Century)* appeared two years before Stone's book, but belongs to the same Anglo-Saxon school as far as definition of the problem, methodology, subject, and conclusions are concerned. Shorter opposes the exclusive attention to literary sources which are not representative of the lower classes and radically opts for a study of the daily life of ordinary people, relying on documents such as medical reports by doctors from the country, administrative documents, and folklore. For him too domestic love and intimacy, romantic love, and the privacy of the nuclear family unit are 'inventions' of the eighteenth and nineteenth centuries. He convincingly sketches family life in large and open village communities, which were marked by geographical stability, social control, and lack of privacy (mainly due to their architecture). Affection and romanticism were non-existent in such communities, or at least not presupposed. It all changed in the second half of the eighteenth century, when there was massive migration to the towns during the Industrial Revolution. With the disappearance of social control, love and sexuality became more and more a matter of personal choice. The barriers of social control were gradually dismantled: people married outside their own social class or profession, the age difference between partners grew smaller, free choice became an important issue. Newly-weds often sought another residence than their parents' house. According to Shorter, this was the first sexual revolution, which may be explained by the rise of capitalism. The rising standard of living as well as the boom of the industrial working classes proved unstoppable. Freed from the bonds of local communities, townspeople developed their 'egoism': they married the partner they preferred; they tried to enhance the status and comfort of their own little family. Stone situates the second sexual revolution around 1960. Since love and sexuality were no longer viewed in terms of procreation, they were upgraded, as it were. People diligently searched for the ideal partner, in a marriage or relationship that should ideally come as close as possible to perfection from every point of view: relational, emotional, and sexual.

Stone's book in particular was severely criticised in the same way that Ariès' work had been: Stone was said to incline towards a model of 'invention'; he almost unconsciously assumed that the mentality and lifestyle of the ruling class is adopted by the lower classes; he used his sources arbitrarily; and he was influenced by economic or demographic determinism.[14]

1.4 Philosophers, psychologists, and sociologists on the invention of youth

Some 150 years before Mead, the French philosopher Jean-Jacques Rousseau (1712–78) 'discovered' the life stages of childhood and youth in his novel *Émile*, published in 1762. According to Rousseau, children below the age of twelve should be treated differently from adults. They live in a world of their own. He also mentions a period of crisis in the transition from childhood to adult life. In a certain sense, education only begins at that stage, since young people, supervised by a teacher, must learn to control

---

[14] See the extremely critical review essay by Macfarlane 1979.

their passions. From this point of view, childhood and youth are inventions of the Age of Reason and Romanticism, preparing the way for modern paedagogy in the nineteenth century. This point of view also implies that preceding civilisations did not recognise childhood or youth.[15]

In the middle of the twentieth century the Dutch phenomenologist and psychiatrist Jan Hendrik van den Berg (1914–2012) took up the challenge of defending the philosophical theory of the invention of youth. Van den Berg has been a very controversial scholar and much-read author. In his *Metabletics or Theory of Change: Principles of an Historical Psychology*, first published in Dutch in 1956, he discerns a crisis of psychology in the middle of the twentieth century. Psychologists had lost their inner peace and were confronted with a bewildering number of questions and problems, the solutions to which were left to their competent judgement. In the same period, doubt and uncertainty characterised contacts between practitioners and their patients. The self-assured psychology of the nineteenth century and the first half of the twentieth century, when psychologists undisturbedly wrote momentous treatises sitting at their desks or working in their laboratories, had yielded to uncertainty. According to van den Berg, the main cause of the twentieth-century impasse was a hidden axiom of classical psychology: the idea that human beings are essentially unchanging. Contrary to this axiom, he states that people in the past were fundamentally different in thought, perception, imagination and feelings. The object of study therefore radically changes. He illustrates this change in various fields: the rise of developmental psychology (with its attention to childhood and puberty), clinical psychology (which points to the existence of neuroses), and psychology of religion (which seeks to understand the disappearance of the sense of wonder and of unity between humans and the cosmos). In what appears as a rather loose and associative exposition, but which is actually part and parcel of his 'metabletic' method, van den Berg treats the relationship between adults and children in the works of various philosophers. According to Montaigne children should study philosophy as soon as possible. Locke aimed to be able to reason with a child from an early age. Child prodigies frequently turn up in literature. Blaise Pascal is just one such: he read the Euclidian *Elements* as a children's book, wrote a treatise on sound at the age of twelve and one on conic sections at the age of sixteen. From a moral point of view, there was no such category as childhood. Childhood and adolescence arose only in the eighteenth century, with

---

[15] See Musgrove 1964: 33–57, Horn 1998b: 3 and Kleijwegt 1991: 23, 27 on the invention theory ascribed to Rousseau.

Rousseau arguing for viewing children as children and speaking for the first time about adolescence as a second birth. At about the same time, writers such as Goethe objected to making precocious children cope with adults' subject matter. However, the separation of the adult world from the world of children and adolescents is not evaluated positively by van den Berg. It is, rather, a loss. Youngsters were alienated from the world of adults: integration into this world happens slowly and laboriously. Once children began attending school, labour and their fathers' trades became alien to them, a fact reinforced by the rise of factories. Sex and death were previously omnipresent: adults and children slept in the same rooms, marriages between children were contracted and prudishness towards children was virtually non-existent. Epidemics and high infant mortality rates caused children to be confronted with corpses or the carrion of animals which died on the streets. This newly created distance between adults and children was the main reason that children were rendered infantile. Fairy tales became prudish moralising stories in order to educate young children, although they originally contained a considerable dose of sex and violence when both adults and children made up the audience. This same attitude of moralising and prudishness appears in the concealing of the biological facts of procreation and childbirth. Van den Berg does not shy away from bold statements. As for the invention of adolescence, he claims that Rousseau discerned the process of the coming of age not because he observed more carefully than his predecessors, but because before his time there simply wasn't anything to observe. According to van den Berg, puberty and adolescence are not biological phenomena, but simply a response to a changing world, in which people and the way they look at their surroundings have fundamentally changed. In this sense, he calls developmental psychology the smallest compensation for the loss of the naturalness in the interaction between young and old which had prevailed up till then.[16]

Van den Berg has always been out on a limb and his theories have not found a significant following. However, his theses on the rise of the concepts of childhood and youth have been endorsed by scholars who based their research on sociology and psychology. John and Virginia Demos pointed to the growth in the number of books and pamphlets on educating children and the problem of youth in the United States during the nineteenth century. This particular concern was endorsed and even enhanced by the fundamental works of the experimental psychologist G. Stanley Hall (1846–1924). In his

---

[16] Van den Berg 1957: 24–124 and Zwart 2002: 67–73 on developmental psychology. For fundamental criticism of van den Berg, see mainly Van Belzen 1997.

encyclopaedic work of 1904, *Adolescence: Its Psychology, and Its Relations to Physiology, Anthropology, Sociology, Sex, Crime, Religion, and Education*, Hall tried to explain a wide range of historical and social aspects of the problem of youth from a physiological angle. (Mead's book, placing nurture above nature, has to be viewed mainly as a reaction against Hall's theories.) John and Virginia Demos explained these new developments in terms of the increasing industrialisation and urbanisation of the nineteenth century and the rise of the nuclear family unit. The fact that parents went out to work in a large factory created a distance between the adult world and the world of the family or the school. In agricultural societies, children watched their parents working, and labour and education were part and parcel of a large process of socialisation. The changes caused children and youngsters in the nineteenth century to live in a world of their own: generational conflicts, youth delinquency, and the peer group with its own youth subculture are direct consequences of this evolution.[17]

John R. Gillis, who published on the rise of adolescence in England, is very much on the same wavelength. He postulated the creation of adolescence among the upper and middle classes shortly after 1850 when school was prolonged till about the age of sixteen or even longer (with the purpose of preparing young people for adult life and a better future). Meanwhile, youths were stuck in a situation of dependence on their parents, deprived of social participation or responsibility: a gap-period before their participation in adult life. Marriage usually took place at the age of twenty-seven, when their physical coming of age had long since been completed. The church imposed sexual abstinence before marriage. All this was felt by young people to be unpleasant and disturbing: adolescence increasingly became a period of crisis. In the twentieth century adolescence reached the lower classes. Special books aimed at adolescents appeared; special clubs for young people were created (which, in the beginning, were pseudo-militaristic, such as Baden-Powell's Scout movement).[18]

1.5 Ancient history and the controversy over youth: Eyben versus Pleket and Kleijwegt

The foundations of Emiel Eyben's work on Roman youth were laid in the tumultuous 'Age of Aquarius'. His publications clearly bear the marks of this particular period.

---

[17] Demos and Demos 1969.   [18] Gillis 1974. On scouting, see also p. 117, n. 40.

1.5 Ancient history and the controversy over youth

> Before delving deeply back into the mists of time, let us begin with the early days ... of the notorious sixties ... when students believed they could change the world, and when this creed indeed accomplished miracles. The golden sixties. It was at the beginning of this decade, in 1961 to be precise, when all this was but announcing itself, that Professor T. Reekmans suggested that I write a dissertation on the 'rowdy' in ancient Rome. (Eyben 1987: 9; translated)

Eyben's approach is basically that of a classicist, who at the same time paid attention to the copious sociological and psychological literature of the sixties. He is convinced of the value of literary sources in describing the inner psychology of Roman youths and in understanding the way Romans thought about youth.[19] Through this choice, his research is inevitably focused on the mainly male aristocratic elite of the Roman Empire. The city of Rome is strongly in the foreground since ancient authors inform us about life in this city. Inevitably, the many hundreds of cities in the East and the West of the Empire receive only marginal treatment: the thousands of Greek and Latin inscriptions about youths are only occasionally mentioned in Eyben's work.

His central thesis is that youth did 'exist' among the Romans. It appears as a distinct phase in ancient divisions of the life span, where the authors discern a period between childhood and adulthood which they call *adulescentia* or *iuventus*. Their criteria for distinguishing this stage of life are either biological (ancient doctors did in fact recognise the biological features of puberty), psychological (they had theories about the development of the human brain and the sense of responsibility that arrived at the age of fourteen), or constitutional (real political responsibility was assumed only at the age of twenty-five). Eyben pays a lot of attention to two laws from the beginning of the second century BC, the *Lex Villia annalis*, which set the minimum age for the holding of first political office at twenty-seven (later at twenty-five), and the *Lex Laetoria*, which gave legal protection to youths up to the age of twenty-five against exploitation in financial transactions, meaning that they could not become fully fledged business partners. These measures led to the distinguishing of a separate life stage of youth. Eyben resorts to terms such as *Jugendraum*, a gap-period in which young people could fully experience their youth, with their own psychological make-up, which is comparable to that of modern adolescents. To the Romans, restlessness (*ferocitas*) was the main feature of the young man. In order to explain the restless nature of young people, they resorted to external

---

[19] For Eyben as historian of ancient mentality, see Van Houdt 2009.

explanations (the lack of real political responsibility as well as the considerable amount of liberty which was restrained only at about the age of twenty-five when young men entered marriage), as well as to internal causes (the psychological weakness of youths was explained by physiological elements).

Eyben describes young Romans' behaviour at length. There were a lot of possibilities for recreation: sports, music and dance, theatres and spectacles, feasts and parties, student life. Vandalism by gangs of youths and the snobbishness of young dandies receive ample attention. Young Romans did not really belong to society: their political and military outlets were clubs or associations such as the *collegia iuvenum* in the West or the *ephebeia* in the East. The reckless behaviour of young lawyers, officers or soldiers is often rebuked by more experienced adults.

According to Eyben, the same restlessness characterised young Romans' intellectual and spiritual life. Their thirst for study appeared in many fields. They were fanatical about rhetoric and eloquence, therefore they opted for the extremes of the lavish baroque of Asianism or the tight austerity of Atticism. To young people, philosophy and religion were not a game but an honest quest for truth, a vocation for life. In Latin literature Eyben finds poets who, with their passionate poems on love, almost crystallised the youthful attitude to life: their poetry was a playful creation of the mind, and a striving after an ideal world which only exists in dreams. Finally, Eyben deals with the sentimental life of Roman youths, discussing love (with a chapter on the restless youthful lover), friendship, idols, parents, and religion.

According to him, the long period from about 200 BC to AD 500 was mainly marked by continuity. However, he tends to view youths from the early Republic as engaged with society, while their peers from the late Republic were revolutionary types, and those of the Empire the serious generation.[20]

As has been mentioned, a full-scale attack on Eyben's theses was launched by the Leiden professor Harry Pleket.[21] The controversy between the two scholars has to be understood in the light of their completely different scholarly approaches. Pleket has attached great importance to comparative historical research, and studied ancient society as one of many pre-industrial societies. He has consequently taken into account what historians of other periods have to say.[22] This also explains his

---

[20] Eyben 1977: 588. [21] Pleket 1979 and 1981a; Eyben 1981a and 1981b.
[22] See mainly Pleket 1990, a survey article which appeared in a handbook on the economic and social history of Europe.

attention to Ariès' theories, which are only rarely mentioned by Eyben.[23] Moreover, Pleket is an internationally acknowledged authority on Greek epigraphy. The study of ancient inscriptions has led him to a different image of youths from the one presented by the literary sources. Inscriptions show how, in the provincial cities and amongst the imperial elite (in the latter case from seventeen years of age), adolescents and even 'pre-adolescents' were integrated into adult life and received adult responsibilities. There was nothing like a gap-period of youth or *Jugendraum* in ancient society. Pleket reproaches Eyben for not taking sufficient notice of the overall structure of ancient cities (including the metropolis of Rome) and thus failing properly to understand the way in which youth was incorporated into this structure. Eyben has all too easily projected the modern adolescent into the Roman world. Moreover, by focusing almost exclusively on literary sources, he has limited his research to a very small segment of the ancient population. Pleket on the contrary states that Roman urban youth was accepted early into the adult world, and that it suffered no crisis of adolescence. As far as terminology is concerned, he notes that the Romans did not sub-divide the period between fifteen and twenty-five/thirty years of age. So there were no ancient adolescents, no teenagers or youngsters in their twenties, no consequent terminology for the age group between fourteen and twenty-one whom we consider adolescents.[24] Latin terms like *adulescens* and *iuvenis* are rather vague and indefinable: they are also in use for people in their thirties in the full prime of their lives. The education and schooling that some youths enjoyed from the age of twelve was short and aimed at a quick integration into adult life.

The psychological features that Eyben considered typical of Roman youths have in fact nothing to do with a crisis of adolescence on the mental or the moral level, but with the commonplace complaint of elders about the impetuous attitude of youngsters (that is, everyone who is 'not yet old', not just adolescents). These complaints by no means imply a systematic demarcation or characterisation of a period of adolescence. Other activities, which Eyben considers as typical of youths, for instance sport or hunting, were not at all specific to youth and did not reflect a youth subculture. To Pleket, it is highly questionable whether dandyism was considered a typical problem of youth. The same applies to the problem of gangs and vandalism: the ancient

---

[23] Pleket 1981a: 140.
[24] According to UNESCO and World Health Organisation definitions, adolescence is confined to the period between ten and nineteen years of age. See for instance http://en.wikipedia.org/wiki/adolescence.

sources do not allow us to state that they really were peer groups of restless adolescents who distinguished themselves from society by their specifically youthful behaviour. Finally, Pleket points out that the emphasis Eyben places on the presumed characteristic restlessness of youths and his marked preference for psychological explanations have distorted his conclusions. In a certain sense, Eyben's main thesis is always the same: whether a young orator opts for austerity or for baroque elegance, his choice is always considered a consequence of youthful restlessness. In reality, these orators were young adults, just like the so-called *poetae novi* from the circle of Catullus, who at the very most were an atypical inner circle of poets. Similar criticisms are made in a review by David Meadows of Eyben's English book *Restless Youth*: these poets are pictured by Eyben as hippies from the 'Age of Aquarius', the Roman version of The Beatles.[25]

Marc Kleijwegt's book *Ancient Youth. The Ambiguity of Youth and the Absence of Adolescence in Greco-Roman Society*, which originated as a doctorate at Leiden University under the supervision of Harry Pleket, is in fact a substantiation of Pleket's theories and a radical rejection of Eyben's. The central thesis of the book is that Graeco-Roman youth has many features in common with other pre-industrial societies from the past, but nothing with modern adolescence. Youth was a protracted and non-defined period; people did not discriminate between teenagers and persons in their twenties, between adolescents and young adults, a stage of life for which specific terms were lacking. Moreover, youth was considered to be a preparation for adult life. Young people were expected to behave like adults as soon as possible, and so they did. They were integrated into adult society in various areas: public functions, office-holding, and professional activities. They often performed the same tasks as adults and they did so alongside them, so they were consistently viewed as adults and treated on a par with them. Why then do we hear so many laments from ancient writers about 'the youth of today'? Because their position was actually very ambiguous: they were not considered fully fledged in a society where adult experience of life and old age were highly esteemed. They did not yet have certain adult features or capacities: 'the child was an adult with defects'. In this context, we occasionally read about deviant behaviour or youthful rebellion. However, these rare cases were, according to Kleijwegt, occasional storms on a usually quiet sea. And even when youths did revolt, they did not go further than the denial of adult values. They never attained a personal

---

[25] Meadows 1993: 3.

1.5 Ancient history and the controversy over youth

standpoint or created anything like a youth subculture. Ancient youths are therefore in no way comparable to modern adolescents.[26]

Kleijwegt elaborates upon his main thesis in eight chapters: the image of youth in ancient society (with a strong expectation of the continuation of the family tradition as well as of adult seriousness), the educational system, young doctors, young lawyers, senatorial youth, equestrian youth, youth and office-holding in the Greek East, youth and political responsibility in the Latin West. We will deal with all these subjects in the chapters of the present book. There we will pay full attention to Kleijwegt's views, and we will compare our opinions with his statements. Suffice it to observe here that Kleijwegt has been criticised on several points. While Eyben's exclusive focus on literary sources has been denounced, Kleijwegt has been subject to the opposite criticism. Owing to his strong emphasis on inscriptions, he has largely failed to notice the evidence offered by literary sources.[27] Furthermore, Kleijwegt interprets the ancient sources (terms, indications of age) preferentially in favour of his own theses, whereas in many cases it might be better to observe more caution in drawing conclusions. Finally, Kleijwegt often draws conclusions about the psychological make-up of youths based on their outward activities. This interpretation opens up the way for a subjective interpretation which endorses his own opinions.

After Kleijwegt, scholarly debate on ancient youth came to something of a standstill. In 1998, however, Johannes Christes published an account of the *status quaestionis*.[28] He reviews briefly the main points of the discussion. Concerning the law and participation in politics, he agrees with Kleijwegt that young aristocratic Romans had ample opportunities to gain experience; their political and military offices (and also their role as *patronus* in private suits) were not without importance, although evidently not bearing the highest responsibility. That kind of office was reserved for mature men with substantial experience, which the youngsters had still to acquire. But the mere fact that young men held functions despite their age is important and made them young adults. They did not oppose the minimum age fixed by law: the authoritarian structure of Roman society prevented this.[29] Concerning the terminology in Latin, Christes identified a problem. On

---

[26] Kleijwegt 1991: xiv–xv. See especially pp. 52–4 for criticism of Eyben.
[27] Garland 1993; Wiedemann 1994.
[28] Christes 1998: 141–66. The view and main arguments of Christes are adopted by Bormann 2006: 72–8.
[29] If there were opposition to the *Lex Villia*, this could be interpreted as an indication of a specifically youthful sense of life, but there was no protest. The lack of a 'revolutionary' attitude does not imply the absence of adolescence, as Kleijwegt argued.

the one hand a term which unequivocally denotes youth did not exist; on the other hand a few texts which we will discuss in Chapter 2 show an emerging consciousness in the late first century BC of a distinctly youthful phase of life: all humans go through such a phase, determined by age, with its own mental characteristics. Around the same time, there were young people who found their own way. This was made possible by the introduction of the Greek educational system (from the second century BC), which offered to scions of the senatorial and equestrian classes aged between eleven and about twenty what Christes calls a *Freiraum*, or period of free time. Comedies inspired by Greek models also played a role. Thus Christes finds indications that some young people of the upper class (after the donning of the adult toga until about the age of twenty) developed a specifically youthful sense of life, which may be compared to modern adolescence. He discerns traces of this youthful feeling in Catullus and the circle of the *poetae novi*, along with the elegiac poets and the satirist Persius; we will discuss these texts in Chapter 8.1. The traces are concentrated in a short period of time, at Rome and among the upper class. This youthful sense of life itself only lasted a short time: the young men soon embarked on a political or military career or turned to philosophy. Although Christes affirms, contrary to Kleijwegt, that this youthful attitude was by no means an atypical marginal phenomenon, he ends by emphasising that the *Jugendraum*, or gap-period of youth, comes to an end as soon as one assumes responsibility.[30]

These opposed scholarly views have encouraged us to undertake a renewed study and interpretation of both the literary and the epigraphic source material.

1.6 New challenges for ancient historians

As an intellectual jack-of-all-trades or a cultural omnivore, a sociocultural historian of antiquity has to take note of the conclusions of his fellow-historians studying other periods of history. However, there is a real danger that, after reading their conclusions, the ancient historian will only dare to speak hesitatingly about 'childhood' or 'youth'.

First of all, ancient historians should be aware of the fact that a book on Roman youth covers an immensely large area. Divisions of human life span and legal regulations are but one side of the coin. Demography, clubs, political office-holding, school and labour, feasts and entertainment, family

---

[30] Christes 1998: 157, 163–4. This is exemplified by the conduct of Scipio Africanus, as related by Livy (see pp. 146–7).

life, marriage and sexuality, documents written in the first person and autobiographies, images and monuments – they are all pieces of the jigsaw enabling us to sketch an overall picture. Moreover, one should reconcile oneself to the fact that this jigsaw will never be completed. Ancient historians can only envy the studies carried out by Stone or Shorter which are marked by social and geographical differentiation. For the Roman Empire, it is almost impossible to distinguish patterns which can be considered typical for the country, the city, one peculiar region or social class – frequently we have to be content with sketching a rather rough picture which we presume to be valid for a greater or lesser part of the population. This certainly seems to be the case for patterns of schooling and education, which display a remarkable uniformity all over the Roman Empire. But an elaborate case-history of the dazzling and tumultuous life of apprentice boys in one particular town of the Roman Empire will never be written, owing to the lack of source material.[31] This does not mean that we are never able to differentiate chronologically or geographically. It is possible to imagine how city life in the Greek East was different from that in the Latin West. And occasionally one encounters vivid case-histories, first-person documents or anecdotes, which unexpectedly shine a light on life as it was lived in antiquity.

What in fact is youth?[32] That was the intriguing question when we began writing this book. It should be acknowledged that the reading of fundamental studies for other periods of history did not make solving the problem easier. There is indeed a widespread consensus that youth begins with the outbreak of puberty. The central question is whether this biological fact is linked with the assumption of social responsibilities, or with their postponement. The upper limit, the end of youth, is also a thorny problem. From a contemporary point of view, we almost spontaneously come up with work and admission into professional life. However, entering a profession as a specialised and privileged position after a period of schooling and study is a modern concept, which does not apply in many cultures where becoming involved in work is a gradual process, without a strict distinction between school and work.[33] Becoming financially independent from one's parents seems another valuable criterion for the end of youth, but is difficult to apply to societies where people live together in large family units as the extended family, alongside parents, adult brothers or sisters or other relatives. Creating your own financially independent nuclear family unit has

---

[31] See Smith 1973 for such a study of apprentices in seventeenth-century London.
[32] Horn 1998b: 3–11 makes excellent observations on the problem of the demarcation of youth.
[33] See Laes 2006a: 132–97 and 2011: 148–55 on child labour, a concept unknown to the Romans.

not always been a possibility, and the way people have lived together has created affective and emotional bonds with persons who do not belong to the nuclear family. Marriage (sometimes connected with financial independence) is often considered the end of youth. In the case of aristocratic girls, early marriage should imply the absence of a phase of youth. There is also, of course, the problem of the unmarried. Should we consider a bachelor in his early thirties as young, whereas his peer who married ten years earlier left behind his youth a decade ago? From a practical point of view, it seems appropriate to impose an age limit in attempting to demarcate youth. But this criterion too poses problems. How is one to cope with societies in which age was not of decisive importance, where people possibly did not know their exact age? Again, the imposition of an age limit seems to be connected with factors such as marriage, financial independence, legal maturity, entering the workforce – factors which have been shown to be problematic.

No matter how difficult the concept of youth seems to be theoretically, this should not deter us from approaching the question for the Roman world. In their discussions of the human life cycle, Roman writers distinguished a period called *adulescentia* or *iuventus*, which roughly corresponds to the late teens and early twenties. And of course it is possible to study work, schooling, the assumption of responsibilities or the daily life of Romans during this period of their lives. Whether it is actually justified to talk about Roman youth or adolescence is an issue for the conclusion of this book. In the same way, a voluminous standard work on the phenomenon of homosexuality among the Romans comes to the conclusion that . . . they had no such concept![34] However, the question of the existence of a concept should not hamper the study of the phenomenon itself. Thus, our hesitant discourse should not end in an obstinate silence, which does not serve scholarship at all.

---

[34] Williams 1999.

CHAPTER 2

Minority, majority: youth, divisions of the human life cycle, and Roman law

2.1 Youth and the division of the life cycle

How many stages are there in human life? Till what age are we considered young? When does old age start? Dividing the human life cycle in order to answer such questions was one of the favourite intellectual pastimes of ancient writers. The first elaborate division of the human life cycle appeared with the Athenian statesman and poet Solon in the sixth century BC. But when one reads the Latin works of the encyclopaedist Isidore of Seville of the seventh century AD, one finds the very same divisions; these were based on symbolic numbers and numerology. The same applies to medieval and Renaissance passages offering subtle divisions of human life based on ancient Greek and Latin texts, which had become the common property of an intellectual elite. The divisions were seldom applied to concrete social reality: the game of numbers prevailed; it was about numerology, more than psychology.

Scholars of the early twentieth century have catalogued and commented upon those ancient Greek and Roman divisions of the life span. In the last decades, the source material has been approached with new questions in mind. It turned out that the ancients had a fundamentally different view of personality and education: the adult male citizen was their point of reference. It was all about adapting oneself and conforming, psychological well-being and introspection being of lesser value. Ancient writers believed that the nucleus of one's personality was already present from early childhood, but at the same time they believed that by strenuous efforts it was still possible to polish it a bit and to offer nature a helping hand.[1]

The division into three phases by the philosopher Aristotle was influential throughout Greek and Roman antiquity. According to his views on the

---

[1] For studies on ancient divisions of the human life cycle, iconography, and the afterlife, see Höhn 1911–12; Boll 1913; Hofmeister 1926; Eyben 1973a, 1973b and 1977: 7–40; Burrow 1986; Garland 1990; Amedick 1991; Harlow and Laurence 2002 and 2007; Minten 2002; Parkin 2003: 15–35; Laes 2006a: 75–87 and 2011: 85–99.

happy medium (*in medio virtus*) adulthood stands as an ideal between the extremities of youth and old age. For Aristotle, young people are restless and impulsive in their desires. They are gullible, full of hope and naive, since they have not yet suffered much evil in their lives. They enjoy the company of friends and fellows. They are not coolly calculating: in their lives, beauty counts for more than utility.[2] Aristotle's description undoubtedly contains striking observations, but the passage can hardly be considered a high point in developmental or youth psychology.[3] There is not even a distinction between childhood and youth. The whole text serves only as the assertion of the Aristotelian point of view: between the naively hopeful young man and the pessimistically depressed old man stands the ideal figure of the realistic adult, carrying all the positive features of youth and old age without lapsing into the weaknesses of these stages.

Divisions into four stages were popular with Greeks and Romans. According to tradition, they went back to Pythagoras, who allegedly divided human life into four periods each of twenty years, the four stages corresponding to the four seasons (see Fig. 2.1). The medical theories of Hippocrates and Galen elaborated upon this division, to which they gave a physical basis, combining the principle of the four seasons with the science of the four corporeal humours (blood, phlegm, yellow and black bile) and the corresponding states of mind. Hence numerous texts stick to the basic scheme as outlined in Table 2.1, in which the phase of youth is interpreted quite broadly and is treated as more or less synonymous with 'years of full corporeal force'.[4]

The description by the Roman poet Horace is well known; he distinguishes four stages (childhood, youth, adulthood, and old age) and offers the following portrait of the young man:

> The beardless youth, finally relieved from his *paedagogus*,
> Finds delight in horses, dogs, and the grass of the sun-drenched Campus Martius.
> He is soft as wax to be seduced into vice, he is troublesome towards his educators,
> Does not foresee what is useful, squandering his money.
> Arrogant and greedy, he suddenly leaves behind what he loved some minutes before. (Horace, *Ars poet.* 161–5)

Johannes Christes has considered this an important text; its point of view corresponds partially with two passages in Cicero's *De Senectute*.[5] These

---

[2] Aristotle, *Rhet.* 2, 12, 3–13, 1 (1389 a 3–1390 b 12). For the text, see pp. 44–6.
[3] Remarkably Eyben 1977: 114 believes this is indeed the case.
[4] See Horstmanshoff 1999 for an introduction and Lloyd 1964 for an elaborate survey.
[5] Christes 1998: 150–3, followed by Bormann 2006: 74. Cicero, *De senect.* 10, 33 and 20, 76.

2.1 Youth and the division of the life cycle

Table 2.1 *The division of the human life cycle into four stages*

Life stage	Quality	Temperament	Season
childhood (till 20 or 25)	humid and warm	sanguine	spring
youth (25 to 40)	dry and warm	choleric	summer
mature age (till 60)	humid and cold	phlegmatic	autumn
old age (from 60)	dry and cold	melancholic	winter

2.1 Sarcophagus of the four seasons, third century AD. From left to right we can see Spring (with flowers in his hair), Winter (with reeds in his hair and ducks in his hand), Autumn (with grapes in his left hand) and Summer (with a cornucopia in his left hand). The authors thank Janet Huskinson for her expert advice on the interpretation.
(Capitoline Museum, Palace of the Conservators, Rome.)

texts are written by authors who, from the vantage point of experience (Cicero being sixty-two and Horace approximately fifty), look back on their lives. They believe that human beings go through not only a biological development, but also a mental evolution. These passages are not about individual development, but about a general human process. Christes believes that in this period, the late first century BC, the awareness of a distinct stage of youth emerged.

The history of the Roman state, too, has been conceived as divided into four stages: *infantia, adulescentia, iuventus, senectus*. This image turns up in

Table 2.2 *The division of the life cycle into five stages (Varro)*

Years	
0–15	puer
15–30	adulescens
30–45	iuvenis
45–60	senior
60+	senex

the work of the historiographer Florus and was also popular with writers of late antiquity.[6]

Divisions into five stages were particularly popular with Roman writers. According to Censorinus, Varro applied the division shown in Table 2.2.[7]

However, in his commentary on Vergil, Servius claims that Varro actually divided human life in the following way: *infantia, pueritia, adulescentia, iuventa, senecta*. In this distinction, it is of course impossible to stick to periods of fifteen years each, unless one is prepared to accept the possibility of childhood from the age of fifteen till thirty. Nevertheless, the numerological value of 5 x 3 is rescued by the suggestion that each stage of life has a beginning, a middle and a period of decline. For a study of Roman youth, the first division by Varro is important as it corresponds well with the social reality of the Roman upper class: the donning of the toga at approximately fifteen years of age, the entrance into the senate at the age of thirty and the exemption from military service in the Republic at the age of forty-six.[8]

It is only in the division into seven stages (Table 2.3) that one finds traces of a further classification of youth based on numbers. Here there appears a distinction between the late teens (referred to by the Greek word *meirakion*) and the twenties (the Greek *neaniskos*). It should be noted that the application of these terms seems somewhat artificial: in other Greek texts it is certainly not the case that *meirakion* exclusively refers to the period from fourteen to twenty-one and *neaniskos* to that from twenty-one to twenty-eight.

The division into ten stages by Solon is also based on the number seven. Solon distinguishes a stage between the ages of fourteen and twenty-one,

---

[6] Florus, *Epit.* 1, pr. See Eyben 1977: 9 on this fragment and its parallels in later Latin literature.
[7] Censorinus, *De die nat.* 14, 2.   [8] Servius, *Comm. Aen.* 5, 295; see Eyben 1977: 22–3.

2.1 Youth and the division of the life cycle

Table 2.3 *The division of the human life cycle into seven stages (Ps.-Hippocrates)*

Years		Features
0–7	little child	loss of the milk teeth
7–14	child	first growing of the beard
14–21	teenager	full beard
21–28	young man	full physical force
28–49	adult	–
49–56	older man	–
56–?	old man	–

Note: Ps.-Hippocrates, *De hebd.* (9, 434 Littré).[9]

Table 2.4 *The division of the human life cycle into seven stages (Pollux)*

Years	
0–7	little child
7–14	child
14–21	teenager
21–28	young man
28–35	adult
35–42	older man
42–49	old man

Note: Pollux, *Onom.* 2, 4.

and one between the ages of twenty-one and twenty-eight, without assigning specific terms to these periods.[10] Stubborn adherence to the regularity of the number seven occasionally led to strange results, as in the division by the Greek sophist Pollux (end of the second century AD), in which old age starts remarkably early (see Table 2.4).

The division into seven stages was popular also with Roman authors. Thus the fifth-century writer Macrobius distinguishes a phase from fourteen to twenty-one years of age, in which the full growth of the beard and of height is accomplished, and a period from twenty-one to twenty-eight, in

---

[9] This division was quite popular; see Plutarch, *De E apud Delph.* 392 c; Philo, *Jos.* 127–129 and *De opif. mundi* 105.
[10] Solon, fr. 19 (ed. Diehl).

which lateral growth is accomplished. He does not use specific terms to denote these stages of life.[11] Specific vocabulary is found in Isidore of Seville, whose writings of the seventh century AD incorporate a massive amount of scholarship of previous centuries, so that we can freely use his testimonies to gain knowledge of the ideas of previous generations. According to Isidore, the period of *adulescentia* ranges from fourteen to twenty-eight years of age. The biological ability to procreate and the development of body power and intellect are crucial at this stage of life. Afterwards, it is in the stage of *iuventus* that one attains full strength. Hence, this 'strong' stage of life covers three periods of seven years, from twenty-eight to forty-nine years of age.[12]

Also based on the number seven, albeit from an astrological point of view, is the division by the authoritative astrologer Ptolemy (AD 87–150). He lists the planets and the celestial bodies in increasing order of distance from the earth (according to ancient astrologers): the moon, Mercury, Venus, the sun, Mars, Jupiter, Saturn. The duration of each stage of life is in proportion to the length of the orbit of the corresponding planet around the earth. As for the moon, four was chosen for the duration of this life stage because of the four lunar phases. Youth is considered the phase of Venus, ranging from fifteen to twenty-two years of age:

> Venus' stage of life, the third period, namely that of the young man, covers eight years by analogy with the number of years of one orbit by Venus. Of course, this phase activates the sperm cells and experiences the explosion of the sex-drive, according to which the soul is pervaded by a sort of rage and lack of self-control, as well as by a longing for sexual activity wherever it may be found. There is also the blindness caused by dominating passion and the inability to acknowledge one's own restlessness. (Ptolemy, *Tetr.* 4, 10)

In total, one can find about fifty Greek texts and 120 Latin passages that contain more or less elaborate divisions of the human life cycle. But what does this study tell us about ancient concepts of youth? Greek and Latin authors did indeed distinguish a phase between childhood and adulthood, a period to which they applied various terms, which in everyday usage were employed with greater fluidity. There were no such things as specific age terms. The distinction between *adulescentia* and *iuventus* as consecutive stages of life was presumably introduced into the Latin language by Varro, although we may safely assume that *iuventus* always covered a wider range than *adulescentia*. Both terms could in any case be employed to denote

---

[11] Macrobius, *Comm. Somn. Scip.* 1, 6, 70.
[12] Isidore of Seville, *Orig.* 11, 2, 2 and *Diff.* 2, 19, 74; *Lib. num.* 7, 31. Isidore's two divisions differ only in details.

2.1 Youth and the division of the life cycle

youth and full physical force: there is no reason whatsoever to equate Roman *adulescentes* with our adolescents (a term from developmental psychology often pointing to the beginning of integration into the adult world from age seventeen to twenty-one, though in the English-speaking world adolescence is thought to begin at about age eleven–twelve and to end about eighteen–nineteen). When demarcating the stage of life referred to as *adulescentia*, ancient writers resorted to numerology. The starting age was fourteen or fifteen (depending on whether they counted in sevens or fives), and the upper limit was twenty-eight or thirty. If this period was further divided, symbolic numbers were once again involved in distinguishing a phase from fourteen to twenty-one years of age and another from twenty-one to twenty-eight years of age.[13]

There is no doubt that these conventional and stereotypical divisions, with their obvious preference for numerology, are somewhat sterile. It was not because of the numerological preference for twenty-one – as a multiple of seven – that the average twenty-one-year-old had the feeling that he was beginning a new stage of life. It cannot be concluded from the fact that someone is called *adulescens* that he actually belonged to the age category of fifteen to thirty. According to Livy, the Carthaginian general Hannibal, for instance, who was forty-four years of age at the fatal Battle of Zama, considered himself an old man (*senex*), in contrast to his Roman opponent Scipio, who was thirty-four years of age and, according to Hannibal, still in his *adulescentia*.[14] In his Philippic orations, Cicero states how he acted as a young man (*adulescens*) against Catiline in the year 63 BC.[15] At the time of Catiline's conspiracy Cicero was forty-two years of age.

So, if one wishes to discover the everyday sociocultural reality of young people in the Roman world, the practical value of such divisions of human life is rather limited. Scholars have indeed questioned the relevance of these divisions ('How on earth can our ancestors possibly have believed in such a load of rubbish?' Peter Laslett unabashedly asks in his study of the medieval versions of the ancient divisions of the human life course).[16] Undoubtedly these divisions are valuable evidence for the existence of strategies of

---

[13] There is, however, one remarkable passage in Philo, *Cher.* 114, which deals with the transition from child to adult (and thus does not provide a full division of the human life span). This passage divides youth into five phases, which, according to Eyben 1981: 139, can be compared to contemporary developmental psychology: pre-puberty, puberty, crisis of youth, adolescence, young adulthood. Undoubtedly, Eyben is far too optimistic in his interpretation. Philo's text should rather be considered a 'special case', as should also the small number of texts which divide old age into several stages. See Parkin 2003: 299–301.
[14] Livy, *Ab Urbe cond.* 30, 30, 10.   [15] Cicero, *Phil.* 2, 46, 118; see Parkin 2003: 20–1.
[16] Laslett 1987: 103.

manipulation and confirm the presence of dominant prejudices and clichés. From the point of view of structuralism, the study of the ideology of age classes is a study of power mechanisms: throughout the generations, adult male citizens try to perpetuate an ideology granting them superiority over weaker members of society such as women, children and older people.[17] As for the everyday reality of Roman youth, we should content ourselves for now with the rather obvious finding that ancient authors discerned a phase between childhood and adulthood to which they did not give a specific name and which they did not demarcate very precisely (and if they did so, it was usually based on numerology). In order to gain a clearer view of the situation, it is necessary to turn to the Roman legal system.

2.2 Roman law

Roman law certainly provides us with revealing information on age categories. At the same time we should approach this source material with care. There was a considerable difference between theoretical regulations and their practical application in everyday life. Owing to the limitations in the means of communication, the Roman state could not possibly impose its system of regulation all over the Empire. Besides, it is doubtful whether a large majority of the people (the relatively well-to-do forming less than 10% of the total population) ever came into contact with a court, not to mention the fact that they were hardly capable of defending their rights if such an occasion did occur.

It is generally assumed that the end of Roman childhood occurred at around the age of fifteen for boys. The transition to adulthood was celebrated by a rite of passage (see Chapter 4): the child removed his *bulla* – an amulet providing protection against the evil eye – and donned an immaculate white *toga virilis* replacing the purple-fringed *toga praetexta*. Generally it was up to the *pater familias* to decide when the right age for the ceremony had arrived. This probably took place on 17 March during the festival of the *Liberalia*, which was celebrated during the imperial period in the Forum of Augustus.[18] However, many other dates throughout the year are mentioned by ancient authors, and the relationship with the Temple of Mars Ultor in the Forum of Augustus is not entirely certain.[19] For girls, the wedding

---

[17] See the approach to the life course adopted by Harlow and Laurence 2002 and Laes 2007.
[18] Cicero, *Pro Sest.* 69, 144; *Ad Att.* 5, 20, 9 (Cicero deciding for his nephew). See Laes and Strubbe 2006: 40–1.
[19] Dolansky 2008: 49–52.

ceremony was considered the rite of passage. There seems to have been no 'costume' attached to a Roman girl.[20]

Roman jurists disagreed about whether the age of fourteen should be a fixed age for going through the ceremony or whether it should rather be the actual age of sexual maturity, or whether a combination of the two should be the deciding factor. The school of the jurists Cassius and Sabinus defended the criterion of physical maturity, except for the cases of eunuchs and impotent men.[21] Others, such as the adherents of the school of the Proculiani, defended a fixed age, namely fourteen for boys and twelve for girls (for whom there was no ceremony of the donning of the toga).[22] Priscus stuck to the principle that one should take into account both physical maturity and actual age.[23] It was only in the sixth century, during the reign of Justinian, that the controversy was finally settled: physical investigation of the sexual maturity of boys was deemed indecent (during the imperial period it was already considered as such in the case of girls, for whom the fixed age of twelve was considered to represent the transition to adulthood); hence the fixed ages of fourteen for boys and twelve for girls were taken as standard.[24]

The following passages testify to the lively juridical discussion on the question of maturity:

> When boys grow into adults, they are freed from guardianship. Sabinus and Cassius and our other teachers have pointed out that those boys are adults who show adulthood in their physical appearance, that is when they are capable of producing offspring. In the case of those who cannot properly reach adulthood, such as eunuchs, one should take into account the age at which they would normally become adults. Teachers of the other school, however, think that adulthood should be measured by the years, that is, he is to be considered an adult who has reached the age of fourteen. (Gaius, *Inst.* 1, 196)

> When under-age boys and girls become adults, they are freed from guardianship. Ancient authorities have it that adulthood should be granted not

---

[20] On the question of whether young free-born girls wore the *toga praetexta*, just as did free-born boys, see Olson 2008, who discusses all the evidence. In fact there is only one source, Arnobius, *Adv. nat.* 2, 67 (late third century AD), that mentions the offering of the toga by girls to Fortuna Virginalis on the eve of their marriage. See also p. 202.
[21] *Tit. Ulp.* 11, 28; Gaius, *Inst.* 1, 196.
[22] *Tit. Ulp.* 11, 28. On these ages in wills, see *Dig.* 28, 1, 5 and 28, 6, 2 pr. (Ulpian).
[23] *Tit. Ulp.* 11, 28. On the combination of age and mature physical appearance, see also Servius, *Comm. Aen.* 7, 53; *Comm. Ecl.* 8, 40 and Ausonius, *Epitaph.* 35.
[24] On fixed ages, see *Cod. Iust.* 6, 22, 4. For an extended study of this juridical controversy, see Schwarz 1952. Eyben 1977: 60 and Fayer 1994: 396–7 offer good summaries.

> only according to the number of the years, but also according to the physical appearance in the case of boys. Our Majesty, however, has considered it appropriate to the good custom of our times to extend immunity towards boys from what has long since been considered inappropriate in the case of women and older people: namely the examination of the physical appearance. Therefore, we have announced and stipulated in our sacred constitution that adulthood for boys begins immediately after the completion of the fourteenth year, while we continue the ancient custom for women, namely that they are considered marriageable after the completion of their twelfth year. (*Inst. Iust.* 1, 22 pr.)

It is thus sufficiently clear that Roman law distinguished between minority and majority. With the coming of age, the new adults acquired new rights. When they were under guardianship, the tutelage was cancelled. They were granted the right to contract marriage and a legal will. However, this does not mean that after the ceremony had been accomplished those young people immediately entered full adult life. Boys usually married in their twenties, girls in their late teens. In politics the minimum age for holding offices with real responsibility, including in the cities and the municipia of the Empire, averaged around twenty-five. And well-to-do young people continued their studies after the age of fifteen. These crucial aspects will be dealt with in separate chapters of this book. For girls, the age of twelve did not bring much change. In Roman law women in a certain sense remained minors throughout their whole life. They fell under the authority of their husbands, their fathers, or any other adult male relative performing the role of guardian.[25]

According to Roman law, a male was only fully adult at the age of twenty-five. In private law, the *Lex Laetoria* (*c.* 200 BC) protected young men below the age of twenty-five against economic exploitation. Before reaching this age, he was a *minor*; only at twenty-five did he really become a *maior*. The law stipulated that every commercial transaction that was harmful to a *minor* could be cancelled by law. Young people were thus protected, not only when they were cheated, but also when they had made a commercial mistake. Theoretically they were fully capable of contracting. In practice, however, many potential business partners baulked at doing business with a young man, since there was always the risk that he would invoke the lack of experience of his young years. Roman law recognised the fragility of young age:

---

[25] Frier and McGinn 2004: 450–6.

> Everyone agrees that the plans of people of this age are fragile and inconsistent, exposed to many traps, the victim of many ambushes. (*Dig.* 4, 4, 1 pr. (Ulpian))

Consequently, it was difficult for young people to do business with someone:

> I am finished! This law concerning twenty-five years of age is my ruin. Everybody is afraid of lending me money! (Plautus, *Pseud.* 303–4)

In order to protect restless youngsters in business matters, a *curator* might be appointed:

> Boys beyond the age of puberty and girls being fertile are granted a *curator* until they reach their twenty-fifth year. Although they are already adults, they are not yet at an age at which they can look after their own financial interests. *Curatores* are to be installed by the same magistrates who appoint guardians. However, a *curator* is not to be installed by will. He is to be confirmed by a decree of the praetor or the governor of the province. Those young people who do not wish it shall not receive a *curator*, unless for a trial. It is indeed possible to appoint a *curator* for just a single purpose. (*Inst. Iust.* 1, 23 pr. 2)

The appointment of a *curator* was apparently never obligatory, although an unreliable source states that the emperor Marcus Aurelius expanded the institution to make it compulsory for all young people.[26] Since a *curator* took care of the commercial interests of a young man and ratified his agreements, a possible business partner received a guarantee that a contract could not simply be cancelled because of youth.

We would like to know how all this worked in practice, whether the *Lex Laetoria* and the legal restraint were strictly applied or remained theoretical constructions, whether this was the case in all parts of the Roman Empire, what happened if a young man stubbornly refused a *curator*, etc. It is certain that these measures were not merely theoretical, since a whole chapter of the *Digest* is dedicated to cases concerning *minores* below the age of twenty-five.[27] In the papyri of Roman Egypt (Roman citizens from this province evidently resorted to Roman law) we read about a young man who had sold at far too low a price and demanded compensation since he had still been a *minor* when he had decided to sell.[28] *Ad hoc* solutions certainly existed. The *venia aetatis* granted men from the age of twenty and women from the age of

---

[26] *SHA Vita Marci Aur.* 10, 12. Modern scholars assume an expansion of the institution, but not that it became compulsory. See Berger 1932: cols. 1870–1; Frier and McGinn 2004: 441.
[27] *Dig.* 4, 4. [28] *P. Mil. Vogl.* 25; *P. Lond.* 113. See Taubenschlag 1944: 124 and 249–50.

eighteen the advantages of full legal majority.[29] The measure, introduced by the emperor Constantine in 321, states that this grant was possible only when, as confirmed by the testimony of truthful witnesses, the young man gave proof of outstanding moral conduct and integrity. This text also mentions five juridical stages of life: childhood (*pueritia*), youth (*adulescentia*), a stage in which stability is reached in rare cases (*firmata aetas*), the usual age of adulthood (*legitima aetas*), and old age (*senectus*).[30]

In criminal law, youthful restlessness did not normally count as an excuse:

> In the case of crimes, one should not offer help to *minores*. (*Dig.* 4, 4, 9, 2 (Ulpian))

> In the case of crimes, *minores* are not defended by their age. Instability of mind is no excuse for bad habits. (*Cod. Iust.* 2, 34, 1)

Although such statements exclude the possibility of juvenile justice, Roman law equally recognised that young children (*infantes*), just as madmen (*furiosi*), were not responsible for damage done:

> If a child or a lunatic loses or destroys something, his deed remains unpunished. (*Dig.* 6, 1, 60 (Pomponius))

> If a child or a madman kills a person, they are not held under the *Lex Cornelia*. Innocence in consciousness protects a child, whereas the lunatic is excused by his unhappy fate. (*Dig.* 48, 8, 12 (Modestinus))

Only if a minor *impubes* (to be distinguished from an *infans*) gives proof of a certain physical and intellectual maturity can he be held responsible for the deed he committed.

> Therefore the following question may be raised: if a lunatic causes damage, is one entitled to compensation according to the *Lex Aquileia*? Pegasus too claims that this is not the case: how is he to blame who does not control his senses? That is completely true. There will be no trial on the basis of the *Lex Aquileia*, just as there is no such trial if a quadruped causes harm or a tile falls from a roof. In the case of a child doing harm, the same applies. But if a minor causes damage, he can be held by the *Lex Aquileia*, since he can also be accused of theft. That is Labeo's opinion. I think this is right, if a minor is capable of committing injury. (*Dig.* 9, 2, 5, 2 (Ulpian))

This passage testifies to a certain refinement and nuance, since an under-age child is not to be compared to a boy approaching puberty. Thus the

---

[29] Berger 1932: cols. 1888–9; Eyben 1977: 57–8.   [30] *Cod. Theod.* 2, 17, 1–4.

category of the *pubertati proximus* ('he who approaches puberty') was introduced in Roman law.

> The question is whether a minor commits a theft if he removes someone's possessions. Most jurists think he does so. Theft is indeed connected to conscience. Thus, a minor is certainly accused of theft if he approaches puberty and thereby understands the crime he is committing. (Gaius, *Inst.* 3, 208)

According to Labeo, a child (*pupillus*) cannot be held responsible for cheating in matters of inheritance, since this presupposes the use of deception. Ulpian states that a young person approaching physical adulthood (*pubertati proximus*) is indeed capable of deception. Deception is certainly conjectured if the young one has the possibility of enriching himself.[31] There seems to have been a wide juridical consensus that those approaching physical maturity (*pubertati proximi*) were indeed capable of deception or premeditation.[32]

In general Roman jurists divided minors (*pupilli* or *impuberes*) into small under-age children (*infantes*) and older children approaching physical and intellectual maturity (*pubertati proximi*). No exact age limits are mentioned. Judges were presumably guided by concrete indications proving a certain maturity. Power of speech was one of those criteria, evidently not the babblings of early speech but the capability of forming sentences and simple reasoning.[33] A strongly developed sense of reasoning was not required. It was sufficient if a child could talk, even if he did not fully understand the subtleties:

> It is necessary that the young boy's slave stipulates if the child is absent or does not possess the power of speech. If he is present and capable of talking, even if he is not of that age that he already understands what he is doing, it is for practical reasons accepted that he can legally stipulate. (*Dig.* 46, 6, 6 (Gaius))

In such cases, *infantia* seems to have been understood in the literal sense as 'the age at which one is not capable of speaking' (*in* = not; *fari* = to speak). The legal age limit of seven appears only in late antiquity, influenced by the magic and symbolic value of the number seven.[34] Fixing an age limit was certainly a more objective criterion for the judges, controllable by means of birth registers and certificates.[35] The first traces of age seven appear

---

[31] *Dig.* 4, 3, 13 (Ulpian).
[32] The same assumptions are to be found in *Dig.* 50, 17, 111 pr. (Gaius); *Dig.* 40, 12, 15 (Paul) and *Dig.* 47, 2, 23 (Ulpian) (*infantes* certainly cannot be involved in cases of deception).
[33] Knothe 1982: 247.   [34] Knothe 1982: 254–6.   [35] Knothe 1982: 249–52.

in *Dig.* 26, 7, 1, 2, where Ulpian poses the question whether guardians (*tutores*) are entitled to start a trial themselves on behalf of their *pupilli*. They could do so if the children were younger than seven or absent at the moment of the trial. In the case of older children, *tutores* could act on behalf of their *pupilli* when the children were present at the trial. Seven years also appears as the minimum age for betrothal.[36]

In order to determine whether a young person possessed a sense of responsibility and could be considered a *pubertati proximus*, concrete observation played the deciding role. Investigation by the court decided if one was still a real child (*infans*) or belonged to the second category. Most probably it was the same juridical practice and the longing for more objective criteria that led the jurists to fix the minimum age of seven – a limit which was well known from the popularity of symbolic numbers and the science of numerology.

Many questions remain unanswered. We do not know about concrete instances in which children or young people were brought to trial accused of committing a crime. In medieval England roughly the same criteria of capability of speech and reasoning were used, both in civil and in canon law. Judges apparently took a decision according to the circumstances of each case. In 1249 four-year-old Catherine Passeavant was sent to the abbey's jail after she had thrown another child from an open window. The child had died as a result of the fall. A boy aged six died in his cell. In the fourteenth century a thirteen-year-old servant girl was hanged after the murder of her mistress.[37] In all likelihood, Roman law did not offer protection to minors as we tend to do, certainly not in the cases of slaves. According to the harsh *senatus consultum Silanianum* all slaves of the *familia* of a murdered master were executed, even if they were absent when the crime was committed. An exception for innocent children was granted, unless they gave proof of the capability of deception (*capacitas doli*), had cooperated in the crime or were found guilty of culpable neglect (like the young slave who slept with his master and did not rouse the family when the murder was committed). These restrictions at least give the impression of considerable arbitrariness.[38] In cases of interrogation, the torture of slaves below the age of fourteen was not permitted, but again exception was made in cases of high treason. Beating such children, with a whip or a rod, was evidently permitted from a Roman point of view.[39]

---

[36] *Dig.* 23, 1, 14 (Modestinus).   [37] Orme 2001: 223–4.
[38] *Dig.* 29, 5, 1, 32 (Ulpian); *Dig.* 29, 5, 14 (Maecianus).
[39] *Dig.* 48, 18, 10 pr. and 10, 1 (Arcadius Charisius); *Dig.* 29, 5, 1, 33 (Ulpian).

2.3 Ages in practice

At first sight the Roman concepts of minority and majority and the protection of youthful recklessness have a modern ring. However, a similarity in concepts should not blind us to fundamental differences. Take the example of a young man reaching the legal age of majority – that is eighteen – in a present-day European country. His rights and duties are clearly defined. He can be a candidate at elections and vote. He is entitled independently to undertake his financial transactions. He is fully responsible for his own deeds, and when he breaks the rules he is no longer referred to a special youth court. Also in matters concerning sexuality he stands on his own two feet, so long as his sexual relations are with those who have reached the age of sexual maturity (sixteen according to Belgian law, for example) and, in the case of those aged between sixteen and eighteen, over whom he does not exercise power. How different was the situation of his Roman peer! (Because slaves were deprived of any personal rights whatsoever, we exclude them from this comparison.) Some of these differences are to be explained by the fact that majority was conferred earlier than it is nowadays. To be sure, young Roman adults too could vote in their town elections – yet according to legal rules and general practice, the holding of offices with real responsibility was usually postponed for some years. Financially the young Roman adult still stood under tutelage. Sexual maturity was a concept unknown to Roman law. And for both young adults and those young people approaching the ceremony of adulthood, accounting for wrongdoing took place before a normal court. Whether or not one was held already responsible for his own deeds rested with the arbitrary judgement of the judge (it is likely that young people were often held responsible because the mere power of speech already seemed to be sufficient proof of competence to act). The moment when one became an adult was not strictly determined by one's birthday. Until late antiquity actual physical maturity was one of the decisive factors as to whether a boy could proceed to don the *toga virilis*. A fixed age of fourteen seems to have become standard only in the Christian Empire. For girls, the legal situation seems to have been far less ambiguous: at the fixed age of twelve they were considered marriageable and thus adults. With the exception of the rich upper class, however, most girls married later – there was no special rite of passage for them. As noted above, one may even ask whether the transition to adulthood made any difference to them, since they remained under the tutelage of one person during their entire life: their father, husband or any other male relative performing this duty.

This brings us to the important question of the role of age in the Roman Empire. Did people know how old they actually were? And if they knew this, was age a decisive factor for their functioning in society, as it certainly is nowadays?

Ancient historians disagree on the question as to whether people in antiquity possessed age consciousness. There was the genre of occasional verse called the *genethliacon*, the birthday poems for members of the self-conscious elite. On these days, offerings were brought to one's personal *Genius*. However, knowing the date of one's birthday does not necessarily imply consciousness of one's exact age. The Roman calendar was full of feasts and festivals, and it was simple to use a festival as a reminder of one's birthday.[40] The bureaucratic system of the Roman Empire was well founded. Yet although birth registers certainly existed, we do not know whether registration was compulsory. The same goes for death certificates.[41] Moreover, the actual operation of censuses and census lists is not well known, although it is certain that such lists did not guarantee the exact reporting of the age of the people registered.[42]

Consider the remarkable case of the North African Pudentilla; if we are to believe the Apologia of her widower Apuleius, it was uncertain whether her age was actually forty or sixty years.[43] Extensive research on funerary inscriptions has revealed a clear preference for age rounding, with ages that are multiples of five being particularly popular.[44] Various explanations have been offered for the phenomenon of age rounding.[45] Some have claimed that age numbers in antiquity mainly had symbolic value: one hundred years meant 'reaching a very high age', forty 'mature age', and so on. This thesis seems barely tenable if one takes into account that thousands of inscriptions contain highly detailed indications of age, which are by no means multiples of five and frequently exactly record the number of days lived by the deceased. Others have explained the preference for five on the basis of the Roman census system – the Republican census taking place every fifth year. Again the question remains why people would have counted

---

[40] Brind'Amour and Brind'Amour 1971: 999 on *genethliaca*. On birthdays and knowing one's age, see Parkin 2003: 33.
[41] Parkin 2003: 175–82.   [42] Parkin 2003: 182–9.   [43] Apuleius, *Apol.* 89.
[44] Salmon 1987: 109 quotes the following numbers: 66% of the age inscriptions of Rome are multiples of five; 40% of the inscriptions for people under the age of thirty from Africa are multiples of ten; multiples of ten are particularly popular in Egypt; inscriptions from Bordeaux have a striking preference for multiples of five starting from the age of thirty. Le Bohec 1987: 62–3 counts 238 multiples of five out of 383 known ages of deceased soldiers of the *legio* III *Augusta* (Numidia). See Laes 2007 for the dossier of the inscriptions from Rome.
[45] Le Bohec 1987: 63–4.

2.3 Ages in practice

exactly the number of *lustra*, when they ignored the three or four years in between. Modern sociology and psychology have pointed to the preference for rounded numbers. When reading the papyri, one notices many examples of carelessness in mentioning one's own age.[46] However, a study by Walter Scheidel on age rounding in Graeco-Roman Egypt has shown that the range of inaccuracy in the reporting of age is by and large reasonable, certainly if one compares it to the situation in present-day developing countries. In official tax documents or the census, which took place every fourteenth year, the results appear to be fairly accurate, compared to what one finds in censuses from the Philippines or Bangladesh.[47] Deviations or rounding are not uncommonly to be explained by cultural habits: the ages of women are more often rounded than those of men, the master of the house makes the declaration for the census and so the rounded numbers for women may imply less attention being paid towards females. Finally, there is also the possibility of fraud: (bastard) children are omitted; age is possibly exaggerated to avoid taxes. This does not mean that people in antiquity had an awareness of age exactly comparable to our own. Since the link between age rounding and illiteracy has been firmly proved, there must have been at least some difference.[48] Moreover, regional differentiation played a role: country people generally have a less accurate age awareness than do city-dwellers, who are governed by the calendar of public life.[49] This last conclusion is not unimportant if one remembers that 80% of the total population of the Empire actually lived in the countryside.

Occasionally one catches a glimpse of how the inhabitants of the Roman Empire coped with the factor of age. As we have shown above, age could be important in some cases. In a petition a certain lady Marciana asked for imperial exemption, arguing that she was not yet twenty-five years of age.[50] The answer of the emperors Diocletian and Maximian was as follows:

> You claim not yet to be twenty-five years of age? Go to the governor of your province and prove your age! (*Cod. Iust.* 4, 19, 9)

---

[46] The best known example is Aurelius Isidorus, who claimed to be thirty-five in April 297, thirty-seven in April 308, forty in August 308, forty-five in June 309 and forty again in June 309. See Salmon 1987: 110. Scheidel 1996: 88 observes that some readings are actually uncertain, and warns against drawing sweeping conclusions from this case.
[47] Scheidel 1996: 63 and 87. See pp. 60–71 for a thorough discussion of the census lists.
[48] See Duncan-Jones 1977. Scheidel 1996: 89 recognises the value of this principle, but warns against an excessive implementation of it.
[49] Scheidel 1996: 70.
[50] During the reign of Diocletian or Constantine permanent tutelage seems to have been abolished. See Kaser 1971–5 II: 222.

According to the *Codex Justinianus* birth certificates were sometimes lost in the archives.⁵¹ Falsifications and miscounting were possible. In the year 293 a certain Livius initially claimed to be a *maior*. Afterwards, he withdrew his statement: he was still a *minor*. The emperors Diocletian and Maximian advised the governor of the province to re-examine the evidence for the age of the young man.⁵² Living witnesses were often more important than written testimonies from the archives: one simply called in some people who were prepared to certify one's age.⁵³ Or physical appearance was decisive, as in the case of the young man who looked older than twenty-five, but who turned out in fact to be younger.⁵⁴

A nuanced view thus seems appropriate. People in antiquity did not have an age awareness comparable to ours, but nor did they live with utter indifference towards the factor of age. On the contrary, age was important in Roman law. Whenever it turned out to be necessary to prove one's age, people resorted to *ad hoc* solutions: one was as old as one claimed to be, *citra causarum cognitionem* – as long as the opposite was not proved.⁵⁵

The consequences for the existence of youth as a separate group in society are clear. On the basis of the criterion of age, it is impossible that young people had the feeling of belonging to a tightly defined group. The same accounts for the lack of fixed boundaries of the phase of youth. The divisions of the human life course also displayed a rather vague demarcation of youth. However, this does not necessarily prove the absence of youth in Roman society, since it is certainly possible that young people manifested themselves in other areas.

---

⁵¹ *Cod. Iust.* 4, 21, 6. See Parkin 2003: 383 for more references.
⁵² *Cod. Iust.* 6, 23, 5 (falsifications); 2, 42, 4 (Livius). *Cod. Iust.* 2, 42 is a whole chapter on age declarations and possible falsifications or uncertainties.
⁵³ Implied in *Dig.* 27, 1, 2, 1 (Modestinus). See Parkin 2003: 181 on the importance of living witnesses.
⁵⁴ *Dig.* 4, 4, 32 (Paul).   ⁵⁵ Parkin 2003: 31–5.

CHAPTER 3

Terminology and characteristics of youth

3.1 Terminology

In the previous chapter, on minority and majority, we discussed the place of youth in the life cycles of the Greeks and Romans. In the literary and documentary sources several words are found to denote youth and youths.

The Greek language contains a remarkably rich variety of words for a young man: *meirakion, ephebos, ko(u)ros, neanias, neos, neoteros, neaniskos*.[1] These words refer in some contexts to a specific age but in most cases they are non-technical and denote rather vaguely the period between childhood and manhood. But not always, because some of these words were also used for adults. *Neos*, for example, normally denoted a young man between approximately twenty and thirty years of age, but could also denote an adult, even up to fifty years. The word *pais*, which means 'child', could be used to denote a young man of seventeen or eighteen years of age.[2] There was no word for puberty but *hebe* comes close to it; one would expect then that *ephebos* denoted an adolescent from about twelve years of age, but in Chapter 7 we will show that the word *ephebos* did not refer to a specific age in the Hellenistic and Roman periods. A *neaniskos* could be younger than an *ephebos*, or of the same age or even older (synonym of *neos*), but the word could also mean 'soldier'.[3] For a marriageable girl Greeks often used the word *numphe*. But this word could also denote a young bride. *Parthenos* and *kore* were other terms for young girls, but these were also used for little children and for adults. Much confusion therefore surrounds the vocabulary. Often the social category (social status, marital state) and the context (epitaph, consolation decree) were more important than the actual age.

---

[1] Garland 1990: 13–15 and 164–7; Kleijwegt 1991: 56 and 2004: 866–7.
[2] Laes 2004: 166; Strubbe 2005: 102.
[3] Prag 2007: 90–1. A striking example is the epitaph of Panticapaeum of Heliodorus, deceased at the age of thirty-two, who in an affective way is called *artichnous neanias* ('a young man with the first bloom on') by his brothers (*CIRB* 134).

In Latin too, terms for youth and youths were often used loosely.[4] The biographer Suetonius, for example, called Caesar, just before being elected as an *aedilis* at the age of thirty-four, an *adulescens*.[5] The same word could be used for adults in their forties, as we have already seen in the case of Cicero, at age forty-three. And *iuvenis*, 'young man', could be used for teenagers and men over fifty.[6] In Chapter 7, on associations of young men, we will encounter a man of about fifty years who was a member of the *iuvenes*. *Adulescens* and *iuvenis* were used in literature roughly as synonyms. The former term was in use mainly until the end of the Republic, while from the Augustan period onwards the latter became more common. The Latin word *puer*, which means 'child', could be used for youths in their late teens, just as in the case of the Greek word *pais*.[7]

The ancient world had no specific terms which clearly demarcated youth. Youth was a long period with no exact beginning and an even less exact ending. There were also no words which denoted phases or subdivisions within youth, as we have today: teenager, adolescence, puberty. There was no specific word in Greek and Latin to denote adolescents from twelve to twenty years old. Does this mean that adolescence was not perceived as a distinct period of life? Things are not that simple: the absence of a specific term does not necessarily imply the absence of a consciousness of the period as a separate phase of life.[8] The lack of exact terms, incidentally, often renders it extremely difficult, if not impossible, for scholars to define the age group about which a source provides information.

3.2 Characteristics of youths and adolescents

When we look at adolescents these days, we generally see a period of 'storm and stress'. Many of them fight fierce battles with parents and teachers over clothing and hairstyles, pocket money, what time they should return home at night, and so on; they fall in love and experiment with sexuality; they idolise sports players, rock 'n' roll musicians and movie-stars. Adolescents

---

[4] Kleijwegt 1991: 55. For Latin synonyms of *adulescens/adulescentia* and *iuvenis/iuventus*, see Eyben 1977: 37–40.
[5] Suetonius, *Jul.* 9, 3.
[6] The epitaph of a fifty-year-old man from Auzia in Mauretania calls the deceased 'flower of youth' (*flos iuventutis*): *CIL* VIII 9158 from AD 247. Or was this man a 'flower' to his parents during his youth? *AnEp* (2003) 814 is the epitaph of a *iuvenis* who died at the age of thirty-six and was married (Forum Traiani on Sardinia).
[7] *CIL* VI 8613, cited in Chapter 10 p. 194.
[8] See the discussion of the absence of a specific word in Latin to denote early childhood in Laes and Strubbe 2006: 36–9.

3.2 Characteristics of youths and adolescents

want to decide their own lives, free from all authority. They search for their own identity and wish to affirm it. Internally, however, they are tormented by violent feelings of uncertainty, alternating with idealism and sometimes also with depression. They hardly know what they want to achieve, but all their desires must be satisfied immediately: 'I want it all and I want it now.'

How did Greeks and Romans characterise adolescents, or – since terminology is usually vague – youths after childhood?[9] To begin with, they observed that in the period after childhood the ability for logical thought (*logos*) emerged. Together with physical maturation (corporal puberty), mental maturation started from about fourteen years onwards. The youth began to think rationally, to reason, to abstract. Maturation also took place in the realm of morality. The youth became aware of good and evil, of justice and injustice, of virtue and vice, of duty and pleasure. But the Romans emphasised that the *logos* was still underdeveloped; and the period was still a phase of weakness with many slips. The young man was thoughtless, licentious, he did not worry about the future, he was easily influenced, playful, prodigal, unrestrained. Vices tempted him. In short, as Cicero said, it was a slippery age:

> For nature itself has produced many temptations that can make virtue rest and cause her to lie dormant at times. She shows youth (*adulescentia*) many slippery paths (*vias lubricas*) on which this age can barely stand or walk without falling or slipping. (Cicero, *Pro Cael.* 17, 41)

In the second place, youth was characterised by passions. Since reason was still underdeveloped, youth fell victim to many violent emotions. Typical of youth were passions and desires, especially for pleasure, love, and money. These were intemperate, frequent, aggressive, and uncontrolled. The young man was impulsive: he strove to satisfy his needs at once and without further thought. At the same time he was fickle. Lastly, youth was characterised by juvenile ardour: the adolescent was heated, fiery, hot-tempered. This characteristic was linked with medical theories about the humours, the body fluids. These theories propounded that the body of the young person was warm and moist and its nature sanguine. The young man's blood was abundant and agile. His heart was pounding. Desires were inflamed by the warmth of the blood. We have mentioned already that astrologers, among them Ptolemy, related this characteristic to the planets. Ptolemy argued that young men from fifteen to twenty-five are characterised by

---

[9] For Greek sources, see Eyben 1999: 396–8 and 401–3; for Latin sources, see Eyben 1977: 66–80; 1993: 9–16 and 1999: 412–13; Harlow and Laurence 2002: 69–71.

lustful desire and lack of self-control, and that they are blinded by overwhelming passion, because that age is in the sign of the planet of Venus.

Aristotle in the *Rhetoric* presents a detailed description of youths (*neoi*); no doubt adolescents made up part of this group (see Fig. 3.1). He describes in sequence the passions, the emotions, the behaviour, and the acts of the *neoi*. This characterisation has been the source for many descriptions of the nature of youth, including by Roman authors.

> The young (*neoi*), by nature, are inclined to desire and capable of realising what they desire. And of all the bodily desires, they are most inclined to pursue those involving sexual pleasures. And they are powerless in this respect. They are changeable and fickle in their desires; their desires are strong but short-lived. For their wishes are impulsive and not long-lasting, like the thirst and hunger of the sick.
>
> And they are hot-tempered and quick-tempered and inclined to give in to their passion, unable to resist their impulses. For, owing to their love of honour, they cannot bear to be slighted, but they are indignant when they think they are being wronged. And they love honour but love victory still more. For youth is eager for superiority and victory is a kind of superiority. And they love both of these, more than they are fond of money. They have very little love of money because they have not yet experienced want, as Pittacus remarks pithily of Amphiaraus.[10] And they are not ill-natured but good-natured because they have not witnessed much wickedness. And they have good faith because they have not experienced much deception yet.
>
> And they are full of hope because the young by nature are hot-blooded, like the drunk, and moreover have not yet experienced much failure. And they live for the most part in hope, because hope is of the future, memory of the past. For the young the future is long, the past short. For in the early years one has nothing to remember but everything to hope for. And they are easily deceived, owing to the aforementioned (trait), because they readily hope. And they are more courageous, because they are hot-tempered and full of hope, the former of which makes them fearless, the latter confident. For no one who is angry feels fear, and the hope of something good inspires confidence. And they are sensitive to shame, for they have not yet conceived the idea of other standards of the honourable but have been educated only according to the established rules and customs of their society. And they are high-minded because they have not yet been humbled by life, nor have they experienced the force of circumstances; moreover, to think oneself worthy of great things is high-mindedness and that is proper to one who is full of hope.
>
> And they prefer to do honourable deeds rather than ones that are to their advantage, for they live more by the rule of moral character than by that of calculation, for calculation aims at the advantageous, virtue at the

---

[10] Pittacus' comment is not extant.

3.2 Characteristics of youths and adolescents

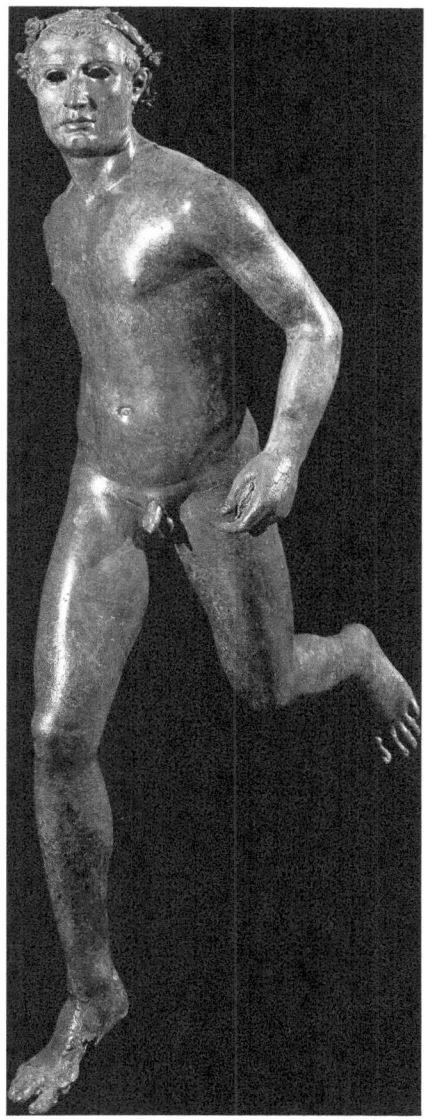

3.1 Bronze honorary statue of a runner from Cyme, late first century BC. The statue was found at sea by fishermen. The runner has a laurel wreath on his head as a sign of victory; perhaps he is running a victory lap. Ephebes competed in various races.
(Archaeological Museum, Izmir.)

honourable. And they love their friends and comrades more than (people of) other ages, because they take pleasure in companionship and as yet judge nothing by its utility, not even their friends. And they commit all their mistakes with excess and vehemence, contrary to the precept of Chilon,[11] for they do everything to excess. They love to excess, and hate to excess, and everything else equally. And they think they know everything, and confidently affirm this. This, in fact, is the root cause of why they do everything in excess.

And if they do wrong, it is with wanton insolence in mind, not small-minded malice. And they are disposed to pity because they deem all men to be of moral valour or better than they (i.e. all men) in fact are. For they measure their neighbours by their own lack of wickedness, so that they think they suffer undeservedly. And they are fond of laughter and hence are witty. For wit is cultivated insolence.

Such, then, is the nature of the young. (Aristotle, *Rhet.* 2, 12, 3–13, 1 (1389 a 3–1390 b 12))

The Romans too characterised youth according to a mixture of negative and positive features. Usually the characterisation is for the most part negative, as in the verses of Horace quoted earlier, in which young persons are reproved for their lightheartedness, vices, rebellion against teachers, prodigality, and other weaknesses. But Seneca, Cicero, and Tacitus on the other hand mention the beauty, charms and elegance, cheerfulness, sincerity, and idealism of youth.[12]

All characteristics of youth may be summarised in one word: *ferocitas*, impetuosity or restlessness. Just as childhood is characterised by weakness, impetuosity is the main characteristic of youth, to quote Cicero again:

Human life follows a fixed course. Nature has only one single path, which is run but once. Each stage of life has its own character, so that the weakness of children (*infirmitas puerorum*), the impetuosity of young men (*ferocitas iuvenum*), the seriousness of middle age (*gravitas constantis aetatis*), and the maturity of old age (*maturitas senectutis*) are all natural. One has to submit to it at the right time. (Cicero, *De senect.* 10, 33)

It is obvious that the Romans predominantly spoke in a negative way about youth. We recognise many of these characteristics in modern adolescents. And developmental psychologists describe youths in the same way: fiery and prone to mood swings, critical and recalcitrant, desiring to act independently. They generally also point to the fact that adolescents usually do not get enough sleep (which is the result of changes in sleep patterns caused by changes in melatonine production during growth spurts) and that as a

---

[11] Allusion to the Delphic maxim 'nothing in excess', attributed to Chilon, one of the Seven Sages.
[12] Tacitus, *Ann.* 3, 8, 4; Seneca, *Epist. mor.* 108, 12 and 27; Cicero, *Top.* 7, 32. See Eyben 1977: 125–6.

3.2 Characteristics of youths and adolescents

consequence they are often tired and listless, often interpreted as laziness. This aspect is not stressed in ancient literature. There are only a few general remarks on the idleness of the youth (*desidiosa iuventus*).[13]

The negative judgement of the ancients is the reason why Emiel Eyben has characterised the period of youth as an age of crisis. But was it really so? Are not the most negative judgements uttered by adult Romans, prominent figures and writers, who are characterised themselves by the opposite quality, seriousness (*gravitas*)? The image of youths in literature is indeed constructed by older men who precisely emphasise the differences between youth and maturity, and do not value them.[14] These are often the well-known and almost stereotypical complaints made in every age – including our own – by the older generation which looks down pityingly on the behaviour of the younger generation and finds that everything went better 'in the good old days'. The 'youths' criticised in such complaints are often in their late twenties or early thirties, not in the phase of life we call adolescence. Pliny, for example, wrote of the deceased Junius Avitus that he did not behave like other contemporary *adulescentes*, who are pedantic and arrogant and show no respect for age and authority. Avitus had already been quaestor, so he was at least twenty-six years old![15] Christian authors in late antiquity have contributed much to the negative image arising from Christian ethics. But their complaints are mainly isolated and often moralising statements about the vaguely defined group of youths, not specifically about adolescents. It is certainly possible to collect all such texts and to find out how the Romans thought about youth and to call this a period of mental and moral crisis. And it is possible to collect texts which present social, physical or psychological explanations of the alleged crisis. But if a scholar does so, he fails to do justice to the ancient texts. He makes the ancient sources say more than they mean, just by putting them together and creating a cumulative image of what in reality is scattered over an enormous area and period of time. As we have said, the existence of a large number of passages in which characteristics of youths are described does not imply that *adulescentes* were perceived as a distinct group, comparable to modern adolescents.

The period between childhood and adulthood was seen as a transitional phase during which a young man had to be and could be educated by an

---

[13] Eyben 1977: 86 n. 96; for example Seneca the Elder, *Contr.* 1 pr. 8 (see p. 139 below). This is of course a different theme from that of the *otium* of youth.
[14] Eyben 1977: 66–76 and 1993: 11–14; cf. the criticism by Pleket 1979: 185; Meadows 1993.
[15] Pliny, *Epist.* 8, 23.

elder to become a morally responsible citizen, no longer subject to desires and excesses unsuited to manhood, including in the realm of sex. So the education of the young Caelius Rufus was placed in the hands of Cicero and Marcus Crassus, older men. They looked after him, advised him, and chaperoned him whenever he received guests. But when Rufus was about nineteen years old, supervision ended and things went wrong. Rufus began to indulge himself in pleasures, new passions, love affairs; his way in this direction was paved by his proximity to the disreputable Clodia, a fashionable and frivolous aristocratic lady, sister of the tribune Clodius, who had rallied around her a host of young admirers. If the teachers did not restrain the impetuous character of the young man and he fell into the hands of an evil person, things could turn out badly, even for the state. The historian Sallust describes the bad influence of Catiline, who in 63 BC organised a conspiracy against the state. It is true that Sallust was a moralist, who took the moral decay of Roman society of the first century BC as his guide to the writing of history. But throughout his work, we catch glimpses of the aristocratic *jeunesse dorée* who were carried away willingly into dubious adventures.

> Most of all, Catiline sought the friendships of the young (*adulescentes*). Their minds, still pliable and soft, were easily seduced by temptation. He carefully noted the passion that burnt inside each of them, according to his years. He supplied harlots to some; he bought dogs and horses for others. In short, he spared neither expense nor his own decency, provided he could make them submissive and faithful to himself. (Sallust, *Cat.* 14, 4–6)

The Roman state was indeed threatened by the danger of conspiracies in the turbulent times of the late Republic whenever young men from the elite, impressionable as they were, were led astray by corrupt leaders. Strict teachers wished to keep young people far away from vice and to watch over them continuously. But most parents and teachers seem to have been rather more understanding. As we will see later, they were convinced that the restless behaviour would burn itself out. It comes as no surprise to learn that strict moralists and church fathers were less indulgent.

CHAPTER 4

Rites of passage

Even when adolescence is not perceived as a distinct phase of life, a society can celebrate the physical coming of age of a youth in a public ceremony. The onset of puberty or the transition to adulthood can be marked by a ritual (rite of passage). Such rituals are often determined by local traditions and rules. Since the Roman Empire was a conglomerate of many different peoples and cultures, there existed very many different rites of passage or initiation.

4.1 In the Greek East

In the Greek world of the Hellenistic and Roman periods it is not clear whether rituals marking the end of the period of childhood were performed systematically. In classical times rites of passage existed in many places to symbolise the transition of a boy to adulthood,[1] mainly in conservative and backward areas: on Crete, in Arcadia, at Sparta. In the latter there was the notorious *krypteia*, which has been abundantly discussed by many scholars but remains surrounded by many uncertainties.[2] According to tradition (a small number of?) young Spartans were sent away from time to time into the countryside where they had to survive. They were armed with just a dagger and had to find or steal their food. Some sources report that during the daytime they hid themselves and at night killed every (?) helot (state slave) they were able to catch. The *krypteia* may have been an initiation rite but its character apparently changed in the late third century BC, when it turned into some kind of training for military scouting.[3] Another Spartan tradition which is sometimes interpreted as an initiation rite was the stealing

---

[1] Garland 1990: 174–83.
[2] Burkert 2004: 122–3 with ancient sources and literature; Christien and Ruzé 2007: 298–301; Berger 2008.
[3] Berger 2008: 157; Plutarch, *Cleom.* 28, 4.

of cheeses from the altar of Artemis Orthia, while other young men defended the altar with whips. In the Roman period this rite had become a rather bloody public spectacle. Cicero and Pausanias apparently witnessed the savage flogging.[4] At Athens the transition of a youth to adulthood gradually took place during the period from sixteen to twenty years. Around the age of sixteen a boy was introduced into his *phratria* (family group) for the second time (the first time occurred shortly after birth). This ceremony took place on the third (last) day – called *Koureotis* – of the *Apatouria* festival, celebrated in autumn.[5] The youth's hair was cut in a ceremonial way. It was sacrificed to Artemis, probably together with an animal and wine. In the course of his eighteenth year the young man was officially enrolled in the register of the members of his *deme* (local district). This happened at an annual ceremony in the city (probably in late summer) for all candidates at the same time. The *boule* (council) conducted an examination beforehand into their age and descent. Those registered were judged to be adults, no longer subject to the authority of their father. The young men could marry without parental consent and could be brought to court for their actions. The young Athenians, however, did not yet receive full political rights. They still had to complete the *ephebeia*, a two-year period of compulsory military training. At the end they were enrolled on the register of the citizens as *neoi*. Only then did they acquire full rights as citizens and become entitled to attend the people's assembly.

What rituals survived into the post-classical period is unclear. The *ephebeia* was instituted in almost all Greek cities but its character changed fundamentally, as will be argued in Chapter 7. It is probable that everywhere (except in Egypt) boys were considered adults and received full political rights when they turned eighteen. It is quite possible that the ritual act of cutting the hair took place at some point in the transition to adulthood. Hair-cutting rites are indeed well attested in the Greek world, even in the imperial period. The hair could be offered to various gods, often river gods or nymphs who were thought to protect children. The ritual act of cutting the hair of adolescents is invested with many different meanings by scholars. Each of these interpretations certainly contains something of value.[6] Some scholars see the rite as a magical means of avoiding the

---

[4] Singor 2008: 144–5; Cicero, *Tusc. disp.* 2, 34 and Pausanias, *Perieg.* 3, 16, 10–11. Libanius (fourth century AD) writes in his Autobiography that he attended at Sparta 'the Festival of the Whippings' (*Or.* 1, 23).

[5] Garland 1990: 179–80; Legras 1993: 121–2, but Leitao 2003: 112–13 has pointed out that hair-cutting at this festival is rather weakly attested. A comparable rite also existed in other poleis, such as Delphi, in the Classical period; see Cole 1984: 235; Legras 1993: 122.

[6] Leitao 2003: 114.

pollution or evil spirits that threaten the adolescent in transition by symbolically transferring the pollution or the attention of the spirits to a lock of hair that is cut and removed. Others see the offering as the restitution of the child – the hair symbolises the entire person, being a *pars pro toto* – to the deity who protected the child during childhood now left behind. Others again see the cutting as the symbolic closing off of the old status and the passing over to a new one, comparable to the laying aside of a dress, for example. The rite was usually a private family affair, which demonstrated and confirmed the family's identity and solidarity. Epigraphic records derive from, among other places, Thebes in Thessaly (early imperial period?) and from the island of Paros (third century AD).[7] At Panamara, near Stratoniceia (Caria), 100 inscriptions from the late second century AD onwards are preserved, mentioning offerings of hair made by boys to Zeus *Panemer(i)os* at the *Komyrion* festival.[8] However, it is not absolutely certain that this ritual was a rite of passage. In some instances a father offered his hair along with his sons. One boy dedicated his hair in three successive years. One inscription mentions that five brothers offered their hair all together. Not a single dedication, incidentally, records the age of the dedicants. Maria Girone has therefore assumed that the offering had a different meaning: an annual commemoration of the miraculous help provided by Zeus of Panamara to his sanctuary at the time of the attack of Q. Labienus in 40 BC; this disloyal general had started a revolt against the Romans, without much success. The offering aimed at winning the god's favour for the sanctuary and the dedicants.[9] David Leitao, on the other hand, who published his work at the same time as Girone, does believe that the ceremony was a rite of passage. He argues that fathers may have decided to offer their hair along with their sons in a burst of enthusiasm. The fact that several brothers dedicated their hair together may be explained by the fact that there was no specific age at which one cut one's hair: the family decided. Leitao further stresses that the hair-cutting rite is usually associated with youths, and that some dedicants at Panamara are in fact young.[10] Not all of

---

[7] Leitao 2003: 115; for Paros, see Melfi 2002: 350–5.

[8] *I. Stratonikeia* 1, 401–500, republished by Girone 2003: 24–34; a new dedication from Lagina in the neighbourhood of Stratoniceia: *SEG* LII (2002) 1070.

[9] Father along with his sons: *I. Stratonikeia* 1, 402, 428, 463; repeated offerings *I. Stratonikeia* 1, 414–16; five brothers together: *I. Stratonikeia* 1, 434. For earlier interpretations, among others in the context of initiation into a mystery cult, see Girone 2003: 37. Rumscheid 2004: 43–7 connects the lock (as depicted on the grave monument of the (slave?) boy Cinnamus at Mylasa, Caria; *SEG* LIV (2004) 1144) with a dedication to Isis; see n. 18 below.

[10] Leitao 2003: 115–18; young persons offering: *I. Stratonikeia* 1, 412 (but the central word, *neaniskoi*, is largely restored!).

these arguments convince. Whatever the case may be, if the ceremony was a rite of passage, it is clear that the performance had nothing to do with the acquisition of citizenship, because the hair of slaves was also sometimes offered to the god. In other cities than Panamara rites of passage with the hair-cutting ritual no doubt displayed regional and local variants. Such *kourosyna* are still mentioned in the fourth century AD by the church father Gregory of Nazianzus.[11]

The suggestion has been made that Athenian girls in the distant past performed the rite of the *arkteia* at the onset of puberty: they performed certain ritual acts as 'she-bears' (*arktoi*) at the festival of Artemis Brauronia at Brauron (East Attica). But in the classical period the nature of the rite had completely changed: the age of the girls was lowered to ten years and their number was limited. Perhaps it had become a ceremony of a private nature, the transition of the girl to the condition of marriageable *parthenos*, and thereby the preparation for marriage, motherhood and household tasks, or maybe it was a public ceremony in order to propitiate the goddess Artemis.[12] It seems that no general ritual took place for girls at the onset of puberty. Marriage marked for them the transition to womanhood. This transition was accompanied by a number of rites. Just before marriage the girl cut her hair and dedicated a lock to Artemis. She could offer her girdle, which she would have worn as a *parthenos* since puberty, to the goddess known as *Lysizonos*. She also dedicated her toys – doll, ball, knucklebones – to Artemis or other deities.[13] It looks very probable that such rites continued to exist in the Greek cities in post-classical times. The offering of a lock of hair and the donation of toys are rites of passage which are found in most ancient populations. Pausanias (second century AD) says that he saw in the temple of Hera in Olympia a small doll's bed, decorated with ivory; it was said to be the toy of Hippodameia, daughter of Oinomaus, legendary king of Elis.[14] At Panamara a father dedicated the hair of his daughter Apphion to Zeus *Panemeros*, probably in a ceremony of passage, such as described above.[15]

---

[11] Gregory of Nazianzus, *Or.* 40, 1. See Eyben 1999: 435.
[12] Cole 1984: 238–42; Garland 1990: 187–91; Dillon 2002: 93–4, 220–1; Faraone 2003. For comparable rites outside Athens, such as in Thessaly, see Cole 1984: 242.
[13] Dillon 2002: 215–16. Faraone 2003: 60 argues that every girl made an offering to Artemis before marriage, often in a temple of the goddess (at Brauron, Mounychia), in order to protect herself against that goddess – often identified with the dangerous Hekate – either in general or specifically during childbirth. The object offered could be hair. This private ritual was not a rite of passage.
[14] Pausanias, *Perieg.* 5, 20, 1.
[15] *I. Stratonikeia* 1, 485; the father dedicated statues of Perseus and the Gorgo at the same time, and demonstrated in this way the socioeconomic standing of his family. For a possible female rite of passage in Hellenistic Thessaly, see *SEG* LVII (2007) 496.

4.1 In the Greek East

More information on rites at the end of childhood survives from Graeco-Roman Egypt.[16] Strabo, writing at the beginning of our era, states the following about the customs of the Egyptians:

> One of the customs they (= the Egyptians) observe very strictly is that they raise all children who are born, and that they circumcise the boys and trim the genitals of the girls, as is also customary among Jews. (Strabo, *Geogr.* 17, 2, 5)

But the account of Strabo is not reliable. It is true that in Pharaonic Egypt boys were circumcised, but the custom died out in the Graeco-Roman period, except for members of the priestly caste. For boys of the Hellenised urban elite the transition to adulthood went hand in hand with admittance to a social class, according to which their social identity was defined. In the year a boy reached thirteen or fourteen, a written declaration was drafted, called *epikrisis* or *eiskrisis* ('scrutiny'), containing the affirmation of his status and the request to admit him to the class of the 'metropolites' (the citizens of a metropolis, the capital of a *nome*, who enjoyed fiscal privileges). At the same age a petition could be presented requesting that the boy be enrolled in the 'gymnasial' class, the Hellenised elite who frequented the gymnasium. Such an application stated that the parents and ancestors (sometimes going back several generations) were members of that class. A boy with Greek forebears was then admitted to the Greek *ephebeia* and the gymnasium. A specimen of such a status declaration comes from Tebtynis in the Fayum, from AD 181:

> To Sarapion and Serenus, ex-gymnasiarchs and officials for the *epikrisis*, from Eudaemon, son of Heron, and from his wife and sister Sarapias both from the metropolis (*sc.* Arsinoë) and registered in the 'Treasuries quarter'. Sarapias acts under the guardianship of Eudaemon.
> Since Heron, the son that has been born to us, is in the present third year of (the reign of) Marcus Aurelius Commodus Antoninus Caesar the lord approaching the age of fourteen and ought to be selected, we append our claims. We were both returned in the census of the twenty-third year of the deified Aelius Antoninus and of the fourteenth year of the deified Aurelius Antoninus in the aforesaid 'Treasuries quarter', returning with ourselves only our son Heron who is now a candidate for selection. Accordingly we present this petition.
> Signed by me, Sarapion, ex-gymnasiarch, through Antoninus, scribe. In the twenty-first year of Marcus Aurelius Commodus Antoninus Augustus, on the 7th day of the month Epeiph. (*P. Tebt.* II 320 with minor omissions)

---

[16] For rites of passage for boys, see Montserrat 1991 and 1996: 36–40. For the procedure of *eiskrisis* ('scrutiny'), see Lewis 1983: 41–3; Legras 1999: 151.

On the occasion of the *epikrisis* a banquet was held in the private home or in a public building. The boy was the guest of honour and was crowned with a garland.

Besides this, another ritual presumably took place in Egypt, the cutting of the hair. A very small number of papyri from Oxyrhynchus mentions a festival, *mallokouria* (rather than *mellokouria*); unfortunately, little is known about it. *Mallokouria* means 'the occasion of cutting the hair-lock' (*mellokouria* would mean 'the occasion when one is about to become a *kouros* or youth'). A papyrus found at Oxyrhynchus contains the declaration of a certain Heracleides. He informs various officials at Alexandria who regulate ephebate admission that his son Theon has had his long hair cut off in the Great Serapeum (the sanctuary of the god Serapis) in the presence of the priests and other officials.[17] This was apparently a public ceremony at which the long lock of hair worn by boys of the Greek elite was cut.[18]

According to Strabo, girls were circumcised too, but it is doubtful whether this was common practice.[19] Certain literary texts seem to confirm that (parts of) the genitalia of Egyptian girls were indeed excised. Apart from Strabo, the church father Ambrose, for example, who wrote in the late fourth century AD, said that the Egyptians circumcise their daughters in their fourteenth year when their monthly periods begin.[20] However, Dominic Montserrat thinks it improbable that the practice was widespread in Graeco-Roman Egypt, because we do not find evidence of it in the gynaecological texts (from the Dynastic period onwards) nor in the medical papyri of the Roman period, nor do we find any other clear sign (on mummies, for example). It cannot, however, be excluded that the practice was indeed regular.[21] Another custom related to girls at the onset of puberty and the beginning of their monthly periods may have been the organisation

---

[17] *P. Oxy.* XLIX 3463 from AD 58. For the other texts (second and third centuries AD) and a discussion, see Legras 1993: 114–18.
[18] For the typical lock of hair (*mallos*) of boys, to be seen, for example, on mummy portraits, see Legras 1993: 123–7. It is a long tuft of hair which was left uncut from a certain age until fourteen years, usually behind the right ear and braided into a tress. Children of the indigenous Egyptian elite had a similar lock. The same lock, called 'lock of Horus', was worn by boys who had been initiated into the mysteries of Isis, as can be seen on several monuments, also outside Egypt; see Goette 1989.
[19] For rites of passage for girls, see Montserrat 1991 and 1996: 41–6. All texts on circumcision of girls are collected and commented upon by Knight 2001.
[20] Ambrose, *De Abr.* 2, 11, 78.
[21] Today circumcision of girls is still the norm in Egypt, irrespective of religion: over 90% of all women aged fifteen or older have been circumcised. See the *Final Report on the Egypt Demographic and Health Survey 2008*, which can be consulted on the internet.

of a feast called *therapeuteria*. A few papyri from Oxyrhynchus from the Roman period mention that a father has invited guests to a dinner in honour of his (unmarried) daughter.[22] The girl had probably performed some kind of ritual or an offering in a sanctuary at an important moment of her unmarried life, quite possibly when her monthly periods began (or as a preliminary to marriage?). This affirmed the important transition and the new status of being marriageable, but this cannot be proven.

4.2 In Rome and the Latin West

In the earliest history of Rome a young man became liable for military service at seventeen. This age, then, marked the end of childhood. Later, from around the first century BC, most Roman citizens no longer served in the army. The moment for coming of age was then lowered to the onset of puberty. In practice it was his father (or guardian) who decided whether a boy had reached manhood on the basis of the physical changes to his body. That was usually around fourteen or fifteen years.[23] But it could happen some years earlier or later, roughly between thirteen and eighteen years. Octavian, for example, reached adulthood shortly after his sixteenth birthday.[24] Age limits were thus much more flexible than in our society. Late Roman jurists on the other hand wished for clear limits, and fixed fourteen years (that is the end of the fourteenth year of life) as the beginning of adulthood in judicial cases, as we have seen.

Rituals marked the transition to adulthood in the Roman world.[25] These did not imply that the young man became an adult and responsible citizen all at once: the period of youth was a transitional stage to the adult world. At a moment determined by his father, a free-born boy laid aside the attributes of childhood: the *bulla*, the protective charm he had worn around his neck since his birth, and the *toga praetexta*, the toga bordered by a purple stripe. He dedicated these to the household gods, the Lares. Before donning the man's toga, the boy put on a special tunic, the *tunica recta* (or *regilla*), that his father had given him. Then he received the *toga virilis* (or *pura* or *libera*)

---

[22] Among others *P. Lond.* 3078 (*SB* XIV 11944) from the second century AD. For the other texts, see Montserrat 1990: 206–7.
[23] Dolansky 2008: 49 has stressed that puberty was not a formal requirement for the ceremony; however, it was common practice to celebrate the rite when the boys were already in the process of maturing physically.
[24] Suetonius, *Aug.* 8. See Laes 2006a: 253 and 2011: 279–80 for variations in age.
[25] Néraudau 1984: 251–6; Eyben 1985: 411–16; Harlow and Laurence 2002: 67–9; Rawson 2003: 142–4; Laes 2006a: 251–4; Dolansky 2008.

from his father, the plain white adult toga. This usually took place on 17 March, the festival of the *Liberalia* in honour of Liber Pater (a very old deity of fertility), but other dates were also possible (Octavian, for example, assumed the toga on 18 October). Ovid devotes a few lines of poetry to this day in his *Fasti*, in which he describes the Roman calendar and its festival days. The name of Liber summons up for him associations with *libertas*, freedom:

> It remains for me to discover, shining Bacchus, why the gown of liberty is given to boys on your day. Is it because you seem to be always a boy and a youth and your age is in the middle between the two? Or is it because you are a father (*pater*) that fathers commend their pledges, their sons, to your care and divine protection? Or is it because you are Liber that the gown of liberty is assumed and a freer life starts under your custody? (Ovid, *Fasti* 3, 771–8)

The day had a private as well as a public aspect. In the morning an offering and a meal took place in the home. Then the boy went to the Forum and the Capitol together with his father, family, and friends. He sacrificed to Liber, and perhaps also to Jupiter and Juventas on the Capitoline Hill. His complete name may then have been registered in the *album* of the citizens at the *tabularium*, the records office. In the evening a party was held for family, friends, and relatives and the boy received presents from all of them.[26]

From Augustus' reign the public ceremony at Rome probably took place in the Forum of Augustus. Fanny Dolansky has pointed out that it is not clear whether the boys who had donned the toga were required or simply encouraged to come to the Temple of Mars Ultor in that forum.[27] In any event, that particular setting was very significant, for it was loaded with symbolism. The Temple of Mars Ultor, the war god, was vowed by Augustus on the occasion of the battle against the murderers of his adoptive father Julius Caesar and dedicated in 2 BC. More generally, Mars alluded to the military victories of Augustus: the new citizen ought in principle to fight in wars for the Roman state from his seventeenth year onwards. In the centre of the Forum stood Augustus' statue as the Father of his country; around him in niches stood statues of famous Roman mythical and historical heroes. They were *exempla*, or role-models, for the behaviour of the new citizen towards the state. But familial bonds and the duties of the young

---

[26] After donning the adult toga, adolescents were allowed to recline at banquets in contrast to children, who were usually seated; see Roller 2006: 169–75.
[27] Dolansky 2008: 52.

man towards his parents, family and ancestors were also stressed by the statues, in particular by those of the trio of Aeneas, Ascanius, and Anchises: father, son, and grandfather. According to legend they helped each other when they fled from Troy.

The day of the adoption of the adult toga was very important. A new citizen was 'born' for the state. The young man received full citizen rights (political, juridical), although these were restricted on some points by the *Lex Laetoria* and the *Lex Villia*, as we have seen. It marked the beginning of the young man's public life. In the private sphere he still remained under the authority of his father (the *patria potestas*) until the latter's death.

From the day the young man donned the *toga virilis*, he could contract a marriage (but not without parental consent). Alongside puberty, fertility had started. A young man wearing the adult toga was seen as capable of penetrative sex, unlike a child. The putting aside of the child's *toga praetexta* led to the removal of protection in the public sphere. The *toga virilis* brought freedom and the period after its adoption was associated with violence, drinking, and sex. The young man was free to wander through the Subura, the red-light district of Rome with its innumerable brothels and prostitutes. The satirist Persius describes his anxiety at the beginning of this new phase of his life and his newly acquired freedom. He found a mentor and spiritual guide in the person of the Stoic philosopher, Cornutus.

> I was shattered when I had lost the protective purple and had suspended the *bulla*, offered as they had been to the short-girt household gods. My friends were gentle and my gown, now white, permitted me to cast my eyes with impunity over all of Subura. (Persius Flaccus, *Sat.* 5, 30–6)

After Rome's conquest of the East Roman customs and laws were introduced there too. This meant that youths who belonged to elite families in the Greek cities which happened to possess Roman citizenship adopted the adult toga around the age of fourteen to fifteen. This ceremony was celebrated publicly. When Pliny was governor of Bithynia, he reported in a letter to the emperor Trajan that 'it is customary there, when a person dons the manly toga or contracts marriage or enters an office or dedicates a public building, to invite the entire city council and a large part of the citizenry, and to distribute one or two *denarii* (to each)'.[28] Pliny was of the opinion that this went too far because sometimes a thousand people or more were invited. The emperor agreed that this was an unreasonable number of people. It is clear that the wealthy municipal elite used the ceremony for

---

[28] Pliny, *Epist.* 10, 116, 1.

self-aggrandisement, for an exuberant display of its wealth and its adoption of the new Roman customs. A Latin papyrus from Alexandria, dated to AD 110, states that lists of recent recipients of the male toga living in the provinces were displayed in the Forum of Augustus at Rome, while copies were kept in the local record-offices in the provinces.[29]

In the imperial period the offering of hair is sometimes mentioned on the occasion of donning the *toga virilis*.[30] This custom may have been derived from the Greeks. The hair did not come from the beard but was rather a lock from the head. On the morning of the ceremony the hair of the adolescent was cut short. In Rome it was common practice not to shave the first beard until it had fully grown. Down on the chin was the sign of adolescence. The beard was shaved at some time between fourteen and twenty-four years of age, and usually in the early twenties. Octavian shaved his beard for the first time when he was twenty-three. The young *decurio* C. Laetilius Gallus from Iulium Carnicum (northern Italy) died of fever after living for twenty years, seven months, and seven days, before shaving his beard.[31] The dedication of the first full beard (*depositio barbae*) to a god of one's choice probably took place at the festival of the *Iuvenalia*. This had been instituted by Nero on the occasion of his *depositio* when he was twenty-one years old in AD 59. The beard was kept in a precious small box in the sanctuary of the household gods. The ritual marked the symbolic transition into a more adult period of life. From that moment a young male shaved regularly until the beard became fashionable again during the reign of the emperor Hadrian. The rite incidentally marked the end of sexual availability in any paedophile relationship. Not only literary texts record the rite of the *depositio* but inscriptions as well. It is even mentioned in the Christian period.[32]

In the late Roman period the ritual of donning the adult toga seems to have persisted. It is still mentioned in the fourth and even fifth centuries.[33] Although the celebration included a sacrifice to pagan gods, Christians such

---

[29] *P. Mich.* VII 433; see Dolansky 2008: 64 n. 26 and 69 n. 68. There is some evidence that sons of the local elite in the western part of the Roman Empire performed the same rite as the boys at Rome; see Derks (2009) 209–11.
[30] Eyben 1985: 414; Harlow and Laurence 2002: 72–5.   [31] *CIL* v 8652 (*CLE* 629; *IulCarnicum* 42).
[32] *CIL* vi 38425 (*CLE* 1948) from Rome; Pauline of Nola, *Carm.* 21, 377 (end of the fourth century); cf. Eyben 1999: 435.
[33] Dolansky 2008: 59, with sources in notes 24 and 71 (Servius, Augustine). The fact that attending the ceremony is not mentioned by the Roman senator Symmachus as part of his social obligations (late fourth century), which Kunst 2006: 80 considers proof of the dwindling of the institution, may not be significant.

as Tertullian had no problem in attending it (and other family rituals): it was just a social duty.³⁴

Similar rites of passage are not recorded for Roman girls.³⁵ The age at which puberty began for girls varied of course, but was fixed by jurists at the end of the twelfth year. From that age a girl (called *virgo*, virgin) could marry. At around the same age menstruation and fertility started. Ancient physicians observed that sexual maturity occurred earlier in girls than in boys. They proposed several explanations. One was that the female body was somehow inferior to the male. It matured more swiftly, just as inferior fruits ripen more quickly than the hardy.³⁶ Once the physical signs of puberty appeared, the girl was watched over even more closely than before, and was always accompanied (by her former nurse). She had to preserve her virginity until her first marriage. The ancients saw that adolescent girls, just like boys, developed a desire for sexual relations. Since the general idea prevailed that women have little self-control but an excessive sexual appetite, measures had to be taken. Physicians recommended physical exercise or a diet that was not very nourishing.³⁷ When girls in puberty experienced physical or psychological problems, doctors in general advised that they should be allowed to marry as quickly as possible; all problems would then be solved at once.

There was no public ritual at the onset of puberty. Marriage, which was sometimes contracted even before puberty, marked the transition to adulthood for girls. We can only guess what a girl experienced on her wedding day. But we should not forget that in antiquity marriage and motherhood were a girl's aims in life. She was brought up with this expectation, she was prepared for it, and she no doubt longed for it. On the evening before her wedding she probably dedicated her toys, such as dolls and nuts, to the household gods or to Venus or Juno, as well as her *bulla* and her *toga praetexta* if she wore one.³⁸ This symbolised the end of her childhood. She also made an offering to Mutunus Tutunus, a very old deity of coupling and conception. On the day of the wedding she was not conducted to the

---

³⁴ Dolansky 2008: 51, contra Kunst 2006, who argued that in late antiquity a young man took up the white toga (without a special ritual) at around fifteen to sixteen years, after his schooling with the *grammaticus* and at the beginning of his higher education.
³⁵ Néraudau 1984: 256–61; Harlow and Laurence 2002: 54–64; Rawson 2003: 145; Dolansky 2008: 60 n. 3 agrees with Dixon 1992: 101, 215 n. 12 that the assumed absence of rites may be due to the failure of male sources to record them.
³⁶ Macrobius, *Saturn*. 7, 7, 11. See Eyben 1985: 406–7   ³⁷ See p. 144.
³⁸ On the question of whether young free-born girls wore the *toga praetexta*, just as did free-born boys, see p. 31, n. 20.

Forum but to her husband's residence, where she began an entirely new life. She put on a new dress, that of the *uxor* or *matrona*, the married wife.

The end of the period of youth of a young male cannot be fixed so easily: sometime in his twenties, when he married, founded his own home, and assumed social and political responsibilities. This happened at different times for young men and was not marked by any rite of passage.

CHAPTER 5

Youth and ancient medicine

5.1 Medical observations concerning young people: similarities and differences

Modern medicine is surely not the first to observe physiological changes at the onset of puberty, nor did twentieth-century doctors develop the first theories and explanations of these changes. Ancient physicians also treated these questions; they wrote about almost every change in the pubescent human body and tried to offer a physiological explanation.[1] They situated the moment of important bodily change at approximately the age of fourteen, based on the symbolic value of the number seven and numerology (see Chapter 2).[2] Only Galen (second century AD; see below) seems to have understood that coming of age does not happen for everybody at the same moment, and that each division inevitably involves simplification.

> It is not possible to restrict those phases of life with a number, as some have done, except approximately. Coming of age happens for some after the completion of their fourteenth year, for others one year later, sometimes even later. (Galen, *De san. tuenda* 6, 2; 6, 387–8 Kühn)

Sexual maturity was the preeminent criterion for the beginning of puberty:

> Puberty is the adult age, the age at which one is capable of producing offspring. It is named after the full growth (*pubes*), a word that is related to the private parts (*pudenda*), because the first pubic hair starts at this place. (Isidore of Seville, *Diff.* 1, 460)

---

[1] For the most exhaustive studies, see Eyben 1972 and 1977: 42–56. See also Cootjans 2000 and Corvisier 2001.
[2] See for instance, besides the divisions in Chapter 2: Heraclitus 22 A 19 (1, 149, 6–9 Diels); Aristotle, *Hist. anim.* 5, 544 b 25–7; Galen, *De san. tuenda* 6, 2 (6, 387 Kühn); Philo, *Leg. alleg.* 1, 4, 10; Philo, *In Gen.* 2, 5; Aetius, *Plac.* 5, 23 (435 Diels); Censorinus, *De die nat.* 7, 2; Tertullian, *De an.* 38. Galen, *Comm. in Hipp. Aph.* 5 (17, 2, 791 Kühn) situates puberty between fourteen and twenty-five years of age. Cf. Hippocrates, *Aph.* 5, 7 (4, 534 Littré). On Galen's divisions of the life span, see Laes 2006b. On fourteen as a liminal age, see Eyben 1977: 59.

The Roman poet Lucretius informs us about the circumstances of the first seminal discharge. The semen ripens and begins to spread all over the body. In a dream the young boy is titillated by the images of beautiful girls – in this way he has his first nocturnal emission of sperm.[3]

Etymologically the Latin word for adolescence refers to growth and change:

> Adolescents (*adulescentes*) are so called because of the link with the verb 'to grow' (*ab alescendo sic nominatos*). (Varro in Censorinus, *De die nat.* 14, 2)

One often reads that a human being completes his growth in height at the age of twenty-one, after the completion of the third hebdomad. His lateral growth is completed at the age of twenty-eight, after the fourth hebdomad.[4] Some doctors linked this growth with the life spirit, which was also called *pneuma*. Others claimed that body warmth was the main cause of growth: since children and young people are endowed with a warm constitution, their bodies grow steadily.[5] The period of youth is also one's strongest phase of life: one's blood is still unspoiled, fervid, abundant, and movable:[6]

> Only with young people the blood is still unspoiled. Doctors claim that the blood diminishes with age. That is why old men tremble. (Isidore of Seville, *Orig.* 11, 1, 123)

Of course, ancient authors took notice of the most remarkable physiological changes: the growth of the penis and the curving of the breasts, the latter in both girls and boys. According to Aristotle, the humid constitution is the main cause of pronounced breasts and the well-developed genital organ, although in other passages he claims that it is the life spirit or *pneuma* which is mainly responsible for this.[7]

Ancient doctors had various explanations for the breaking and changing of the voice. Aristotle stated that the sperm canals were connected with a vein close to the heart, close to that part of the body which also sets the voice in motion. When the sperm canals widen, the human voice automatically alters, especially in boys.[8] However, in his fourth-century collection of his predecessors' medical theories, the Greek doctor Oribasius sees a connection between children's weak voices and their pores which are still closed in

---

[3] Lucretius, *De rer. nat.* 4, 1030–6.
[4] Pliny the Elder, *Nat. hist.* 11, 87, 216 (height); Macrobius, *Comm. Somn. Scip.* 1, 6, 72 (girth).
[5] Galen, *De temp.* 2, 2 (1, 584 Kühn); *Comm. in Hipp. Epid.* 4, 25 (17, 2, 204 Kühn).
[6] Aristotle, *Hist. anim.* 3, 521 a 31–3. Celsus, *De med.* 3, 22, 8 claims that a human being is in his strongest phase of life from the age of eighteen until that of thirty-five. On this phase, see also Hippocrates, *Aph.* 5, 9 (4, 534 Littré).
[7] Aristotle, *Hist. anim.* 7, 582 a 6–16; *De gen. anim.* 1, 728 b 27–30.
[8] Aristotle, *De gen. anim.* 5, 787 b 26–33. The ancients believed that girls had sperm.

that period of life. The breaking of the voice might thus possibly be connected to the opening of the pores.⁹ Oribasius also explains women's and children's shrill voices by reference to their narrow and short trachea. The expansion of the trachea during adolescence causes the irregularity of the voice.¹⁰ Both Greek and Latin had a specific term for the breaking of the voice: *gallulascere* (a word which could fittingly be translated as 'crowing') and *tragizein* or *irquitallire*, two words connected with terms for the male goat, an animal that was not only notorious for its foul stench, but also for its lust. It is as if a male goat lived under the armpits of the adolescent:

> And that is the reason why pubescents are also called *irquitalli*, because of their body stinking like a male goat. (Censorinus, *De die nat.* 14, 7)

The growth of body hair was another sign of coming of age. According to Aristotle, the first body hair was the pubic, then the hair under the armpits and finally the first beard on the chin.¹¹ When, during a visit to the baths, Augustine's father perceived his son's first pubic hair, he was delighted and rushed to his wife to tell her the good news.¹² The first blossom of the beard was obviously a clearer sign to the public.

> A child is called *puer*, because of its purity: it is still pure and does not yet possess the first down or the first blossom of the beard. (Isidore of Seville, *Orig.* 11, 2, 10)

Once again, ancient medicine is eager to offer various explanations. As the earth carries most fruit at the end of the spring and the beginning of the summer, when the ground is dry and humidity draining away, so is the warm and dry skin of the young man the ideal soil for the growth of body hair. It grows most abundantly in those places where the skin is soft and warm, under the armpits, on the chin, and near the genitals. Besides, children's pores are too weak to make the growth of hair possible.¹³ Even youth pimples are mentioned, albeit very rarely: they appear during the coming of age together with the first beard and they emit a watery fluid if one starts scratching. If they become hard, they can mutilate the face.¹⁴

---

⁹ Oribasius, *Coll. med. rel.* 6, 10, 10–17 (1, 161–2 Raeder).
¹⁰ Oribasius, *Lib. inc.* 62, 40–3 (4, 170 Raeder). Applied to adolescence: Alexander of Aphrodisias, *Problem.* 1, 125.
¹¹ Aristotle, *Hist. anim.* 3, 518 a 21–3; see also Macrobius, *Saturn.* 7, 7, 3.
¹² Augustine, *Conf.* 2, 3, 6.
¹³ Galen, *De temp.* 2, 5 (1, 611 Kühn); *De usu part.* 11 and 14 (3, 901 and 907 Kühn); *De temp.* 2, 5 (1, 619 Kühn).
¹⁴ Cassius Felix, *De med.* 7. Celsus, *De med.* 5, 28, 15 B deals with pimples containing pus, but situates them in the period of childhood.

The most prolific writer of antiquity, and after Hippocrates the most famous doctor of Graeco-Roman antiquity, was undoubtedly Galen. Born in Pergamum, he lived and worked at the end of the second century AD as a court physician in Rome.[15] The influence of his monumental oeuvre, edited in twenty-two ample volumes, reached far into the nineteenth century and can hardly be underestimated.[16] In one passage, Galen carries systematisation to its limits in drawing a parallel between puberty in boys and in girls:[17]

> Hippocrates claimed the following symptoms of puberty: breasts, sperm, and the womb. Two of those symptoms are equal for men and for women, namely sperm and the breasts. The third symptom, the womb, is typical of women. During the transition from childhood to puberty, the production of sperm and the growing of pubic hair begins in boys. Also the testicles start growing. In the same way, the growing of the breasts starts in girls, as well as menstruation and the changing of the voice – the latter mainly in boys. (Galen, *Comm. in Hipp. Hum.* 2, 36; 16, 338–9 Kühn)

These various texts clearly show how sexual maturity, physical growth, enhancement of physical force, developing genital organs and breasts, the changing of the voice and body odour, and body hair were the subject of speculation and observation by various ancient authors. However, the initial comfortable feeling of recognition should not blind us to obvious differences from contemporary ideas. These differences do not lie primarily in the sometimes strange physiological explanations, which of course need to be understood in the context of less developed medical knowledge. What should rather attract our attention is that ancient theorists almost never linked these physiological changes to psychological consequences. Ancient medicine has virtually nothing to say about shame, inner confusion or a crisis of identity (there is only one indirect comment of Rufus of Ephesus on girls who abandon their childhood games out of shame as they grow up).[18] Physiological explanations of the moral crisis of youth do arise in early Christianity, but need to be understood in the context of the condemnation of sexual lust, the desire of the flesh which hampered the young Christian in

---

[15] For an excellent sociocultural introduction, see Schlange-Schöningen 2003; see Chapter 10.3. See also Laes 2006b and 2008; Hankinson 2008b; Lloyd 2008.
[16] These volumes were edited by Karl Gottlob Kühn in the 1820s and 1830s and are still the only complete edition. The *Corpus Medicorum Graecorum* has been gradually replacing Kühn since 1914.
[17] For a similar text, see Galen, *Comm. in Hipp. Epid.* 4, 27 (17, 2, 212–3 Kühn).
[18] Rufus in Oribasius, *Lib. inc.* 18, 10 (4, 107 Raeder). Eyben 1977: 126–7 offers numerous passages on *pudor* or shame as one of the main characteristics of the young man, but this sense of shame needs to be understood as a social phenomenon (the morally high-minded young man knows his right place in relation to his social superiors), rather than inner confusion due to a lack of self-confidence. For excellent studies on ancient shame, see Barton 1999 and 2001.

his ideal life of asceticism and self-restraint. In this sense, one may say that the vexed and sexually frustrated young man is an invention of Christianity, a question to which we will return in the last chapter of this book.

Ancient literature certainly offers a large number of passages dealing with the young man in search of his destiny, and the moral crisis of youth, and presents manifold explanations such as the influence of the environment or the newly acquired freedom of adulthood.[19] But these are loose and often moralising passages. It is only when they are brought together in an anthology and seen through contemporary eyes that one is inclined to see strong resemblances with our twentieth-century crisis of adolescence. The context, however, is fundamentally different. There is not a single ancient author who reached a view on youth in which medical and physiological, social, and psychological factors were profoundly integrated. Nor do we find opinions which led to the collective perception of a separate social group somehow similar to our pubescents or adolescents. Indeed, ancient doctors thought and speculated a lot on childhood and youth – yet their divisions of the human life span cannot simply be equated to our phases of life.

5.2 Sickness in teenagers: some examples

It was important to ancient doctors to be in direct contact with their patients. Hence, their works regularly offer us concrete cases, snapshots from their daily practice.[20] This is certainly the case in Galen's writings, which confront us with some telling cases of sick teenagers.[21]

As a practitioner, Galen was often confronted with epileptics, and as a young doctor he talked with his young patients. One was a boy aged about twelve years; he was surrounded by the best physicians of his age, including Galen:

> I heard the boy telling of his pains which started in the vicinity of the legs, then spread about the thighs and the socket of the hip, then around the ribs. As soon as the pain reached his head, so he said, he lost consciousness. When the doctors asked him about the nature of the pain he felt in his head, he could not provide them with an adequate answer. (Galen, *De loc. aff.* 3, 1; 8, 194 Kühn)

---

[19] The most exhaustive collection is in Eyben 1977: 63–90. He also recognises the lack of a physiological explanation (Eyben 1977: 106–10). However, he does not sufficiently think through the consequences of this lack.
[20] Horstmanshoff 2006.
[21] For such telling cases, see mainly Gourevitch 2001. Hummel 1999 too offers valuable information.

66   5 Youth and ancient medicine

Another young epileptic proved more capable of talking about his disease in front of a group of doctors:

> He was quite intelligent and able to explain precisely what was going on with him. He expressed himself better than the first patient and explained that what rose to his head resembled a cold breeze. (Galen, *De loc. aff.* 3, 1; 8, 194 Kühn)

More than once, Galen was called in to help sick women or young children. It is remarkable how these groups of patients appear as silent patients in his writings. They never speak for themselves, and the diagnostic conversation is held with the caring fathers or husbands. In the case of a thirteen-year-old boy, things appear to have been different: the doctors took notice of his stories.[22] Even clearer is the case of the sick teenager Sestus, who presumably was one of the prominent young men at Marcus Aurelius' court. He contracted a long-lasting fever, but did everything he could to prove the error of Galen's prognoses. Galen had predicted that if his illness reached a peak on the sixth day a relapse with high fever would follow. As this in fact happened on the sixth day, Sestus did all he could to avoid the predicted relapse. When he finally developed a tremendous fever on the fourteenth day, he did his utmost to conceal this from Galen. It looks as if the arrogant Roman aristocracy was eager to show Galen, the 'wonder doctor from Pergamum', to be in the wrong. When he was proved right, they only reluctantly recognised his intellectual superiority.[23] Young people were quite often awkward and priggish patients; this is highlighted by an autobiographical testimony from Galen. At the age of seventeen he was a zealous student. Day and night, he concentrated on his studies at Pergamum, even during the tremendously hot dog days of August, when his father sought refuge in the coolness of the country. Together with his fellows, the young student gorged himself on seasonal fruit. In autumn he became so ill that bloodletting was inevitable. His father returned to the city, reminded his young son of the diet he used to be given when he was still under his father's wings, and urged his beloved child to stick to his former habits of eating, and not to those of his reckless peers. The following summer, his father diligently observed his son's nutritional habits. No problems occurred. The following year (when Galen was nineteen years old) his father died. Once again, the young Galen stuffed himself with seasonal fruit along with his fellow-students; once again illness and the inevitable bloodletting were the

---

[22] Gourevitch 2001: 43 and 52 on women and children as silent patients.
[23] Galen, *De praen.* 10 (14, 651–7 Kühn). This passage is translated and commented upon by Nutton 1977; see also Gourevitch 2001: 53–6.

5.2 Sickness in teenagers

consequences. So this carried on, year after year, until Galen developed serious trouble with his liver at the age of twenty-seven. He then decided to consume grapes and figs only in moderation and to abandon all other fruit. A friend of his, who was two years older, followed the same regimen, with great success, since for many years he had no complaints. Galen even mentions patients who stuck to the same diet and were free of disease for a period of twenty years. So, his father proved to be right ... but, as a stubborn young man, his beloved son had refused to listen to him.[24]

Galen also informs us about typical activities of young people. A patient suffered from contusions in the nose and the mouth:

> He told me how he had had fun with others during the summer in a pond in the country, playing games in the water, as young people like to practise water sports. But I knew that there were leeches in that water. (Galen, *De loc. aff.* 4, 8; 8, 266 Kühn)

In another passage, we read about a healthy student of philosophy who was burnt by the fierce summer sun.[25]

It would be rash, however, to claim that young people appear as a separate category in Galen's writings. When he mentions their illnesses and cures, he is mainly concerned about his self-promotion, which is quite apparent throughout the whole of his work. Galen was indeed the best doctor in town, capable of curing the fifteen-year-old son of a fellow citizen who suffered from a tumour in the ear, or able to heal the young prince Commodus from his tonsilitis.[26] The following fragment is almost symptomatic of Galen's conceited approach:

> During my first visit to Rome, I examined a young man suffering from heavy fever, alongside the prominent physicians of the city. They disagreed amongst each other and had an argument about the possible consequences of bloodletting. After their endless discussion, I said: 'Your discussion is useless. Nature will not refrain from breaking a blood vessel. The redundant blood will find its way out of the boy's body through his nostrils.' Indeed, they did not have to wait long to watch the bleeding of his nose with their own eyes. They stood there with their mouths open and didn't say a word. From then on, I was deeply hated by them and they gave me the nickname of 'seer'. (Galen, *De opt. med. cogn.*; transl. A. Z. Iskandar)[27]

---

[24] Galen, *De prob.* 1 (6, 755–7 Kühn).   [25] Galen, *De meth. med.* 6, 3 (10, 402–3 Kühn).
[26] Galen, *De comp.* 1, 7 (13, 402–3 Kühn) on tumours of the ear; Galen, *De praen.* 12 (14, 661–5 Kühn) on Commodus. See also Gourevitch 2001: 49–52.
[27] This story is preserved only in an Arabic version; see the edition by Iskandar 1988: 60–3. On young people and fever, see Gourevitch 2001: 80–2.

5.3 Excursus: Aristotle on puberty

Undoubtedly the most extensive description of puberty is offered by Aristotle in his *Historia Animalium*, a work that during the Middle Ages in the West was considered to be the reference encyclopaedia of the biology of humans and animals, albeit in Latin translation. Because of the great cultural and historical importance of this text, we offer the complete passage in translation.

> The male first begins to produce seed, in most cases, when twice seven years have been completed. Simultaneously, the growth of hair starts on the pubes, just as plants that produce seed must first flower, as Alcmaeon of Croton says. Around the same time, the voice begins to change, becomes rougher, more uneven, no longer shrill but not yet deep, nor yet all of one pitch, but resembling badly strung and rough strings. They call this 'goat-bleating'. It is all the more apparent in those who attempt sexual intercourse. For in those who indulge in this intensively, the voice changes into the voice of a man. But in those who abstain (from intercourse), the opposite happens. And if they try to check it through exercises, as some do who devote themselves to choruses, the voice remains unbroken for a long time and undergoes an altogether small change.
>
> And a swelling of the breasts and of the private parts occurs not only in size but also in shape. And at about this time those who try to rub themselves in order to provoke an emission of the seed not only experience pleasure when the sperm is discharged, but also pain. At around the same time, the swelling of the breasts occurs in the females, and the so-called *catamenia* (menstruation) start to flow. This is blood like that of the recently killed. But a white discharge also occurs in girls, when they are quite young, and the more so when they follow a liquid diet. This impedes their growth and emaciates their bodies. In the majority of cases, menstruation starts when the breasts have grown to the height of two fingers. And around this time, the voice in girls also changes to a deeper tone. For while, in general, a woman's voice is higher pitched than that of a man, young women (have higher voices) than older women, just as boys (have higher voices) than do men. But the voice of female children is higher than that of male children and a flute for a maiden is tuned higher than that for a boy.
>
> They are also in very great need of surveillance around this time. For they feel a very strong impulse to perform sexual activities when they begin, so that – if they do not arm themselves against further changes beyond those their bodies themselves make, even when not indulging in sexual activity – (that habit) is likely to continue into later life. For young girls who are sexually very active become more intemperate and so do males, if they are not guarded either in one direction or in both. For the channels become dilated and make open this part of the body with pores and passages. And at the same time the old memory of the accompanying pleasure creates a longing for the intercourse that once took place.

5.3 Excursus: Aristotle on puberty

Some men grow up congenitally impotent and sterile because they are malformed in the genital region. Similarly, women too may grow up congenitally infertile.

Both males and females undergo changes in condition, in becoming more healthy or more sick and, in the body, leaner or fatter or better developed. For after puberty some boys who were previously thin put on weight and become healthier, and vice versa in others. This is also the case for girls. For in all boys or all girls who had residues in their bodies, after these have been discharged, with the sperm in the case of boys, with the *menses* in the case of girls, their bodies grow healthier and thrive, for that which had been impeding their health and nutrition has been removed. But for those who are in the opposite case, their bodies grow thinner and sicklier. For the discharge through the sperm in the case of boys and through the *menses* in the case of girls occurs at the cost of the natural state and the right condition.

Furthermore, in the case of girls, the development of the breasts proceeds differently in one girl from another. For some develop very large breasts, others small. The former in general happens in girls who, being children, tended to residues. For as the menstruation comes nearer but is not yet there, the more moisture there is, the more it compels to flow upwards, until (the menstruation) breaks out. So the breasts at that moment acquire bulk and remain the same in the future. In the males, too, the breasts become more conspicuous and more like those of women, both in young and old men, in those who are moist and smooth and without large blood vessels, and all the more so in those who are dark rather than fair.

Now up to the age of thrice seven years, the seeds are at first infertile. Then they are fertile, but young men and young women produce small and imperfect offspring, as is the case in most other animals. Young women conceive more quickly, but when they have conceived they labour more in childbearing. And the bodies become less developed in general and age faster, both in men who indulge in sexual activities and in women who give birth several times. For it seems that growth stops after the bearing of a third child. Those women who are intemperate towards intercourse and sexual activities become more sedate and restrained after they have given birth several times.

After thrice seven years, women are favourably shaped for childbearing, but men still go on improving. Thin seeds are infertile, but granular ones are fertile and tend to produce male offspring. But thin and unclotted seeds generate female children.

And it is around this age that the growth of the beard occurs in the males. (Aristotle, *Hist. anim.* 9 (7), 581 a 13 – 582 a 33)

CHAPTER 6

Youth and education: the rhetor and 'university'

6.1 The schooling system in the Roman Empire

The general outlines of the Roman schooling system are well known and have been extensively studied.[1] When boys and girls were about the age of seven, they were entrusted to the schoolmaster or *ludimagister*, from whom they would learn, at the very best, the basic skills of reading, writing, and arithmetic. Since this kind of instruction often took place in primitive conditions, and as it involved large groups of children from mixed social backgrounds, parents of the elite often opted for their sons and daughters to be taught at home. For the second phase of their education, boys of reasonably well-to-do families (girls stayed at home) were sent to the school of the *grammaticus* or grammarian, where they would study Greek and Latin literature. Other subjects featured hardly at all on the curriculum, unless they could serve as an aid for understanding literary texts. The pupils of the grammarian were approximately twelve to fifteen years of age. Only a very small minority subsequently moved on to study with the rhetor, and they were aged between fifteen and twenty.

On the face of it, the Roman educational system seems quite familiar. Somewhat anachronistically, one could regard it as a three-tier system, consisting of primary school, secondary school, and higher education. However, this comparison does not hold, for several reasons. First and foremost, there was no state-run education in the Roman world. Consequently, education was not only relatively expensive, but it also lacked any form of quality control, regulation, and certification. Secondly, the three-tier system was never applied uniformly across the Empire. Depending on local customs and needs, various systems existed side by side. Some grammarians also

---

[1] Marrou 1964; Bonner 1977; Wiedemann 1989: 143–75; Vössing 1997, 2002, 2003, and 2004a and 2004b; Cribiore 2001; Too 2001; Laes 2006a: 97–131 and 2011: 107–47; Pernot 2008. For a recent collection of sources, see Joyal, McDougall, and Yardley 2009, which includes translations of several of the sources used in the present chapter (nos. 8.17a, 8.30, 9.14a, 9.15a, 9.17).

provided what we would term primary education. And, in more remote settings and small villages, schoolteachers offered more than just a basic introduction to reading, writing, and arithmetic, tackling more advanced literary texts with their pupils. Finally, unlike in a modern educational system, there were no clearly defined age groups. In fact, the custom of putting children of the same age in the same class was an innovation by the Jesuits in the late sixteenth and early seventeenth centuries. Roman classrooms, by contrast, consisted of children of different ages. Moreover, as any official structure and state control were lacking, it was entirely up to parents to decide when their children should make the transition from one phase of schooling to the next. If they deemed their children to have completed their studies with the *ludimagister*, they could move them on to the grammarian. This, of course, explains why our sources rarely mention precise ages of pupils or students.

For the same reason, there is no genuine Greek or Latin equivalent for the modern notion of a 'student'. Inscriptions speak of *discipulus, litteratus, eruditus* or *educatus* in Latin; *philologos* in Greek. But these designations could also refer to those who had already graduated, to adults who took pride in representing themselves as participants in the ancient rhetorical culture, as individuals of sophistication and education.[2] On the other hand, the mere lack of a specific term to denote a 'student' is in itself not insignificant. It seems to suggest that academia was not perceived as a separate realm by the cultivated elites, which, from our perspective, would clearly have major implications in relation to whether there was any such thing as a separate youth culture. In order to answer this question, one needs to consider two aspects of higher education in the Roman Empire in greater detail. First and foremost, one must look at whether education with the rhetor offered room for a specifically youthful perception. Secondly, due consideration must be given to the aspect of student mobility: if the evidence is that youngsters travelled to study at recognised centres of learning, then there is every likelihood that a youthful subculture did indeed develop in such ancient 'university' towns.

In the following sections we will discuss firstly higher education (oratory, philosophy, and law) in the Greek East in the cities and in the so-called 'university' towns, then higher education in Rome and the Latin West,

---

[2] Kleijwegt 1991: 118–19 offers a list of inscriptions relating to young people from ages thirteen up to twenty-two who are referred to as *philologos*. The individuals concerned may have been students of literature (e.g. in the case of young people studying abroad). However, the term *philologos* may also denote literacy and cultivation, irrespective of age.

including the topic of non-intervention by the state. Next we study the content of the instruction provided by the rhetor and Libanius' teaching at Antioch. The chapter is concluded by two specific themes: students' lives at 'university' and the instruction of girls.

6.2 Higher education in the Greek East

At around twenty, a male city-dweller in ancient Greece would have entered the age group commonly referred to as the *neoi*, meaning young men. Other attested names are *neoteroi* and *neaniskoi*, though the latter often appears in a military context and is sometimes used to denote soldiers.[3] As explained in Chapter 3, these words are rather vague, their semantic boundaries rather fluid: *neos*, for example, could also denote a man in middle age. As a group noun, the word *neoi*, which is frequently attested in the Hellenistic and, even more so, in the Roman period primarily in Asia Minor, usually refers to young men between *c*. twenty and thirty years of age. The *neoi* were one of the age groups that visited the gymnasium, along with the ephebes and, in some places, the *paides* (see 7.1). In some towns, the *neoi* had their own gymnasium. They were sometimes organised as an association, a *synodos* or *koinon* or *synedrion*.[4] Membership was voluntary and open to citizens as well as non-citizens. Most members, however, belonged to the leisure class, as membership implied a financial contribution to cover one's use of the accommodation at the gymnasium, including the cost of oil, heating, maintenance, and the like. As with the ephebes, this financial burden was sometimes alleviated by generous donations from rulers or benefactors, often gymnasiarchs.[5] We will not go too deeply into this group, since it consisted of more than strictly juveniles, and will concentrate instead on the possibilities for further education within this organisational structure.

At the gymnasium, the *neoi* were under the authority of the gymnasiarch, the director of the institution. In many cities a gymnasiarch was appointed whose duty it was to supervise in particular the *neoi* or the *neoi* and other age

---

[3] Forbes 1933; Dreyer 2004; D'Amore 2007: 166–9; for a register of records of the three words, see Kennell 2006: 153–5. On the ambiguity of the term *neaniskos*, see Chankowski 2004a: 64; Prag 2007: 90–1. There were also organisations of female *neai*, as documented by Gauthier and Hatzopoulos 1993: 157–8, but these were religious associations.
[4] On *neoi* as an organisation, see Forbes 1933: 38–9, Dreyer 2004: 232–6. On the finances, see D'Amore 2007: 167–8. On the magistrates – secretary and treasurer – of the *neoi*, see Forbes 1933: 34–7. A new attestation of an archivist, keeper of records of the *neoi*, has been found near Hierapolis (Phrygia); see *SEG* LV (2005) 1417. The organisations of *neoi* may be compared to the Latin *collegia iuvenum*.
[5] Ameling 2004: 158; Dreyer 2004: 216. In years when a generous citizen was serving as a gymnasiarch, the number of young men visiting the gymnasium would generally be large; see p. 109.

6.2 Higher education in the Greek East

groups, such as the ephebes.⁶ The *neoi* would primarily train their bodies, just like the ephebes, who were younger (see Chapter 7): they received a military training and did physical exercises.⁷ The military training of the *neoi* focused on javelin-throwing, archery, catapult-shooting, and other skills, to which they had previously been introduced as ephebes. The frequency and intensity of this training are, however, unknown.⁸ The *neoi* would regularly demonstrate their military skills at contests and during parades. Their training, like that of the ephebes, was part of their general education as citizens, but it clearly also served another practical purpose: in cases of genuine emergency, the *neoi* could be deployed to perform military tasks.⁹ The *neoi* would also undergo athletics training at the gymnasium and participate in contests in these skills too. Occasionally, there were opportunities for intellectual education, specifically in oratory and philosophy. There were occasional lectures to attend at the gymnasium, delivered by itinerant orators, philosophers, historians and physicians. As a rule, students would have to pay to attend such public lectures (*akroaseis*).¹⁰ In the Greek city of Argos, the rhetor P. Anteius Antiochus from the Cilician town of Aegeae is known to have given a public lecture on how Argos and Aegeae were connected through the mythological figure of Perseus. And the city of Seleuceia (in Pamphylia or Cilicia) is known to have honoured the extraordinarily skilful doctor and surgeon Asclepiades of Perge for his lectures, in which he had given much valuable counsel concerning the health of the citizens.¹¹ From this example, it is clear that such lectures were attended not only by young people, but also by other interested members of the public who had time and money to spare, including ephebes and citizens from

---

⁶ Some sources mention other leaders of the *neoi/neaniskoi* besides the gymnasiarchs, namely the *neaniskarchoi*. Little is known about their responsibilities (possibly sports and games-related?); see Zoumbaki 2004.
⁷ On *neoi* and sports, see Forbes 1933: 45–8; cf. the honorary decree for Menas of Sestus, in 7.2.
⁸ Chankowski 2004a: 59–61. A law from Coresia on Ceos informs us that the *neoteroi* trained three times a month: *IG* XII, 5, 647 (*Syll.*³ 958) (document probably dating from the beginning of the third century BC).
⁹ The *neoi/neaniskoi* could defend the city against external or internal threats (e.g. pirates, tyrants); they were sometimes called upon to assist the Roman army. There is only one fairly certain record of *neoi* patrolling the countryside (at Apollonia on the Salbace in Caria; see Robert and Robert 1954: 281–3 no. 162, late second or early third century AD), yet this may not have been exceptional; for evidence, see D'Amore 2007: 169–71; Brélaz 2005: 187–93; Chankowski 2004a: 63–70 and 2004b: 278. Note that ephebes never performed these tasks. During the Hellenistic/Republican era, in Sicily in the West, there was also a close link between gymnasial culture (of *neaniskoi*) and civic military activity; see Prag 2007: 87–96.
¹⁰ Scholz 2004: 117–24.
¹¹ Antiochus: *SEG* XXVI (1976) 426, c. AD 160–230, cf. *SEG* LV (2005) 1992; Asclepiades: *I. Perge* 1, 12 from the Hellenistic period.

neighbouring towns. As an act of generosity, the wandering scholar could waive the payment. The Peripatetic philosopher Epicrates of Heracleia, who spent a long time on Samos instructing local *neoi*, made his lectures accessible to poorer citizens who could not afford his fee.[12] Travelling scholars could visit a city on their own initiative or by invitation. Sometimes the local gymnasiarch would invite a scholar to visit his town, or even to reside there for a longer period of time. He would pay for the visit (rarely for the actual lectures) or contribute to the costs of accommodation and dining. The gymnasiarch Agias, for example, was honoured in Pergamum for his reception of foreign lecturers and for contributing to their fees:[13]

> He considered his leadership of the gymnasium to be extremely important, and he took care of the education of the ephebes and the *neoi*. Honour and reputation were significant values to him. He rigidly devoted himself to the cause of just behaviour at the gymnasium, and he despised all wrongdoing. He encouraged and watched over discipline at the gymnasium, in accordance with the will of the king and the wishes of the people. He received the scholars, who came from abroad and gave their lectures, with his whole heart and paid them out of his own pocket, on top of the contributions of the *neoi*. He thereby relieved the other city dignitaries from this financial burden. (*MDAI(A)* 33 (1908) 379–81 no. 2)

In exceptional cases, a scholar would lecture for a longer period of time at the gymnasium of one particular town. Usually, he would have been hired by the gymnasiarch to teach different age groups. In Sestus, a teacher of mathematics was honoured by *paides*, ephebes and *neoi*. In Eretria on Euboea, the gymnasiarch Elpinicus appointed a rhetor and an *hoplomachos*, at his own expense, to instruct the *paides*, ephebes, and anyone else who wished to benefit from their teaching. In the same town, the gymnasiarch Mantidorus appointed an 'Homeric philologist', who provided lectures at the gymnasium for the benefit of ephebes, *neoi*, and all others with an interest in culture (*paideia*).[14]

---

[12] *IG* XII, 6, 1, 128 (*c*. 200 BC?); see Scholz 2004: 119; Haake 2006: 185–94.
[13] The text dates from the reign of King Attalus III, i.e. prior to 133 BC. For other examples (including Menas from Sestus; see 7.2 below), see Quass 1993: 287 with nn. 1193–4; Scholz 2004: 118–19; Dreyer 2004: 218 n. 35.
[14] Sestus: *I. Sestos* 5; Eretria: *IG* XII, 9, 234 and 235, both from *c*. 100 BC. The fact that different age groups were taught by the same teacher is strongly emphasised by Pleket 1981b: 165. He points to the absence of clear 'age segregation' in the educational system and hence to the absence of any clearly defined category of youth in antiquity and also of adolescence in the modern sense of the word. In our opinion the latter assertion lacks foundation; moreover, there is no indication that the teachers instructed all age groups at the same time; cf. the strict segregation of age groups in the gymnasiarchical law of Beroea (see below).

6.2 Higher education in the Greek East

Young men from the local elite could further enhance their knowledge by reading books, which were available in libraries. Indeed, quite often these libraries were attached to the gymnasia, not only in large centres such as Pergamum or Rhodes, but also in smaller towns. Benefactors sometimes sponsored such libraries. Gaius Julius Longianus, poet and travelling scholar, donated his books to the library of his hometown Halicarnassus 'in order that the *neoi* could be instructed with these copies as they had been with the older books'.[15]

The principal tasks of a gymnasiarch were to maintain good order and to control the behaviour of visitors to the gymnasium (*eukosmia*).[16] The inscription in honour of Agias from Pergamum, cited above, and other testimonies show that gymnasiarchs sometimes had to apply harsh discipline. An honorary decree for the gymnasiarch Metrodorus from Pergamum explicitly mentions the large number of *neoi* and the ensuing problems of conduct. Metrodorus took appropriate action and punished those who did not obey. He praised those who behaved properly and treated them kindly.[17] Internal issues of discipline are, of course, rarely mentioned in public epigraphical documents. Hence, it is quite possible that any material pointing in that direction indicates merely the tip of the proverbial iceberg, and that the young men who attended such institutions actually behaved quite rowdily. On the other hand, *neoi*, just like ephebes (see below), were trained at the gymnasia in civil virtues such as *eutaxia* (disciplined behaviour), *euexia* (fitness and physical harmony), and *philoponia* (endurance).[18] Through this training, they were undoubtedly prepared for a strictly organised civil life during adulthood. Moreover, by their public appearance in parades or processions for the gods, emperors or deceased benefactors, they participated in urban life, often in association with the ephebes and sometimes also together with the *paides* of the city.[19] In this manner, the *neoi*, like the other age groups in the city, were effectively socialised and taught to behave as decent citizens.

Clearly there were few opportunities for the *neoi* to receive further and regular intellectual education in their cities. The amount of intellectual

---

[15] On libraries, see Nilsson 1955: 51–2, Marrou 1964: 282–3; Scholz 2004: 125–7; Longianus: *LBW* 1618 (*c.* AD 127).
[16] Schuler 2004: 168 and 171; Dreyer 2004: 221 with n. 48.
[17] *MDAI(A)* 32 (1907) 273–8 no. 10 from 133 to 130 BC. On gymnasium and gymnasiarchy in Hellenistic Pergamum, see Wörrle 2007. The gymnasiarchical law of Beroea also provides for the punishment of anyone insulting or striking the gymnasiarch at the gymnasium; see p. 117 and n. 41.
[18] Forbes 1933: 25; Dreyer 2004: 230. On these moral virtues, see pp. 117–18.
[19] Forbes 1933: 52–3; Dreyer 2004: 230–1.

training provided at gymnasia should not be exaggerated. It would appear that it was mainly up to individuals, like certain gymnasiarchs, to promote intellectual endeavour at the gymnasium. Yet, in public documents the emphasis is very much on education and culture (*paideia*). This would however appear to be an expression of a social ideal rather than an image of reality, as we will argue in the discussion of the *ephebeia*.[20] We may safely assume that most young men were more interested in sports and athletics than in literature or oratory.

If a young man wished to pursue an education in oratory or philosophy, then he had to call on a private teacher or move to one of the intellectual centres of the Greek world or, in late antiquity, to one of the large centres of learning, 'university' towns if you will.[21] The earliest records of individual young men studying abroad appear in late Hellenistic honorary inscriptions from cities near the west coast of Asia Minor (Ionia). Not surprisingly, these students belonged to the urban elite. In Metropolis, Apollonius, son of Attalus, was honoured in 145/4 or 144/3 BC.[22] As a youth, he had organised his life in a zealous way (*philoponos*) and with discipline (*met' eutaxias*). He moved abroad, where he would gain high esteem; his good fame was recorded in writing. He subsequently returned to his home town and embarked on a political career. Although the purpose of Apollonius' stay abroad is not specified, it is clear from similar decrees that it was to obtain a higher education. The period of study must have been in the first half of the second century BC. Two other testimonies of young men seeking education abroad come from nearby Colophon.[23] The first of these students is Polemaeus. The decree in his honour (*c.* 130–110 BC) mentions in a rhetorical manner how he continued to attend the gymnasium after the *ephebeia*. He exercised his body intensively and nourished his spirit by studying the finest arts. But still he was not satisfied. He longed for the beauty brought by political government in words and deeds. Therefore, he travelled to Rhodes and sought instruction from the best teachers. The inscription does not mention which teachers taught at Rhodes, but we do know that the library contained rhetorical works by various famous orators. Later, Polemaeus would be sent by his city as a *theoros*, an envoy on cultic matters, to Smyrna. He stayed there longer than necessary and, again, studied with the best teachers. Indeed, Smyrna was a cultural capital in those days and a metropolitan centre of rhetoric. The city honoured Polemaeus for his excellence

---

[20] Van Nijf 2004, especially 214.   [21] Scholz 2004: 114–17.
[22] *I. Metropolis* 1, inscription B (*SEG* LIII (2003) 1312 B); see the commentary on pp. 46–7.
[23] Robert and Robert 1989; *SEG* XXXIX (1989) 1243 and 1244, cf. *SEG* LV (2005) 1247.

and good behaviour. Some years later, some time after 120 BC, another young nobleman from Colophon, Menippus, was sent to Athens as a *theoros*. He, too, stayed on in the city for a long while and benefited from instruction by the best teachers. In those days, many famous scholars, mainly philosophers, taught in Athens. Undoubtedly, all three young men were prepared during their higher studies for subsequent political leadership roles.

During imperial times, Athens was a well-known centre of learning attracting many students from abroad. So too did many cities in Asia Minor, a region famous for its schools of rhetoric.[24] From a funerary inscription, we know of a certain Theodorus from the city of Agrippeia (= Crateia?) in Bithynia. The young man, whose exact age is not given, travelled to Claudiupolis (in Bithynia), a less well-known centre of education, in order to study rhetoric, but died in the latter city and was buried there. The *strategoi* of the city commemorated him with a rhetorical consolation decree.[25] Another student from abroad is recorded in an epitaph at Ephesus: Lucius Calpurnius Calpurnianus, whose father originated from Prusias on the Hypius in Bithynia; after studying for five years in Ephesus, he died at the age of twenty.[26]

By late antiquity some cities in the Greek East – more so than in the Latin West – had developed into veritable 'university' towns. Examples include Athens (where the 'university' was called Museum), the island of Rhodes (famous for the study of oratory), Egyptian Alexandria, Constantinople, Beirut (famous for its Latin law school), and Antioch (the city of the famed rhetor Libanius). In the West, Rome, Carthage, and Marseille were the most renowned 'university' towns. When historians of antiquity speak of 'university towns' in the Roman Empire, they refer to educational centres that attracted large crowds of students from far and wide. Scholarly activity gravitated around professors with high fame and reputation. Of course, the term 'university' is somewhat misleading: there were neither official curricula nor official degrees or certificates to be obtained. The subject matter on offer was by and large the same in all towns but in the East the language of instruction was Greek, the language of culture. The instruction by the professors was for the most part privately funded, with students' parents often paying considerable sums. Those who travelled far in order to study in

---

[24] Puech 2002 offers a list of rhetors from Asia Minor. Cribiore 2007: 47–82 presents a list of cities in the Greek East that were known for providing instruction in rhetoric.
[25] *I. Klaudiupolis* 71, from the late first century AD.
[26] On these centres of learning, see Pleket 1981b: 174–7; Calpurnianus: *I. Ephesos* v 1627 (*SGO* 1 03/02/61) from the third century.

a 'university' town were a very small minority among the population of the Roman Empire.²⁷ In another section, we will take a closer look at students' lives in the 'university' towns.

Why would young men opt for instruction in oratory? They did it with a view to a career in politics. True, by Hellenistic and imperial times, democracy had long perished, and the art of oratory had ceased to be the tool *par excellence* for convincing fellow-citizens at public meetings. Nonetheless, in the city council, an important decision-making body that was commonly comprised of over a hundred local dignitaries, the art of persuasion continued to be absolutely crucial. Moreover, skill in oratory was required in diplomacy between the cities and in maintaining the relationship with Hellenistic rulers and later with Rome. Embassies sent by the cities to the Roman leaders and emperors were of vital importance. There were various reasons for sending such missions: to ensure protection in times of war, to settle disputes, to acquire financial privileges, to enhance the political or legal status of the city, or to gain prestige through exclusive honorary titles.²⁸ Most ambassadors were orators or sophists, but philosophers and other intellectuals from the elite could also be entrusted with such roles. To them, this presented an excellent opportunity to confer a benefaction upon their city by financing their own missions. Moreover, ambassadors could obtain private benefits: Roman citizenship, sky-high prestige, even godlike honour and personal protection afforded by the Roman emperor.²⁹ No surprise, then, that young would-be politicians were keen to follow training in oratory. Furthermore, rhetorical skills came in handy during lawsuits and personal literary production. Finally, it was an established custom on special or festive occasions for skilful rhetoricians to deliver panegyrics and discourses on mainly historical topics to an attentive audience.³⁰ When youngsters returned to their home towns after having completed their studies, they were expected to demonstrate to a large public audience that they had truly mastered the craft and were ready to offer their services to their cities. Gregory of Nazianzus recounts how he felt almost sick with tension at this crucial moment in his young life. And Libanius mentions that a professor of rhetoric would be evaluated on the basis of the active participation of his alumni in city councils.³¹

In addition to oratory, a young man could study philosophy. In Hellenistic times and during the early Empire, Athens and Rhodes were

---

[27] Watts 2004. [28] Quass 1993: 125–37 and 168–78. [29] Quass 1993: 139–49 and 151–64.
[30] Cribiore 2001: 239–44.
[31] Gregory of Nazianzus, *Carm.* 2, 1, 11, 265–76; Libanius, *Or.* 1, 86–9. See Cribiore 2007: 84–8 and 202–5.

the best-known centres of philosophical learning. Undoubtedly there were also local schools. One possible example comes from the Carian town of Stratoniceia: in an honorary inscription from the second century AD, the *boule*, *demos*, and *gerousia* mention Hierocles and his two sons, Thrason Leon and Leon Thrason. The two brothers are referred to as 'sons, on the way to adulthood, philosophers', clearly implying that they were trained in philosophy from adolescence.[32]

In late antiquity, Athens and Alexandria in Egypt were the intellectual capitals of philosophy. The renowned Neoplatonist school of Athens remained a bastion of pagan philosophy until it was closed down by the emperor Justinian in 529.[33] The intellectually bustling town of Alexandria was the scene of a fruitful exchange of ideas and culture between paganism and Christianity from the third century onwards. The Alexandrian philosophical school survived up into the early seventh century; it never fully opposed Christianity and – thanks to the typically conservative attitude that prevailed in ancient education – was tolerated, respected and even taken over by the Christian intelligentsia.[34]

Next to oratory and philosophy, there were several other specialisations that vied for popularity with the happy few who were in a position to embark on higher studies. The most famous law school of the Roman Empire, for example, was established in Berytus, present-day Beirut. Law students were required to have at least a passive knowledge of Latin, the language in which all legal texts were composed. Whether or not law was actually taught in Latin is not entirely clear though.[35] There were also medical schools, as will be discussed in the chapter on professional training. And the steadily increasing army of civil servants in late antiquity meant that training as a stenographer became an excellent tool for achieving social advancement.[36]

6.3 Higher education in Rome and the Latin West

Whereas the Greek East had for centuries had a tradition in rhetoric, things were quite different in Rome. Admittedly, the study of oratory had always been a crucial element in the education of the young Roman aristocrat. But as long as Rome remained a relatively small city-state, any such training would have been strongly associated with a smooth and relatively direct

---

[32] *I. Stratonikeia* II 1028; see Kleijwegt 1991: 129, who cites some other examples in n. 340 (all twenty years or slightly older).
[33] Watts 2006: 24–142.   [34] Watts 2006: 143–256.   [35] Cribiore 2007: 207–13.
[36] Cribiore 2007: 207.

initiation into adult life. In origin, this kind of training was very much like an apprenticeship, not institutionalised within a school context. Once a young man assumed the adult toga, his father would entrust him to the care of a famous statesman under whose personal guidance he was prepared for his future function as an orator and a politician. Tacitus, in the *Dialogus de oratoribus*, makes the orator Vipstanus Messala look back with nostalgia, in around AD 80, on the 'good old days' of this practical training, known as *tirocinium fori*.

> So, then, this was usual with our ancestors: when the young man who was being prepared for legal practice and oratory was fully trained by home discipline and his mind was expanded by the fine arts, he was conducted by his father or a relative to that orator who held the highest rank in the city. The young man used to follow him continually, to attend on him, to be present at all his speeches in the law-courts as well as in the assemblies. In this way, he picked up the art of legal repartee and became habituated to verbal disputes, and he learned, I daresay, to fight in battle. From this, young men acquired from the outset great experience, much self-possession, and a vast reservoir of sound judgement. For they studied in broad daylight and in the very midst of conflicts, where no one can, without impunity, say anything stupid or inconsistent lest he be rebuked by the judge and ridiculed by the opponent, or, last of all, repudiated by his own counsel. In this way, they were imbued from the start with true and unspoiled eloquence. And, although they followed just one orator, still they became acquainted with all the advocates of that time in a multitude of civil and criminal cases. And they had abundant experience of the very divergent tastes of the people, and so they could easily ascertain what in each speaker was liked or disapproved. Thus they were not deprived of a teacher, indeed they had the best and choicest, who thus could show them the true face of eloquence, not a mere semblance. They had opponents and rivals, who fought with an iron, not with a wooden, sword. They had an audience that was always plentiful, always different, made up of hostile and well-disposed people, so that neither good nor bad speech passed unnoticed. You know, of course, that the great and lasting fame of eloquence is won as much among the benches of the opposing side as amongst those of one's friends. Indeed, it rises more steadily from there; grows strong more lastingly.
>
> It was under such teachers, indeed, that the young man, of whom I am speaking, the pupil of orators, the listener in the Forum, the attendant to the law-courts, was trained and gained experience through the practice of others. He learned the laws by hearing them every day. The faces of the judges were not unfamiliar to him. The practice of popular assemblies was frequently before his eyes. He often got to know the tastes of the people. And whether he undertook a prosecution or a defence, he was from the outset all alone, ready for any kind of case, on his own. (Tacitus, *Dial. de orat.* 34, 1–6)

Training in oratory at a specialised rhetorical school was originally a Greek phenomenon. Although there had been contact between Romans and Greeks for a few centuries, it was not until the second century BC that Rome was overrun by Greek influences (Greece being definitively annexed into the Roman Empire in the year 146 BC). Hence, the first rhetors in Rome were Greeks. The attitude of the Roman state towards these new and strange influences was not in the least favourable. A senatorial decree from 161 BC even urged the expulsion from Rome of all orators and philosophers. The edict was most probably inspired by fear of the possible consequences of this new instruction rather than by an aversion to the Greeks who taught it. Besides, the decree does not mention schools. And, as it turned out, the Romans had good reasons to fear these Greek innovations. The philosopher Carneades was a member of the philosophical delegation that travelled to Rome in the year 155 BC: on the first day of his visit, he extolled justice; the next day, in an exercise designed to prove that justice was an inherently problematic notion, he called it into question by refuting all the points he had made the day before by equally strong counter-arguments. Cato the Censor was shocked by Carneades' success and recognised the danger of his art, and it was at his instigation that the visiting philosophers were expelled from Rome.[37]

The first state intervention aimed against a school is believed to have taken place in 92 BC, with an edict targeting the school of Latin oratory of Plotius Gallus.[38] The censors Crassus and Domitius Ahenobarbus ordered its closure, but apparently to no avail, as there are references to Plotius Gallus helping young advocates with their pleas in the year 56 BC.[39] Roman aversion to the schools of oratory was inspired mainly by conservatism. It was an aversion to a form of education provided by politically independent teachers; a form of education, moreover, that offered even non-aristocrats the possibility of making progress in rhetoric, traditionally a subject of private instruction in aristocratic circles. The Roman establishment also feared that these schools, where instruction was consistently in Latin, would produce an ever-increasing number of orators who would aggressively and fiercely attack traditional values in their speeches in the Forum. And it goes without saying that traditional Romans looked down on the low social status of the new teachers of oratory. Plotius Gallus was most probably a

---

[37] Pliny the Elder, *Nat. hist.* 7, 112–13; Cicero, *De orat.* 2, 155. See also Quintilian, *Inst. or.* 12, 1, 35.
[38] Gellius, *Noctes Att.* 15, 11, 1–2 (decisions from 161 and 92 BC). See Corbeill 2001: 272–3; Vössing 2003: 465–7.
[39] Suetonius, *De rhet.* 2.

freedman, was as a certain Lucius Voltacilius Plotus, who, as a slave, had served as a chained doorkeeper.[40]

However, even the most traditionally minded Romans soon came to realise that the tide could not be turned. By the first century BC, the schools of oratory were already well established: instruction by a rhetor had become part and parcel of the education of young Romans from the elite. Handbooks now appeared in Latin. The state, too, gradually came to recognise the importance of rhetorical training. The emperor Vespasian (AD 69–79) thus provided the lavish sum of 100,000 *sestertii* to fund a chair in Greek rhetoric and another in Latin.[41] The state also provided accommodation so that these professorial functions could be carried out. However, conservative protests continued: complaints about the decline of oratory and criticism of the senseless games at rhetorical schools are rife in Latin literature.

If instruction in rhetoric was indeed considered so very important, at least by a small elite, then why did the Roman state fail to acknowledge this? We have already mentioned the favourable measures by the emperor Vespasian. Previously, in 46 BC, Caesar had tried to entice foreign doctors and teachers to the city of Rome by offering them Roman citizenship.[42] In the early 30s BC, Caesar also granted certain tax exemptions to teachers (*grammatici*), sophists (*rhetorici*), and physicians.[43] In the so-called Pergamum edict of 27 December AD 74 Vespasian went even further. Across the Roman Empire, doctors and teachers, with the exception of schoolmasters, were granted special privileges: exemptions from any contributions to the public coffer whatsoever and from the obligation to provide lodging for soldiers and other officials passing through (see 10.1). Moreover, they were offered protection against any form of molestation by persons under imperial command. Such offenders were punished with a fine. Teachers and doctors were also granted the right of association and assembly, though, according to some interpretations, the latter merely implied the right to teach at a temple.[44] From the second century through to late antiquity, these imperial edicts were reissued on various occasions: the legal corpora contain ten or so such edicts concerning teachers and other professions.[45] Clearly, though,

---

[40] Suetonius, *De rhet.* 3. On Plotius Gallus' school and on Voltacilius Plotus, see Bonner 1977: 71–4.
[41] Suetonius, *Vesp.* 18 and Cassius Dio, *Hist. Rom.* 53, 60.   [42] Suetonius, *Jul.* 42, 1; cf. *Aug.* 42, 3.
[43] *I. Ephesos* VII, 2, 4101 (*SEG* XXXI (1981) 952; Samama 2003 no. 206).
[44] Text of the edict and commentary by Herzog 1935. See *AnÉp* (1936) 128; cf. *AnÉp* (1940) 46. See Sherk 1988 no. 84 and Samama 2003 no. 189 for a translation; Wes 1981: 203 for a summary; Pleket 1981b: 176 for the interpretation concerning the right of association and assembly.
[45] For the best discussion of immunity, see Kaster 1988: 223–7. For a survey of all texts concerned, see Marrou 1964: 110–11.

this apparent generosity on the part of the Roman state should be placed in the correct context. First of all, the present-day notion of education and schooling funded and supervised by the state was unheard of: parents were invariably required to cover the costs of instruction. The fact that teachers were exempt from taxes and liturgies did not, after all, imply that they were remunerated by the city where they taught.[46] Furthermore, the frequent reiteration of the decrees would seem to point to an unwillingness on the part of the cities to implement such measures. Their reluctance is easy to understand, since the local authorities, not the Roman state, ultimately had to foot the bill.[47] One text explicitly mentions that the privileges concerned could be revoked in the event of financial trouble.[48] Grammarians or rhetors who did not perform satisfactorily faced the risk of being struck off the list.[49] Moreover, the benefits of immunity did not extend beyond one's home town, so that they did not apply to travelling physicians or teachers. Despite this rule, several teachers chose to work outside their home town. Lucius Memmius Probus taught in the Spanish town of Tritium Magallum, although he actually originated from Clunia, 75 km to the south. The small town of Tritium probably had no sufficiently qualified grammarian of its own, and consequently had to rely on a young and inexperienced teacher from elsewhere, who we are told died at the age of twenty-five.[50] Finally, the question arises how many grammarians and rhetors actually benefited from such imperial privileges. It was probably in consequence of unremitting opposition from the cities that the emperor Antoninus Pius set a *numerus fixus* for exempt teachers: three grammarians and three rhetors for smaller towns, four of each for medium-sized towns, and five for the large urban centres.[51] Assuming that every teacher who benefited from support from the city could take on fifteen students a year, the total number of students benefiting from their education in a town of ten thousand inhabitants would still have been very small. Machinations and disputes were undoubtedly rife. Those who were considered 'exceptionally learned' could be added as supernumeraries to the list, though this will often have involved an element of favouritism.[52]

---

[46] Vössing 2002: 258 n. 62.   [47] Marrou 1964: 111; Wes 1981; Vössing 2002: 247–8.
[48] *Dig.* 50, 4, 11, 2 (Modestinus).   [49] *Cod. Iust.* 10, 53, 2.
[50] *Dig.* 27, 1, 6, 9 (Modestinus). On Memmius, see *CIL* 11 2892 (*ERRioja* 25); cf. *AnÉp* (1987) 617 and Fear 1995.
[51] *Dig.* 27, 1, 6, 2 (Modestinus); the text has been translated by Parkin and Pomeroy 2007: 143–4 no. 4.7. The large towns are probably provincial capitals, the medium-size towns those with legal assizes, and the small towns the rest.
[52] *Dig.* 27, 1, 6, 10 (Modestinus), on which see Kaster 1988: 226.

But were there really no state-funded schools in the modern sense? Some cities provided grammarians and rhetoricians with teaching accommodation beside the Forum. It goes without saying that such *scholae publicae* were rather limited in space. Moreover, the city provided only accommodation, no remuneration.[53] Nonetheless, some passages explicitly mention that teachers were paid by the city government. According to Pliny the Younger, this was actually quite common.[54] With some sense of exaggeration, Juvenal asserts that even Thule (supposedly the world's most northerly country) was thinking about hiring a rhetorician.[55] We know of teachers of rhetoric who were appointed by the cities of Milan and Marseille. Gaul was famous for its rhetoric, including in cities such as Arles, Autun, Bordeaux, and Toulouse. The same holds for Trier, as well as for various cities in Hispania (Saguntum and Asturica) and Africa.[56]

There were some state-funded chairs of learning in the cultural capitals of Rome, Athens, and Constantinople. Only a handful of professors would have been housed by the state though; the rest would have needed to seek private teaching accommodation. Thus, there was no such thing as a 'university' in the modern sense of the word.[57]

All these instances of 'subsidising' were connected with higher forms of education. Again, the costs were borne by the cities or by foundations established by local benefactors. In his oration *Pro instaurandis scholis*, a paean to the emperor's liberality presented in the city of Autun in the winter of the year AD 297–8, the orator Eumenius proudly mentions his appointment as an official city orator for the princely, rather exorbitant salary of 600,000 *sestertii* a year. In fact, though, it was the city that footed the bill for this imperial generosity![58] Since there is not a single town where mention is made of more than one grammarian of Greek, one grammarian of Latin, and one rhetorician on a municipal salary, the obvious implication is that only a very small minority of the already small elite could enjoy their services.[59] Besides a fee from the city treasury, these teachers also received payments from the parents of their

---

[53] Vössing 1997: 325–35.
[54] Pliny, *Epist.* 4, 13, 6; the letter has been translated by Parkin and Pomeroy 2007: 142–3 no. 4.6.
[55] Juvenal, *Sat.* 15, 112.
[56] See Kaster 1988: 100–6 and 455–62 on Gaul. For Trier, see Vössing 1997: 335–41. On Hispania, see *CIL* II 2892 (commented upon by Vössing 1997: 343 n. 1205). On Africa, see Vössing 1997: 343–9.
[57] Vössing 2002: 246 (Athens) and 261 (Constantinople).
[58] Eumenius, *Pro inst. scholis* 9, 21. See Vössing 2002: 255. The same holds for the schooling decree of Trier; see Kaster 1988: 116–17.
[59] Vössing 2002: 257–8.

6.3 Higher education in Rome and the Latin West

students.[60] An enlightened treatise on the education of children falsely attributed to Plutarch argues that the poor and the less-well-off should do their utmost to ensure that their children received the best possible education. Should they fail, then the blame should be laid on Fortune rather than on the author giving them this advice.[61] Clearly, then, we are far removed from any state concern with the literacy of the population in general.

A young man in Rome who wished to study philosophy rather than rhetoric could attend one or several of the schools of philosophy in the city. These schools, too, were private undertakings, without state involvement. Each school provided teaching in Greek on a specific set of doctrines: Stoicism, Epicureanism, etc. Alternatively, the prospective student could leave Rome for an established centre of philosophical learning, especially Athens, as did the young Marcus Cicero. In Rome, just as in the Greek cities, there were also wandering philosophers who gave lectures (*akroaseis*) open to people of all ages who could afford to attend. However, it seems such lectures increasingly came to resemble meaningless demonstrations of rhetorical virtuosity.[62]

In sum, the Roman state completely neglected schooling and education.[63] What is more, the supposed tendency during late antiquity towards greater state involvement in education would appear to be a myth. Little changed during imperial times: cities still had their benefactors who bore most of the costs of education, while wealthy parents also continued to contribute financially.[64] Quite remarkably, the system proved to be adequate for those for whom it had been designed, and for the Roman state, which relied heavily on a steady inflow of adequately trained officials. Problems began to arise only during the economic crisis of the third and fourth centuries AD. The decrees in the *Digest* appointing scholars and exempting teachers from local taxes were most relevant to the late Roman period. These examples may be seen as modest attempts by the state to tie

---

[60] Vössing 1997: 334 n. 1185. For examples from everyday life, see Augustine, *Conf.* 9, 2, 2 (Augustine being paid by parents and receiving a salary from the city of Milan); *Epist.* 118, 2, 9 and 159, 4; *De civ. Dei* 1, 3.
[61] Ps.-Plutarch, *De lib. educ.* 8 d–e.   [62] Armisen-Marchetti 2004.
[63] A devastating criticism on the efficiency of ancient education is provided by Atherton 1998: 222–3 n. 29. See also Saller 2012: 84 on the low investment in education (total expenditure of about 0.1% of the minimum Gross Domestic Product on basic education). Public expenditure on education in the EU-27 in 2009 was equivalent to 5.4% of GDP. The poorest countries of sub-Saharan Africa nowadays have education levels of one to two years, while Saller estimates that the average number of years of formal education across the whole population of the Empire was less than half a year per person.
[64] Vössing 2002: 253–60 and 2004b.

young men to their home towns and to provide them with a local education, so that their future services and wealth would not be lost.

6.4 Instruction provided by the rhetor

Instruction by the rhetor was, in general terms, not just a continuation but also the culmination of the training with the grammarian. Students would have to write down a fable that had been read aloud by the rhetor. They would be required to write compositions on prescribed subjects. And they would be asked to comment on concise sayings, and to compose eulogies for or criticisms of a given person. Other subjects of written exercises were the elaboration of comparisons and the writing out of descriptions and characteristics of an object or subject and of variations on a given theme. Many of these types of exercises would already have been undertaken under the grammarian. After these preparatory *praeexercitamenta*, the students were ready for the oral exercises. The *suasoriae* or 'deliberations' were intended for novices in rhetoric and were conceived as a preparation for political oratory. The student was expected to imagine himself in the shoes of an historical figure or legendary hero who faced an important decision in his life: Alexander the Great considering a conquest of the West, or Cicero contemplating the burning of his own books in order to elicit mercy from his enemy Antony.[65] The *controversiae* or 'pleas' were exercises in juridical oratory, fictitious lawsuits that were held in an imaginary world governed by laws that did not apply in the real Rome. Such an imagined law might state that a woman who has been raped can either demand the death penalty for the rapist or that he marry her. Students would then be asked to imagine a situation where a man has raped two women in a single day; the first woman demands his death, the second marriage. After a written preparation, the student would be required to argue in favour of both plaintiffs.[66] In the first century AD, the conservative elite severely opposed the imaginary situations and playful nature of such exercises. Their criticism of this approach chimed with the more general Roman dislike of innovations that were deemed to subvert traditional Roman values.

> But nowadays we have our young men taken to the schools of those whom we call rhetors. These first appeared on the scene not long before Cicero's day. Our ancestors did not approve of them. This is evident from the fact that the censors Crassus and Domitius ordered the closure of what Cicero calls 'the school of impudence'. But, as I was just saying, our young men are

[65] Seneca the Elder, *Suas.* 1 (Alexander the Great); 6 and 7 (Cicero). [66] Seneca the Elder, *Contr.* 1, 5.

taken to schools where it is hard to tell what does most harm to their minds: the place itself, their fellow-students, or the nature of the studies undertaken. For the place commands no respect, as nobody enters it who is not as ignorant as the rest. The fellow-students do not contribute to progress, because boys and young men speak and listen among boys and young men with equal complacency. The actual exercises are largely counter-productive, for two kinds of subject matter are dealt with before the rhetors: the deliberative (*suasoriae*) and the controversial (*controversiae*). Of these, the deliberative exercises are assigned to the boys because they are deemed to be easier and to require less skill. The *controversiae* are assigned to more mature students, but, heavens, of what poor quality and how inadequately composed they are! Hence the declamations cover subjects that are far removed from real life. Thus, the reward of tyrant-slayers, or the choice of outraged maidens, or remedies against pestilence, or incest by mothers, or any other topic that is discussed every day in the schools but rarely if ever in the Forum, are described in grandiloquent phrases. (Tacitus, *Dial. de orat.* 35, 1–5)

Thanks to the extraordinary memory of the rhetor Seneca the Elder, we have at our disposal fragments of some fifty declamatory exercises performed by over a hundred different orators. Indeed, such exercises were extremely popular. According to Pliny the Younger, adults commonly attended classes to listen to the students, to applaud them, or even to speak themselves.[67] Trivial as this fact may seem, it is telling about the essence of Roman rhetorical training. At first sight, these declamatory exercises would appear to be products of adolescent fantasy, playful outbursts of juvenile and restless imaginations, expressions of a purely aesthetic admiration of the beautiful word. Undoubtedly, young people were enticed by the fire of rhetorical play and the popularity and success they could gain with their peers and parents by showing off their verbal skills. Some were attracted by the truly baroque and exuberant style of the Asianists, whereas others turned to the opposite extreme in the form of tight austerity, as preferred by the Atticists. As a mature orator, Cicero thought back with embarrassment to the grandiose baroque style of his earliest speeches. It was only after his time in Rhodes with the orator Molo that his restless style calmed down.[68] In his exhaustive handbook on the training of the orator, the prominent teacher Quintilian considered it normal that the language of a young orator should be somewhat overloaded. He also approved of the practice whereby young people were presented with subject matter that was stimulating to the imagination.[69] In Fronto's correspondence with the

---

[67] Pliny, *Epist.* 2, 3.   [68] Cicero, *Brut.* 91, 316. See Eyben 1977: 322–30.
[69] Quintilian, *Inst. or.* 11, 1, 31–2 and 2, 10, 4–6.

88   6 Youth and education: the rhetor and 'university'

young prince and future emperor Marcus Aurelius, we read about the joy that young Marcus derived from looking up the meaning of uncommon words, from paraphrasing ancient authors, from embellishing his own style with figures of speech or synonyms, and from practising linguistic purism.[70] Young people found it amusing to produce literary pastiches such as the *Testamentum Porcelli*, in which a piglet draws up its will. Before being slaughtered, it bequeaths the various parts of its body to various legatees:

> Here begins the piglet's will. Marcus Grunnius Corocotta the piglet has made his will. Since I was unable to write it myself, I have resorted to dictation ...
> As for my body parts, I bestow my bristle upon shoemakers, my head/muzzle on squabblers, my ears on the deaf, my tongue on advocates and blabbermouths, my innards on sausage-makers, my hams on sellers of cold cuts, my kidneys/testicles on women, my bladder on young boys, my tail/penis on young girls, my muscles/rectum on the unmanly, my ankles on messengers and hunters, and my hooves on robbers. (*Test. Porcelli* 1–3)[71]

However, it would be wrong to regard the schools of oratory as isolated pockets of youth subculture. After all, it was at these schools that young boys were directly instructed in the kind of skills that would be eminently important in their future lives, namely the ability to impress others by the power of speech and performance. A training in rhetoric was a life-long learning process, involving the continuous assimilation and imitation of literary examples. The skills acquired at a school of oratory would be applicable throughout one's life, as expressed in Quintilian's famous adage, *Non scholae, sed vitae* – 'not for school, but for life'.[72] Hence, the training with a rhetor provided pupils with practical know-how: its purpose was to instil the kind of intellectual flexibility and eloquence that were deemed useful to a cultivated aristocrat throughout his career, or whenever he should wish to present himself as a man of arts and literature. Those who had the ability to speak quick-wittedly, those who possessed the gift of the *bon mot*, were admired as heroes.[73] Adult life was permeated with fragments of ancient texts that one had studied in one's school days. *Veni, vidi, vici* ('I came, I saw, I conquered') was as famous an adage in antiquity as it is today, and one to which a visitor to a brothel at Pompeii wittily

---

[70] Fronto, *Eloq.* 2 (135–45 van den Hout). See Eyben 1977: 314.
[71] According to Jerome, *Comm. in Isaiam*, praef. (p. 493 Vall.) and *Adv. Rufinum* 1, 17 the Piglet's Testament was a favourite text in schools. See Baldwin 1984: 137–48 and Champlin 1987: 174–83.
[72] Quintilian, *Inst. or.* 1, 8, 12: *non scholarum temporibus, sed vitae spatio*. On this crucial aspect of Roman education, see Eyben 1977: 311–13 and Vössing 1997: 40.
[73] Cribiore 2001: 238–44.

6.4 Instruction provided by the rhetor

alluded in a graffito: *Hic ego cum veni, futui, deinde redei domi* ('I came here, I fucked, then I returned home').[74]

To be sure, completing one's rhetorical studies was compared to reaching the summit of a steep mountain. Ancient authors were well aware that education was a laborious process, which often went hand in hand with toiling and sweating. Only after strenuous effort, kept up to the very end, would the happy few reach the summit of the challenging ascent.[75] Similar views were held in the Greek world. In a papyrus, a student says the following prayer, possibly uttered at the end of a school year:

> I bring the offering of the school feast. I yearn to reach very soon the full measure of youthful vigour and to live a long time listening to my teacher ... Would that I could complete my general education. I long to rise up and come near Zeus' abode. (*P. Laur.* II, 49; transl. R. Cribiore)

In a passage by the second-century writer Lucian, himself an accomplished rhetor, we hear Lady Paideia addressing the young man:

> 'Come at once and mount this car' – she pointed to a car with winged horse that resembled Pegasus – 'in order that you may know what you would have missed if you had not followed me'. When I had mounted, she plied whips and reins, and I was carried up into the heights from the East to the West surveying cities and nations and people. (Lucian, *Somn.* 15; transl. R. Cribiore)

Both texts refer to the accomplishment of one's education, understood here as the study of eloquence.

The rhetor Libanius lived in fourth-century Antioch, a dazzling city and one of the foremost cultural centres in late antiquity.[76] His voluminous correspondence and his extended collection of speeches offer a unique insight into the daily life of a 'professor' of rhetoric.[77] Libanius started his teaching career at Constantinople and Nicomedia. As he mentions himself, he was so successful in the latter city that the whole town could in a way be considered his classroom.[78] In Antioch, he started out with some fifteen students, but the number soon grew towards fifty. The professor proudly mentions that he had so many students to oversee that he hardly had time for lunch.[79] Life also brought him misfortune: the severe famine of AD 385 and the street riots of AD 387 drastically reduced the number of his students, so that in his old age he lamented the small number of people attending his

---

[74] *CIL* IV 2246 (*CLE* 955).   [75] Cribiore 2001: 220–5.
[76] Cribiore 2007: 24–30 offers a vivid description of the city.
[77] Petit 1956 and the magisterial book by Cribiore 2007.   [78] Libanius, *Or.* 1, 53–5.
[79] Libanius, *Or.* 1, 104; *Epist.* 405, 6.

courses.⁸⁰ In fact, it is very difficult to estimate accurately the number of students whom Libanius attracted. Thanks to his correspondence, we know of 196 students, 134 of whom are to be attributed to a period of fifteen years. While this may not seem particularly impressive, one has to take into account the fact that students who came from Antioch itself are hardly ever mentioned in the letters. Modern estimates put the number of students at the height of his career at eighty, and at fifteen in his final teaching years.⁸¹ Libanius' school was probably located in the large public town hall: a covered auditorium with four adjacent colonnades surrounding a luxuriant garden.⁸² The master was assisted by five or so rhetors.

Students applying to study with Libanius were required to show him a formal letter of recommendation, written by their parents or other relatives or by their former teachers. Most of his students were boys from families belonging to the extended social network of Libanius' friends.⁸³ A father who had sent his son to Libanius without the required letter, believing that residents of his town were sufficiently well known to the teacher, received a slightly reproachful reply which stressed that letters of recommendation are part and parcel of good etiquette.⁸⁴ When candidates first met their new teacher, they were expected to prove their literary acumen by reciting passages of Greek poetry, but there was no such thing as a thorough entrance examination. Upon first meeting his new students, Libanius would often remark that a son resembled his father. On one such occasion he was subsequently required to write a letter of apology for having asserted that a boy had a Syrian hooknose, just like his father!⁸⁵

Libanius taught classes of around ten pupils. The previously mentioned teaching assistants would provide most of the instruction, although students would, from the first year of study, also come into contact with Libanius himself, as he commented on and corrected their initial attempts at oratory. Instruction was provided only in Greek. The main focus was on the classic Attic orators and Demosthenes, Plato, and the literary corpus written by Libanius himself. In this Greek teaching tradition, preparatory exercises were referred to as *progymnasmata*. The mythical hero Achilles seems to have been the most popular subject of such writing exercises at Libanius'

---

⁸⁰ Libanius, *Or.* 1, 233 (famine); *Or.* 34, 14 (riots); *Or.* 3, 27–33 (few students).
⁸¹ Cribiore 2007: 95–100.
⁸² Cribiore 2007: 43–7 on the archaeological setting of Libanius' school.
⁸³ Cribiore 2007: 104–10.
⁸⁴ Cribiore 2007: 112–17. See Libanius, *Epist.* 768, 1–3 (letter with rather reproachful tone).
⁸⁵ Cribiore 2007: 120–2. She makes a telling comparison with similar entrance examinations at Harvard in 1636. See Libanius, *Epist.* 93, 1–3 on the Syrian hooknose.

6.4 Instruction provided by the rhetor

school. Students were taught to write both eulogies for and invectives against Achilles, and they were also required to present their orations before wider audiences beyond their class. In his paedagogical approach Libanius attached great significance to competition. Sometimes the best students would be allowed to take over from Libanius in teaching certain courses.[86]

Parents evidently desired the best for their children. During the summer (students would stay on in their 'university' towns even during vacations, since travelling took a long time or was simply dangerous), Libanius was burdened with the task of writing 'reports'.[87] These reports were no formal instruments of evaluation, but rather short written messages in which he informed parents of the progress of their beloved sons. Many of the surviving letters are quite formulaic. Libanius was well aware that it was customary for teachers to praise their students, even if their achievements were not that brilliant. Sometimes, a professor had to say that they were like sons of gods, even if they were, in actual fact, so intractable that they seemed to be made of stone! This should not come as a surprise, since teachers were paid primarily by the students' parents. In his writings, however, Libanius often succeeds in steering a middle course between flattery and the harsh truth. Quite often, he does not mention the negative traits of a student, but the simple omission of a particular quality can of course be equally revealing. He sometimes diplomatically conveys that there is still room for improvement. But sometimes he harshly proclaims the truth. To a father of two sons, he praises the first to the skies, but says about the second that he 'should not have been born'.[88] In any case, Libanius considered adult behaviour and maturity important qualities in a student. The ideal student was also self-restrained, modest, and respectful. In one letter, Libanius argues that a young man should be judged on the basis not of his age but of how his behaviour ranks him vis-à-vis his seniors.[89] The following passage is significant in this context:

> There was a man who wanted to praise your excellence of character. He said: 'About which Honoratus are you talking? The old young man?' He spoke of you in this way not because you experienced the same as what Erginus experienced – hair turning grey at a young age – but because you already

---

[86] Cribiore 2007: 143–7 (*progymnasmata*); 149–50 (instruction in class groups); 150–2 (programmes of instruction); 199–202 (final examinations). See Libanius, *Epist.* 249, 1 on the best students.
[87] Cribiore 2007: 122–9 on reports and Libanius' comments in reports. See also Libanius, *Epist.* 650 (writing reports during the summer holidays).
[88] Libanius, *Epist.* 547, 1 (habit of teachers); *Or.* 25, 47 (sons of gods); *Epist.* 346, 1–2 (possibility of improving); *Epist.* 465, 1–2 (better not born).
[89] Libanius, *Epist.* 571. See Cribiore 2007: 127–9.

conducted yourself as senior folk do before having completed your period of youth. (Libanius, *Epist.* 300, 3; transl. R. Cribiore)

For their final evaluation, students had to give a rhetorical performance in front of a large audience of peers. Afterwards, Libanius would publicly comment upon the speech. From Libanius' work as a whole it emerges that the orators themselves were public figures *par excellence*. Being intellectual superstars, they were constantly concerned with protecting their reputation with the public at large. Indeed, even non-intellectuals, who were not the kind of people to send their sons to the schools of the orators, had to be instilled with awe about the reputation of the rhetorical school. One way of managing their image was for Libanius and his colleagues/rivals to give demonstration orations before large public audiences.[90]

6.5 Students' lives at 'university'

The sources, which mainly consist of the extended correspondence of Libanius and his large collection of speeches, suggest an average age of fifteen to twenty for those students studying with a rhetor.[91] This fits well with legislation by the emperor Valentinian in the fourth century which prescribed that foreign students in Rome should end their rhetorical studies at the age of twenty. Since a course of study with a rhetor could take five years on average, a starting age of fifteen seems quite plausible.[92] Of course, there were exceptions. Among Libanius' youngest students were Euphemius and Hieron, both aged approximately eleven.[93] Arbitrariness in the organisation of education seems to have been rife. School careers with Libanius varied in length from one to six years. Personal circumstances and the whims of fortune could result in some students leaving school prematurely, while others might spend many years with their teacher. Of the fifty-seven students of Libanius for whom we know the exact length of their studies, fifty-three left his school after their second year.[94] Not surprisingly, such drop-outs were a concern for the rhetors, as they resulted in the loss of a considerable amount of potential income. Libanius writes about a certain Severus, who was dragged out of the classroom by his father in his second

---

[90] Cribiore 2007: 202–5 on the rhetor as a public figure. See Libanius, *Or.* 5, 46 (public speeches); *Or.* 25, 48 (taking into account all citizens, not just the cultural elite).
[91] Petit 1956: 63–6 and 139 on prosopographical lists of Libanius' students and their ages. See also Watts 2006: 5; Cribiore 2007: 31.
[92] *Cod. Theod.* 14, 9, 1. See Petit 1956: 139.   [93] Petit 1956: 139–41.
[94] Petit 1956: 62–5; Kaster 1988: 26–7; Watts 2006: 5.

year. Much too soon, according to Libanius, yet within the next year the young man would triumphantly win a trial as a fully fledged lawyer![95]

There was, in any case, no such thing as an age-based system of differentiation in education.[96] Quintilian aptly summarises ancient thinking on such matters: a student was deemed ready to move on from the grammarian to the rhetor as soon as he had provided evidence of possessing a sufficient degree of intellectual maturity.[97]

The young men studying abroad, whether in Athens, Rhodes or elsewhere, formed groups around their teachers, especially students of philosophy. The previously mentioned Epicrates from Heracleia took care of the spiritual and material well-being of the young men who were continually joining his group of students at Samos (*suscholazontes*). Wandering philosophers were often followed around by a group of pupils. The students were recognisable by their attire. According to an anecdote about the philosopher Bion of Borysthenes (Olbia), he persuaded some sailors to put on students' clothes (*scholastikai esthetes*) and to accompany him to the gymnasium of Rhodes as if they were his students in order to impress the citizens. It is tempting to assume that these groups of students of the Hellenistic period, living far away from their home town and forming a distinctly recognisable group, developed typically youthful behaviour, just as would students in the late imperial period (see below). Unfortunately, there is no indication that this was indeed the case.[98]

There are three important sources of information about the students' sometimes tumultuous lives in the late Republic and the imperial period: the correspondence of Marcus Tullius Cicero, some texts on papyri concerning Egyptian Alexandria, and texts by late antique Greek rhetoricians such as Libanius and Eunapius or church fathers such as Augustine and Gregory of Nazianzus – which bring us to the 'university' towns in the Eastern part of the Empire. These sources immediately give rise to the question of the possible existence of a youth subculture in these towns.[99]

For students from abroad, the temptations in the new environment would have been numerous: chariot races, amphitheatre games, brothels, parties, initiation ceremonies, and nocturnal rambling. The view that young people should be given an opportunity to experiment and that they should

---

[95] Libanius, *Or.* 57, 3–6. See Cribiore 2007: 147. [96] Petit 1956: 63–6.
[97] Quintilian, *Inst. or.* 2, 2, 1 and 2, 1, 7.
[98] Epicrates, see above n. 12 (*c.* 200 BC); Bion: Diogenes Laertius, *Vitae philos.* 4, 53 (*c.* 325–255 BC); see Scholz 2004: 120.
[99] Elaborate and vivid descriptions of the instruction offered by the rhetorician and of life as a student can be found in Eyben 1977: 199–215 and 292–338; Cribiore 2001: 102–23 and 2007.

94   6 Youth and education: the rhetor and 'university'

be allowed to learn from their own errors would appear to be common to all periods. The distances involved meant that fathers rarely came to visit their sons during their studies. Most students also stayed on in the town where they were studying during summer breaks.[100] So there was little control. Students were often accompanied by a slave paedagogue, who was supposed to keep an eye on the young master and to keep his family updated on the progress made in his studies, but this system obviously did not work. Marcus Cicero, son of the famous orator from the first century BC, is known as the prototype of the alcohol-guzzling student. His father invested enormous sums of money in his education, amounting to about a 100,000 *sestertii* a year. During his stay in Athens, the twenty-year-old revealed himself as a notorious partygoer and soon became known as the biggest drinker of his time. His father ignored the initial negative reports on his son's behaviour and chose to believe some of the more flattering, but unfortunately inaccurate, accounts. In the end, however, the worried father could not but open his eyes to reality and even considered travelling to Athens personally to deal with matters. From Cicero's correspondence, we know of one letter by the hand of young Marcus himself, in which he speaks repentantly of his youthful sins. Or was the shrewd young man simply trying to soften the heart of his gullible father in order to persuade him to send even more money?[101]

From the papyri, we know of a father called Theon who, in the first or second century AD, sent his son Nilus to Alexandria, together with a younger brother. The boys were accompanied by a paedagogue called Isidorus and a slave known as Heraclas. The latter was required to perform all kinds of jobs in the city in order to fund the studies of his young masters. In the first part of his letter, Nilus complains vehemently that he had been unable to find suitable teachers in Alexandria (or did he just want his father to believe that there were none?). In the second part, we read about an incident involving the slave Heraclas, who had been beaten up by Isidorus. With unmistakable pleasure, Heraclas had gossiped about a certain event in the theatre, which contributed to the spread of lies and rumours about his young masters. Nilus was indignant at the behaviour of his slave, but nevertheless urged his father to allow him to continue to work with a view to funding his masters' studies. Moreover, he and his brother were

---

[100] Cribiore 2007: 117–20. She points to interesting parallels with Paris in the year 1501.
[101] See Cicero, *Ad Att.* 14, 7, 2 and 14, 13, 4 (the indulgent father considering the trip); *Ad fam.* 16, 21, 2 (the letter by young Marcus; see 8.3). See Eyben 1968: 44–5 and 52–3; 1977: 214–15; Bradley 1991: 103–6.

intent on moving to a bigger house, since their present accommodation was too cramped. From the end of the letter, it is apparent that Theon had generously sent food to his two 'diligent' sons in the city of Alexandria![102]

The most vivid accounts of tumultuous student life are found in texts from late antiquity. According to Eunapius, competing groups would await the arrival of new cargoes of students at the Athenian harbour of Piraeus. The young men would be 'abducted' and recruited into the group of a particular professor, who would thus secure his income. Sometimes, a sophist would arrange with the captain of a ship to supply him with a whole cargo of new students at once.[103] When the sophist Lollianus wanted to buy a shipload of grain, he had his students pay in advance for the whole academic year in order that he could finance his purchase.[104]

The process of initiation through ragging was part and parcel of student life in antiquity. In a procession involving much jostling and pulling, the freshmen would be led to the bathhouse. Here, they had to take a ritual bath and suffer mockery from older peers before being fully accepted into the fraternity of students. Only then would they be allowed to put on the traditional student gown, known as a *tribon*.[105]

Riots and brawls between the groups of students of different 'professors' were frequent. These groups, or *choroi*, were organised according to a strict hierarchy, with older students commanding the freshmen. Loyalty towards the sophist was considered to be of crucial importance.[106] Sometimes such student organisations would function as a national faction. When Prohaeresius, an Armenian, applied to succeed his master Julian to the chair of rhetoric, the Armenian students in Athens supported his candidacy.[107]

Deep friendships could develop between the members of a *choros*. A touching account of bidding farewell to his life as a student is provided by Gregory of Nazianzus. He describes how teachers and students flocked together at the quay. Tears flowed as farewell speeches were made. The students begged their friends to stay just a little longer. Nothing is more painful, writes the author, than saying farewell to Athens and to the fellow-students with whom one has shared so many joys and sorrows.[108]

---

[102] *P. Oxy.* XVIII 2190; for a translation, see Parkin and Pomeroy 2007: 140–1 no. 4.5. See Legras 1999: 39–43; Cribiore 2001: 57–8 and 121–2.
[103] Eunapius, *Vitae sophist.* 485–6.   [104] Eunapius, *Vitae sophist.* 526–7.
[105] Eunapius, *Vitae sophist.* 486; Olympiodorus of Thebes, fr. 28; Gregory of Nazianzus, *Or.* 43, 16.
[106] Watts 2005: 239–40.   [107] Eunapius, *Vitae sophist.* 487. See Watts 2006: 55–6.
[108] Gregory of Nazianzus, *Or.* 43, 24. See Eyben 1977: 212.

Libanius makes mention of pitched battles between groups of students in the centre of Athens with adversaries wielding clubs and knives and throwing stones at each other. In a subsequent text Libanius asserted that professors in Athens were more like soldiers, and that many students returned home from their studies with scars to remind them of battles fought in support of 'their' sophist.[109] Such disturbances would result in reciprocal recriminations and numerous trials. It even happened that the members of a student group were punished collectively. In one such instance, the sophist Julian the Cappadocian and his students ended up in an Athenian prison after a brawl with the members of the group of the Spartan Apsines. Subsequently, however, one of Apsines' students failed to plead convincingly before the proconsul, who was acting as a judge in the dispute. By contrast, Prohaeresius, Julian's student, argued masterfully. Consequently, the defendants were freed and the Spartans condemned to a severe beating. Prohaeresius would later succeed Julian and become the intellectual superstar of fourth-century Athens.[110]

Teaching in quiet and easy circumstances would appear to have been virtually impossible at Athens. Philostratus recounts how the sophist Philagrus was ridiculed during a public lecture by the students of his rival Herodes Atticus. He had been pretending to be improvising, but Herodes Atticus' crew had laid hands on the prepared text and began to recite it simultaneously with the teacher. The large crowd burst out laughing.[111] Augustine, too, recalls how gangs disturbed his classes in Carthage.[112] Students would sometimes switch professors to avoid having to pay a fee: they would claim to have learned nothing with the sophist they had left. Some students made a 'grand tour' of all the teachers in town.[113] What is more, the teachers themselves were often not safe. Libanius mentions how a professor from Arabia was dragged through the mud by two hired thugs. He also recounts how an Egyptian teacher was almost drowned in a well. Fearing for his life, he migrated to a faraway region and switched professions.[114] Ordinary citizens could also fall victim to the rowdy behaviour of students: verbal and physical abuse were commonplace. Gangs of students, known as *eversores* or 'destroyers', would break into the homes of the poor and cause mayhem.[115] The authorities hardly ever intervened.

[109] Libanius, *Or.* 1, 19; *Epist.* 715, 3.
[110] Eunapius, *Vitae sophist.* 483–5. See Eyben 1977: 206; Watts 2005: 240; Watts 2006: 48–78 on Prohaeresius' school (fourth century AD).
[111] Philostratus, *Vitae sophist.* 2, 8, 578–9. [112] Augustine, *Conf.* 5, 8, 14.
[113] Augustine, *Conf.* 5, 12, 22. See Eyben 1977: 210. [114] Libanius, *Or.* 1, 85. See Eyben 1977: 208.
[115] Libanius, *Or.* 1, 21–2; Augustine, *Conf.* 3, 3, 6.

6.5 Students' lives at 'university'

Libanius writes openly about his own life as a student. As a youngster, he had always dreamt of living it up in Athens, attending parties and spending his money lavishly. However, things turned out quite differently once he became a student. He did not participate in ballgames, and steered well clear of the 'loose' girls who broke the hearts and ruined the studies of many of his fellow-students. In another passage, he warns against the squandering of parents' money on games of dice, drinking sprees, and other unspeakable acts of debauchery.[116] At his own public lectures in Athens, things did not always go well:

> When I start declaiming, they keep on nodding to each other in regard to charioteers, mimes, horses, dancers, and past or future combats. Even better, some stand up as if they were made of stone with their hands crossed, others pick their nose with both hands, others sit down even if many get up with enthusiasm, others force people who would like to get up to sit down, others start counting the new arrivals, and others are content to look at the leaves. (Libanius, *Or.* 3, 12–13; transl. R. Cribiore)

In the following part of this speech, we read about students walking ostentatiously through the auditorium or enticing listeners to leave, by inviting them to the bathhouses.

An edict of the emperor Valentinian I from the year AD 370 proves that the sophists' complaints were not at all unjustified. It concerns the red tape which a student had faced before being allowed to study in Rome or Constantinople. Upon arrival, the young man would have to check in with the *magister census*, the chairman of the commission for good manners. Not only was the candidate required to submit credentials from an authorised magistrate of his own province; he also had to provide details about where he would be residing during his studies as well as about his plans for the future. The prospective student would be warned not to join any of the barely legal gangs and not to attend too many theatre or amphitheatre performances, and to refrain from licentious merrymaking. Failure to abide by these rules could result in a public beating and instant expulsion. As previously mentioned, the maximum age for studying was fixed at twenty.[117] Of course, this imperial decree should be understood in its proper context. The economic crisis of the fourth century had created an enormous need for *decuriones* who were able to provide the necessary funds to keep the cities going. As taxes and other financial burdens became increasingly heavy, youngsters of the local aristocracy tried to evade them by spending long

---

[116] Libanius, *Or.* 1, 19 and 1, 22 (on his own life as a student), *Or.* 3, 6 (spending parents' money).
[117] *Cod. Theod.* 14, 9, 1.

periods studying abroad. Hence, Valentinian's legislation was probably more concerned with controlling and limiting the numbers exempt from municipal duties than with keeping in check students' behaviour.

During their stay in a 'university' town, young people were in effect unleashed on a new social environment. Their teachers and fellow-students served as their models in their lives abroad. Separated from normal society, they lived according to their own values, customs, and traditions, which included a general rowdiness, excessive drinking, and lewd behaviour. They were also set apart from the rest of society by their attire.[118] Students were well aware that the transition to 'university' marked the beginning of a new phase in their lives.[119] Traditionally, they would get away with acts that would have been regarded as crimes had they been perpetrated by other people.[120] Nowhere does one seem to come closer to witnessing a separate youth subculture than in the case of the lives of young students in ancient 'university' towns.[121] However, Harry Pleket has cast some doubt on this view.[122] He argues that, for these young people, the future was assured: they were young aristocrats, prospective bureaucrats. Hence, they experienced nothing like a crisis of adolescence or a period of self-doubt or uncertainty, or of searching for a destiny in life; they knew all too well what would be expected from them after their studies. While this is undoubtedly partly true, the fact that their future had already been planned does not in our view make them into wise and responsible students. Most of the available evidence for tumultuous student life comes from late antiquity. This does not imply that the phenomenon was merely typical of the state-controlled society of the fourth century: the earlier evidence of Cicero and the papyri proves otherwise. It is worth noting that many of the texts cited were written by Christian authors. Did they choose to overemphasise the sins of youths in pagan society in order to contrast them with their own devout Christian behaviour? One can hardly imagine that these writings did not, in one way or another, touch upon reality. Moreover, non-Christians such as Eunapius and Libanius tell similar stories, even though this has been questioned by some historians. Libanius' accounts of youthful misbehaviour, while similar, invariably relate to Athens. Hence it may well be the case that the rhetor from Antioch intended to cast the teachers and students in this competing 'university' town in a bad light. Besides, Libanius did not have good

---

[118] Eunapius, *Vitae sophist.* 487; Eusebius, *Hist. eccles.* 6, 9, 12–14. See Watts 2005: 249.
[119] Watts 2005: 237.   [120] Stated explicitly by Augustine, *Conf.* 5, 8, 14.
[121] See also Kunst 2006: 88.   [122] Pleket 1979: 188–9.

6.6 The instruction of girls

memories of his own time as a student in Athens.[123] But we think that the stories, possibly exaggerated, have a kernel of truth.

6.6 The instruction of girls

We possess far less information on the instruction of girls in the Roman Empire. Of course, in this respect too there were great differences between the social classes. Primary schools were in any case mixed, so that girls of low social status would have been part of the motley hotchpotch of pupils instructed by a single schoolteacher. There they were taught the basics of reading, writing, and counting in basic and noisy classrooms.[124] When their parents felt they had acquired sufficient knowledge, they would leave school. At most they might have mastered some elementary skills, but barely enough to distinguish them from an illiterate. According to estimates, just 10–15% of the population was actually literate. Illiteracy was most probably much more prevalent among women, though we have no data or statistics to prove this assumption.[125] After a short period of schooling, if any, girls from the less well-to-do classes would learn a trade. This happened gradually and most commonly within the domestic sphere. There was no choice to be made: one simply performed the tasks that one's parents (or at least one's mother) performed. Most girls in the Roman world married in their late teens. At that age, they would have familiarised themselves with the skills required for marital life and for meeting the social expectations that had long since been outlined. In a sense then the male head of the family and the social environment determined how the course of education of young women was completed. They simply followed the traditional pathway that had been mapped out for them for centuries and that many had followed before them.

Just like upper-class boys, girls from the elite tended not to attend the disdained school of the *ludimagister*. Instead they received instruction at home from a private tutor. Like young boys, girls were supervised by a slave paedagogue. They were instructed in Greek and Latin literature by their private teacher. 'You have returned from the war. I wish you had died over there.' With these words, nine-year-old Pompeia welcomed home her father Pompeius on his return from a four-year campaign in the East. The little girl

---

[123] Watts 2006: 42–7 considers student riots as typical of fourth-century Athens. See Cribiore 2007: 81 on Libanius' preference for 'his' Antioch.
[124] Laes 2006a: 109–13.
[125] Harris 1989: 175–284; Hemelrijk 1999: 20. For a more positive view on ancient literacy, see Corbier 2006: 77–90.

was, of course, proudly reciting verses which she had learned from the *Iliad* and was blissfully unaware of the inappropriateness of her greeting. The anecdote does, however, at least indicate that girls could receive a training in Greek literature in their homes.[126] Unlike boys from the upper class, aristocratic girls did not attend the schools of the grammarians.[127] They could, however, acquire the same knowledge through private instruction. We know of some women of the imperial house who possessed a greater than average skill in composition. Both Julia, Augustus' infamous daughter, and Agrippina Maior, one of Augustus' granddaughters, were praised for their writing style.[128] Among the senatorial class, Pliny's young wife Calpurnia was capable of writing poetry that was pleasing to her husband, in addition to well-composed letters.[129] We have but scant information, though, on eloquent women. In the Greek world, there is a single exceptional case of a female rhetor, Auphria from Delphi, who delivered many speeches at the Pythian games (second century AD).[130] Cornelia, mother of the Gracchi, the icon of all Roman *matronae*, gave birth to twelve children, only three of whom reached adulthood. As a virtuous widow, she took care of the education of her two famous sons, Caius and Tiberius, all by herself. There was no need for her to rely on teachers, as her own style of writing and eloquence were so excellent that she was said to have provided her sons with rhetorical instruction almost from the mother's breast.[131] Of course, this image of Cornelia is an idealised picture from later centuries. Moreover, in her day, during the second century BC, rhetorical instruction was not institutionalised at all. Hence, Cornelia could expand her knowledge and skill by contacting scholars around her.[132] Another woman to be explicitly praised for her rhetorical talent was Julia Domna (AD 170–217), wife to the emperor Septimius Severus and the strong female *par excellence* of the Severan dynasty. In the imperial palace she was surrounded by sophists and philosophers. She was herself fanatically engaged in rhetorical exercises. Most probably, this group was essentially an informal gathering of intellectuals who had flocked together at the imperial court only around the year AD 200, when Julia Domna was about thirty years of age.[133] Ultimately, it is hardly surprising that we know so little about the eloquence of Roman

---

[126] Plutarch, *Quaest. conv.* 9, 1, 3. The quote is from Homer, *Il.* 3, 428. See Hemelrijk 1999: 22.
[127] Vössing 2004a. *AnÉp* (1994) 1903 (1996, 1903) is an extraordinary record of a woman *grammat(ica)* at Caesareia in Mauretania (second to fourth centuries AD).
[128] Macrobius, *Saturn.* 2, 5, 2; Suetonius, *Aug.* 86.
[129] Pliny, *Epist.* 4, 19 (interest in literature); *Epist.* 6, 7 (Calpurnia writing her letters herself).
[130] *FD* III 4, 79.   [131] Cicero, *Brut.* 58, 211; Quintilian, *Inst. or.* 1, 1, 6. For a survey, see Dixon 2007.
[132] Hemelrijk 1999: 64–7.
[133] Philostratus, *Vita Apoll.* 1, 3; Cassius Dio, *Hist. Rom.* 75, 15, 6–7. See Hemelrijk 1999: 122–6.

6.6 The instruction of girls

matronae: they were neither expected to engage in politics, nor to deliver speeches in public. Moreover, aristocratic girls generally married at a very young age, often in their mid-teens or even younger. Their very short period of youth, if they enjoyed any at all, was also one of the reasons why they did not attend the schools of the grammarians. As for girls of the middling classes, this did not imply that they could not acquire further knowledge and skills after marriage. Much more so than in the case of boys, instruction may have been provided in an informal way. The husband, who would usually have been older than his wife, could act as an instructor. Alternatively, married women could have their own private teachers (the philosopher Nicomachus of Gerasa from the second century AD wrote a moralising treatise for a young lady whom he taught; and there are some accounts of teachers falling in love with already married young pupils). And newly wed young ladies could pick up from other women the social skills required in their new roles as matrons.[134] In the end, the social lives of women of the upper class involved a sophisticated exercise in balance. They needed to be charming, to possess musical skills, to have a sound literary background, and to be capable of responding wittily in conversation.[135] At the same time, they had to guard their reputation meticulously, avoid drawing too much attention to themselves, not give cause for gossip, respect the female dress code (a tunic and *stola*; a cloak reaching to the ankles, and even a kind of shawl or headscarf known as a *palla*). Above all, they had to exude a sense of chastity and respect for the ancient Roman values. The domestic tasks *par excellence* of the Roman *matrona* were weaving and the working of wool.[136] A testimony by the biographer Suetonius mentions how the emperor Augustus gave his daughters and granddaughters a conservative education, undoubtedly partly inspired by a concern that his own family should embody the principles of the new Augustan era as well as a return to the time-honoured Roman traditions. We should not imagine that all Roman girls from the elite were educated in this way, but Suetonius' text at least offers a model of good paedagogical practice to the public of Augustus' day.

---

[134] Hemelrijk 1999: 36–47. For the relationship between teacher Caecilius Epirota and his young pupil Attica, a married lady: Suetonius, *De gramm.* 16.

[135] This ideal picture is painted by Ovid, *Ars amat.* 3, 315–70, on which see Scholz 2007: 38–9.

[136] For a portrait of the Roman matron, see Foubert 2006: 18–26. For the same reasons, philosophy was not considered suitable for a young woman; elderly *matronae*, however, sometimes read (moral) philosophical treatises: see Hemelrijk 1999: 51–2. We know of one woman philosopher in the Greek East: Magnilla from Apollonia in Mysia (*IGR* IV 125; second to third centuries AD); she was the daughter of the philosopher Magnus and the wife of the philosopher Menias.

> He raised his daughter and granddaughters in such a way that they became accustomed to spinning wool. He forbade them to say or do anything other than openly and such as might be recorded in the day-books of the household. He kept them away from all contact with non-family members. Once he wrote to L. Vinicius, a young man of good position and reputation, that he had acted presumptuously in coming to Baiae to greet his daughter. (Suetonius, *Aug.* 64, 2)

6.7 Excursus: Ovid's education

It rarely happens that a Roman author informs us about his own youth and education. We are therefore exceptionally fortunate to possess an autobiographical poem by Ovid (*Tristia* 4, 10). There is no reason to question the essential veracity of Ovid's account, although there is undeniably an element of literary *aemulatio* in that it was probably inspired, at least in part, by a similar autobiographical story of the discovery of the vocation of a love-elegist and the abandonment of a potential career in the Roman establishment, as related by Ovid's older contemporary Propertius.[137]

Born in Sulmo on 20 March 43 BC, Ovid became a celebrated poet in Augustan Rome, but he was suddenly banned by the emperor in the year AD 8 to remote Tomis on the Black Sea. The reason for his exile has been much debated. Ovid himself only ever alludes to it in his poems.[138]

From his place of exile, Ovid wrote grieving elegies to his friends and family, known as the *Tristia* and the *Epistulae ex Ponto*. In *Tristia* 4, Ovid looks back on his own life. He writes the following verses about his youth and his schooling:

> We began our education while still of tender age. Through our father's care we went to men in the city distinguished in the liberal arts. My brother leant towards oratory from his early years; he was born for the stout weapons of the noisy Forum. I, even as a boy, took delight in the service of the divine and the Muse was drawing me secretly to her work. Often my father said: 'Why do you pursue useless studies? Even the Maeonian himself (= Homer) left no wealth.' I was moved by his words and, forsaking Helicon, tried to write words free of metre. But verse came, of its own accord, in the right measures, and whatever I tried to write was poetry. (Ovid, *Tristia* 4, 10, 15–26)

Ovid describes his first literary experiments with great pride and an almost religious seriousness: 'higher spheres', service to the Muses, a reference to

---

[137] Propertius, *Eleg.* 4, 1, 119–34. See Verstraete 2008.
[138] See Claassen 2008: 2–4; 232–4 and Volk 2010, who offer bibliographical guidance into this vast debate.

6.7 Excursus: Ovid's education

Helicon, the sacred mountain of the Muses. We will never know for sure whether he intended to be entirely serious on these matters or whether he was writing with a certain sense of irony.

In the following excerpt, Ovid is about fifteen years of age, the age of donning the toga:

> Meanwhile, as the silent-footed years slipped by, my brother and I assumed the toga of a freer life. Our shoulders carried the broad purple stripe, while our studies remained the same as before. My brother had just doubled ten years of life when he passed away, and, from then on, I was bereft of half myself. Still I received the first honours, granted to tender youth, since at that time I was one of the *tresviri*. The senate awaited me; I narrowed my purple stripe. But that burden was too heavy for my shoulders. I had neither the strength of body, nor a spirit suited to that vocation, and I shunned the worries of an ambitious life. The Aonian sisters (= Muses) urged me to seek the safety of seclusion that I had always cherished. (Ovid, *Tristia* 4, 10, 27–40)

Ovid and his brother had received a toga with a broad purple stripe. This was the privilege of youngsters of the equestrian class with considerable ambition, pointing to a possible senatorial career. Around age twenty, Ovid held office with the commission of the *tresviri (capitales)*, responsible for the prison system, among other duties. This minor office was to be held before a man could become a quaestor and enter into the senate. But Ovid gave up his political career and so became a simple knight, entitled to wear only a small purple stripe. He devoted himself to the art of poetry.

> I cherished and reverenced the poets of those times; I thought all bards so many present gods. (Ovid, *Tristia* 4, 10, 41–2)

By rejecting a political career and explicitly choosing poetry, Ovid proved an exceptional case in antiquity.[139] He would indeed publish several works before the age of thirty, including the mildly erotic and light-hearted *Amores*. However, it would be wrong to consider him a modern *poète maudit*. He was very successful socially as he found himself within the exclusive inner circle at the imperial court. He entered into his first marriage at a young age, still 'almost a child'.[140] He was a rich aristocrat, with plenty of spare time on his hands, and was thus able to assume the exclusive aura of a great poet. He was certainly not an adolescent in search of his identity and prepared to give up everything to pursue his vocation as a poet.

---

[139] Eyben 1977: 405 offers some other examples. [140] Ovid, *Tristia* 4, 10, 69–70 (*puero*).

CHAPTER 7

Associations of adolescent youths

7.1 Greek ephebes

During the Hellenistic and Roman periods, there were associations of adolescent boys in almost all cities in the Greek East. Known as the *ephebeia*,[1] it was an institution centred on the gymnasium whose precise nature could vary from city to city.

In post-classical Athens, after the reforms of the third/second century BC, the *ephebeia* became a training school for the sons of the elite. The term of service was one year and it was not compulsory. The Athenian *ephebeia* served no military purpose but provided intellectual education (rhetoric, philosophy) in combination with sports training (including horse-riding). In Egypt, access to the *ephebeia* was restricted to the sons of the small Hellenised elite. Following an official request by the father or the guardian and an investigation by officials, a Greek boy could be admitted at the age of fourteen, on condition that he was registered as a citizen. In most Egyptian cities (*metropoleis*), the father of the candidate had to be a former ephebe himself. The *ephebeia* in Egypt was not so much about education as about citizenship and the consolidation of power by the reigning social elite.[2] We will leave aside here these extraordinary forms of *ephebeia*, and will focus instead on the *ephebeia* in the average Greek city of Greece, Asia Minor, and elsewhere. In fact, by the second century BC, the *ephebeia* had spread to every corner of the Greek world and become an integral part of the education of young men.[3]

---

[1] There were no comparable associations of adolescent girls. If girls ever visited the gymnasium, they stopped doing so at the onset of puberty; cf. also p. 120 n. 49 below.
[2] For Athens, see Marrou 1964: 168–70; Nilsson 1955: 21–9; Burckhardt 2004; Perrin-Saminadayar 2007. For Egypt, see Legras 1999: 133–94; Habermann 2004 esp. 341.
[3] Kennell 2006: XI with a complete register of all records (at least 190 Greek cities). Chankowski 2004b: 279 calls the *ephebeia* 'une institution grecque par excellence qui véhiculait un type particulier de civilisation'. One should bear in mind that there was considerable variability across the Greek world.

7.1 Greek ephebes

Before discussing the *ephebeia* in further detail, let us first consider the gymnasium where the ephebes assembled (see Fig. 7.1). The gymnasium was a place of training and instruction, not only for ephebes but also for other age groups, such as *neoi* (see 6.2) and sometimes *paides*. In larger cities, such as Pergamum, each of these groups had a gymnasium of its own. Some

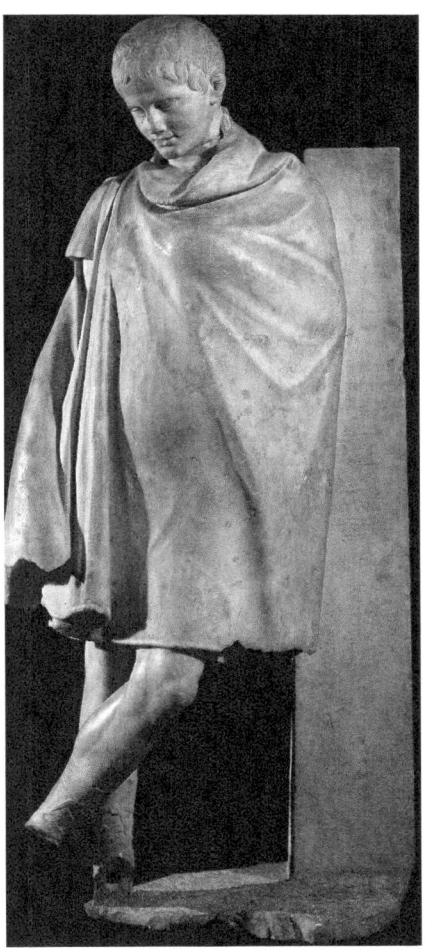

7.1 The Ephebe of Tralleis, late first century BC, marble statue of a young ephebe. He is dressed in a cloak of thick fabric, a *chlamys*. Tired, he leans against a pillar, perhaps the starting or finishing post at a race in the stadium. Ephebes competed in many sports. (Archaeological Museum, Istanbul.)

towns provided gymnasia for other groups, too, including the *gerousia* (the elders) and even women.[4] All gymnasia were based on the same ground plan. The central part was the palaestra, a square or rectangular open court for athletics, boxing, and other sports. The palaestra was lined on all sides with colonnades; the rooms behind were for changing and washing, and there were also classrooms for teaching and lecturing. In the imperial period, one of the rooms was usually dedicated to the cult of the emperor; here, a statue of the deified emperor would adorn a niche. Another room may have housed a library. Next to the gymnasium, there was often a stadium with a track for racing and sometimes one for horse racing too. In the Roman imperial period (from *c.* AD 50), a bathhouse was commonly added.

In the Roman imperial period, the gymnasium became the most important place for social contacts between cities' inhabitants; it is often referred to by scholars as 'a second agora'. Here people would meet each other, engage in conversation, or listen to a lecture by an itinerant scholar. It was also a venue for a variety of contests, as well as feasts and banquets, quite often courtesy of local benefactors. The gymnasium developed into the busiest urban hotspot and indeed came to symbolise its city. A benefactor who had a gymnasium built or thoroughly restored would often come to be regarded as 'a second founder of the city' and receive the highest cultic honour. He would sometimes be buried inside the gymnasium, an exceptional honour reserved for the greatest benefactors.

It is not always entirely clear how gymnasia were financed, but almost certainly this involved various sources of income, which may have varied from place to place.[5] The gymnasium could have funds of its own; it could receive money from the treasury of the city; visitors paid contributions; benefactors donated money or land or created foundations, the yearly interest from which defrayed the operational costs. Often gymnasiarchs

---

[4] For the Hellenistic gymnasium, see Kah and Scholz 2004. For the gymnasium in the imperial period, see van Nijf 2004: 207–8 with references. For gymnasia in Egypt, see Cribiore 2001: 34–6; Habermann 2004. For Egypt, there is no proof that gymnasia were places of intellectual education: neither classrooms nor libraries have been found; there are no documents that shed light on how the gymnasia functioned and on the responsibilities of the gymnasiarch.

[5] Pleket 1981b: 161; Quass 1993: 287 and 318; Schuler 2004: 178–89; Kennell 2009: 327–9. An important document from Beroea (Macedonia) from the beginning of the second century AD recounts that the gymnasium's funds had diminished considerably and that the wealthy citizens were unwilling to assume the expenses of the gymnasiarchy. This led to the occasional closure of the gymnasium, an 'utterly disgraceful' situation, which the proconsul L. Memmius Rufus had to resolve; see *I. Beroia* 7, republished with commentary by Nigdelis and Souris 2005 (*SEG* LV (2005) 678). As a counterweight to this extraordinary situation, one may point to a wealthy gymnasiarch at Mylasa (Caria), who remained in charge for no less than eighty months (*SEG* LIV (2004) 1101, late Hellenistic period).

7.1 Greek ephebes

acted as benefactors; they provided free oil for the physical exercises or prizes for the contests, they paid for the heating of the baths, they kept the building in good repair or embellished it, they established foundations; the latter benefaction was often rewarded with the title 'eternal gymnasiarch'. A good example of a generous gymnasiarch is Menas from Sestus (in Thrace), as evidenced by the decree in his honour (see 7.2; from *c.* 133–120 BC), especially lines 61–82. The gymnasiarch was, as a rule, not concerned with the actual education of the youths at the gymnasium: he was not a teacher, nor did he appoint teachers or instructors. His main responsibility lay in keeping good order at the gymnasium; he was the guardian of proper behaviour by the visitors (*eukosmia*). He also looked after the building and was in charge of the daily routine at the gymnasium: the offering of sacrifices, the staging of festivals with contests, and the administration of the finances. Holding the gymnasiarchy was always very expensive but it became even more so during the imperial period, to the extent that the spending of money became the position's primary purpose. Hence gymnasiarchs often remained in charge for just a few months, rather than an entire year. Wealthy women and children could also hold the office.[6]

Some scholars, including Harry Pleket and Marc Kleijwegt,[7] have argued that the *ephebeia* in Greek cities was an elitist institution: its purpose was to prepare the sons of the upper class swiftly to take over their fathers' tasks in the political and social life in the city: 'a school for the well-to-do, by the well-to-do and with the purpose of continuing the role of the well-to-do in city government'.[8] Pleket and Kleijwegt assume that the age of entry into the *ephebeia* tended to drop, so that the *ephebeia* came to follow immediately after the primary education of the *paides* (children), which ended at the age of about fourteen. Depending on the city, the length of the *ephebeia* varied from one to three years, though in most cities the duration was limited to one year. The ephebes were trained in various sports, including light and heavy athletics and horse-riding. They received education in a variety of intellectual fields, such as literature and music. Membership of the *ephebeia* was expensive: one had to pay for the numerous teachers, for oil and other amenities in the gymnasium, for offerings etc., so that only children of the wealthy upper class, who had time and money to spare,

---

[6] Quass 1993: 286–91 and 317–23; Dmitriev 2005 *passim*; Schuler 2004: 166–72; an important document on the duties of the gymnasiarch is the Hellenistic gymnasiarchical law of Beroea (Macedonia), *I. Beroia* 1; see n. 41 below. For benefactions, see also Ameling 2004: 147–57; Schuler 2004: 189–90.

[7] Pleket 1981b: 169–74; Kleijwegt 1991: 91–101; Marrou 1964: 170–3.

[8] Pleket 1981b: 172. In later publications Pleket modified his position and argued that middle-class boys also engaged in athletics in the gymnasium: see Hin 2007: 143 n. 4.

were able to participate. In a word, the *ephebeia* was an educational institution which provided schooling for only a short period; it was aimed at preparing elite boys quickly to assume responsibilities in public life and to follow in their fathers' footsteps in pursuing a municipal career. At least, this was the case according to Pleket and Kleijwegt, who believe that adolescents commonly held political and religious office in the cities during their teens. For these youngsters, there was, in their view, no *Jugendraum*, no time to be young, between childhood and adulthood. New research, however, has revealed that it was unusual for youngsters to hold public office (see Chapter 9 on youths in public office). And a recent re-examination of epigraphic materials by Saskia Hin has shed new light on the nature of the *ephebeia*.[9]

Let us first consider the age of the ephebes. There are very few sources that provide indications regarding their age. In fact, we know of only ten, primarily epitaphs, some of which are problematic and difficult to interpret. The unequivocal records (eight) yield the following information: one ephebe was thirteen years old, another was fourteen, and a third was fifteen; two were sixteen; another was seventeen, and two were eighteen. The gravestone of Dionysius from Chios, for example, tells us:

> Passing through the seventeenth year of my life ... whilst I, Dionysius, was just blooming at the heights of the *ephebeia* and the brightness of the Muses, I went to Hades. (Vérilhac 1978–82 no. 77; second century AD)

Although the source material is extremely scant and quite unworkable from a statistical point of view, the historian of antiquity must of course make do with whatever is available to him. On this evidence, the average age of the ephebes appears to have been sixteen rather than fourteen. What is certain, though, is that there was no fixed age. As a consequence, sometimes brothers of different ages served together as ephebes.[10] It is possible that, as Nigel Kennell has recently suggested, not all *ephebeiai* in the Roman period were annual. In some cities they were only held when a sufficient number of adolescents had reached approximately the qualifying age.[11] It is also possible, we believe, that many adolescents did not join the *ephebeia* until a generous gymnasiarch had been appointed, making participation

---

[9] For the ages, see Hin 2007: 143–6, who carefully discusses all the evidence (the uncertain texts record an ephebe of sixteen or seventeen years and a young man of eighteen years who had not yet reached the initial or the final age limit of the *ephebeia*). Since the study of Hin, one new relevant source has been published: *AnÉp* (2008) 1335 from the necropolis of Marmarotus on Cos. It is the epitaph of the ephebe M. Aeficius Chryseros, who died at the age of thirteen (second to third century AD).
[10] Kennell 2009: 330–1.   [11] Kennell 2009: 331.

more affordable. Two late Hellenistic decrees from Eretria on Euboea for the gymnasiarchs Elpinicus and Mantidorus mention how the *paides*, ephebes and others (i.e. the *neoi*) who fell under the gymnasiarch's authority convened (at the gymnasium) in larger numbers thanks to his generosity.[12] The fact that the age of the boys on entering the *ephebeia* was lower than in classical Athens, where the *ephebeia* consisted in a two-year period of military service for boys of eighteen–nineteen years, is presumably due to a decline in the importance of military training as a component of the *ephebeia* from the late Hellenistic period (see below): physical maturity was no longer required.[13]

Next, there is the duration of the *ephebeia*.[14] This, too, varied from city to city: from one to three years. Two- or three-year *ephebeiai* were not exceptional. S. Hin has argued that there is no point in trying to determine the average duration, as it could vary within the *ephebeia* of a single city, with some boys participating for a year and others for two or three years. The case of the city of Apollonis in Lydia (in western Anatolia) is very informative in this respect. An ephebic list from this city mentions at least sixteen ephebes of the first year (*epheteoi*) but only three of the second year (*dieteis*).[15] Conceivably most boys left the *ephebeia* after the first year and only a small select group continued with a second year. But if this was indeed the case, then who belonged to the select company that continued? The inscription from Apollonis again may provide a clue. One of the three ephebes of the second year was a certain Apollonides. In the aforementioned list, he is described as ephebarch (leader of the ephebes); his father was Apollonius, who held the civic offices of gymnasiarch and *stephanephoros* (the eponymous magistrate of the city) in that same year and paid for oil out of his own pocket throughout that period. This indicates that the ephebe Apollonides belonged to one of the city's wealthy aristocratic families.

---

[12] *IG* XII, 9, 234 and 235 (*c.* 100 BC; for a translation of the latter text, see Joyal, McDougall, and Yardley 2009: 144 no. 6.19); cf. Ameling 2004: 140 n. 59. Compare *SEG* LV (2005) 1251: at Colophon no fewer than 153 *neoi* frequented the gymnasium in the year Euelthon served as gymnasiarch, no doubt thanks to his generosity (early second century BC).

[13] The data on the ages of the ephebes come mainly from the first century BC and the first and second centuries AD; the record of the fourteen-year-old ephebe (from Thasos) dates from the third or fourth century AD: see Hin 2007: 144 n. 11; the record of the thirteen-year-old ephebe (from Cos) dates from the second or third century AD; see above. Perhaps the age tended to drop in the third to fourth century. The uneven physical development of the ephebes meant that often a distinction was made in sporting contests between younger and older competitors.

[14] For the length of the *ephebeia*, see Hin 2007: 147–50. Since her study, some new documents have emerged: *SEG* LVI (2006) 1193 (ephebes of the second year at Caunus); *SEG* LVII (2007) 365 (ephebes of the third year at Asine, Messenia); *AnÉp* (2008) 1254 (ephebes of the third year at Messene).

[15] *TAM* V, 2, 1204 from *c.* 150–100 BC.

Other examples confirm that boys who enjoyed a longer membership came from truly aristocratic backgrounds. The boys whose membership ended after one year apparently came from a broader population group, the middle classes, if you will.

Participation in the *ephebeia* clearly required a certain level of wealth, particularly as the city did not finance such institutions. Boys from poor families most definitely did not participate: their parents simply could not afford it. Moreover, they were expected to work to boost the family's income and hence did not possess the luxury of leisure time. Middle-class parents, on the other hand, apparently were able to afford the contribution for their sons, not least thanks to the generosity of rich ephebes and other wealthy citizens, often gymnasiarchs, who frequently mitigated the costs through donations. For example: M. Vettius Philon from Stuberra (in Macedonia) made a very generous gift, large enough to secure the ephebes' oil for at least thirty-five years.[16] Permanent funds were also established. The annual interest from such funds would help pay for oil, offerings, the salaries of teachers, and the like. So despite the cost involved, it would apparently be wrong to think of the *ephebeia* as an exclusively aristocratic institution.

The numbers of ephebes found on several membership lists would appear to confirm this. The numbers are simply too great for them all to have been the sons of elite families, citizens and non-citizens. A list from the above-mentioned city of Apollonis in Lydia contains the names of at least fifty-six ephebes. A small city such as Apollonis would typically have had a population of around five thousand. On this basis, one would expect there to have been around fifteen aristocratic boys of ephebic age at any one time. All the evidence therefore suggests that the ephebes were a mixed group, comprised of upper-class adolescents as well as boys from less wealthy families, without aristocratic pedigree and not participating in the city government.[17]

The ephebes from the elite distinguished themselves from their fellow-ephebes not only by their longer participation, but also by performing certain offices, such as that of the ephebarcheia, and by acting as benefactors towards the ephebes of less wealthy families. This gave rise to an internal hierarchy among the ephebes; the *ephebeia* in effect mirrored the social

---

[16] *SEG* XXXVIII (1988) 684–5, Babamova 2005: 15–6, 18–20, catalogues of ephebes whose oil was paid for by the city from the *denarii* given by Vettius, from AD 87/88 to 121/122.

[17] It is possible that, in very small cities, there were not enough young men available to organise the *ephebeia* every year. This may explain why three or even four brothers are registered in the list of ephebes at Icaria (*SEG* LIII (2003) 888 from the first century AD).

structure of the city.[18] This way, all ephebes were familiarised with their positions in society. The rich boys learned to behave in the manner that would be required of them once they became magistrates or *euergetai*. The boys who stood a few rungs below them on the social ladder were likewise prepared for their place in society. In other words, the *ephebeia* was a means of socialisation.

The next question to arise is what kind of training did the ephebes receive at the gymnasium?[19] There were three different kinds of activities: military training, athletics, and intellectual training. During the Hellenistic period ephebes were taught the following military skills: javelin-throwing, archery, catapult-shooting, slinging, *hoplomachia* (man-to-man combat with round shield and javelin, as practised by hoplites), *thyreamachia* (man-to-man combat with long shield and sword, as practised by Roman soldiers), and some other, minor, skills. Javelin-throwing and archery were intended for lightly armoured soldiers; catapult-shooting and slinging were skills required for laying siege to a city. *Hoplomachia*, on the other hand, was useless in real battle, in which soldiers fought in the order of the phalanx.[20] The military aspect of the *ephebeia* is also demonstrated by the fact that weapons were commonly offered as prizes to ephebes in agonistic competitions, for example at Sestus (see 7.2, Excursus).[21] But what, then, was the purpose of this training? Marc Kleijwegt has argued that the ephebes in regions outside Attica frequently engaged in semi-military activities:[22] patrolling the countryside on horseback, commanding police or security forces, participating in armed uprisings and revolution. But this would appear to be incorrect. In fact, the generally accepted view today is that the ephebes did not fulfil a military role, unlike *neoi* or *neaniskoi* (see 6.2). Indeed, there is not a single document to prove that ephebes were ever called upon to defend their city with arms, or even to patrol the territory.[23] At most, there is one indication from Ephesus that the ephebes were

---

[18] In three cities of mainland Greece (Argos, Corone, Tegea), an *archephebos* is recorded, the head of the ephebes or the first among the ephebes; see Kennell 2006: 139; add the ephebic catalogues from Messene, AD 177: *SEG* LII (2002) 385, *AnÉp* (2003) 1617 (incomplete text); AD 188: *SEG* LVI (2006) 481, *AnÉp* (2008) 1258.

[19] See Hin 2007: 154–61.

[20] Kah 2004: 54–64; Chankowski 2004a: 59; Hin 2007: 155 n. 47. D'Amore 2007: 158 mentions that sometimes even *paides presbyteroi* (older children, near the age of becoming ephebes) started military training. For the *hoplomachia*, see Kah 2004: 70. Chankowski 2004a: 59 rightly remarks that ephebes also trained outside the gymnasium, where they may have learned to operate as a phalanx.

[21] Chankowski 2004a: 71–2; D'Amore 2007: 159.   [22] Kleijwegt 1991: 94–6.

[23] Chankowski 2004a: 62; D'Amore 2007: 157; Kennell 2009: 333–5. Some authors cause confusion by using the term 'ephebic' in a broad sense. Brélaz 2005: 187, for example, uses it for all organisations modelled on the *ephebeia*, including *neoi*, *neaniskoi*.

expected to contribute to the defence of the sanctuary of Artemis and the city.[24] Kleijwegt's conclusion that young men from ephebic age onwards frequently served as security forces, and thus played a vital role in society and were not marginalised, is altogether lacking in foundation. This is not to say that the military training of the ephebes served no practical purpose. Rare though such eventualities were, it was preparation for their possible armed action in the future, as *neoi*. In the meantime, the ephebes displayed their military skills only in contests and armed parades. The military training also had an ideological purpose, as it was seen as an integral part of the identity of the citizen. The citizen body had, from time immemorial, been a body of warriors. A good citizen was a good soldier. Hence military training remained, for long time, a traditional component of the education of young men to citizenship, while it also tied in with the Greeks' general disposition towards competition. At the same time, the public display of military skills by the youths was a symbol of the continuous renewal of the civic community. And through such military education, the cities of the East were able to present themselves as civic communities with a Greek cultural identity.[25] In the late Hellenistic period, however, military education lost its significance. Evidence of military training in the imperial era is almost non-existent outside Athens.[26] Kennell has argued that scarcity of evidence is in itself no proof that military training was completely abandoned in the Roman period; perhaps it was not recorded in the inscriptions. For one thing, the number of records of *ephebeiai* drastically diminished under the Principate. Secondly and perhaps more importantly, the nature of the evidence changed fundamentally. Many ephebic inscriptions were no longer set up at public expense, recording names and activities of the ephebes, but by wealthy private citizens, magistrates or even ephebes, often testifying to their own generosity.[27] Be that as it may, military training was no longer prominent in the ephebic curriculum in the imperial period. Some scholars, such as Peter Scholz and Lucia D'Amore, connect this with a change in mentality. They argue that around the middle of the second century BC the

---

[24] *I. Ephesos* IV 1382, an Hellenistic decree containing an oath of the citizens and the ephebes; see D'Amore 2007: 156. Cf. the Greek honorary inscription for the gymnasiarch Antallus, *IG* XIV 311 (cf. *SEG* XXXVIII (1988) 964 and XLVII (1997) 2277) from Soluntum in Sicily (probably first century BC; see Prag 2007: 86). It was set up by three units of infantry and the ephebes, but the text does not explicitly mention any military action on the part of the ephebes.

[25] Kah 2004: 69–74; Chankowski 2004a: 70–3 and 2004b: 277–9, who argues that the uniform character of the military training in the Hellenistic cities proves that its primary aim was not practical.

[26] Kennell 2009: 332–3. Almost all records of ephebic military training in the Greek cities in that period (just four!) date from the early first century AD.

[27] Kennell 2009: 325–6; he calls this 'privatisation'.

7.1 Greek ephebes

notion of 'the good citizen' had changed: he was now a man who cared for public matters, acted as a benefactor, was well educated.[28] This at once implied that the non-military activities in the gymnasium became more prominent: sports and intellectual *paideia*.

Ephebes were trained in various athletic sports at the gymnasium: foot races over various distances, endurance and torch races, wrestling, boxing, *pankration* (a mixture of boxing and wrestling), etc. They did not engage in the same sports in every city though. Some ephebes, no doubt the richest, also practised horse-riding, but there is no proof that this was a regular part of ephebes' training. Athletics competitions were held in all the cities in the East; the names of the victors were often publicly engraved, on the walls of the gymnasium or on other public buildings. A good example can be found at Heracleia Pontica on the south coast of the Black Sea. Here, the ephebes were arranged into groups for their sporting contests on the basis of age rather than the number of years they had been in training, since the physical strength of younger and older adolescents can evidently vary considerably.

> Short distance (*stadion*):
> Among the younger ephebes: Tryphon, son of Heraclides
> Among the older ones: Ponticus, son of Titus.
> Middle distance (*diaulos*):
> Among the younger ephebes: [–]
> Among the older ones: Dorotheus, son of Lucius.
> Long distance (*dolichos*):[29]
> Among the younger ephebes: Demetrius, son of [–]
> Among the older ones: Diocles, son of Dionysius.
> Wrestling:
> Among the younger ephebes: Longinus, son of Hypsigonus and [–] and Dorotheus, son of Lucius.
> Pankration:
> Among the younger ephebes: [–]
> Among the older ones: Stratonides, son of Apollodorus and [–us], son of Heracleon.
> Long distance with shield and sling:
> Longinus, son of Hypsigonus.
> (*I. Heraclea Pontica* 60 B lines 1–11 from the imperial period; here somewhat shortened)

---

[28] D'Amore 2007: 171–3, after 188 BC; Scholz 2004 *passim*, e.g. pp. 110, 119, 128, who detects a new *Bildungsbedürfnis* (demand for good education); cf. Gehrke 2004: 416.

[29] The *stadion* is comparable to the 200 m sprint, the *diaulos* (= two stadia) to the 400 m sprint, the *dolichos* (varying from seven to twenty-four stadia) to the 1,500 m to 5 km race.

So did ephebes receive a thorough intellectual education in fields such as literature, poetry, rhetoric, philosophy, music, and science, including mathematics? Saskia Hin has recently pointed out quite compellingly that there are very few documents mentioning intellectual courses during the *ephebeia*, while there are large numbers of inscriptions relating to sporting activities.[30] In Priene, the benefactor Zosimus was honoured because he had appointed, at his own expense, a *grammatikos* for all subjects pertaining to literature (*philologia*).[31] At Eretria on Euboea, the gymnasiarch Mantidorus, likewise on his own initiative, appointed an Homeric philologist, and the gymnasiarch Elpinicus appointed a rhetor for the *paides*, ephebes, and all those interested.[32] We further know of one teacher of mathematics (*geometria*) at Sestus, who was crowned by the *neoi*, ephebes, *paides*, and 'the teachers'.[33] Only in these three cities are courses in literature and science recorded, usually as a result of the private generosity of gymnasiarchs. This implies that in years when there was no gymnasiarch or *euergetes* to pay for them teachers of these subjects were not at hand. There is no or only very meagre evidence that ephebes took courses in other sciences, such as medicine and music; intellectual disciplines are not found on the lists of victors in the gymnasium. One must assume that this instruction, if it took place at all, was provided outside the structure of the *ephebeia*, most likely through private education by home tutors and in private schools. Young men could also attend lectures by itinerant scholars at the gymnasium (see Chapter 6.2). There were many philosophers, historians, rhetors, and other scholars who travelled from city to city and lectured in the gymnasium to anyone who was willing to pay, including youngsters. Some gymnasiarchs or other *euergetai* invited, and paid for, these lecturers to come. Ephebes who were eager to improve their intellectual capacity may also have visited the libraries that were often attached to the gymnasium.

---

[30] Hin 2007: 155–7; her view is corroborated by several scholars who devoted a (somewhat earlier) profound study to the Hellenistic gymnasium, in Kah and Scholz 2004. Many of them emphasise that the gymnasium is not a centre of culture and intellectual life, e.g. Scholz 2004: 103–4.

[31] *I. Priene* 112, lines 73–4, after 84 BC. Zosimus also organised contests in the same subjects: *I. Priene* 113, line 28.

[32] See p. 74, n. 14. Other sources mentioned by Scholz 2004: 113 nn. 38, 40 are highly uncertain, because the texts are much damaged. The decree for the ephebarch Melanion from Iasus does not provide convincing proof of intellectual education of ephebes either (*I. Iasos* 1 98; first century BC; see Scholz 2004: 114 n. 42 and the next note).

[33] See p. 74, n. 14. It is a fact observed by many scholars that gymnasiarchs rarely gave benefactions for intellectual education in the gymnasium; see Scholz 2004: 112–14; Ameling 2004: 154–5 (who rightly points out that terms such as *mathemata* and *paideutai* are vague and may also apply to military training); Schuler 2004: 186.

It may sound strange that intellectual education was not an essential component of the curriculum of the *ephebeia*. After all, the ideals of education (*paideia*) and literacy were significant to the civic aristocrats. They frequently emphasised their intellectual abilities in honorary decrees, in funerary texts and on reliefs. Education set them apart from the rest of the population, which was largely illiterate; it made them the right people to govern the cities. That superiority justified and consolidated their position of leadership.[34] Onno van Nijf, however, has argued that the *paideia* on which such praise was lavished was in fact merely an ideal, part of the idealised self-representation of the higher-ranking members of society. It was commonly mentioned when a politician was praised and when a prematurely deceased child was remembered by his parents, who wished to present an idealised image of their promising offspring. If one looks more closely at the contests held at festivals in cities and at gymnasia, it soon becomes clear that there were relatively few in music, rhetoric, theatre, and other cultural fields. Athletics contests were much more common. Monuments commemorating victories in cultural events are rather rare. Victories in athletics, on the other hand, are very frequently recorded in funerary texts. And statues and honorific monuments for victors in boxing, wrestling, and other sports were ubiquitous in cities to the point of dominating the urban landscape. In the real world, sports were apparently deemed much more important than intellectual activities.[35] Inscriptions rarely tell a different tale. Yet these few texts probably paint a more truthful picture of the real interest and behaviour of the youths concerned. One example is the epitaph of Cladus from Hadriani in Mysia, who died at the age of thirteen. The epigram is presented as a dialogue with the passer-by:

> If you ask: 'Who are you?' – my name is Cladus.
> And: 'Who raised you?' – Menophilus.
> 'Of what did you die?' – of fever.
> 'At what age?' – thirteen.
> 'So you did not like the Muses then?' – Not quite. They did not love me very much, but Hermes cared a great deal for me. For in wrestling contests I often received the praiseworthy garland. Apphia, my nurse, buried me. She set up my portrait and placed this monument on my tomb. (*I. Hadrianoi* 77; *SGO* 11 08/08/10; from the late Hellenistic or early Roman period)

The imaginary voice of the boy concedes that he was better at wrestling than at intellectual pursuits. So why were sports so important and popular? There

---

[34] Kleijwegt 1991: 85–8; van Nijf 2004: 212–13.   [35] Van Nijf 2004, 2003 and 1999–2000: 182–6, 191.

is no single answer to this question. Sports were a traditional pursuit and an integral part of Greek culture. The Olympic and other famous games were time-honoured and venerable occasions. Athletics were essential to the Greek cultural identity; it was a characteristic element of the Hellenic culture, of which the urban elites of the East were so eager to be part. Moreover, athletic excellence was central to the masculine identity of members of the Greek elite under Roman rule. For some talented young men, training could be a springboard to a professional athletics career. Victors in sports contests were held in very high regard, as they were considered to enhance the glory of their city. They were honoured with statues, crowns, honorific seats, ritual dinners, and sometimes even a triumphal entry into their home town and a form of 'state pension'. Elite victors were also seen to enhance the prestige and renown of their families. Athletics contests may also have offered the young aristocrats an outlet for their drive for competition. In the cities of the Greek East, with their oligarchic aristocratic governments, public life was a highly competitive arena. Young men from elite families were generally excluded from the city government (see Chapter 9.1 on public office). Since they had limited opportunities to gain honour and status in this way, athletics was the main area where they could prove their excellence and compete with each other.[36]

Whatever the reasons for the popularity of sports, clearly intellectual education was not an important item on the curriculum of the *ephebeia*. That is not to say that culture was deemed unimportant; athletics and literature were two complementary ingredients of traditional Greek *paideia*, and they were both integral parts of the educational curriculum at the gymnasium, though not on a par.[37] Several gymnasiarchs are indeed praised for having taken care of the *paideia* (or *agoge*) of the ephebes (and *neoi*). And ephebes are sometimes referred to as being 'fond of learning' (*philomatheis*).[38] The relative unimportance of intellectual training within the *ephebeia* opened the door to middle-class children, who had not enjoyed years of 'primary education' as a *pais*. The *ephebeia* did not require advanced intellectual skills; it cannot rightly be called a form of 'secondary education' (all the more so since it did not follow on from 'primary education').

---

[36] Van Nijf 2004: 221–2 and 2003: 270–1. At 1999–2000: 197 he calls athletics 'an alternative passport to Greek identity'.

[37] Van Nijf 2003: 282–3.

[38] Gymnasiarchs, for example Chares at Themisonium in Phrygia: *Michel* no. 544 (see Schuler 2004: 186 n. 141; 67/66 BC?); Menas at Sestus (see 7.2 line 76); several gymnasiarchs at Pergamum: e.g. *MDAI(A)* 32 (1907) 273–8 no. 10 line 45 and 278–84 no.11 line 47 (all from the Hellenistic period). For *philomathia* of ephebes, see D'Amore 2007: 161–2; Scholz 2004: 110–11. This is part of the idealised picture.

However, the *ephebeia* was not all about physical training. Considerable attention was also paid to developing the social skills and the proper conduct of the ephebes.³⁹ They were trained in endurance (*philoponia*), in bodily harmony or fitness (*euexia*), and in discipline or orderly behaviour (*eutaxia*).⁴⁰ Competitions were staged in all of these skills. A jury would monitor the boys at festivals or over a longer period of time. An illustration is provided by the gymnasiarchical law from Beroea in Macedonia which governed the Hermaea, the festival in honour of Hermes:

> The gymnasiarch shall hold the Hermaea in the month of Hyperberetaeus ... He shall draw up a list of seven men from those on the spot, who are to judge (the competition) of fitness. Then he shall draw lots from those and make the three, who are selected, swear by Hermes that they will judge fairly the youth who seems to them to be in the best physical condition, without favouritism or hostility of any sort ... As for (the contests of) good discipline and hard training, the gymnasiarch shall swear an oath by Hermes and choose in respect of good discipline the one who seems to him to be the best-behaved of those younger than thirty, and in respect of hard training the one who seems to him to have trained hardest during the current year of those up to the age of thirty. (*SEG* XLIII (1993) 381B, lines 45–57, *c.* 200–170 BC or shortly after 168 BC)⁴¹

While some of the skills (e.g. *eutaxia*) obviously had practical military application, they were first and foremost regarded as integral to the proper conduct of the citizen in the *polis*. A citizen had to conform to the ordered life of the community, and be obedient to the magistrates and the laws of the city (*eutaxia*); he was expected to devote himself to public affairs, sparing no pains (*philoponia*); he was required to act in public in a self-restrained manner (*euexia*). It is important to note that these skills were taught not only to ephebes but also to younger *paides* and older *neoi* (see 6.2).⁴² Hence the gymnasium may rightly be seen as a place of social education, of socialisation of youth. It played an essential role in the formation of the

---

³⁹ Hin 2007: 161–2; the major study on this topic is by Crowther 1991: 301–4 (reprinted in Crowther 2004: 341–4); see also Gauthier and Hatzopoulos 1993: 102–8.

⁴⁰ The emphasis in the *ephebeia* on physical fitness and the right mental attitude is reminiscent of scouting in its earliest phase, as instituted by R. Baden-Powell (in 1908); see Gillis 1974: 145–8; Wilkinson 1969: 7–18. Baden-Powell wished to educate youngsters (boys between eleven and fifteen) in good citizenship and physical fitness; in general terms, he tried to achieve this via a paramilitary organisation: athletics, drill, open-air activities. But that is as far as the similarity between *ephebeia* and scouting goes. Baden-Powell's aim was to preserve the British Empire and to strengthen national defence; in its earliest days, the movement was carefully designed and led by influential members of the political and military elite. Comparable aims and organisational structures are not demonstrable for the *ephebeia*.

⁴¹ Republished in *I. Beroia* 1; cf. *SEG* LIV (2004) 602 and LVI (2006) 691. Translations by Austin 1981 no. 118; Bagnall and Derow 2004 no. 78.

⁴² For records of these terms, see Kennell 2006: 144, 157.

Greek citizen through its focus on developing qualities and attitudes that were fundamental to public life, and hence also to Greek civic identity.[43] It would be mistaken to think that the training of the adolescent ephebes in *eutaxia* was necessitated by the fact that they tended to behave in a disorderly manner, although it is not inconceivable that this aspect also came into play.

What other activities might ephebes have engaged in? For one thing, they participated in cult ceremonies, inside and outside the gymnasium.[44] Within the walls of the gymnasium, several gods were worshipped, especially Hermes and Heracles. Festivals and contests were often named 'Hermaea' after Hermes, as in the above-cited inscription from Beroea. Several 'lower' gods were also worshipped at the gymnasium. In the Hellenistic period, some benefactors enjoyed cultic honour at the gymnasium, including a dedicated altar, special offerings, and a procession; the ephebes would participate in such ceremonies, too. In the imperial period, the emperor was usually worshipped in a dedicated room of the gymnasium. Outside the gymnasium, the ephebes as a group were frequently involved in publicly performed cultic activities: offerings, banquets, processions in honour of a variety of gods. This could take up a considerable amount of the boys' time. A 'school calendar' from Cos, even in its incomplete state of preservation, mentions twelve such occasions within a period of just eight weeks.[45] In the city of Ephesus, Gaius Vibius Salutaris donated thirty-one golden and silver statues to his town. Many of these represented the goddess Artemis, often combined with a civic institution such as the *boule*, the city council, or the *gerousia*, the council of elders. Salutaris stipulated that these statues be carried through the city centre at the monthly assemblies, the games, festivals, and other special occasions. It was the task of the ephebes to carry them from the city's southern gate (towards Magnesia) to its northern gate (towards Mount Coressus). Along the road, they would pass numerous historical monuments. The procession took place at least twenty-seven times a year, more than once a fortnight. In this way, the ephebes were thoroughly familiarised with the political, economic, and religious history of their home town. This contributed considerably to their socialisation.[46]

Marc Kleijwegt concludes that the ephebes played a role of some importance in the field of religion, as well as in military affairs. However, the supposed military role of the ephebes is dubious, as shown above, and their

---

[43] Gehrke 2003: 232–3, 242–4 and 2004: 415; Wörrle 2007: 502.
[44] Nilsson 1955: 61–75; Hin 2007: 162–5.   [45] *Syll.*³ 1028 between 159 and 133 BC.
[46] Rogers 1991, lines 52–5.

role in religion would appear to have been representational rather than substantial. Kleijwegt links to his conclusion the psychologising remark that in these fields the ephebes were expected to behave like 'social adults' and apparently did thus behave: they did not even remotely resemble today's marginalised and protesting adolescents.[47] It goes without saying that this opinion is unfounded.

On many occasions, the ephebes took part in public life outside the walls of the gymnasium, for example when honours were bestowed upon kings, emperors or local benefactors. They sometimes walked along in procession or sang hymns or assisted the solemn crowning of an *euergetes*. When a deceased benefactor was carried to his grave, in the agora or in the gymnasium, they served as members of the cortège. They sometimes shared this role with other groups: the magistrates, the *neoi*, the *paides*, and citizens. The ephebes were an important element in a city's social make-up, and as such they could even come to symbolise that city. They constituted the core of the gymnasium and this institution played a central role in community life (see above). Hence they were frequently called upon to assist in public ceremonies and were seen to represent their city. There are several records from the city of Priene that testify to this practice, including one of the many honorary decrees for Thrasyboulus:

> (It is decided) that the *paidonomoi* with the *paides* will follow the funeral procession, and the gymnasiarch with all ephebes and the *neoi*, and the *strategoi* with the other officials. (*I. Priene* 104, lines 9–12, around 100 BC)

A marked feature of the *ephebeia* is that its structure mimicked that of the municipal institutions. The ephebes had their own magistrates. Their leader was the ephebarch, who could be an ephebe himself, sometimes still a child, sometimes slightly older.[48] Nigel Kennell has argued that the ephebarcheia was an ordinary office in many cities in the imperial period, and that it was performed by young men (*neoi*) of between twenty and thirty who were at the beginning of their municipal career. The latter claim is however unsubstantiated. In our opinion, it is not inconceivable that ephebarchs generally were mature adults and supervised the conduct of the ephebes. In Iasus in Caria, a certain Melanion, son of Theodorus, was honoured because, in his

---

[47] Kleijwegt 1991: 101.
[48] Kennell 2000; for a register of *ephebarchoi*, see Kennell 2006: 142. The number of records grows every year, e.g. *SEG* LVII (2007) 1037; *AnÉp* (2007) 1431 (Heraclea on the Salbace: the ephebe Papias is honoured by the ephebarch), *TAM* v, 3, 1446 and 1489 (Philadelpheia or its territory; no. 1441 records a child-ephebarch). At Cyzicus, there is a record of an *hypephebarchos*; see Kennell 2006: 150. He was probably an assistant, not an official magistrate; see Dmitriev 2005: 228–9.

capacity as ephebarch and head of the gymnasium, he had devoted himself to the orderly conduct (*eukosmia*) of the ephebes and the *neoi*. In some cities of the East, there was a magistrate known as the *ephebophylax*, who most probably also supervised the ephebes.[49]

The ephebes sometimes had their own treasurer, secretary, and gymnasiarch, and, in some cities, even a priest. They held their own assemblies, at which resolutions and decrees were passed. They gave benefactions to their fellow-ephebes. In sum, the *ephebeia* was a city in miniature, a replica of the municipal institutions, and so it prepared the boys for their eventual participation in civic life. In the concluding remarks (7.4), we return to the question of the role of the *ephebeia* in the Greek cities.

7.2 Excursus: the honorary decree for Menas of Sestus

This decree dates from shortly after the death of King Attalus III of Pergamum, who bequeathed his kingdom to the people of Rome (133 BC), prompting a revolt by the pretender Aristonicus. In that same period the Thracians invaded Sestus. This explains the emphasis on military exercises in the text.

> 1–2. [In the priesthood] of Glaucias son of Cillaeus, in the month [of Hyperberetaeus . . . resolved] by the council and the people; Menander son of Apollas made the proposal:
>
> 2–10. [Menas son of Menes] has [from] his earliest manhood believed it the finest course of action to make himself useful [to his native city]. He has not spared any cost or expense and has not avoided any hardship or danger, nor has he taken into account the losses to his private fortune which those serving as envoys suffer. But he considered all these things of secondary importance and attached the highest priority to loyalty and devotion to his native city. He wished always to achieve some useful advantage for the people through his own enthusiasm and to secure for himself and his descendants everlasting fame through the gratitude of the people . . .
>
> 31–39. When he was appointed gymnasiarch, he showed concern for the good discipline (*eutaxia*) of the ephebes and the young men (*neoi*), and took charge of the general good order of the gymnasium honourably and in a spirit of emulation. He built the bathing-room and the building [next to it], and he dedicated a statue of white stone. He built in addition the unfinished parts which were required. And at the birthday feast of the king, when sacrificing

---

[49] Melanion at Iasus: *I. Iasos* I 98, first century BC. *Ephebophylax* at Nicopolis (Epirus) and Priene; see Kennell 2006: 144; add *IGR* IV 396 from Pergamum. Nothing is known about this function. In Pergamum, an overseer of the good order (*eukosmia*) of the girls (*parthenoi*) is recorded (*I. Pergamon* 463; Robert 1937: 56–9), but not within the context of an association.

7.2 Excursus: honorary decree for Menas of Sestus

every month on behalf of the people, he instituted parades (or: races) for the ephebes and the young men, and celebrated javelin and archery contests, and provided oil for anointing. And through (the example of) his own emulation he encouraged the young men to exercise and to train hard (*philoponia*).

39–43. The people welcomed his zeal and eagerness and allowed him to commemorate his deeds in inscriptions, and deemed him worthy of being praised in decrees. And the ephebes and young men crowned him and the ephebarch. And though he accepted the honour, he freed them from the expense involved, and made the dedication of the weapons at his own expense ...

53–54. When he was invited a second time to act as gymnasiarch, he submitted to this in difficult circumstances ...

61–86. When he entered office on the new moon, he celebrated sacrifices for Hermes and Heracles, the gods consecrated in the gymnasium, on behalf of the safety of the people and of the young men. He organised races and contests of javelin and archery, and on the last day he offered a sacrifice and invited to the sacrificial rites not only those who have access to the gymnasium but all the others as well, giving a share in the sacrificial rites even to the foreigners. And every month, when celebrating the appropriate sacrifices on behalf of the young men, he treated with generosity and magnificence the gods who preside over the gymnasium, by instituting javelin and archery contests and organising races. He gave to the young men a share in the victims sacrificed by him, and encouraged through his zeal the young men to exercise and to train hard (*philoponia*), which would cause the minds of the younger men to receive a suitable training in moral excellence by competing for bravery ... He dealt in a friendly way with all those who gave lectures, wishing in this too to secure for his native city glory through men of education. And he looked after the education (*paideia*) of the ephebes and the young men, and showed care for the general good order of the gymnasium. He provided scrapers and supplied oil for anointing, and celebrated a contest in honour of Hermes and Heracles in the month of Hyperberetaeus. He offered as prizes for the competitions for the young men and ephebes weapons with an inscription and bound in shield-cases, on which he inscribed the names of the victors and (which he) immediately dedicated in the gymnasium. He offered second prizes, and he offered prizes for the boys (*paides*) and prizes for armed combat for the ephebes and the men, and similarly for archery and javelin-throwing. And he offered weapons as prizes for the long race, good discipline (*eutaxia*), hard training (*philoponia*), and fitness (*euexia*). And after celebrating a sacrifice to the aforementioned gods and after promoting fitness (*euandria*) in accordance with the law, he invited to the sacrificial rites all the members of the gymnasium and the foreigners who share in the common rights, and entertained them in a magnificent way and worthily of the gods and of the people.

86–100. The people wishes to be seen honouring excellent men and welcoming those who from their earliest manhood have shown zeal concerning matters of public interest, and not to fall short in returning gratitude, so that others who see the honours which are paid by the people to excellent men should emulate the finest deeds and be encouraged towards excellence, and public interest might be furthered when all are striving to achieve glory and are always securing some benefit to their native city. Therefore, with good fortune, be it resolved by the council and the people to praise Menas son of Menes for all the services mentioned and for the goodwill which he constantly displays towards the people, and to allow him to dedicate the weapons with his name inscribed and (mention of the fact) that he was crowned by the ephebes and the young men; and to have him crowned by the people every year at the gymnastic contest during the religious festival with a gold crown, with the following proclamation being made by the herald: 'The people crowns Menas son of Menes, who held the office of gymnasiarch twice honourably and zealously, and showed himself a good man towards the people.' His bronze statue will be set up in the gymnasium with the following inscription: 'The people and the young men honour Menas son of Menes, who held the office of gymnasiarch twice honourably and zealously, and showed himself a good man towards the people.'

100–106. He and his descendants are to be invited to a seat of honour at all the competitions celebrated by the people. The agonothete who is in charge every year shall organise the proclamation of the crown. And since (Menas) wishes in these matters too to do a favour to the people on account of the present tight circumstances of the public finances, and (is willing to) assume the expense for the statue from his private means, he shall take care that the statue set up is as beautiful as possible, and he shall inscribe the present decree on a stele of white stone and place it in the gymnasium. (*I. Sestos* 1; transl. after Austin 1981 no. 215)

7.3 Roman *iuvenes*

During the imperial period, many cities in the Latin West had associations of youths that were known under names such as *iuvenes* or *iuventus*.[50] If anything, there is even more uncertainty about the nature of these institutions than about the *ephebeia*. While numerically there is no lack of sources, these consist for the most part in inscriptions that, unfortunately, offer little concrete information. They were, moreover, often erected for special occasions, so that the picture they provide is rather blurred and one-sided. Many questions remain. Are we aware of all of the activities in which the *iuvenes*

---

[50] This was also true of provinces lying between the Latin West and the Greek East. See Bouley 2003 on the Balkan provinces, where Augustus 'exported' his reforms of the senatorial and equestrian youth to the ephebic organisations and the *iuventus*.

engaged? Are the activities that are most frequently mentioned in the sources really the most important ones? Do the scarce concrete data on the participants offer a representative picture? Scholars have put forward divergent views on such matters, which we cannot discuss exhaustively here. We therefore restrict ourselves to the views of arguably the three most prominent scholars in this field: Maria Jaczynowska (1978), Pierre Ginestet (1991), and Marc Kleijwegt (1994). The first contests the old theory that the *iuvenes* served a regular military role, arguing instead that their main emphasis was on sports, games, cultic activities, and political involvement in civic life. The second argues that participating in games was not the most important activity of the *iuvenes*, and that they played a political role only in periods of unrest; the cult was prominent, and only the *iuventutes* in the frontier provinces had any real military significance. The third rejects the notion of almost any political and military role on the part of the *iuvenes* and interprets the organisations as entertainment clubs.[51]

Organisations of *iuvenes* are found all over Italy, where they are indeed recorded most frequently, in about sixty localities. They are also attested in most Latin-speaking provinces, in around forty places. The epigraphic sources date from the second century BC (?) to the first half of the fourth century AD; they reach a peak in the second and third centuries AD. This pattern corresponds with the general diffusion of Latin inscriptions. The associations of *iuvenes* in the city of Rome have a long history. In the regal and in the early Republican periods, the *iuventus* was an important military organisation. Later its significance dwindled: in the late Republic military service was no longer compulsory and hence the organisation all but disappeared. But at the beginning of the imperial period it re-emerged. Whether Augustus played an active part in this development is still much debated. In any case, the suggestion by Michael Rostovtzeff that Augustus modelled the *iuvenes* on the Greek *ephebeia* is now generally rejected. As will become apparent in the course of this chapter, there are indeed some marked differences between the two.

For one thing, there is a difference in terms of gender: girls could also join a *iuventus* in some places, including in Reate, Tusculum, and possibly

---

[51] In the sources one finds many similar words; the term *collegium iuvenum*, which is often used in modern literature, is recorded only from the end of the second century AD onwards. There is much debate about whether the different terms refer to different types of associations. And of course there were regional and chronological variations. Jaczynowska 1978: 67–107 presents an appendix of the epigraphic sources; Ginestet 1991: 211–75 contains a collection of all sources. For supplements and corrections, see Kleijwegt 1994: 80–1 and 94 n. 1. This article by Kleijwegt presents a view that diverges from that in his book (1991: 101–16).

Ficulea (all in central Italy), as well as at Tebessa (North Africa). Here the memberships of the associations were apparently of mixed gender. But the fact that the evidence is restricted to a limited number of locations need not imply that female membership was all that exceptional. After all, the inscriptions mentioning female names come from different parts of the Roman Empire and, moreover, they do not sound unusual. For example, the inscription from Reate is an ordinary epitaph for a girl called Valeria Iucunda; it was erected by the magistrate of the *iuvenes* (the *magister iuvenum*) and mentions quite plainly that she was a member of the *iuvenes*. In Mediolanum (Milan), there was a separate association for girls, known as the *iuvenae*; such organisations may have existed in other cities too.[52]

Evidence regarding the age of the *iuvenes* is inconclusive. One may assume that a boy could become a member after the donning of the *toga virilis*, which generally happened around the age of fourteen or fifteen. We do not know at what age girls entered.[53] Grave inscriptions inform us of the age of only three *iuvenes*. At the time of their death, they were respectively seventeen (a girl), eighteen and almost twenty years old. Sources indicating the duration of their membership are altogether lacking. Most scholars believe there are a number of sources mentioning older members, but in our view just one of these records is certain: a member of the *iuvenes* at Aricia (central Italy) died after having been married for thirty years, suggesting he must have been around fifty years of age.[54] It is impossible to assess whether or not this person was an exception. Hence it is not clear whether there was a strict age limit at which one was required to quit the association. Be that as it may, any middle-aged members will probably not have been much inclined to participate in the (essentially sporting) activities of youths. Dieter Ladage has pointed out that some leaders of the associations were just over twenty years old: two priests were aged twenty-three and twenty-five years. It is, however, conceivable that these men were, strictly speaking, not members of the association. Based on this evidence, it seems reasonable to assume that most members were under or around twenty years of age.[55] In

---

[52] On girls as members and their activities, see Saavedra-Guerrero 1996; for the *iuvenae* at Mediolanum, see Boscolo 2003: 262–5. The inscription from Reate can be found in Ginestet 1991: 237 no. 120 (*CIL* IX 4696) from the end of the second century AD (?); it is unclear why the gravestone was not erected by the family of the girl (but see below n. 81).

[53] It is very uncertain whether Flavia Vera, who died aged almost seven years, was a priestess of the *sodales* (= *iuvenes*) at Tusculum (Ginestet 1991: 220 no. 22; *CIL* VI 2177), as Rawson 2003: 324 believes. Her epitaph merely states that she was a priestess of the Tusculani.

[54] *AnÉp* (1912) 92; cf. *AnÉp* (1991) 382.

[55] For the ages, see Jaczynowska 1978: 39–40; Ladage 1979: 326–7; Kleijwegt 1994: 84–5. We do not follow these scholars but agree with Saskia Hin (in an unpublished study, Leiden 2004) that the man

his book *Ancient Youth*, Marc Kleijwegt gives much weight to sources that he believes mention older members. He argues on their basis that the *iuvenes* were not teenagers but adults aged roughly between eighteen and fifty.[56] He feels that this mix of younger and older members and the lack of distinction between them would have strongly affected the psychological make-up of the adolescents. However, if there were only a few older members, as we believe to have been the case, any such influence can only have been limited. Moreover, this at the very least leaves open the possibility that the youths behaved in a typically youthful way within their peer group.

The social composition of the *iuventutes* is fairly clear. All scholars agree that the organisations included youths both of the municipal elite and of the social classes below that elite. This is apparent from the three surviving membership lists of *iuvenes*. Two lists include one or more freedmen (*liberti*); the names of several members strongly suggest that the individuals concerned were freed slaves. Moreover, the number of members is simply too high for them all to have been sons from elite families (at Virunum, for example, there were at least 120 members).[57] Two freedmen of the emperors Caracalla and Commodus were also included as honorary members in the cities of Lanuvium and Mediolanum.[58] *Liberti* did not belong to the elite of city dignitaries, but they often possessed considerable wealth. It remains unclear, though, whether slaves could also participate in the *iuventutes*. One membership list, from Pagus Fificulanus (central Italy), very probably contains the names of five slaves, but this would appear to have been an exception.[59] A slave would have entered the *iuventus* only if his master allowed him to and was prepared to pay on his behalf.

of forty-four years, commemorated at Rome by his *coniuvenes*, was no longer a member of the *iuvenes* (Ginestet 1991: 215 no. 3). His comrades from earlier times honoured him, just as *synepheboi* honoured their former comrades in the Greek world; see Strubbe 2005: 103. We are similarly convinced that the man of thirty-five years from Burdigala (Bordeaux) was not a *iuvenis* (Ginestet 1991: 255 no. 200; *CIL* XIII 785). The epitaph was established by his brother, whose name was Iuvenis (a common personal name): *Iuvenis Iuliano fratr(i) d(e)f(uncto) ann(orum)* XXXV *ponend(um) cur(avit)* (thus also the text in *EDCS*). The inscription from Nursia (central Italy) in which a *magister iuvenum* of twenty-four years is mentioned (Ginestet 1991: 237 no. 118), is possibly not genuine; see *Supplementa Italica* n.s. 13 (1996) 91–3 no. 23. For the twenty-three-year old priest, see p. 179.

[56] Kleijwegt 1991: 101–6. He sees a parallel with the upper age limit of the *neoi*, which in his view was probably fifty years; this is highly implausible, though: see p. 72.

[57] See particularly Ginestet 1991: 123–8; Kleijwegt 1994: 83–4. The freedmen associated with the *iuventutes* (e.g. an *aedilis*, a *sacerdos*, and even some *patroni*) who are mentioned by Jaczynowska 1978: 35–6 were probably not members of the association, though they had an important role in it.

[58] Ginestet 1991: 128; the emperors' interference in the admission of the two men had nothing to do with their social origin but concerned their profession of pantomime, which was not highly regarded.

[59] Ginestet 1991: 235 no. 112 (*CIL* IX 3578), undated. *Contra*: Ladage 1979: 333. Jaczynowska 1978: 31 points out that this is the only source mentioning slaves as members.

A *iuventus* organisation then was typically a broad group of youngsters who participated of their own free will and who, as a group, were representative of the whole population of the city. But there were exceptions. In cities like Ostia there were several associations of *iuvenes*. One of these groups consisted of *iuvenes decurion(um)*, the youths of the decurial class (*decuriones* were city councillors). Hence, this group must have been of an aristocratic character, distinguishing it from other groups in the city.[60]

Adolescents of the lower classes were able to participate courtesy of benefactors, whose generosity could reduce the costs substantially. Wealthy citizens (and probably *iuvenes* too) paid for the games and provided prizes. They distributed money and food, donated estates, and established funds that yielded an annual interest, which was used to defray the costs of festivals and other activities. Many associations had *patroni*, patrons, who usually belonged to the richest and most influential circles in town – often Roman knights or senators – and donated lavish gifts. An inscription from Beneventum (southern Italy) from AD 257 speaks in plain terms of such gifts:[61]

> The magistrates (of the *iuvenes*) have reported upon the co-opting of a patron. We hope that in future even more abundant benefactions will follow from the man whom we have considered worthy of the highest esteem in the past. Therefore we co-opt Rutilius Viator as our patron. We do this together with those whose names follow: Nonius Gratilianus, senator, and Egnatius Sattianus, senator, and several eminent Roman knights and fellow-councillors of the same Viator, who excited us by their honour and merits. (*CIL* IX 1681)

Boys (and girls) from the poorest families did not participate in the *iuventutes* owing to the costs involved and because they lacked spare time.

To sum up, the composition of the Roman *iuventutes* differed from that of the Greek *ephebeia* in terms of gender, age, and social background. All these peculiarities fall into place if one approaches the Roman *iuventus* not as a municipal institution but rather as an association.[62] Frank Ausbüttel (1982) has studied the associations in the western Roman Empire, more than two thousand of which are attested. They went by different names, including *collegium*, *corpus*, and *sodalicium*, and they brought together people of the same profession, or individuals who worshipped the same

---

[60] Kleijwegt 1994: 83–4.
[61] Jaczynowska 1978: 46–7; Ginestet 1991: 141–2. The text is at Ginestet 1991: 233–4 no. 109.
[62] Ladage 1979 *passim*, especially 345–6; for the legal background of the right of gathering of *collegia* (*ius coeundi*), see de Ligt 2001. Kleijwegt 1994: 93 interprets the *iuventutes* as 'entertainment clubs' on the grounds that the role of the associations in political, military, and governmental matters is negligible. He does, however, not elucidate the correspondence between *iuventutes* and associations.

gods, or soldiers, etc. Ausbüttel has established that the memberships of associations were usually not homogeneous. For one thing, they sometimes included women, especially in the case of cultic associations, and in Rome and elsewhere there were also associations intended exclusively for women. Most members were free born, but freedmen often participated, and in a small number of cases slaves, too, especially in professional and cultic associations. In some cities, associations were restricted to persons of similar legal status, for example Roman citizens.[63] The members of the associations were usually not poor, and their governors and patrons, as well as other rich citizens, often donated gifts.[64] The *iuventutes* resembled associations in other respects, too, including their leadership, administration, and position in the municipal hierarchy.

But in what kind of activities did *iuvenes* engage within these associations? A good starting-point in trying to answer this question is provided by the activities of associations in general. First, however, let us consider the principal available sources on the *iuventutes* themselves, because one may expect the youngsters to engage in specific activities that are typical of their age. Unfortunately, these sources are scarce and it is moreover questionable whether the attested activities were typical of the *iuvenes* in general and in all places. One inscription from Paestum (southern Italy) states that the *iuvenes* had a *summarudis*, presumably a referee at gladiatorial fights. In Lucus Feroniae (northern Italy), a *summaruda iuvenum* is mentioned in a hitherto unpublished inscription.[65] A funerary inscription from Spoletium (Spoleto) records a *pinn(irapus) iuvenum*, most likely a professional instructor in gladiatorial combat techniques. Of course, *iuvenes* did not fight to the death – nor for that matter did professional gladiators necessarily – and presumably no blood was shed. Their combats were most probably demonstration fights with blunt weapons.[66] This seems to be corroborated by the story of Cassius Dio, who recounts how Titus, later to be emperor, engaged in a mock fight with a certain Alienus during games for youngsters in his native city of Reate.[67]

---

[63] Ausbüttel 1982: 25 and 40–2. [64] Ausbüttel 1982: 43–8.
[65] Paestum: Ginestet 1991: 234 no. III (*AnÉp* (1935) 27); *EAOR* III 64, from AD 245; Lucus Feroniae: *EAOR* II 36, from AD 216. For the meaning of *summarudis*, see Ville 1981: 367–72; Ginestet 1991: 142 prefers to see this man as a 'maître d'armes' who gave demonstrations.
[66] Ginestet 1991: 243 no. 145; *CIL* XI 7852; *EAOR* II 39, late second or third century AD; see Ginestet 1991: 142–3; Kleijwegt 1994: 87. For more connections between *iuvenes* and weapons, see Ville 1981: 216–18; Kleijwegt 1994: 86.
[67] Cassius Dio, *Hist. Rom.* 65, 15, 2. See Ginestet 1991: 155; Kleijwegt 1994: 86. Titus was then in his thirties and no doubt not a member of the association of *iuvenes* (called *neaniskoi* in the Greek text of Dio); he was allowed to participate in the games because he was the son of the emperor.

Another activity of *iuvenes* appears in an inscription from Aquae Sextiae (Aix). It mentions a *iuvenis* who was *comes ursari(u)s*, that is, in charge of the bears. He was also well versed in games in the arena and frequently fought wild beasts. This refers to wild animal hunts (*venationes*), which were commonly staged in amphitheatres. A few other sources also refer to such hunts.[68] During such activities, the *iuvenes* may well have ridden horses. A relief from Virunum (Zollfeld in Noricum) shows a parade of young men on horseback and bearing a standard (*vexillum*). Possibly it is a parade of *iuvenes*, but this is by no means certain.[69]

Marc Kleijwegt attaches great importance to the hunting by *iuvenes*, in amphitheatres as well as out in the open,[70] even though the latter activity is not attested in the sources. He stresses that young as well as older members of the *iuventus* participated in hunts. On this basis, he concludes that the young men did not act separately from the adults, so that their associations did not constitute a distinct group, characterised by its own distinctive activities and culture. It goes without saying that this conclusion is unfounded. The fact that young and older men engaged in a similar activity does not imply that their mental attitude was identical or that there was no psychological distinction between them.

It is quite possible that the *iuvenes* in the Roman Empire were occupied chiefly with combat sports, unlike the ephebes who engaged mainly in athletics. However, given the small number of sources, it is by no means certain that physical training really occupied such a central place in the lives of *iuvenes*. It would, for example, be wrong to think that *iuvenes* were trained to become gladiators. Gladiators were generally not free citizens. And we can certainly not agree with Mark Vesley's argument that girls, too, were trained to perform as gladiators.[71] In fact, we have no way of telling what girls got up to in the *iuventutes*. Did they participate in the same sports as boys or were they involved only in cultic activities (see below)? The

---

[68] Ginestet 1991: 253–4 no. 188 (*CIL* XII 533; *CLE* 465), *ILN* III 41, from c. AD 200; see Ginestet 1991: 142; Kleijwegt 1994: 87–8. For more indications of hunting by *iuvenes*, see Ville 1981: 218–20. There is no proof that *ursarii* hunted bears in the wild, as Kleijwegt 1991: 110 claims. His assertion (on p. 111) that *iuvenes* fought bulls in the amphitheatre is also speculative.

[69] Ginestet 1991 Pl. VIII Fig. 4. Standards belonging to *iuvenes* have been found at, among other places, Pollentia (Mallorca); the top is adorned with a small statue of the *genius iuventutis*. The relief at Virunum may show not *iuvenes* but children at the *lusus Troiae* or just a military parade; *ibid.*, 153–4. The sources adduced by Kleijwegt 1991: 112–15 as proof that *iuvenes* engaged in horse-riding and older *iuvenes* in chariot-racing are not convincing.

[70] Kleijwegt 1991: 109–16.

[71] Vesley 1998. Vesley started from the erroneous assumption that the *iuventutes* were training places for upper-class boys who wished to perform in the arena (p. 89); he assumed this same function for noble girls.

7.3 *Roman* iuvenes

combat sports required much training, which took place at a designated training ground or *campus*. The *iuvenes* would demonstrate their skills at games known as *lusus iuvenum* or *iuvenales*, or also *iuvenalia*, which presumably had nothing to do with the *Iuvenalia* that were celebrated at Rome.[72] Often a special magistrate, referred to as the *curator lusus iuvenalis*, would be appointed to supervise these games.

The nature of the activities of the *iuvenes* and the mention in a few literary sources of young men in military action have given rise to the question of whether the *iuventutes* (at least in some instances, or in specific regions or periods) were essentially of a military nature. Were the *iuventutes* a training ground for future recruits into the army? Were these boys being prepared for positions of military command? Were they deployed to maintain order in the provinces? Did they act as a reservist army in cases of emergency? Kleijwegt rejects any such notion categorically and argues convincingly that *iuvenes* were involved in military operations only in exceptional cases.[73] A few years ago, Cédric Brélaz re-examined all the available evidence and came to the same conclusion:[74] not a single source provides evidence that the *iuventutes* were of a specifically military nature. In times of emergency the *iuvenes* may occasionally have helped defend a city or assisted a Roman legion, thanks to their para-military training, but they most definitely did not perform a permanent military role. The activities of the *iuvenes* in the first place involved combat sports. Why these sports were so popular with the *iuventutes* is unknown. Perhaps they were a relic from the early Roman era, when the *iuventutes* clearly did serve a military purpose. It is in any case significant that the boys were trained not in Greek athletics but in combat, which was a distinctive element of Roman culture and identity, even in the provinces.

A second field in which the *iuvenes* were apparently very active was religious worship.[75] Many of their organisations bore a name that pointed to the cult of a particular god, as in the case of 'the *iuvenes*, worshippers of Hercules Fificulanus' in the small town of Pagus Fificulanus. The *iuvenes* often put up dedications to the gods and brought offerings; they also participated in religious feasts. In Italy, the most commonly venerated god among the *iuvenes* was Hercules, the god of youth and physical

---

[72] For the games, see Jaczynowska 1978: 52–5; Ginestet 1991: 151–8, who argues that the games were restricted to central Italy. This claim has been refuted by Kleijwegt 1994: 85–6. Ginestet further argues that *iuvenes* were often not competitors in the games but merely spectators and that the games cannot be regarded as the principal activity of the *iuvenes*. This too is rejected by Kleijwegt 1994: 86–8.
[73] Ginestet 1991: 159–68; Kleijwegt 1991: 107–8 and 1994: 81–3.   [74] Brélaz 2005: 183–6.
[75] Jaczynowska 1978: 55–9; Ginestet 1991: 168–76.

strength, followed by one or more deified emperors. In the provinces, the *iuvenes* primarily honoured the emperor, and also commonly Jupiter and Hercules. The following dedication from Vicus Aurelius (Oehringen in Germania Superior) dates from AD 222:[76]

> For the well-being of imperator Severus. The *collegium iuventutis*, which is very devoted to his *numen*, puts up (this dedication to his *numen*) on the Kalends of November, when imperator Severus Alexander Augustus was consul. (*CIL* XIII 6549)

The *iuvenes* had their own priests, known as *sacerdotes* and *flamines*. The sources for the religious activities of the *iuvenes* are numerous and far outnumber references to other activities. This, however, does not necessarily imply that worship was the most important activity of the *iuvenes* or that it represented their primary role in society. It may simply be the case that this activity was deemed more appropriate than others to be recorded in public inscriptions.[77]

Now that we have established the main activities of the *iuvenes*, were there any other areas in which they became involved? They are mentioned once in relation to granaries and to the imperial postal service (*cursus publicus*).[78] They sometimes participated in the public life of the city, for example during the honouring of an emperor. They occasionally joined the city magistrates and citizens in the unveiling of an honorary inscription for an emperor. And they frequently rendered thanks to benefactors by erecting a statue or through a public inscription. Unlike in the case of the ephebes, there are no records to suggest that the *iuvenes* took part in public processions, to honour a (deceased) prominent citizen, for example. But during the distribution of money in a city, they were sometimes treated as a separate group, usually ranking below the *ordo* of the *Augustales*, who were rich freedmen, on a par with the city's other associations.[79]

The activities of the *iuvenes* indeed fit well the interpretation of the organisation as an association.[80] One of the most important activities of *collegia* in general was the practice of a cult. Many *collegia* bore names

---

[76] Ginestet 1991: 257 no. 211.
[77] Kleijwegt 1994: 91. Ladage 1979: 327, 339–41 argues that the associations of *iuvenes* were in fact 'Kultvereine'. The *iuvenes* formed a *collegium* in order to enhance their prestige and to obtain better financial facilities, for example on occasion of distributions in the city, at which they quite often received a special share. For a priest of the *iuvenes* at Milan, see p. 179.
[78] Kleijwegt 1994: 80. There are no firm indications that the *iuvenes* played a role of any great significance within the machinery of state.
[79] Jaczynowska 1978: 38–9; Ladage 1979: 328–9. On the ranking of associations behind the *decuriones* and the *Augustales*, for example at distributions, see Ausbüttel 1982: 48.
[80] Ausbüttel 1982: 49–59 (cult), 59–71 (burial).

derived from gods; they had priests; they set up dedications and celebrated religious festivals in honour of the gods and the deified emperors. They also organised communal meals. Another important activity, according to F. Ausbüttel, was the interment of members and the cult of the dead, including through memorial banquets. Almost one-fifth of all *collegia*, irrespective of their composition, were involved in such activities. There are plenty of indications that the *iuvenes*, too, engaged in such actions.[81] In contrast, other likely activities for such organisations, including the performance of public tasks, political duties, and mutual assistance, are barely recorded, though the involvement of the *iuvenes* with granaries and the imperial post may be regarded as an example of the former. Sports activities are not attested in the Roman Empire for organisations other than the *iuventutes*. Sports were typical of the *iuventutes* and may – alongside the social life of the association, the communal meals, and the prospect of mutual help – have held a great attraction for the young men. There are no indications at all that *iuventutes* functioned as schools. In fact, there are very few sources that refer to any intellectual activity whatsoever; there is one hint that the *iuvenes* may have performed theatre plays (comedies) in Vienne (southern Gaul), but it is very doubtful whether this was a general feature.[82] No sources speak of the moral training of the young men in diligence or discipline, as with the ephebes. Much as ephebes appear not always to have behaved correctly, so the *iuvenes* in certain cities are mentioned in the *Digest* as having quite frequently displayed rebellious and turbulent behaviour (*seditiose et turbulente*).[83]

Like all associations,[84] the groups of *iuvenes* had their own magistrates, *magistri* and *praefecti*. Some were governors who were part of the *iuventus* themselves; others were representatives of the city. Those who themselves belonged to the association were called *magistri iuvenum* or *iuventutis* (or similar titles). This office was collegial: every year, two (or more) *magistri* were appointed. Some *magistri* were known as *(magistri) quinquennales*. They held office in census years in the city (censuses were conducted every five years), or perhaps they carried out censuses (registration) within the organisation of the *iuvenes*. It appears that the *magistri* could be elected by

---

[81] Most scholars have devoted little attention to this fact. See Ausbüttel 1982: 59 with n. 5, 68 with n. 54; Ginestet 1991: 176 who, in nn. 120–1, collates the evidence (twelve items). The funerary activities of the *iuvenes* may account for the fact that the epitaph of Valeria Iucunda at Reate (see p. 124) was erected by the *magister* of the *iuvenes*.
[82] Ginestet 1991: 158–9; Ladage 1979: 335–6; Kleijwegt 1994: 90 and 101 n. 72.
[83] *Dig.* 48, 19, 28, 3 (Callistratus); the period is around the early third century AD.
[84] Jaczynowska 1978: 42–5; Ginestet 1991: 131–9.

the *iuvenes* or appointed by the city (see below). Technically speaking, they may not have been members of the *iuventus*. Apart from the *magistri*, there were governors, appointed by the city and most definitely not *iuvenes* themselves. Invariably, these individuals were prominent dignitaries of the city and most had previously served as municipal magistrates. They usually bore the title *praefectus iuventutis*, but other titles are also attested, including *praetor, curator, procurator*. It is not clear what exactly their tasks were. The *praefecti*, who are in any case recorded in just a few cities, probably performed a general supervisory role. The *curatores* (and *procuratores*) presumably supervised financial matters and were concerned with games and contests, the *lusus iuvenum*. F. Ausbüttel has pointed out that *decuriones* frequently held executive offices in associations.[85] It would, however, be a mistake to believe that an executive office in the *iuventus* functioned in general as a gateway to a municipal career and that aristocratic youths were prepared in the *iuventus* for holding office in the city administration; in fact very few governors of the *iuventutes* moved up to municipal positions.[86] Still, we cannot deny that the few aristocratic *iuvenes* who held the office of *magister* thereby acquired experience in governing. But as M. Jaczynowska notes, about half of the *magistri* who moved up to municipal positions had performed one or more of these functions before they became *magister* of the *iuvenes*. Caius Annaeus Pastor, for example, erected a tombstone for his beloved father at Vallis Canera (central Italy), mentioning in the epitaph that he himself had initially been a member of the board of four judges (*quattuorvir iure dicundo*) invested with aedilician power; only subsequently had he become *magister* of the *iuvenes*, and ultimately quaestor of the public treasury.[87] The other half of the *magistri* moved up to municipal magistracies only after serving as *magister*. So it was not the primary goal of the associations of *iuvenes* to train young men for administrative positions in the city or the Empire.[88]

So did young Roman men (aristocrats, free born, freedmen) learn about their place in society from the internal hierarchy in the *iuventutes*, as was the case with the Greek ephebes? It is quite possible that aristocratic *iuvenes* displayed their higher status and wealth by their armour, by their generosity towards the association, and possibly also by riding on horseback. Yet there is an important difference between the organisations of *iuvenes* and the real

---

[85] Ausbüttel 1982: 96–7; Ladage 1979: 330 n. 86. *Decuriones* often also acted as *patroni*.
[86] Ginestet 1991: 177–83.
[87] Ginestet 1991: 238 no. 123 (*CIL* IX 4754), end of the first or second century AD.
[88] Ginestet 1991: 190; Kleijwegt 1994: 91, 93.

world of the city, namely the fact that, in the *iuventutes*, freedmen could also hold the position of *magister*. In the municipal administration, by contrast, freedmen were excluded from all governing posts. The only two cities where freedmen are recorded as *magistri* are Reate and Lucus Feroniae, both in northern Italy:[89]

> For Manius Silius Epaphroditus, patron of the *seviri Augustales*, *magister* of the *iuvenes* for the second time. The *iuvenes* of Lucus Feroniae set up (this statue?) for their patron because of his merits, because he built and dedicated the amphitheatre of the colonia Julia Felix Lucoferensis from his own pocket. The place is assigned by decree of the *decuriones*. He was content with the honour and paid back the costs (of the honouring). (*CIL* XI 3938; *AnÉp* (1962) 86; probably *c*. AD 100–150)

The fact that freedmen were able to hold executive offices with the *iuvenes* ties in perfectly with the notion of *iuventutes* as associations. According to F. Ausbüttel, there is a long list of records of freedmen performing governing roles in *collegia*.[90] In so doing, they could acquire social prestige, which they were unable to gain through municipal offices, from which they were excluded. And in this manner they were also able to act as benefactors, for which they would receive honours in return.

7.4 Concluding remarks

The *ephebeia* was neither an educational institution nor a 'secondary' school, but rather a broad group of boys (usually aged around sixteen years) from the upper and middle classes who gathered in the gymnasium on a voluntary basis. For between one and three years they received physical and (irregular) intellectual training; this emphasis on sports appealed to most youths, for whom they were, moreover, a typically Greek activity. For the young men in the aristocratically ruled cities, athletics contests provided an arena for competition in honour and status. Sporting activities may also have served as a safety valve for any tension and aggression that may have existed, though such activities may themselves have occasionally resulted in unwholesome competition and undesirable behaviour. But the *ephebeia* also served other important goals: social education, development of civic virtues, participation in and preparation for civic life. The boys were prepared for their later roles in society, either as ordinary citizens or as leading officials.

---

[89] Reate: Ginestet 1991: 237 no. 120 (*CIL* IX 4696), end of the second century AD; Lucus Feroniae: Ginestet 1991: 245 no. 156; *EAOR* II 65.
[90] Ausbüttel 1982: 40; Ladage 1979: 333.

The new generation was thus familiarised with the prevailing structures of society and imbued with the values of civic life. Ultimately, this helped consolidate the power of the elites and thus contributed to maintaining the oligarchic regimes that prevailed in the Hellenistic–Roman cities.

The organisations known as *iuvenes* differed in many ways from the *ephebeia*, though there are also several similarities. The three main points of difference are that the *iuvenes* were less active in the field of sports than the ephebes and that the focus was primarily on combat sports. They were less oriented towards municipal life than the ephebes and not organised as miniature cities. The *iuventutes* were (sometimes?) mixed groups, comprising boys as well as girls, and could even include adults. In other words, *iuventutes* and *ephebeiai* were quite distinct from one another in several ways. On the other hand, they were similar as organisations in that they were not schools for general physical and cultural education. The associations of *iuvenes* are perhaps better described as 'entertainment clubs', where young people of the same age met on a voluntary basis. Here they could engage in (combat) sports, which apparently appealed greatly to youngsters and which moreover constituted a distinctive element of Roman identity. Sporting activities may also have served as an outlet for tension and aggression, as was the case with the Greek ephebes. Additionally, the *iuvenes* engaged in various religious activities. They were not, however, prominent as a group within the make-up of cities: their involvement in politics was negligible. The purpose of the organisations of *iuvenes* was not to prepare young men for their future roles in society, neither as civic magistrates nor as army recruits. The purpose was rather grounded in social life: maintaining social contacts through communal dining and participation in religious and funerary activities, as well as by forging bonds of solidarity.[91]

Admittedly, many questions about the organisations of Greek ephebes and Roman *iuvenes* remain unanswered. What influence might participating in such organisations have had upon young people aged between fourteen and twenty-one, considering that membership lasted only one or sometimes a couple of years and that the activities pursued did not fill the whole day? It is not clear whether or not this sufficed to shape their attitude and mentality, to temper their restlessness, and to mould them to expectations of adult behaviour. How did youngsters' behaviour prior to and after their membership period differ, and how did they behave during the time

---

[91] Kleijwegt 1994: 93. The author argues that the *iuvenes* were able to find an outlet for tensions between the generations in their organisations, though there would seem to exist just a single, rather late, reference to their involvement in 'farcical upheaval'.

7.4 Concluding remarks

spent outside the associations? Did the sporting activities provide an outlet for possible tensions? It is also unclear to what extent the participation of boys in public events provided an incentive for them to act as responsible citizens. Nor is it known whether the constant emphasis on 'norms and values' in the Greek *ephebeia* was effective in preventing undesirable behaviour on the part of the youngsters. What influence did ephebarchs, *magistri* and *praefecti iuvenum* have? Did they supervise and impose discipline? Did their presence curtail the *ferocitas* of the adolescents? Neither the ephebes nor the *iuvenes* apparently performed structurally significant tasks in society, but it is unclear whether or not this may have instilled a sense of marginalisation in the minds of the young men. If so, may youth in antiquity have been similar to adolescence today?

All these questions remain open. Every possible answer is speculative. Unfortunately, we do not possess written sources informing us of the intimate lives of young people in the cities of the Roman Empire: no diaries describing their feelings, no accounts of their behaviour in groups.[92] Our main source of information consists of inscriptions, which often paint an official and idealised picture, and which inform us about activities and forms of organisation, but not about the psychological make-up of the individuals concerned.[93] Were the urban youths of antiquity decent young people imbued with an adult spirit, or were such offspring of the upper classes and the wealthy elites spoilt brats who generally behaved badly? The study of the youth associations unfortunately provides no answers to such questions.

---

[92] Compare the accounts of noisy parades of young people, known as *charivari*, in medieval France, often on the occasion of a marriage (that was deemed of a morally dubious nature); see Kleijwegt 1991: 30–8.

[93] Wörrle 1995.

CHAPTER 8

Youthful behaviour

8.1 'Restlessness'

Were Roman youths typically impetuous or restless? Certainly Emiel Eyben, who chose *ferocitas* as the leitmotiv for his entire oeuvre on young Romans, thinks they were. There are indeed good arguments for believing that adolescents in ancient society must almost inevitably have behaved differently from, more 'restlessly' than, their adult counterparts. After all, the conduct of youngsters is determined largely by biological factors. With the onset of puberty, certain hormones begin to surge through young people's veins. Moreover, as mentioned in Chapter 1, neuropsychologists of the Leiden Institute for Brain and Cognition have demonstrated that the brain of an adolescent is not yet fully developed: it reaches full maturity only around the age of twenty-four. The part of the brain that develops the latest is the frontal lobe, including the prefrontal cortex, which plays an important role in cognitive functions such as planning, organising, thinking in abstract terms, controlling impulses. This may explain why adolescents tend not to take due account of the long-term consequences of their actions and to ignore the potentially negative impacts of their behaviour, such as loss or punishment. They enjoy risk-taking and impulsiveness. There is no balance yet between the amygdala in the temporal lobe, which controls emotional responses, and the prefrontal cortex. That is why emotions often prevail over rational thinking and decision-making: the controlling part of the brain is unable to resist. The (medial) prefrontal cortex also plays a crucial role in social behaviour: in understanding and appreciating the point of view of others, and in selfish and reciprocal conduct.[1] Hence, there would appear to be a biological reason why adolescents like to take risks and find it difficult to act with moderation. However, biology is not an absolute determinant. Other

---

[1] Westenberg 2008: 8–11; Crone 2008. Crone and Dahl 2012 now argue that developmental neuro-imaging studies do not support a simple model of frontal cortical immaturity. Rather, it is a question of cognitive flexibility. Growing evidence suggests that use of the prefrontal cortex is variable and

8.1 'Restlessness'

aspects, such as personality, education, social interactions, and the structure of society, also play an important role. Did Roman society give the young people time and space to be young, as Eyben contends? In this chapter we investigate the ancient sources on the behaviour of youths, taking as our lead the work of Eyben, who has extensively discussed their supposedly impetuous conduct, thinking, and feelings.[2] Eyben considers leisure an important aspect of their lives which provides much information about the conduct of youths. He also considers attitudes towards love and sex significant indications of their emotional life, and youthful poetry a major element in the field of their thinking. We therefore restrict our study to these three aspects, rather than attempt to be comprehensive. Instead of analysing every detail, we set out to examine whether these activities were indeed characteristic of Roman youths and whether society allowed youngsters to develop their own subculture. First we consider Roman society, which is relatively well documented, and then we briefly turn our attention to the Greek setting.

*****

Roman youths filled their leisure time by participating in and watching athletics (e.g. running and wrestling), hunting, engaging in other sporting activities (e.g. horse-riding), bathing, music and dance, and by attending performances at the circus (e.g. chariot racing), the theatre (especially mime and pantomime) or the amphitheatre (gladiator fights and wild animal hunts). These activities were not equally popular: athletics, music, and dance, for example, were not in vogue with conservative Romans. Hunting and combat-training, on the other hand, were highly thought of, particularly as they were seen as an excellent preparation for military service. But these activities were not engaged in exclusively or even predominantly by youngsters.[3] Of course, it could happen that certain young men took an extreme and even a fanatical interest in a particular form of recreation, and that their fanaticism erupted into violence and caused disturbance at public shows or events.

We come closer to a possible youth culture when we discuss feasting and love of luxury. Eyben provides extensive descriptions of dandies, revellers,

---

depends primarily on what motivates adolescents. This motivation is in turn influenced by social and affective processes in the environment. Changes in social and affective processing begin around the onset of puberty and are crucial to understanding adolescent vulnerabilities.

[2] Eyben 1993: respectively 81–127, 128–202, 203–55; 1999: 413–20; a more elaborate discussion is found in Eyben 1977: 133–268, 269–464, 465–572.

[3] Pleket 1979: 186–7 pointed out that many of the 'restless' youths were not adolescents but young adults; see below.

spendthrifts, and vandals.⁴ From the large number of cases, we present but a few examples. Young men frequently indulged in merrymaking, paid visits to brothels, and drank too much wine. They purchased expensive horses, dogs, and other pets. They sprinkled themselves with costly perfumes and dressed in expensive and effeminate garments. Conservative Romans such as Seneca did not approve. In a letter, he fulminates against all

> Those who pluck out their beards completely or partially, who closely shear and shave the (upper) lip while they keep and let grow the rest of their beard, who choose cloaks with frivolous colours, who wear a transparent toga, and who refuse to do anything that might escape notice of the people. They excite them and draw their attention to themselves. They are even ready to be criticised, provided they attract notice. (Seneca, *Epist. mor.* 114, 21)

Young men could be profligate, spending the money they had sometimes earned in a dishonest or ignominious way, and losing fortunes gambling. Bands of young thugs could create havoc: at night after a party, intoxicated with alcohol, they would sometimes roam the streets and beat up innocent passers-by.⁵ According to ancient accounts, certain 'bad' emperors, including Caligula and Otho, also used to indulge in such excesses. Nero, too, is said to have engaged in forays after dark. He apparently used to pay incognito visits to common taverns, break into shops and loot them, and attack revellers on their way home late at night. His escapades almost led to his death, as one night he himself was beaten up badly by a senator whose wife he had accosted; the man had not recognised his emperor. Observations by the imperial biographer Suetonius on Nero's behaviour are revealing: 'In the beginning his acts of wantonness, lust, extravagance, avarice, and cruelty were gradual and secret and might be condoned as defects of youth. But even then no one doubted that these vices were due to his character, not to his age.'⁶

Reading the numerous examples of extravagant and irresponsible behaviour in Roman young men, one could get the impression that this is a consistent pattern. In fact, though, these are isolated references dating from the second century BC well into the fifth century AD. The image created is cumulative and thus an exaggeration: in reality, these reports span a very broad geographical area and an extensive period of time. Moreover, many of

---

⁴ Eyben 1993: 98–112.
⁵ See McGinn 2004: 91. Known as *comissatio*, this was a kind of 'after-dinner entertainment' for befuddled young men, often resulting in casual acts of aggression against persons and property and forced entry into brothels.
⁶ Suetonius, *Cal.* 11; *Otho* 2; *Nero* 26, 1.

the examples adduced by Eyben originate from the same sources, which are, moreover, not particularly objective. They include the comedies of Terence and Plautus, Cicero's description of the followers of his political arch-rival Catiline, Tacitus and Suetonius' account of the behaviour of Nero, who in their eyes was most unsuitable as an emperor, and the writings of the church father Augustine, who confesses to errors committed during his pagan youth. Other texts are expressions of the aversion of older authors to the supposedly improper conduct of the young: as we have pointed out before, older individuals often despised the behaviour of the young because they felt it did not come up to their standards of gravity, austerity, and wisdom. Quite revealing in this respect are the words of Seneca the Elder, who painted the following picture of youth (*iuventus*) in his lifetime, the first century AD:

> See how the spirit of the idle youth is, so to say, paralysed. They do not stay awake over the study of the one and only honourable art (i.e. eloquence). Sleep and indolence and enthusiasm for acts more shameful than either of these have seized hold of their minds. An ignominious passion for dance and song keeps the effeminates in its hold. They braid their hair, they refine their voices in order to approximate to the charms of women. They compete with women in softness of the body. They beautify themselves with utterly filthy fineries. That is the appearance of our youths. (Seneca the Elder, *Contr.* 1 praef. 8)

But which young men had the time and money to feast and to show off their riches? Clearly only those belonging to the wealthy elite. 'Restless' behaviour was apparently restricted to a small, well-off social group. For the most part, it occurred in the Roman metropolis, rarely in other cities. Hence, it is a generalisation to speak of *the* restless behaviour of *the* Roman youth.

Impetuousness could turn to riotous behaviour and violence. A passage in the *Digest* mentions organisations of *iuvenes* who joined local public protests and revolts. In the *Metamorphoses*, written by Apuleius of Madaura, the girl Photis begs her lover Lucius not to return late after supper:[7]

> 'Now take care', she said, 'and come back early from supper because a frenzied gang of aristocratic young men is out to disturb the public peace in our city. You will see the bodies of their victims lying everywhere in the streets. The troops of the governor are far away and cannot help our city in this disaster.' (Apuleius, *Met.* 2, 18)

---

[7] *Dig.* 48, 19, 28, 3 (Callistratus); see p. 131, n. 83. See Meadows 1993 and Veyne 2001: 85–7, who suggests that the gangs may have consisted of groups of wealthy young men with an abundance of leisure time on their hands (a *jeunesse dorée*) who, in a carnival-like atmosphere, behaved indecently; cf. the *charivari* processions mentioned on p. 135, n. 92.

It is unclear whether or not young men of the lower classes joined in such acts of violence. All we know is that, in late antiquity, there were wandering gangs of so-called *vagantes*, a term that most probably refers to young men who refused to pursue the same occupations as their fathers.[8] But this issue would appear to have been associated with the economic distress of the late Roman period.

*****

Next, let us consider how young Romans experienced sexuality between puberty and marriage.[9] Young men may be assumed generally to have had strong sexual desires. We have spoken earlier about ancient astrological and medical theories of the bodily fluids, which in the eyes of the ancients explained why young men were naturally inclined towards lust, lack of self-control, and passion. Were young men obliged to suppress their sexual desires and did this lead to problems and even crises, or were there accepted sexual 'outlets' in Roman society? It is well established that the Romans were broad-minded in the realm of love and sex. However, certain forms of sexuality and certain deeds were not tolerated. This is formulated quite unequivocally by a slave in Plautus' comedy *Curculio*. He says to his master: 'Love anyone you want, provided you keep away from married women, widows, virgins, young innocents, and children of respectable families.'[10] This would seem to imply that there were certain accepted outlets for the sexual impulses of the young: masturbation, prostitution, and sex with male and female slaves and freedmen. Masturbation was not considered an ignominious practice. Although it was rarely spoken about openly, very few ancient physicians actually opposed it.[11] Prostitution in Rome was ubiquitous.[12] There were brothels on every other street corner, so to speak, particularly in the popular district of Subura, which had a high concentration of lower-class housing and residential buildings in general. Besides brothels, there were 'cribs' (*cellae meretriciae*), one-room venues for sexual encounters with direct access to the street, usually provided with a masonry bed. Prostitutes could be found in the streets, in commercial establishments such as inns and taverns, near all places of public

---

[8] Veyne 2001: 30. [9] Eyben 1993: 231–8; see also 1977: 469–75.
[10] Plautus, *Curc.* 37–8. On acceptable and unacceptable conduct in sexual intercourse, see Van Houdt 2003: 109–13.
[11] Masturbation was not considered the cause of physical and mental diseases, as the Swiss physician Tissot argued in his influential work *L'onanisme: dissertation sur les maladies produites par la masturbation*, published in 1760. See Krenkel 1979; Laes 2006a: 235; cf. p. 223, nn. 37–8.
[12] Kolb 1995: 493–4. For a general overview, see McGinn 2004; Faraone and McClure 2006.

8.1 'Restlessness'

entertainment, including the circus, theatres, and baths, and even in the Forum, in and near temples and among tombs along the roads. Outside the metropolis, there were brothels too. At Pompeii, for example, several houses have been identified as serving this purpose. Some scholars count as many as thirty-five brothels in the town. Mary Beard has calculated that this is roughly one brothel to every seventy-five adult males, which is an 'over-generous ratio'. Much depends, though, on the criteria one uses for identifying a brothel. The most conservative estimates actually identify just one at Pompeii: the famous 'lupanar' near the Stabian baths. Be that as it may, there are many rooms in Pompeii that are decorated with erotic paintings and plenty of examples of sexually oriented graffiti providing details such as the names of prostitutes, their price and quality, sexual positions, and other useful tips or warnings for the visitors.[13] It is obvious that, in Pompeii, sex for money was available all over town: the upstairs or backrooms of bars, for example, often provided accommodation for commercial sex.[14]

Several ancient writers, including Cicero and Seneca the Elder, considered it normal for a young man to visit prostitutes, be they female or male,[15] though some moderation was apparently called for. Cato the Elder recounts how a young man left a brothel just as he walked by. The youngster ran off, but Cato called him back and congratulated him. Later, however, after having seen that same young man leave the brothel on quite a few more occasions, he told him: 'I praised you because you came here, not because you lived here!'[16] In other words, a degree of restraint and decency was required. And young men should not waste too much money on such diversions.[17] However, Thomas McGinn has argued that many Romans found it dishonourable for persons of rank to set foot in a brothel. When an elite Roman entered or exited such an establishment, he might have covered his head in order not to be recognised.[18] A certain *odium* was attached to visiting a brothel for members of the upper classes: these were places of

---

[13] Younger 2005: 97–103 s.v. Pompeii; Johnson and Ryan 2005: 101–3, 108–9; see McGinn 2004: 267–302 for evidence on Pompeian brothels (forty-one, about half of which uncertain), 'cribs' (thirteen) and names of prostitutes (160).
[14] Beard 2008: 232–3, 236–7 on the 'Pompeian Brothel Problem'.
[15] Williams 1999: 38–47; Hermans 1995: 135–8.
[16] Ps.-Acro, *Schol. In Hor. Serm.* 1, 2, 31–2; see Williams 1999: 43. McGinn 2004: 237 offers an entirely different interpretation of this passage.
[17] According to Eyben 1993: 113, it was decreed by Augustus that brothels should not open their doors before the ninth hour (1:30 to 2:30 p.m. depending on the season), so that young men would not neglect their military training (*Schol. ad Pers.* 1, 133). McGinn 2004: 149–51 does not find this and other evidence credible, but acknowledges that the *aediles* may have stipulated opening hours for brothels with a view to maintaining public order.
[18] McGinn 2004: 84–5.

social mixing, associated with disorder and criminality; prostitution was linked with low social status and looked down upon.[19] Therefore, it seems that elite Romans relied on other sexual outlets than the prostitutes who were at their disposal in brothels (see below). But for low-status males venal sex was readily accessible: clients of brothels were mainly of the lower classes if not of servile status. Not only were brothels usually located in lower-class lodgings, the prices charged by prostitutes were quite affordable.[20]

It could also happen that a young man became the object of the love of an adult male. The emperor Hadrian had as lover an adolescent boy called Antinous (see Fig. 8.1), who drowned in the Nile near Hermopolis during

8.1 Antinous, lover of the emperor Hadrian, came from Claudiupolis in Bithynia. When he was eleven or twelve years old, he was discovered during Hadrian's travels in the area and ended up in the imperial paedogogium in Rome. He was the favourite of the emperor in a pederastic relationship. Antinous was beautiful, intelligent, athletic, and Greek.
(Archaeological Museum, Delphi.)

[19] McGinn 2004: 71–2, 86.
[20] McGinn 2004: 20–1, 40–55 on prices. On p. 72, McGinn points to the somewhat surprising lack of evidence for upper-class brothels.

the emperor's visit to Egypt in AD 130. It is conceivable that the boy took his own life to stop the relationship, which was on the verge of ending. A homosexual relationship with a young man had to come to an end when the young man had grown a full beard. At the time of his death, Antinous was twenty or slightly younger. Hadrian bestowed many marks of honour on his departed lover and had him deified. He also had innumerable statues in his image erected all across the Empire. These perpetuated the memory of the handsome young man and immortalised the beauty of his youth. Be that as it may, the relationship of Hadrian and Antinous was far from unproblematic. There are no indications that Antinous was born as a slave, but the fact that he was not a Roman citizen made it easier for the emperor to display publicly their intimate relationship. This outing in any case tied in with the Greek aura that Hadrian was keen to adopt.[21]

Elite Romans found sexual outlets with the slaves in their *familia*. Slaves were considered to be the property of their master and their own will to be irrelevant. The master had absolute power over them and was free to have sex with them if and when he so wished. Wealthy people often owned large numbers of slaves, and a master could abuse them sexually, female slaves as well as male ones. This was an accepted custom and even permitted by law. The abuse of male slaves, usually (but not always) boys, is recorded in many literary texts from the second century BC onwards.[22] Slaves who had been manumitted remained socially in the power of their former master and had the moral obligation to obey him and to render him sexual services, if so desired. But it was not deemed acceptable by society to abuse male or female slaves and freedmen unrestrictedly. The prevailing norm prescribed that a man should exercise self-control. He was required to temper his sexual desires. Otherwise, he risked incurring moral disapproval and public derision, and being given a name like *ancillariolus* (pursuer of slave-girls). During the Empire, a stricter ethical code came to the fore under the influence of Stoicism. Philosophers such as Musonius Rufus (first century AD) and later Hierocles (second century AD) set the same standards for husbands as for wives. The husband was no longer allowed to have sexual intercourse outside wedlock; sex was permissible only within a legal marriage (with the aim of procreation). Still, it is doubtful that the teachings of

---

[21] On Antinous, see especially Birley 1997: 247–50; Vout 2005; Boymel Kampen 2007.
[22] Williams 1999: 30–8; Hermans 1995: 133–5. On the preference for smooth-skinned boys, see Williams 1999: 72–7. Adolescents without a fully grown beard were considered extremely sexually attractive. On paedophilia and pederasty in Roman society, see Laes 2006a: 199–249 and 2011: 222–68.

these philosophers brought about any real change in conduct, particularly outside the circle of the Roman aristocrats.[23]

Hence, in the realm of sexuality, there was an element of permissiveness and, at the same time, a strict moral boundary; outlets for sexual urges were in any case available for upper- and lower-class males. Sexual frustration, of the kind which modern adolescents may experience in our Christian-based society, was less likely to occur. It should of course be noted, though, that all of the above applied to young males only. Girls were required to keep their virginity until marriage. Herein lies the so-called 'double sexual standard' of the Romans. Medical writers found that unmarried girls at the onset of menstruation often experienced psychological problems, and were even prone to suicide. According to the Hippocratic Corpus, *parthenoi* experiencing such symptoms should marry as soon as possible and become pregnant. The physician Soranus proposed that girls at the onset of puberty could control their sexual desires by taking gentle walks, swinging in a hammock for prolonged periods of time, performing not-too-arduous gymnastics exercises, taking massages with plenty of oil, daily bathing, and exposure to enough distractions to keep their minds occupied.[24] Other physicians prescribed a strict diet. Rufus of Ephesus advised girls during puberty to moderate their intake of food, to avoid wine, and to spurn meat and other excessively nourishing food altogether.[25]

*****

In his chapter on youthful thinking, Eyben explores the characteristic features of poetry composed by young authors.[26] The first feature that catches his eye is a striking tendency to express personal feelings. Traditionally, Romans abhorred expressing their feelings. But a group of young poets from the first century BC, known as the *poetae novi*, broke new ground, inspired by Alexandrian examples. Among them was Catullus, whose poetry reflected his inner moods, especially those associated with deep love and intense hatred. Others, too, described such strong personal emotions, their innermost turbulent feelings. Later, elegiac poets, such as Propertius, Tibullus, and Ovid, followed their example. Their elegies gave expression to the whole gamut of human emotions. Many of these authors castigated the

---

[23] Van Houdt 2003: 124–9. The term of abuse *ancillariolus* is encountered, for example, in Seneca, *De ben.* 1, 9, 4.
[24] Garland 1990: 168–9; Soranus, *Gyn.* 1, 25, 2.
[25] Harlow and Laurence 2002: 57; Rufus is cited by Oribasius, *Lib. inc.* 18, 10.
[26] Eyben 1993: 176–202; more extensively in 1977: 405–60.

Roman establishment: they criticised the prevailing norms, provoked the respectable classes, and exceeded many a literary convention. A second similarity between these young writers is that they approached poetry as an intellectual game. They liked to display their erudition, e.g. in the field of mythology, and made deliberate use of complex and unusual vocabulary so that their verses became obscure and impenetrable. The third feature that catches Eyben's eye is that these poets longed for another, ideal world. In a negative sense, they displayed their dislike of public life with its corruption and scandals, and particularly the atrocities and proscriptions of the civil war. They were 'pacifists' of sorts. They longed for peace and wished to flee from daily reality into a dream-like world of fantasy; they longed for a vague and distant past, and the tranquil sanctuary of nature. Eyben, in a reference to The Beatles, writes that Propertius and Tibullus might easily have adopted 'Make love not war' as their motto. Persius believed in the ideology of the Stoa; he was convinced that it could change what he considered to be a degenerate society. Lucan was politically aware: he hated the monarchy and was a firm believer in the restoration of the Republic, with its respect for the principles of liberty and justice. In a positive sense, many poets, especially Catullus, strove for a better world of peace and prosperity, without avarice, governed by new norms and standards; a world detached from that of the adults.

This description of the young Roman poets is in many ways reminiscent of the views and lifestyle of modern adolescents, particularly the outpourings of the young countercultures in 'the golden sixties' of the twentieth century: hippies, starry-eyed idealists, and, indeed, The Beatles, Bob Dylan, and The Doors. It is no wonder that Eyben's image provoked severe criticism. Harry Pleket, for his part, considers the *poetae novi* to have been 'angry young men' of sorts; young adults aged between twenty and thirty who reacted against the society of their elders, but not displaying the typical psychological profile of adolescents. He emphasises that they constituted only a small atypical group; their mentality was not characteristic of all youngsters in the Roman world. Marc Kleijwegt does not discuss the topic explicitly. He appears to interpret what Pleket regards as the opposition of the young poets to the society of their time more as intergenerational conflict. The period of the late Republic was an exceptional age in this respect; it was a chaotic era of civil war and of social, economic, and cultural upheaval. He asserts that the young poets merely concluded that the older generation had failed, but that they did not present a revolutionary programme or innovative ideas to replace traditional concepts. Finally, David Meadows has criticised Eyben for projecting his own experiences as a young adult at the dawn of the *Age of Aquarius* on to the history of Rome.[27]

Johannes Christes, on the other hand, agrees to an extent with Eyben (see Chapter 1.5).[28] He observes that the development of a Hellenistic–Roman culture, and particularly its system of higher education based on the Greek model, opened up a *Freiraum*, or period of freedom, for the youths of the senatorial and equestrian order. These youths, he claims, grasped the opportunity. He concurs with Eyben that there are signs of a specific youthful sense of life, comparable to modern adolescence, from the late Republic onwards. Christes mentions Catullus, who set himself free from the values of the adult world and developed a new poetic vocabulary in which he expressed his personal world of peace, love, and friendship. The elegies of Tibullus and Propertius overturned the traditional concepts of love and marriage and shocked the conservative Roman establishment. They protested against the degeneration of society and the corrupt politics, and provocatively sang the praises of *otium*, that is leisure, spare time; they rejected serving the commonwealth and took pride in idling. In the well-known verses from the fifth *Satire* of Persius (cited in Chapter 4.2), Christes perceives evidence for the existence of a separate *Jugendraum* (time to be young) at the beginning of the Principate. In these verses, Persius describes his sense of freedom after having shed the child's toga and the *bulla*: he is free to cast his eyes over all the Subura (the red-light district of Rome). The notion of possessing the freedom to live one's life to the full encapsulated the sense of vitality of some Roman youngsters, according to Christes, who further argues that this specific youthful feeling was limited in time, and occurred only in Rome and within a small group of the upper class.[29] This 'alternative outlook' on life was temporary, fleeting, like youth itself. The elegiac poet Cornelius Gallus later became a politician, a soldier, and an administrator. Propertius developed into a poet who fully embraced society and supported Augustus' reforms. Others took to philosophy. Christes points to the story of Livy about Scipio Africanus.[30] Scipio, invested with proconsular *imperium* at the age of twenty-five (209 BC), asserted in an address to the Spanish prince Allucius that the *res publica* demanded that he forsake youthful behaviour (*ludus aetatis*, i.e. *iuventutis*). Scipio was a young

---

[27] Pleket 1979: 190; Kleijwegt 1991: 66, 67; Meadows 1993.
[28] Christes 1998: 153–64. Christes' view is adopted by Bormann 2006: 75–8.
[29] Persius Flaccus, *Sat.* 5, 30–6; see p. 57. Christes 1998: 163 calls this *die Lizenz eines freizügigen Sich-Auslebens* ('the licence to live one's life freely to the full').
[30] Livy, *Ab Urbe cond.* 26, 50, 3–7.

adult; his *Jugendraum* came to an end as soon as he assumed responsibility.[31] Diana Bormann adds that the process of 'emancipation' from the old Roman values was facilitated by a change in the political situation.[32] Ovid, the last of the elegists, who lived during the quiet reign of Augustus, also retired from politics, but not in protest against society (see 6.7). Under Augustus, politics had become less important and the tendency to withdraw into the private realm had grown stronger. The notion of protest faded away.

It is not easy to adopt a position in this debate. It is obvious that many of the assertions made are largely unproven, and that scholars use them selectively to support their own views. Was Catullus, who had actually already reached the age of thirty-three, really reacting *against the adult world* when he expressed his longing for peace and prosperity in the new poetic vocabulary? Was criticism of society and unconventional, even provocative, behaviour really the mark of *a youthful sense of life*? Nobody knows for certain what the answer is to such questions. Two points must however be borne in mind. First, it is utterly problematic to connect a supposedly 'youthful' sense of life with any particular age group. The poets concerned were not adolescents but young adults, already in their late twenties or even early thirties. Second, to the extent that the sources are indicative of a specific type of behaviour among the young, then invariably this was limited to a very small circle of the wealthiest in society, those belonging to the senatorial and equestrian classes, as Pleket rightly observes. Tibullus and Propertius belonged to the *equites*, Ovid to the *senatores*, and the other poets were all members of the wealthiest classes in the metropolis of Rome and hence could afford the luxury of cultivating *otium*. The literary sources thus highlight a very select section of Roman youth. So was any youthful sense of life and behaviour induced by a lack of empowerment, by the fact that these youths were not entrusted by the adults with real responsibilities in politics and society? Most definitely not: the fact that some youths stood aloof from society was a matter of personal choice. Youngsters as a group were not banned from the adult world. There are after all examples of other upper-class youths who did not lead an idle life but filled their time with education (rhetoric, philosophy), with training as lawyers or

---

[31] Livy has highly idealised Scipio's moral qualities; see Walsh 1961: 96–100. In our view, the story says nothing about the actual behaviour or feelings of youths. It shows, at best, the ideal in Livy's era of a youth overcoming the deficiencies of his age. What Scipio rejects is passionate love (which was never valued in Roman society), not a general attitude towards life, politics or society.

[32] Bormann 2006: 77–8.

other meaningful activities. As for similarly aged members of the lower classes, the largest population group in the Roman Empire, they would already have been participating fully in an adult society of work and marriage.

*****

So what does the evidence say about possible 'restless' behaviour by young males in the Greek world during the Hellenistic and Roman periods? Does it point to the existence of similar characteristics to those in the Roman world? The truth is that hardly anything is known about this subject. A thorough study of the literary sources (as Eyben has conducted for Rome) simply does not exist. Some facts are known about the conduct of wealthy young men in Athens in the fifth and fourth centuries BC.[33] Apparently they behaved in much the same way as wealthy Roman youths. There are numerous references to revellers, spendthrifts, and vandals, to extravagant and effeminate clothing, drunkenness, visits to harlots, possession of expensive horses and other animals, acts of hooliganism at night on the way to and from parties. One such well-known reference occurs in Ariston's speech against Conon, written by Demosthenes:[34]

> He (= Conon) will say that there are many people in the city, the sons of gentlemen, who, in the manner of young men (*neoi*), have playfully given themselves nicknames, such as *Ithyphalloi* ('Erect-penises') or *Autolekythoi* ('Self-stimulators'); and that some of them have intercourse with prostitutes; and that his own son is one of them; and that he has often given and received blows on account of a prostitute; and that his behaviour is customary among young men. As for me (= Ariston) and all my brothers, he will make out that we are not only drunken and insolent fellows but also unfeeling and vindictive. (Demosthenes, *Or.* 54, 14)

The age of these young men is not entirely clear, though they are referred to in the text as *neoi*, suggesting they were beyond adolescence. They clearly belonged to the wealthy upper classes. Unlike in Rome, there are no indications in Athens of the existence of youthful poetry. As regards sexuality, young males in Athens enjoyed certain 'outlets' for any erotic tensions prior to marriage, just as did their counterparts in Rome: prostitutes and slaves, female as well as male. We thus find a striking parallelism between the impetuous conduct of well-to-do youths in classical Athens and Rome, but

---

[33] Eyben 1999: 404–6.
[34] For the trial (some time around the 350s BC), see Carey 1997: 84–97; the translation of the names of the gangs is by Garland 1990: 207; Carey (p. 88) translates *Autolekythoi* as 'down-and-outs'.

this was unlike modern adolescent behaviour as we know it with sexual tensions. As for the Greek cities in the East during the Hellenistic and Roman periods, again there were accepted sexual 'outlets' and, as in Athens, there is no attested youthful poetry. It is as yet unknown whether evidence exists for impetuous behaviour by youths because the literary sources have not as yet been scrutinised for this aspect. We can however cite an opinion on youths expressed in the treatise 'On Education', written by a follower or student of Plutarch, probably in the second century AD:

> For who does not know that the faults of children are trivial and can be corrected completely? But the vices of early manhood are often monstrous and wicked: unlimited gluttony, theft of the money of parents, gambling, revelling, heavy drinking, love affairs with young girls, and seduction of married women. (Ps.-Plutarch, *De lib. educ.* 12b (16))

It is very rare for a non-literary source from the Greek world to mention disorderly conduct by youths. Sometimes a gymnasiarch felt the need to rectify inappropriate behaviour. And very exceptionally, young men (*neaniskoi*, who were probably not ephebes) became involved in acts of violence: armed uprising or revolution, especially the overthrow of a tyrant.[35] In fact, it is hardly surprising that such behaviour does not appear in epigraphic documents, as these were intended for public display. Hence they always portray aristocratic young men as the natural successors to their fathers, imitating the older generation and adopting their values and attitudes.[36] We will probably never know how these young men felt deep down in their hearts and how they behaved, as there are no first-hand witness accounts of their conduct in the 'depth of the night', so to speak. Unfortunately, autobiographical documents from antiquity, written by the youths themselves, are extremely rare.

8.2 Conflict

Did general antagonism between younger and older people, of the kind we would refer to today as 'generational conflicts', also occur in the Roman Empire?[37] For the Greek world of the Hellenistic and Roman periods, research in this field is almost non-existent. There are some well-known

---

[35] Kleijwegt 1991: 95: *neaniskoi* in Lycia, *neoteroi* at Amyzon in Caria.
[36] Kleijwegt 1991: 68–71; Wörrle 1995.
[37] Starting from very different perspectives, both Vatai 2004 and Isayev 2007 have offered nuances concerning the likelihood of strong inter-generational tension in ancient Rome.

sources from the earlier period, originating in classical Athens.[38] In the fifth and fourth centuries BC, it was customary to show respect for one's elders, but in the second half of the fifth century this seems to have dwindled. Conflicts between older and younger generations spread to public life, perhaps under the influence of the Sophists. The political debate on the leadership of the Sicilian expedition (415 BC), claimed by both Nicias (about fifty-five) and Alcibiades (thirty-six years old!), is often adduced as evidence. Nicias argued that Alcibiades was too young to hold high military office; Alcibiades reproached his opponent for attempting to create a division between young and old instead of striving for consensus between the generations, as in the 'good old days'.[39] In this debate, young and old were represented as distinct and opposing groups. But these arguments may have been merely rallying cries from self-interested politicians who were eager to win support. As regards the Hellenistic–Roman period, M. Kleijwegt has argued that the structure of society became more aristocratic. Unlike in the democratic city-states of the classical period, men were no longer regarded as equals, and a strict social hierarchy arose. As a result, tensions between generations ceased to be a problem. Respect for one's elders again became part of the prevailing ideology. A good example appears in the honorary decree for Agreophon from Caunus (Caria), issued by the city after his death (beginning of the second century AD):

> Also as a private citizen he showed the magnanimity of a generous man. All in all, he demonstrated excellence of soul and character, which in lustre was even more brilliant than the generosities he was able to confer thanks to his personal situation. He lived a proper life, without insolence. He paid respect to the elderly as fathers; he treated all persons of all ages in an affectionate and friendly way. (*SEG* L (2000) 1109 lines 15–17; *I. Kaunos* 30)

Of course, we must be on our guard for exaggeration and take due account of the tradition that no ill should be spoken of the dead. Nonetheless, the decree is illustrative of the ideal conduct of young people towards their elders.

In Rome, inter-generational tension arose during the late Republic. This was induced by civil war, economic crises, and cultural revolution. Some individuals, such as Pompey and Octavian, succeeded in rising to positions of extraordinary power at a young age, despite resistance from the older generation. Octavian was not even twenty when he became a consul. The

---

[38] Eyben 1999: 407–9 with references; Garland 1990: 203–6; Kleijwegt 1991: 65–6 with a definition of generational conflict by M. Reinhold.
[39] Thucydides, *Hist.* 6, 18, 6.

conspiracy of Catiline (63 BC) brought the clash of the generations into the spotlight. Sallust put the following words into the mouths of the young supporters of Catiline:[40]

> For certain – I swear it by the faith of gods and men – victory is within our grasp. We are in the prime of life; our strength has reached its summit. They on the contrary have become utter dotards through the burden of the years and their wealth. (Sallust, *Cat.* 20, 10)

Young poets also reacted against the society of the elders, as described above. But this was very much a temporary phenomenon. During the Principate, tensions faded away. In Rome and in the Latin cities, an aristocratic society developed with a strict hierarchy in which everyone knew his place.

Within the Roman family, the father wielded unlimited power (in theory at least) over his legitimate children, under the principle of *patria potestas*. This authority remained in force as long as the father lived, unless he ended it of his own volition. Rome was unique in this respect. In the Greek world (in the classical but probably also in the post-classical period), the authority of father over son ended when the latter either reached the age of eighteen or married.[41] In Rome, the *patria potestas* continued to be in force irrespective of the son's age and of whether or not he got married. This paternal power meant that the father had absolute right over life and death: *ius vitae necisque*. When a new child was born, it was up to the father to either adopt or to dispose of the baby. He even possessed the power to put to death an adult child. In the ancient literature, one finds several examples of fathers who had their sons executed, for example on the charge of gross disobedience.[42] One of the most famous such stories is that of T. Manlius Torquatus, consul in 340 BC, who had his son decapitated because the youth had, in contravention of his father's orders, engaged the enemy in an episode during the war against the Latins.[43] However, new research has demonstrated that in each of these cases the father acted not on the grounds of his private *potestas* but in his capacity as magistrate. Brent Shaw has argued that authors of the imperial period *believed* deeply that the right of the father over life and death was very ancient, a relic of the ancestral constitution, as it were. It was a rhetorical image with which they tried to affirm and enhance the authority of the family head; an ideal of unlimited paternal power, asserted over and over again in response to constant threats to that authority by other members of the family.[44] In reality, the punitive

---

[40] Later Cicero, too, was reproached for inciting young men against their elders; see Eyben 1993: 61.
[41] For Greek society, see Kleijwegt 1991: 58; Eyben 1991: 115.   [42] See Harris 1986.
[43] Livy, *Ab Urbe cond.* 8, 7–8.   [44] Saller 1994: 115–18; Shaw 2001: 56–77.

power of a Roman father was restricted. Grave cases had to be brought before the court. Imperial edicts affirmed these constraints: from the second century AD, a father who had killed an adult child without consent of the family council could be tried for murder.[45]

In fact, the father's powers in other matters under the *patria potestas* were also limited by various imperial laws. One of these paternal powers concerned a complete monopoly over property rights: only the father of the family was formally entitled to own property. All those who were under his *potestas* had no property of their own: everything they earned or obtained belonged to the family father. But it was good custom for a father to grant his son an allowance, known as a *peculium*. This enabled the son to pay for his own expenses, for example to finance a public career. But the father had the right to adjust or to revoke the amount at any time. A young man from an upper-class family had few other honourable means at his disposal for raising money. His mother (or mistress) could slip him some cash, but it was not easy for young men to borrow money (under Claudius lending to minors was prohibited altogether),[46] while paid labour was considered a disgrace. The father of a family had a good deal of latitude in disposing of family property in his will and could even disinherit a child completely. But in the imperial period, a child who had been disowned without adequate and just cause could challenge such a decision in court.[47]

A final aspect of the *patria potestas* concerns the power over the marriage of children. The formal consent of the fathers of both partners was required for a legally valid marriage to be contracted. Moreover, the father had the right to break up the marriage of any child under his power at any moment. But Augustus forbade fathers from preventing the marriage of their daughters. And from the mid-second century AD, fathers forfeited the right to dissolve the marriage of a daughter living in harmony with her husband.[48] We will discuss in Chapter 11, on marriage, how all this worked out in daily life. But it is safe to say that, in theory and in the ideology current at the time, the notion of paternal power lost much of its significance during the imperial period. Inscriptions, too, demonstrate that the principle that a child belonged completely and uniquely to its father was gradually eroded. Epitaphs from the beginning of the imperial period show that, after a divorce of their parents, children sometimes continued to live with the

---

[45] Shaw 2001: 75 with sources in n. 119. Saller 1994: 116–17 mentions the story of Seneca, *De clem.* 1, 15, 1 that a certain Tricho, a knight in the time of Augustus, had his son whipped to death; the background is not clear. The crowds at Rome became incensed and attacked the man with their styluses.
[46] Tacitus, *Ann.* 11, 13. [47] Saller 1994: 118–19. [48] Saller 1994: 119; Evans Grubbs 2005a: 112–22.

mother. In many inscriptions, children bear the family names (*gentilicia*) of both their father and their mother.⁴⁹

As we have mentioned, a father could end his *potestas* of his own free will. This procedure was known as emancipation (*emancipatio*). The result was that the son became *sui iuris* and that he acquired the right to own property under his own name.

It has been contended that the oppressive authority of the Roman father almost inevitably provoked hostility from his children. Did not Seneca assert in *De clementia* that, under the reign of Claudius, 'filial piety was truly at its lowest ebb after the sack (*culleus*) became a more common sight than the cross'?⁵⁰ The *culleus* was the leather sack in which a patricide was sewn up before being thrown alive into the Tiber; the cross was the method *par excellence* for executing a criminal slave. Seneca seems to imply, then, that patricide occurred frequently in his time, and this could perhaps be accounted for by the nature of the *patria potestas*. However, in recent decades, several scholars, most notably Richard Saller, have asserted that paternal authority caused few problems in everyday life.⁵¹ A first indication that this was the case comes from the demography of the family. Average life expectancy at birth was low and many men married in their (late) twenties, so that the difference in age between a father and a son could be well over thirty years. This meant that many adolescents had no living father. Among the elite, about a third of the children would have lost their father by age fifteen, about half would have no father by age twenty, and this proportion would reach six in ten by age twenty-five.⁵² Among the non-elite, the corresponding proportions were even higher. This implies that many young men were *sui iuris*: they could make free use of their property and they were also free to choose a partner. A second argument is that fathers did not always exercise their *potestas* very strictly. We have already discussed a number of legal restrictions, and the notions of *peculium* and *emancipatio*, which were applied more frequently under the Empire. Social pressures and customs also played a role. It was, for example, a matter of honour for members of the wealthy elite to ensure that their sons were provided with sufficient money to maintain a lifestyle in keeping with their rank. The disinheritance of children was generally frowned upon. And it was not

---

⁴⁹ Evans 1991: 188–9; Rawson 2003: 228 on children left in the care of the mother.
⁵⁰ Seneca, *De clem.* 1, 23.   ⁵¹ Saller 1994: 114–32.
⁵² Saller 1994: 121; cf. Kleijwegt 1991: 60, who used an earlier version of Saller's study. Of course, younger children too faced the possibility of being fatherless. See Huebner and Ratzan 2009 for various studies on being fatherless in antiquity. Imber 2008 has argued that, in the absence of a living father, young people 'learned' to become *patres* by the practice of declamation.

usually in a father's best interest to expel his children from the parental home, as this could destroy his *domus*. Obligingness towards one's children cannot have been unusual in poor families, either, as poor parents must have been aware of their own impending dependency on their offspring in old age: there was, after all, no welfare system to fall back on.[53] And there are other factors that must also have contributed to the low prevalence of intergenerational conflicts: boys sometimes left the parental house at a young age, in order to work as apprentices, for example; and girls often left home early in order to marry. Boys from wealthier families sometimes moved to distant properties of their father's or they went away to perform military service, to study abroad, or to assume an office in a province.[54] Moderation in exerting parental power was praised as the social norm. Moreover, many ancient sources, including letters by Cicero, Fronto, and Pliny, corroborate the view that fathers did not exert their power excessively severely in everyday life. Besides, children also had good reason to gain their father's favour, not least to secure their share of the inheritance.

New research has thus demonstrated that the notion of excessively dominant fathers is exaggerated. But it would be wrong to think that conflicts between fathers and children were rare. Tensions between father (or, as the case may be, mother) and son are ubiquitous in the history of the western family, in all periods and all regions.[55] In Polynesian Samoa, such conflicts occurred much more rarely if ever, as we argued in the first chapter, but family structures were also very different from the western nuclear family. In western society, as in Rome, conflicts between parents and their offspring are the norm, so to speak. Adolescents feel they have to struggle for their position and role within the family. They are keen to acquire a certain status during puberty and to demonstrate that they are no longer infants. By their behaviour, they are able to explore boundaries and familiarise themselves with them. And a certain amount of recalcitrance is also necessary for discovering and developing one's own identity. All this is considered entirely normal and does not usually pose a threat to the family. But in the Roman world familial conflicts may have been more common and more serious than elsewhere as a result of the fact that some adolescents lived very much under the authority of their fathers. There are indications in the sources that some fathers exerted their *potestas* very strictly, including in the *declamationes* by Pseudo-Quintilian, where a rhetor

---

[53] Saller 1994: 122–7. [54] Kleijwegt 1991: 64; Saller 1994: 131.
[55] Dixon 1997: 151 and 1992: 146; Saller 1994: 131; Kleijwegt 1991: 63. This is not sufficient for concluding that youth was an age of crisis, as did Eyben: 1993: 11.

says about a father: 'Frequently you do wrong by your children to show off your *potestas*, as if it were some kind of majesty.'[56] And one can well imagine that one half of those aged twenty, whose fathers were still alive and who were still under his authority, looked with envy at the other half, whose fathers had died and who consequently were free to act as they pleased. This contrast may have induced the former to agitate against paternal power.[57] Many father–son conflicts revolved around the *patria potestas*: money, inheritance, and choice of marriage partner. On the other hand, one might expect the authoritarian aspect of the *patria potestas* to have nipped such conflicts in the bud.

Eyben has published several extensive studies of conflicts between Roman fathers and sons.[58] He has collected many instances from Latin literature, starting with the comedies of Plautus in the second century BC. Once again, it should be noted that, if one considers together all the examples from Rome's long history, a cumulative and hence exaggerated picture emerges, as if the Roman household were a hotbed of conflict. Clearly this is again a very one-sided view. As a counterweight, one may point to the innumerable examples of expressions of parental love towards children, both in literature and in inscriptions, as well as instances of *pietas* of children towards their parents.[59] Seneca's words about *cullei* and crosses are most definitely a gross exaggeration. There is no denying that during the early Empire there were a number of documented cases of or attempts at patricide, but in reality such crimes were very rare. The statement of Seneca rather reflects the enormous fear and abhorrence of the Romans for such a heinous crime, which embodied a reversal of all cherished values of society.[60]

We refrain from discussing all such documented conflicts here and restrict our study to the most important issues and some striking examples. Of all conflicts, those between Cicero (see Fig. 8.2) and his son Marcus and his nephew Quintus are perhaps best known to us, mainly through Cicero's correspondence.[61] The twenty-year-old Marcus studied in Athens. Cicero did not want his son to have less cash to spend than the sons of other wealthy Romans. So he gave him a generous amount of pocket money. But Marcus did not take studying seriously, as we have described in the chapter on student life (see 6.5). He liked to paint the town red. Again and again he

---

[56] Vesley 2003: 161–2; Ps.-Quintilian, *Decl.* 8, 7.   [57] Vesley 2003: 178–9.
[58] Eyben 1977: 526–40; 1991; 1993: 206–13.
[59] Eyben 1991: 116–21; Saller 1994: 102–14; Vesley 2003: 161 n. 6.
[60] Vesley 2003: 176–7. Perhaps a son resorted to patricide and not to a juridical trial because a father and a son could neither sue nor testify against one another: Gaius, *Inst.* 4, 78; *Dig.* 22, 5, 4 (Paul).
[61] Eyben 1977: 535–6; 1991: 139–40; 1993: 210–12; Dixon 1997: 159–61.

8.2 Marcus Tullius Cicero, from Arpinum in Latium, was a lawyer, orator, politician, writer, and philosopher. His most famous achievement is the destruction of Catiline, who had set up a conspiracy (63 BC) against the state. Through his correspondence we know much about the private life of this statesman, who was a Republican at heart. (Capitoline Museum, Rome.)

had to ask his father for additional funds (as appears from his letter to his father's secretary Tiro, cited in the Excursus (see 8.3): Marcus casually mentions his empty purse and, at the end, fleetingly asks Tiro to send him a secretary). Father Cicero initially did not (want to) believe that his son was squandering his money but gradually became aware of the deceit. Circumstances, however, meant that he was unable to take appropriate measures. Cicero was really put through the mill by his nephew Quintus, whom he had largely raised. The young man drove Cicero to despair with his depravity, bad character, and lapses. There were not only problems with money and debt, but there was also the controversial matter of his choice of partner and marriage. The confused political situation of the late Republic added fuel to the flames. The headstrong young man, only sixteen years of age, succeeded in getting an audience with Caesar himself at the beginning of the civil war between Caesar and Pompey (49 BC). He warned him that his uncle's sympathies were with Pompey!

8.2 Conflict

A rich source of information on conflicts are the *declamationes* or *controversiae*, speeches delivered by students at schools of rhetoric (see 6.4). The issues discussed were often imaginary and exaggerated, as we have already explained, but there were also numerous topics with a foundation in real life, as stated explicitly by Quintilian: practical problems concerning money, inheritance, and relations.[62] According to Mark Vesley, more than a third of all *controversiae* deal with father–son conflicts.[63] The speeches often present negative portrayals of the fathers and open father–son hostility. One flashpoint of conflict was money. A young man would have expected a decent *peculium*, but his old man may have been a penny-pincher. Or a father might have opposed the way his son spent the money he had provided. Literary sources confirm that these kinds of conflict also occurred in real life, evidently mainly in wealthy families. A letter by Pliny the Younger addressed to Terentius Junior deals with this issue:[64]

> To Terentius Junior.
>
> Someone reprimanded his son for wasting too much money on horses and dogs. 'And you', said I when the young man had left, 'have you never done anything yourself, that could be rebuked by your father? Have you never done and do you never do anything now, that your son – supposed that he suddenly became your father and you his son – might reprove you with the same severity? Do not all people make mistakes? Does not one person indulge himself in this, another person in that?'
>
> Warned by this example of unreasonable severity, I wrote you this letter because of our mutual love, so that you will never treat your son too harshly and too strictly. Remember he is still a boy and you have been one yourself. Exert, therefore, your rights as a father, remembering that you are a human being and the father of a human. Farewell. (Pliny, *Epist.* 9, 12)

Another money-related topic of conflict was inheritance: many *controversiae* feature sons who have been disinherited by their fathers, for a variety of reasons, including adultery or incest, or an excessively prodigal lifestyle, or the son's refusal to marry the partner his father has selected for him. However, there are indications that in the real world disinheritance was rare. The choice of marriage partner was another common source of conflict, as will be discussed further in a later chapter (see 11.4). The incorrigible Quintus, Cicero's nephew, reported in a conversation with Cicero that his

---

[62] Quintilian, *Inst. or.* 7, 4, 10–11. [63] Vesley 2003.
[64] The theme of the prodigal son, who moreover falls in love with a prostitute, is already present in the early comedies of Plautus (*Mercator*). The father complains about this, sometimes loudly, sometimes merely muttering.

choice of partner had infuriated his maternal uncle Atticus and that his mother too was disgruntled.[65]

Potential sources of conflict were manifold and could extend to very ordinary matters: wild parties or drunkenness, expensive pastimes, love affairs, obsession with shows, aversion to a stepmother or, conversely, too intimate a relationship with her.[66] Not all conflicts escalated. Consultation and mediation by brothers, sisters or other family members not infrequently offered a way out. Romans, in this matter, believed that the best way of preventing undesirable behaviour and conflicts was for parents to set the right example.[67]

What was the best course of action for a father to take in the event of a conflict? If the literary sources are to be believed, fathers tended to be indulgent.[68] The comedies of Plautus and Terence (and particularly in the *Adelphoe*) already feature lenient parents. And the above-cited letter by Pliny contains unequivocal advice. The father of the spendthrift son firmly reprimanded the young man, but took no further action against him and did not exercise his paternal *potestas*. But to Pliny, that was already too harsh. Other authors, like Cicero and Plutarch, also endorsed a 'lenient' approach. They argued that no one should begrudge a young man his pleasures. By accommodating the youngster, worse could be prevented and alienation between child and parents avoided. The occasional misconduct of youths was unmalicious, perfectly normal, and unavoidable; it was simply part and parcel of growing up. Time would remedy such shortcomings. Every young man would eventually calm down and return to the straight and narrow and no doubt become a virtuous citizen. That was the gist of Cicero's plea for Caelius Rufus:

> And, gentlemen judges, in the present days and within the memory of our fathers and ancestors, there have been many very important men and very illustrious citizens, who, after the passions of youth had simmered down, displayed excellent virtues in adulthood. I do not care to mention any of them by name; you will remember them for yourselves . . . If I wished to do so, I could mention many very important and very distinguished men who in their youth were notorious: some for extreme licentiousness, others for extravagant love of luxury, vast debts, prodigality, and lasciviousness. These vices were later covered over by numerous virtues, so that anyone could excuse them on the plea of youth. (Cicero, *Pro Cael.* 18, 43)

---

[65] *Cod. Iust.*: Evans Grubbs 2005a: 93–112. Quintus: Cicero, *Ad Att.* 13, 42 (45 BC).
[66] Problems involving stepmothers are frequently mentioned in *controversiae*; see Vesley 2003: 162–6; cf. also Dixon 1997: 161–4; 1992: 143–4.
[67] Rawson 2003: 221–2; Eyben 1991: 135–6. [68] Eyben 1991: 121–43 and 1993: 16–19.

8.2 Conflict

Cicero certainly seems keen here to clear Caelius' name. The accuser had soiled the character of Caelius by pointing to his liaison with the disreputable lady Clodia (see 3.2) and his youthful misconduct. Cicero responds to this charge with the argument that Caelius, like many other young men, had indeed misbehaved but that he was essentially good-natured.

According to Pliny, a father should think back to his own youth and realise that he had behaved no better than or differently from his son today. Excessively severe parents became rare in the late Republic and the Empire. Livy lamented that, in the Augustan era, the notion of paternal authority had become 'cheap and light'.[69] In the third century AD, the jurist Marcian argued that paternal power should be based on love, not cruelty.[70] But excessive indulgence was also dangerous: it could result in parents bending over backwards to accommodate the whims of their children and not daring to take a strict line even when necessary. Numerous authors from the imperial period warned against both an excessively lenient and an excessively strict attitude on the part of parents. What was required was the golden mean between the two extremes.

These interesting thoughts and words of advice should not, however, tempt historians into making generalisations that are not supported by the sources. Drawing up reliable statistics about violence within the family and in education is a very difficult undertaking, even for our own time.[71] Clearly the relevant data for antiquity are lacking altogether. What we do know is that beatings and other forms of corporal punishment were common practice in Roman society: in the family, at school, at work, towards children, and towards slaves.[72] There are also many sources talking about severe fathers who imposed harsh punishments. It was a generally acknowledged principle that a father had the right to chastise his children physically. Even beyond childhood, young men would not necessarily escape a beating from their father. We know, for example, that the future emperor Otho received a sound thrashing for his nocturnal escapades as a young man.[73] Apart from these real-life testimonies, there was an extensive literature on education describing the new ethos that emerged in the first and second centuries AD in which self-control was highly praised. Moderation was

---

[69] Livy, *Ab Urbe cond.* 26, 22, 15. [70] *Dig.* 48, 9, 5 (Marcian).
[71] Laes 2005: 87–8 on the topic of the beating of children.
[72] On corporal punishment of children and more generally, see Laes 2006a: 123–31 and 2011: 137–47; Saller 1994: 133–53. On the violent nature of Roman society, see Laes 2005: 76–8; Kyle 1998.
[73] Eyben 1991: 121–4 on harsh fathers. See Laes 2005: 79 on the widespread approval of chastisement (for example, Seneca, *De const. sap.* 12, 3). See Suetonius, *Otho* 2, 1 on the young Otho. Other examples of youths who received a thrashing can be found in Quintilian, *Inst. or.* 6, 3, 25.

regarded as a virtue, whilst the unrestrained behaviour of raging fathers was dismissed as a vice. In Christian literature, frequent reference is made to the fear of God and to the Lord of the Old Testament, who punishes sinners. In this context the chastisement of children is often recommended.[74] But for both the pagan and the Christian world it is impossible to draw firm conclusions about the realities of daily life merely on the basis of literature. Just as we should not readily assume that Roman aristocratic education suddenly became less strict during the imperial period, so we should not speculate that Christians treated their children more harshly than did pagans. The preaching of an ideal does not imply that this ideal was readily implemented; some forms of behaviour are very resistant to change, and inevitably the personalities of the parents in question also played an important role.[75]

Thus far we have dealt with conflicts between fathers and children, but conflicts between mothers and children could also arise. Unlike fathers, mothers had no legal power over their offspring, only social and moral authority (*auctoritas*). That authority could be exercised strictly. 'Mothers and teachers correct children not only with words (*verbis*) but also by the whip (*verberibus*)', asserts Cicero.[76] A mother could certainly put pressure on a child if she possessed wealth and the child were financially dependent on her. She could ultimately disinherit a child.[77] Conflicts between mothers and sons are not frequently recorded, except in the imperial family. The nature of our sources may account for this, and perhaps also the fact that many adolescents had already lost their mothers. According to the Coale-Demeny demographic tables, used by Saller (1994), just under three-quarters of adolescents had a mother alive by the age of fifteen, just under two-thirds by the age of twenty, and just over half by the age of twenty-five.

Some mothers were strict, like Atia, the mother of Octavian, the future emperor Augustus. After he had donned the *toga virilis*, she continued to control him meticulously. In the end, Octavian went his own way. Against Atia's advice and even without informing her, he left to raise an army after Caesar's death.[78] Conflicts usually arose when mothers were too ambitious and interfered too much in the lives of their sons, especially in politics.[79] It was normal for a mother to support the career of her son and to offer him advice and assistance. But some pushed things too far and tried to use their

---

[74] De Bruyn 1999. [75] See Laes 2005: 88–9 on discourse and reality.
[76] Cicero, *Tusc. disp.* 3, 64. [77] Dixon 1988: 173 and 189.
[78] Eyben 1991: 123; Dixon 1988: 180–1. [79] Dixon 1988: 175 and 179–87.

8.2 Conflict

sons to achieve their own ambitions. Examples that come to mind are Livia with Tiberius and Agrippina Minor with Nero. In upper-class families too conflicts could arise over the degree of meddling by a mother in the affairs of her sons. Seneca considered himself fortunate with his mother:

> For I know that your heart loves nothing in your beloved ones except themselves. You are not like other mothers who make use of the power of their sons with female lack of self-control. Who realise their ambition through their sons because women cannot hold office. Who spend the patrimony of their sons and at the same time try to obtain it. Who use their eloquence through the mouths of others.
>
> You, on the contrary, have always found the greatest happiness in the well-being of your children, and you have used them not at all. You always set a limit to our generosity, but never to your own. You, a daughter in your father's household, spontaneously gave presents to your wealthy sons. You managed our fortune with such great care as if it belonged to yourself, with such scrupulousness as if it belonged to a stranger. You sparingly used our influence as if you were using the property of a stranger. From our offices nothing accrued to you, except pleasure and the expenses. Your love never looked to self-interest. (Seneca, *Ad Helv.* 14, 2–3)

Among the lower classes, the typical conflicts with mothers over money, conduct, marriage etc. must certainly have occurred, but no confirmation is found in the sources. Conflicts between mothers and daughters are not recorded at all.[80] As a rule, children respected their mothers, though there were no doubt ungrateful adolescents. The young Augustine was rather dismissive towards his mother Monica, rejecting her counsel as prattle.[81]

Little is known about family conflicts in the Greek world of the Hellenistic and imperial periods, as systematic research into this matter has not yet been undertaken. As previously mentioned, a son came of age and gained independence at the age of eighteen. Before then the usual conflicts between parents and children must have occurred. The picture for Egypt is slightly clearer, as some private correspondence on papyrus between parents and children has survived. However, the legal context in Egypt was different from that in the rest of the Greek world. A boy probably came of age when he was only fourteen and the authority of the mother (*materna potestas*) was much greater than elsewhere, particularly in respect of the management of

---

[80] Evans Grubbs 2005a: 118–19 mentions some cases in the Code of Justinian where a mother attempted to dissolve the marriage of her daughter though she had no right to do so, as in *Cod. Iust.* 3, 28, 20. Dixon 1988: 189 cites several instances where a mother refused to pass on an inheritance, as in Valerius Maximus, *Fact. et dict. mem.* 4, 2, 7.
[81] Eyben 1977: 539 and 1993: 213.

property and the contraction of marriage.[82] Bernard Legras has studied several private letters originating in the imperial period, from youngsters to their parents or vice versa. The whole range of emotions is expressed by the writers: from deep respect and love to gross ingratitude and disobedience. One of these letters is addressed by the father Cornelius, a wealthy landowner and Roman citizen, to his 'sweetest son' Hierax. It talks about the expensive clothes he has sent the boy, his monthly allowance, and pocket money. The young man was studying in Alexandria and clearly lived a luxurious life. But the father also had a warning for his son: 'Give your undivided attention to your books, devoting yourself to learning, and then they will bring you profit.' Presumably, the young man had been distracted by the theatre, the shows, and other temptations of the metropolis.[83] Another letter was written by a young man, Antonius Longus, who fared badly in Alexandria. The penitent boy implores his mother Neilous, who lives at Karanis: 'I beg you, mother, be reconciled to me. Well, I know what I have brought on myself. I have received a fitting lesson. I know that I have sinned.' We do not know precisely what the circumstances were, but the source makes it clear that the young man was living in poverty. Perhaps he had turned a deaf ear to his mother when she had tried to warn him about his prodigal and licentious life in the capital.[84]

8.3 Excursus: letter of Marcus Cicero Jr

In 44 BC, Marcus Cicero sent the following letter from Athens to Tiro, secretary to his father M. Tullius Cicero. The latter had told his son to stop seeing his teacher Gorgias, because he felt he had a bad influence on the young man and encouraged him to drink and to behave licentiously. There is no doubt that the letter was also intended for the father. The young Cicero makes use in his letter of several Greek words, which we have rendered in French.[85]

> Cicero Junior greets his beloved Tiro.
> 1 I was anxiously expecting your letter-carriers every day; at last they arrived, forty-five days after they left your home. Their arrival rejoiced me. The letter of my most kind and very dear father gave me very great pleasure. But your most agreeable letter put a crown to my joy. I no longer regret having made a break in our correspondence, but rather rejoice at it, since

---

[82] Age of majority in the imperial period: Legras 1999: 252–3; *materna potestas*: Modrzejewski 1955: 355–7.
[83] *P. Oxy.* III 531 (second century AD); see Legras 1999: 43–6; Eyben 1991: 141–2.
[84] *BGU* III 846 (second century AD); Hunt and Edgar 1970: 316–19 no. 120; see Legras 1999: 50–1.
[85] Translations are provided by Shackleton Bailey 2001: 124–31 (Letter 337) and Joyal, McDougall, and Yardley 2009: 180–1 no. 8.15.

8.3 Excursus: letter of Marcus Cicero Jr

the fact that my letters fell silent has brought me this precious example of your kind nature. I am really delighted that you have accepted my apologies without hesitation.

2 I have no doubt that you are pleased, my dearest Tiro, with the rumours that reach you about me, and that they correspond with what you wished to hear. I shall make every effort to ensure that this tiny new image of mine gets better every day. Therefore, you may with full confidence fulfil your promise to be my publicity agent. For the mistakes of my youth have caused me so much grief and agony that I am not only tormented when I think of what I have done, but also when I hear it talked about. I know very well that you have had your share in worry and grief, and I am not surprised at it. For you wanted all things to go successfully for me, not only for my sake but for yours too, because I have always wished that you should have a part in any prosperity of mine.

3 Since I caused you grief at that time, I shall now make sure that I will give you double joy. I must tell you that Cratippus and I are very close; I am not so much like his pupil but rather like his son. I enjoy attending his lectures and I am quite delighted by his charming personality. I spend whole days with him and often part of the night, for I beg him to dine with me as often as possible. Now that we have become intimate, he often drops in on us unexpectedly, while we are at dinner, and he puts off the austere philosopher and jokes with us in the most genial way. You must try to meet him as soon as possible, Tiro, a man so agreeable and so excellent.

4 As for Bruttius, what can I say? There is never a moment I let him out of my sight. He lives a simple and austere life; yet his company is very pleasant. For wit is not banished from our literary *discussions* and daily researches. I have hired a lodging for him in the neighbourhood and I help him as well as I can out of my meagre funds.

6 As to what you write about Gorgias, he was indeed useful to me in declamation practice. But I placed my father's order above all other considerations. He had written to me *en termes précis* to get rid of Gorgias at once. I did not want to delay for fear my excessive *affection* might raise suspicion with my father. It also came to my mind that it is not a light thing for me to judge my father's judgement.

8 I thank you for attending to my commissions. But I ask you to send a secretary to me as soon as possible, preferably a Greek. For I have a lot of trouble in writing out my notes. Above all, take care of your health, so that we may have some *exercices littéraires* together. I commend Antherus to you. Farewell. (Cicero, *Ad fam.* 16, 21 (letter 337))

CHAPTER 9

Youths in public office

Around the age of fifteen, Roman boys assumed the adult toga. But did this entail that they immediately moved on to adult life and to positions of political and administrative responsibility? Any attempt to answer this question must take into account the different social groups in society: the senators, who usually resided in Rome, the knights, who lived in Rome and in the principal provincial cities, and the members of the municipal elites in innumerable other towns. Our focus is on the period of the Principate. We shall not discuss the extraordinary appointments of the late Republic, like that of Octavian, the later emperor Augustus, to the consulate when he was around twenty. Nor will we consider the public role of children from the imperial family, who occasionally participated in religious or military parades, distributions or banquets, and acted as priests and magistrates. Neither will we pay attention to children on the imperial throne like Alexander Severus, who in the early third century AD became emperor at the tender age of thirteen. Their role was primarily determined by dynastic considerations and, moreover, only a few cases are involved, although their public activities may nevertheless have served as an example.

9.1 Youths in central government: senators and equestrians

The senatorial class was a very select group: it comprised two to three thousand individuals in an empire of fifty to eighty million people. The career of a senator was subject to rules on minimum ages. At the beginning of the second century BC, in 180 BC, the *Lex Villia annalis* was passed. This law fixed a minimum age for (non-specified) public offices of the *cursus honorum*. Henceforth, one was eligible for election as an *aedilis* from the age of thirty-six onwards, as a praetor from thirty-nine, and as a consul from forty-two. The office of quaestor, which at the time was not yet a compulsory part of the career path, could presumably be held from the age of twenty-seven, ten years after the beginning of military service. In 81 BC,

Sulla raised the minimum age of the quaestorship to thirty, after which Augustus lowered it to twenty-five. The reason why the *Lex Villia* was passed is unclear. Cicero asserted that it had been implemented 'out of fear of the temerity of the youth' (*adulescentiae temeritas*),[1] but the term *adulescentia* does not point to a specific age group. The law would in any case always remain in force. Maecenas made the following remark to the emperor Augustus in a fictitious conversation reported by Cassius Dio:

> We must register young men as knights when they become eighteen years old, because at that age physical fitness and mental capability can best be discerned. We must enrol them in the senate when they are twenty-five years. For is it not outrageous and dangerous to entrust the public affairs to men who are younger (than twenty-five), when we do not entrust our private affairs to anyone before that age? After they have served as quaestors and *aediles* and tribunes, they can become praetors when they have reached the age of thirty. (Cassius Dio, *Hist. Rom.* 52, 20, 1)

The fixing of the legal minimum ages – such that, after 180 BC, a senatorial son who wanted to embark on a political career had to wait until he reached the age of twenty-seven, then the age of thirty and, under the Principate, the age of twenty-five – led Emiel Eyben to assert that the young man was not fully accepted as an adult before that age. This attitude was, in his view, one of the factors that made Roman society into one that gave youths the space to be young. Young people lived in a no man's land, a void without responsibility, a *Jugendraum* in which they could do as they pleased.[2] Harry Pleket objects that the exclusion from magistracies was not as rigid as appears at first sight.[3] Indeed, from the reign of Augustus the required age for the quaestorship was twenty-five, but prior to that age, a senatorial youth aged seventeen and older could hold junior positions, including those of the vigintivirate and a military command. The vigintivirate encompassed four different positions, among which were the *quattuorviri* for the building of roads and the *decemviri* who judged lawsuits. The military command was that of military tribune, staff officer in a legion. Eyben in turn points out that only a limited number of senatorial sons could hold these positions: no more than twenty *vigintiviri* and about thirty military tribunes (after the death of Augustus just thirty-three legions were maintained). Yet there were

---

[1] Cicero, *Phil.* 5, 17, 47.
[2] Eyben 1977: 92, 129 and 1993: 7–9, 27. Evans and Kleijwegt 1992: 187–8 object that the *Lex Villia* was probably no more than a reflection of how things were in reality and did not introduce a new minimum age for the quaestorship. Hence there is, in their view, no reason to assume the creation of a new life phase, i.e. adolescence, at the beginning of the second century BC.
[3] Pleket 1979: 175–6, followed by Kleijwegt 1991: 187–98.

still not always enough candidates, even though the junior posts were made compulsory in 13 BC for those who wished to embark on a senatorial career. The average age of the youngsters who held the positions was generally around twenty. So clearly a *Jugendraum* of about five years did exist. Eyben further remarks that the junior positions were in fact rather unimportant. The real threshold of acceptance into the adult world was the attainment of the quaestorship and entrance into the senate at the age of twenty-five (under the Principate). Eyben stands firmly by his theory of a *Jugendraum* of ten years, between the ages of fifteen and twenty-five.[4] However, it is evident that he plays down too much the real value of the junior positions.[5]

Apart from the junior positions, other activities were open to senatorial sons, besides a few official and semi-official posts.[6] Sons often accompanied their fathers when they were appointed as governor of a province. Marcus and Quintus, Cicero's son and nephew, then aged around fifteen, thus followed Cicero to Cilicia (in southern Asia Minor) after his appointment as governor.[7] Sons of senators could also become patrons of a city. They were expected to look after the interests of the city at a higher political or administrative level and to confer financial benefactions. Pliny the Younger, for example, became patron of the small town of Tifernum Tiberinum when he was merely a boy (*puer*).[8] Some senatorial sons served in Rome as priests, for example in the college of the Salii or the Fratres Arvales.[9] They sometimes held office and possibly religious positions in their native city. Inscriptions show that three sons of senators held the office of *curator rei publicae* before the quaestorship; this may have been an appointment in support of cities facing financial difficulties.[10] From the reign of the emperor Augustus, it had become common practice for sons of senators who had begun to wear the adult toga to attend meetings of the senate. Known as *praetextati*, they could of course neither speak nor vote. But, as with the above-mentioned positions, it prepared the young men for a senatorial career; these positions offered them an opportunity to engage in

---

[4] Eyben 1981a: 335–7, 350.
[5] Evans and Kleijwegt 1992: 191; Christes 1998: 145. Kleijwegt 1991: 192 further objects that, for the period after Augustus, there are no indications of a shortage of candidates for junior functions and membership of the senate.
[6] Kleijwegt 1991: 193–8; Laes 2004a: 153–4 and 2011: 172–3. Christes 1998: 145 moreover notes for the Republican period that young men could act as patrons in private lawsuits.
[7] Kleijwegt 1991: 193–4. On Marcus and Quintus, see Garrido Bozic 1951: 13–16.
[8] Kleijwegt 1991: 196–7. For Pliny as a patron: Pliny, *Epist.* 4, 1, 4.
[9] On priests in Rome, see Kleijwegt 1991: 195–6. L. Nonius Quintilianus, for example, was augur and Salius Palatinus (the Salii were an ancient priestly order), and died at the age of twenty-four: *CIL* IX 4855.
[10] Kleijwegt 1991: 197–8.

meaningful, sometimes even responsible, activities before entering the senate. The young men were trained as aristocrats and learned the rules of political life.[11]

Ranked just below the senatorial class were the knights (*equites*). Their number is estimated at between ten and twenty thousand. The minimum age was probably seventeen, corresponding with the age at which military service started in ancient times (following the reforms of King Servius Tullius, sixth century BC). But from the middle of the first century AD, this age restriction was not always applied. There are known examples of children who were elevated to the knighthood at the ages of two, four, five, eight, etc. In total, some twenty knights younger than fifteen are recorded in and outside Rome.[12] The very young age of the knights indicates that their promotion was primarily a matter of prestige. Knighthood was bestowed on children as a reward for the extraordinary merits of their fathers, often within the military (for example as a centurion), or in order to honour their families for their prominent role in government and their splendid benefits. Often the father was not qualified for promotion himself because he was a freedman or an immediate descendant thereof. Similar considerations must have come into play in the elevation of adolescents to knighthoods. M. Kleijwegt has collected twenty-two attestations of knights aged between fifteen and twenty-five: twelve aged between sixteen and twenty and ten aged between twenty-one and twenty-five.[13]

Knights could pursue an equestrian career, though most were so-called 'honorary knights' who did not. They were simply satisfied with the very high prestige they had gained and which placed them at the top of the local elite. Their status was reflected in their dress, in titles, in honorary seats, and so on. In the town of Telesia in central Italy, a young knight passed away; his epitaph mentions not a single position, neither in his native city nor in central government:

> To the Spirits of the Dead. For Publius Lalius Gentianus Victor, Roman knight, a young man of unusual integrity and wisdom. Publius Lalius Modestus and Telesinia Crispinilla, his very sad and loving parents, (made this grave) for their dearest son. He lived twenty-one years, eleven months, eighteen days. (*CIL* IX 2228)

Those who did embark on an equestrian career started off as officers in the army. They were on average thirty-six years old. Among the roughly 2,400

---

[11] On *praetextati*, see Suetonius, *Aug.* 38, 2. [12] Laes 2004a: 154–7 and 2011: 173–4.
[13] Kleijwegt 1991: 209–19. The number of records may have increased slightly after this publication.

equestrian officers known to us, there were one fourteen-year-old boy and eight adolescents aged between fifteen and twenty.[14] The youngest of the latter group were eighteen and nineteen years old. One such example comes from Rome: Marcus Macrinius Avitus Catonius Vindex must have held the first of the *tres militiae*, i.e. the position of prefect of a cohort (500 infantrymen) at between the ages of eighteen and twenty.[15] His whirlwind career was presumably due to the fact that his father was a prefect of the imperial guard. Another example comes from Pisa (northern Italy):[16]

> To the Spirits of the Dead. Caius Saturius Secundus, son of Lucius Saturius Picens who was *primuspilus*, from the Fabia tribe, honoured with an *equus publicus* (horse from the state), judge in the five *decuriae*, prefect of the second cohort of the Astyrii, augur, patron of the *colonia* of the Asculani. He lived nineteen years and twenty-seven days. The father made (this grave) for his most loving son. (*CIL* XI 1437; *InscrIt* VII, 1, 124)

The father of Secundus held the high-ranking position of *primuspilus*, the first centurion of a legion. Perhaps the young man's military qualities were in his genes, so to speak, though there is no proof of his military excellence prior to his promotion to the knighthood.[17] The same holds for the other young knights, who were for the most part over twenty and appointed as prefects of a cohort.[18] These adolescents may actually have performed the duties of an officer, but their number was extremely small, as previously mentioned. In the assignment to positions of responsibility, personal qualities, age, and experience all played a major role.

Apart from all equestrian functions, there was one occasion on which knights had to appear in public, namely the annual parade in Rome on 15 July in the presence of the emperor. Unfortunately little is known about this event. We do not know whether all knights paraded, whether they came

---

[14] Kleijwegt 1991: 210–12.
[15] *CIL* VI 1449 (*RHP* I 100; *IDRE* I 17); cf. Devijver 1977, 1987, and 1993, no. M 4, from Rome (second century AD).
[16] Cf. Devijver 1977, 1987, and 1993, no. S 11, from the end of the second century AD. For the ages of these equestrian officers, see Devijver 1974.
[17] Laes 2004a: 155–6.
[18] L. Pompeius Marcellinus, aged twenty-three, was *tribunus cohortis* (*CIL* III 7131; *I. Ephesos* VI 2305b; cf. Devijver 1977 and 1987, no. P 60, from the second century AD?); this was the second *militia* (commander of a cohort of 1,000 infantrymen). He had presumably been appointed to the first *militia* about three years earlier. T. Crustidius Briso was nineteen years old and *praefectus equitum* (*CIL* VI 3516; cf. Devijver 1976, no. C 257, from the first half of the first century AD); this was the third *militia* (commander of a group of 500 cavalrymen). Possibly he was appointed directly to this office, as was sometimes done by Augustus (see Suetonius, *Aug.* 38). The appointment of P. Aelius Tiro from Praeneste, who was similarly appointed *praefectus equitum* by the emperor Commodus at the age of fourteen, must have been honorific (*CIL* XIV 2947, IX 499.1; cf. Devijver 1976, no. A 66).

over from the provinces, etc. We do possess a few grave monuments, though, with reliefs depicting very young horsemen participating in such a parade. Inscriptions tell us that the boys died at the age of eleven, thirteen, and fifteen. It is possible that the young children had participated in the parade together with the adult knights, and that the parents of the deceased youths put on the tomb the image of this event, the only significant deed of their lives.[19] But it is not unlikely that the reliefs had a merely symbolic meaning: they referred to the boys' potential, to the careers they might have pursued had they lived longer.

Since most knights did not embark on an equestrian career, there was for the majority no waiting period prior to a position of responsibility. In the case of youthful knights, it is more relevant to ask whether they could hold governmental and religious offices in their native city, just like other youths from the municipal elite. This matter is discussed in further detail below. Apart from holding municipal offices, young knights could act as patrons of their home cities, just like the sons of senators.[20]

9.2 Youths in municipal office

In the Greek East

As explained in Chapter 7.1, on associations of youths, Harry Pleket and Marc Kleijwegt argue that elite young men would have completed their education, the *ephebeia*, by the age of fifteen or sixteen. From that age on, they were considered adults and began to participate in the administration of their cities. Honorary and funerary inscriptions indeed identify adolescents as civic officials in the cities of the Greek world. One such example is the inscription for M. Aurelius Magas from the small Lycian city of Bubon (in southern Asia Minor):

> The council and the people of the city of Bubon honoured with appropriate honours and with the erection of a statue Mar(cus) Aur(elius) Magas, son of Magas III, great-great-grandson of Troilos, citizen of Bubon, an illustrious young man who served as *hypophylax* and *archiphylax* of the very glorious Lycian League, dead at the age of eighteen, a relative of senators and consuls, a descendant of Lyciarchs without exception, outstanding by his education ... (*I. Bubon* 14 (*Boubon* 24); third century AD)[21]

---

[19] Veyne 1960. [20] Kleijwegt 1991: 218.
[21] See also Kokkinia 2007: 171–4 (*AnÉp* (2007) 1525, *Boubon* 25), an almost identical honorary inscription for the same Magas.

Magas clearly belonged to a very prominent family. He had been a *hypophylax* and *archiphylax* of the Lycian League, probably from the age of fifteen or sixteen, since he died at eighteen. According to Pleket and Kleijwegt, Magas held these offices, which in their view were positions of responsibility with the police, independently from either his father or any other adult. The holding of magistracies and councillorships by youths was, in their view, a common and institutionalised phenomenon in the cities of the East during the Hellenistic and Roman periods.[22]

The cities of the East were governed during the Hellenistic and Roman periods by an elite of wealthy aristocratic families. They held the annual government appointments, like those of *archon* or *strategos* (the highest magistrate), *grammateus* (secretary), and *agoranomos* (superintendent of the market), and sat on the city council (*boule*) for life as *bouleutai*. These were all honourable offices, referred to as *archai* (*honores* in the legal Roman terminology), and requiring personal service. In addition, there were also liturgies (*leitourgiai*; *munera* in the legal Roman terminology), which in principle entailed only a financial commitment. This distinction persisted into the imperial period, though it had become blurred from the Hellenistic period onwards. Liturgies, on the one hand, had become minor offices, elective and annual. The most important among these offices were those of gymnasiarch (the official in charge of the gymnasium), and agonothetes (organiser of games and festivals). Magistracies, on the other hand, had acquired a liturgical significance, because they now also required the magistrates in question to spend money out of their own pockets. In other words, the distinction between the two kinds of service was not always clear.

Recently several new studies of children and adolescents as magistrates have been published.[23] Let us briefly consider the most important findings.

A rich source of information lies in the legal provisions laying down the age limits for magistrates and councillors, which applied in the East and West alike.[24] These are known to us through a number of municipal laws from the West dating from the first century BC onwards and through the late Roman juridical corpora, the *Digest* and the *Theodosian Code*. We will not discuss the evidence in detail, but the overall principle is clear and unambiguous for the imperial period: young men who had not yet taken up the adult toga (i.e. aged less than about fifteen) were not permitted to perform public services of any kind whatsoever. For adolescents who had donned the male toga, a distinction was made between positions requiring

---

[22] Pleket 1979: 173–4; Kleijwegt 1991: 221, 252. [23] Horster 1996; Laes 2004a; Strubbe 2005.
[24] Horster 1996: 228–30; Laes 2004a: 158–63; Strubbe 2005: 90–1; Laes 2011: 174–7.

9.2 Youths in municipal office

only monetary service (*munera patrimonii*, liturgies) and positions also involving personal service (*munera personalia, honores*). The laws provided that young men under the age of twenty-five were permitted to hold the former type of offices (starting from the age of fifteen) but not the latter type (as magistrates, councillors). This is stated quite clearly in the *Digest*:

> Minors must not be admitted to municipal government before they turn twenty-five, nor to public duties which are not financial, nor to honourable offices. As a consequence they are not elected members of the council, and if they ever are, they do not give a vote in the meeting of the council. (*Dig.* 50, 4, 8 (Ulpian))[25]

The *Digest* also reveals that the laws were not always obeyed. Mention is made of persons under the age of twenty-five who were appointed as councillors. It appears that exceptions were possible: cities could issue their own regulations, making individuals under the age of twenty-five eligible for election to positions as holders of *munera* or *honores*. Under-25s could be appointed as councillors if there were good grounds for doing so, for example in cases of emergency. In other instances, ancient local traditions had to be respected. For the cities of Bithynia (in northern Asia Minor), Augustus proclaimed by edict that minor offices could be held from the age of twenty-two.[26] Possibly this regulation applied to other provinces in the East as well.

Only five youths aged between fifteen and twenty-five (or twenty-two) or of the age of ephebes (around sixteen) are recorded with certainty as magistrates. In addition, there are five inscriptions using rather vague terminology (*pais, en paidi* or similar) so that it is unclear whether the magistrate was a child or an adolescent.[27] To sum up, over a period of six centuries and across a very large geographical area, there are ten such cases at

---

[25] The text goes on to say that the twenty-fifth year is considered to have been completed as soon as it has begun, but only in relation to honourable offices and if nothing belonging to the city patrimony is entrusted to the officeholder. So, in certain cases, a young man just over twenty-four years of age would have been eligible to hold office. But other legal texts do not mention this rule; twenty-five years seems the norm. *Dig.* 36, 1, 76, 1 (Paul) mentions the same rule of exemption from municipal public duties, decreed by the emperor Hadrian.

[26] Pliny, *Epist.* 10, 79 and 80.

[27] Strubbe 2005: 92 ff. no. 4 (fifteen–sixteen years old), no. 5 (from eighteen years onwards), nos. 6–7 (before the age permitted by law, twenty-five or twenty-two years), no. 12 (an ephebe). The following numbers are dubious: nos. 8–11 (*paides*: children or youngsters; the term is vague: see Laes 2004a: 166, 174 but see below in the context of priesthoods) and no. 13 (gymnasiarch? 'since the first age'). Most of these sources date from the imperial period. See also Laes 2011: 177–9. In Strubbe 2005: 106 no. 13, T. Flavius Apollinarius is recorded as gymnasiarch *apo protes helikias* (since the first age/stage of life). Strubbe has argued that this phrase is synonymous with *apo paidos helikias* (since the age of childhood), and that the phrases may refer only vaguely to the period of youth. However, *apo protes helikias*

the most. It is therefore unfounded to speak of an institutional phenomenon, as do Pleket and Kleijwegt. On the contrary, there was a great reluctance to entrust honourable offices and liturgies to young people – even greater than to do so to women, who were strictly forbidden by law to hold any office whatsoever but nonetheless quite often served as gymnasiarchs, as *agonothetai*, and as eponymous magistrates (giving their name to the year).

All youngsters who held office belonged to very noble and extremely wealthy families. M. Aurelius Magas is a good example (see above), but so too is Demetrius, son of Hermapias, at Arneae in Lycia:

> Demetrius, son of Hermapias, son of Hermapias, son of Hermadatus, a man originating from the foremost of the (Lycian) League, noble by descent, became *dekaprotos* at the age of eighteen years. He had been *eikosaprotos* since the time *eikosaprotoi* were first appointed. (He passed away) at the age of eighty-six years, when Timarchus was the high priest of the emperor cult . . . (*TAM* II 765, from the beginning of the reign of Hadrian)

The *dekaprotoi* were a group of ten very wealthy citizens who were responsible for the collection of taxes due to Rome. If there was a shortfall, they had to pay the missing amount out of their own pockets. Under the reign of Hadrian, before AD 124, the group in the Lycian cities was extended to twenty citizens, the *eikosaprotoi*. From the second century AD, they were probably also responsible for monitoring all civic finances; in other words, they had to oversee the collection of the set amount of funds into the city treasury. The office was a heavy financial burden: young Demetrius was expected to spend large amounts of money. This was the case with most offices held by adolescent magistrates. Their nature was financial and liturgical, as permitted under Roman law, although even so it was rare for them to be held by youngsters. Magas from Bubon had held the positions of *hypo-* and *archiphylax* of the Lycian League. These were not police-related, as has been contended by some, but offices concerned with the collection of taxes due by the federal Lycian League to the Roman government, very similar to the municipal position of *dekaprotos*.[28] Two other adolescents are known to have held magistracies before the legally permissible age at Aphrodisias; in one of these cases, explicit reference is made to the *argyrotameia*, the office of treasurer. At Apollonis in Lydia, an ephebe served as gymnasiarch, also an expensive position to hold. The five remaining young

---

may be understood to mean 'from early manhood'; cf. Mitchell and French 2012 no. 306. In this interpretation, no. 13 should be omitted from Strubbe's list, so that the number of young magistrates drops to nine cases.

[28] Strubbe 2005: 98 with references; Laes 2011: 177–8.

magistrates (children or adolescents) were gymnasiarchs (at Stratonicia and Aphrodisias in Caria, and at Calindoea in Macedonia), agonothete (at Thyatira in Lydia) and ephebarch (at Philadelphia in Lydia). The latter office was merely a low-ranking function on the municipal career ladder or an office within the gymnasium. Young people did not hold positions of economic responsibility, such as *agoranomos* (overseer of the market and the food supply) or *sitones* (purchaser of grain for the state) or involving policing (*eirenarches*). They did not act as eponymous magistrates and did not hold governmental offices such as *grammateus* (secretary). In short, they were not entrusted with real governmental responsibility but were appointed because of their wealth – or rather: the wealth of their fathers and families – which would thus come to benefit the city. We do not know whether the young men performed the tasks of their offices autonomously or whether their fathers acted in their place. This will most likely have depended on their age, experience, and so on. The young men will most likely also have been assisted by colleagues and by a professional staff of assistants or public slaves. In the city of Apollonis in Lydia, an ephebe was elected as gymnasiarch and, unlike in other years, a hypogymnasiarch was appointed concurrently. No doubt he was supposed to assist that year's young gymnasiarch.[29] The reasons why the wealth of families was sometimes made available to the cities through youngsters rather than adults will be discussed later when we consider young magistrates in the Latin West.

What about other public functions, memberships of city councils and priesthoods, which were also magistracies and a regular part of a municipal career? Nowhere in the Greek world are youths recorded as councillors.[30] In some places, they are attested as priests. A frequently cited example of a young priest comes from the Carian city of Stratonicia (in south-western Asia Minor):

> Thrason Leon, son of Hierocles, from Hieracome, (died) at the age of (. .) years. He was appointed to the high priesthood when he was ten, the gymnasiarchy when he was eleven, the priesthood of the greatest god Zeus Panamaros when he was sixteen, the priesthood of Zeus Chrysaoreios Propator when he was twenty, and the office of *sitones*, for which they (= Thrason Leon and his wife) had promised to the city 10,000 *denarii* as a gift... (*I. Stratonikeia* II 667, second century AD)

The question arises whether it was common for youths to hold religious office. In fact, we have found only a very small number of records. Apart

---

[29] *TAM* v, 2, 1203 from the first century BC; Strubbe 2005: 102 no. 12.
[30] Laes 2004a: 173; Strubbe 2005: 103, 109 *contra* Kleijwegt 1991: 272.

from Thrason Leon, who served as a priest first as a ten-year-old, then as an adolescent of between sixteen and twenty, we know of a priestess to the Egyptian goddess Isis at Megalopolis (Laconia) who was fifteen, and of a priest (to a local deity?) who died at the age of eighteen in the Lydian countryside near the city of Collyda (in north-east Lydia).[31] Besides these records, there are several inscriptions in rather vague terminology (*pais, en paidi*) so that it is unclear whether the priest was a child or an adolescent, as in the case of magistracies.[32] Perhaps these terms should be taken literally as 'child, in childhood', because children, before reaching puberty, were considered by the Greeks and Romans to be pure and innocent. They stood at the fringe of society. For this reason, they were seen to be closer to the gods and therefore made good priests.[33] We further know of some sacred laws concerning the sale of priesthoods stipulating that the buyer (male or female) should not be younger than respectively ten, fourteen or twenty years. At Chalcedon, it is explicitly stated that the buyer may be a child (*pais*).[34] Hence it was possible for adolescents to buy and hold priesthoods, though no such event is recorded. Since adolescents only rarely pursued a municipal career, it is not surprising that they are seldom recorded as priests. If they did hold a religious function, like Thrason Leon, then their duties were chiefly ceremonial and of a liturgical nature. They were primarily expected to spend lavishly. We know that Thrason Leon belonged to a very prominent and no doubt very wealthy family: at one point, his father Hierocles was sent as an ambassador to the emperor in Rome.[35]

There is a great difference between young people and women when it comes to priesthoods: in the cities of the Hellenistic and Roman periods, women very frequently acted as priestesses, often together with their husbands.[36]

---

[31] *GV* 1163 (*GG* 317) from the second to third century AD and *TAM* v, 1, 432 (Samama 2003 no. 237) from AD 214/215. Note that neither priesthood was part of a regular municipal career. The priest from Collyda is referred to as *hiereus neoteros* ('the younger priest'), just like his relative Dionysius who died at the age of ten (*TAM* v, 1, 433 from AD 183/184). This seems to imply that an older priest was appointed alongside them. We have found no other unambiguous records in the existing collections. The text from Damascus (Laes 2004a: 172, no. 9; *GV* 1047; *GG* 421; *SGO* IV 20/17/02) is not clear: the temporal relation between the high priesthood and the shaving of the first beard is uncertain.

[32] See the collection by Laes 2004a: 172 Table 7 nos. 4–7. One may add: *I. Stratonikeia* 1 239; *IGBulg* III 1572 from Traiana Augusta.

[33] Laes and Strubbe 2006: 120–1.

[34] Dmitriev 2005: 52–3: from Cos, Miletus. For Chalcedon, see *Syll.*³ 369.

[35] Pleket 1979: 191 n. 4; Kleijwegt 1991: 129.

[36] By way of comparison: Kirbihler 1994: 55–72 and van Bremen 1996: 306–47 almost simultaneously drew up a list of around 220 women who performed the offices of magistrates, liturgists, and/or priests in Asia Minor and adjacent islands. These priesthoods were also at the provincial level.

9.2 Youths in municipal office

Although adolescents held public office only rarely, they were from an early age frequently associated with the city government in other ways. This is recorded from the Hellenistic period.[37] A father often performed a magistracy on behalf of his son. The father would carry out all the tasks and pay all the expenses, but the honour of the office went to the son, as if he had held it independently. Numerous honorary decrees mention benefactors who had devoted themselves or been useful to their cities 'from their earliest youth', or who, as a *pais* or an ephebe, had, for example, donated money or lent money interest free. The money would, of course, have been the father's. For example, the ephebe Caninius Severus from Rhodes presented 12 *denarii* to each citizen and 24 *denarii* to the councillors, no doubt from his father's pocket.[38] Fathers and even grandparents associated their children and grandchildren with their benefactions and made them jointly with them, so to speak. A child or a young man often promised to hold an office later, or parents made the promise in the name of their son. In many cases, the office in question was exactly the same as that held previously by the father and/or grandfather. Another type of association is found with the *patrobouloi*. This title was borne by the sons of notable families from the late second century AD and indicated that they were destined to succeed their fathers on the council. They often kept the title after doing so, which highlighted the heredity of important offices within elite families. Presumably the young men would already have become familiarised with the work of the council before entering it.[39]

Children and adolescents from elite families in the Greek cities in the East were expected to follow in their ancestors' footsteps. They were considered a link in the familial chain of successive generations of magistrates and benefactors. This is also attested by the so-called consolation decrees. These are official decrees issued by the council and/or the popular assembly on the occasion of the (premature) death of a citizen, male or female, young or old, with the aim of honouring the deceased and consoling the relatives.[40] They date from the imperial period and are found across the Greek world, but most commonly in Caria (in south-west Asia Minor). The decrees often mention that the entire city was distressed at the loss because it had been deprived of the hope that the young man would one day become

---

[37] Kleijwegt 1991: 225–47; Strubbe 2005: 105–6; Dmitriev 2005: 161–3. For the presumed involvement of youths in city government from an early age, as expressed by the phrase *apo protes helikias* (records collected by Strubbe 2005: 105 n. 64), see n. 27 above.
[38] *IGR* IV 1127 from the second century AD.
[39] Kleijwegt 1991: 263–72; Laes 2004a: 173; Strubbe 2005: 106.
[40] Strubbe 1998: 59–75 with earlier literature and all sources.

an office-holder and a benefactor to the community. In other words, the city had hoped that the young man would continue the noble conduct of his meritorious ancestors. In some cases, the decrees ascribed virtues to the youngsters that were actually typical of adult aristocrats. The eighteen-year-old Titus Statilius Lamprias from Epidaurus was praised in an Athenian consolation decree as a 'self-restrained and wise young man, adorned with all virtues'. In another example from Sparta, that same Lamprias is lavishly praised because 'through his physical beauty and through the virtues of his soul he transcended the measure of his age ... In matters of education, wisdom, acuity, judgement, and piety towards his parents, he gave perfect examples of his excellence in everything.'[41] This reflected society's ideals, offered comfort to the bereaved, and provided a model of desirable conduct for other youths. Whether such laudations actually reflected how these youngsters felt inside is an unanswerable question. There is no evidence that, when it came to their mental development, they were truly small adults.

In the Latin West

Cities in Italy and in the Latin West were governed during the imperial period by a small group of wealthy aristocratic families, just as in the Greek East. The aristocrats held the municipal magistracies, including those of *aedilis* and *duumvir* (the highest magistrates). They also sat on the city council, the *curia*, for life. It was customary for the council itself to elect new *decuriones* from the group of the former magistrates. In the imperial period, youths from aristocratic families sometimes held these offices within city governments.

From the West, particularly Spain, several municipal laws are known from the first century BC onwards fixing minimum ages for city officials. Under the Principate, this age was, as a rule, set at twenty-five for magistrates and councillors. Again, though, the rules were not always obeyed.

When we study the ancient sources, mainly honorary and funerary inscriptions, we find evidence in the Latin West for over twenty-five magistrates under the age of twenty-five.[42] Among them are four teenagers. The three youngest were seventeen years old, and, insofar as the inscriptions

---

[41] Strubbe 1998: 60 no. 1 (*c.* AD 38–48): *IG* IV² 84, lines 26–8; *SEG* XXXV (1985) 305, lines 10–13.
[42] Kleijwegt 1991: 273–334 with tables on pp. 318–19 and 325; Laes 2004a: 176–8 and 2011: 180–4. The table in Kleijwegt 1991 p. 325 contains four magistrates aged twenty-five who in fact do not belong there. The Romans counted the years as we do: a person turns twenty-five after having completed his or her twenty-fifth year of life. For young men just over twenty-four, see n. 25 above.

are datable, they all lived in the second century AD.[43] The largest group were between twenty and twenty-five years of age. They usually held the office of *aedilis*. A grave inscription from Barcino, present-day Barcelona in Spain, provides a good example:

> Domitia Lucilia, the mother, (made this grave) for her dearest son L. Porcius Celer, son of Lucius, from the tribe Galeria, seventeen years old, *aedilis* of Barcino. (This) Place allocated by decree of the town councillors. (*AnÉp* (1972) 297; *IRC* IV 71, second century AD)

Six of the twenty-five young magistrates were also *decuriones* at some point between the ages of twenty and twenty-five. Apart from these examples, well over fifty councillors under twenty-five are attested without a magistracy being recorded. About half of these youngsters were under the age of fifteen, and around thirty were between fifteen and twenty-five.[44] Several *decuriones* were very young indeed: just four, five or six years old. Here, we note a major difference with the Greek East, where no young councillors are recorded. The following grave inscription comes from Beneventum in southern Italy:

> For Numerius Afinius Hierax, son of Numerius, from the tribe Palatina, *decurio* at Beneventum, who lived nineteen years and thirty-one days. Numerius Afinius Apulus and Afinia Acte, his parents, in deep grief, erected this grave. (*CIL* IX 1638, second century AD)

According to Kleijwegt, the phenomenon of under-age youths on city councils was a general one in the West. Marietta Horster objects that records of child *decuriones* are often concentrated in particular cities (especially in the third century), suggesting that these places had developed a tradition of their own. While the participation of youths in councils is not infrequently recorded, it was not considered the norm in legal texts.[45] Moreover, one can rightly ask what the participation of youths meant in practice. The answer is: probably very little. Although the municipal council was, of course, the central government of a city, the office of a young councillor was no doubt merely ceremonial. City councils in the West usually consisted of a hundred members. Clearly a young councillor carried little weight, hence he did not need to be experienced in politics, nor indeed will he have borne any real political responsibility. Moreover, we learn from

---

[43] Seventeen years corresponds with the absolute minimum age for magistrates in emergency cases under the law of Heraclia (southern Italy; 80–75 BC?), see Laes 2004a: 160.
[44] The inscription from Iulium Carnicum (northern Italy), concerning a twenty-year-old *decurio*, mentioned on p. 58, n. 31, may be added to the list in Kleijwegt 1991.
[45] Kleijwegt 1991: 309; *contra* Horster 1996: 236 with n. 47; Laes 2004a: 180.

the *Digest* that these minors (*minores*) had no voting rights in the council. The decurionate was primarily a matter of honour. Out of gratitude for his election, the *decurio* was expected to confer benefits upon the city. This explains why the decurionate could be conferred upon small children of four or five years. What mattered was the father's finances and the prestige of the family concerned. In some cases, the father himself could not be elected as *decurio*, for example because he was a freedman; hence the son was elected instead, while the father simply paid all expenses.[46] For magistracies, things were rather different: these positions brought with them real responsibilities. Consequently, they were conferred only upon older individuals aged seventeen or more. But here, too, the financial aspect was central: generous benefactions were expected from the young office-holder.[47] This explains why several youths from the senatorial and equestrian class are among the attested young magistrates. Their families possessed enormous wealth, in addition to great local prestige, as in the case of M. Aurelius Hermogenes. He was a Roman knight and the son of an imperial freedman, and had held the offices of *aedilis* and *decurio* in Salona in Dalmatia before he died at the age of twenty.[48] Roman magistrates, like their Greek counterparts, were in any case often surrounded by a professional staff of assistants, usually municipal slaves and freedmen, who served as writers, messengers, heralds etc. These people remained in place for several years and were wage earners.

Were youths in cities in the Latin West associated from an early age with public political life and benefactions, as were Greek children? It can hardly have been otherwise, though there are very few concrete indications. There are not many inscriptions from the Principate expressing the hope that a youth would pursue a political career and pay the associated benefits, or documenting that someone had made benefactions from his youth.[49] However, reference can be made to the group of the *praetextati* in relation to the preparation for a career in public office.[50] The album of the *decuriones* of the city of Canusium in southern Italy (from AD 223) mentions not only 100 councillors, but also twenty-five *praetextati*. They were presumably youths between sixteen and twenty-five years of age who were permitted to

---

[46] Rawson 2003: 326. One finds an example in *CIL* v 5894 from Milan, cited below, p. 179.
[47] For example: Tib. Claudius Maximus presented games to his native city Aeclanum (central Italy) when he was *duovir quinquennalis* at the age of twenty; the emperor Antoninus Pius had granted permission for this: *CIL* IX 1156 (*EAOR* III 33).
[48] *CIL* III 2077, from the second half of the second century AD. For the case of a senatorial son, C. Vesnius Vindex, in *CIL* XI 6053, see below p. 180.
[49] Kleijwegt 1991: 230–1, 244–6.   [50] Kleijwegt 1991: 304–11; Laes 2004a: 179.

attend the meetings of the city council, albeit without speaking and voting rights, much like the senatorial *praetextati* at Rome. Their names reveal that they belonged primarily to the most prominent decurional families of the town. New *decuriones* were very likely chosen from this group whenever a seat on the council fell vacant, or the *praetextatus* may well have been destined to follow in the footsteps of his father or a relative on the council after his death.

Did Roman adolescents also hold priesthoods in their home cities? This topic remains to be studied, but the impression is that the number of records is very small, as it is in the Greek world. A rare example comes from Mediolanum (Milan); it concerns a youth who is mentioned elsewhere:[51]

> To the Spirits of the Dead. C(aius) Valerius Petronianus, *decurio, pontifex*, priest of the *iuvenes* of Milan, lawyer, who went five times as an ambassador to Rome and to other cities free of charge on behalf of his own city. He lived twenty-three years, nine months, and fourteen days. His father, C(aius) Valerius Eutychianus, *sevir Augustalis*. (made this grave) for his incomparable son and for himself. (*CIL* v 5894, before *c*. AD 275)

Apart from him, we know of a small number of other youths from the municipal elite who held the office of *flamen* (priest).[52] At Ostia, Aulus Fabius Felicianus was *aedilis* in the cult of Vulcan, the principal deity of the city. He died at the age of nineteen, but it is unknown how old Felicianus was when he held the priesthood. In the cult of Vulcan it was not uncommon for children aged between four and twelve to be appointed to such positions.[53] A similar position did not exist in other cities. Furthermore, we have a small number of records mentioning that youths from the senatorial and equestrian class held priesthoods in their home cities.[54] A dedication

---

[51] For this inscription, see Boscolo 2003: 257–61. The youth is mentioned on p. 125, n. 55 and p. 130, n. 77, and the inscription cited again on p. 178, n. 26 and p. 190, n. 26.

[52] *CIL* III 12739+12740 (*AnÉp* (1948) 243; *ILJug* I 83). a *flamen* of twenty-two years at Domavium in Dalmatia; *AnÉp* (1987) 204, a *flamen* of the deified emperor Vespasian of eighteen years at Portus in Italy; both texts date from the first half of the second century AD. At Ostia, a *flamen* of the deified Pertinax and praetor of the cult of Volcanus is also recorded, but the age at death of this priest is not completely preserved; he was certainly over twenty years, possibly twenty-five or thirty: *CIL* XIV 4648.

[53] *CIL* XIV 351. On children as priests of Volcanus at Ostia, see Laes 2004a: 177–8.

[54] On knights, see Kleijwegt 1991: 218; the number of records from the Principate is very small. The Roman knight C. Saturius Secundus died aged nineteen years and was augur at Asculum Picenorum (*CIL* XI 1437; see p. 168); the knight Apuleius Balbinus had been pontifex at Iader and died at the age of twenty-one (Dalmatia) (*CIL* III 9997). It is not clear whether the knight Q. Ceppius Longinus, who died aged twenty at Paestum, had been pontifex: the text is much damaged (*CIL* X 479). On senators, see Kleijwegt 1991: 195–6; but none of the texts adduced mentions with certainty a local priesthood.

from Urvinum Mataurense in central Italy, for example, mentions that C. Vesnius Vindex made generous benefactions to his native city upon designation as quaestor (and thus senator) at the age of twenty-three. He was a patron of the people of Urvinum and of the municipium, and had been *aedilis* and pontifex in the city.[55] Such young priests would generally appear to have been in their late teens or in their twenties. The scarcity of adolescents as priests in the West may have had the same causes as in the East.[56]

So why were youths appointed as office-holders despite their age? We have previously pointed out that a city's laws could diverge from the general rule. It is striking that two very young *aediles*, aged just seventeen and eighteen, are attested in a single city, namely Barcino. Further concentrations of young magistrates and councillors are found in Salona (Dalmatia) and Volubilis (Morocco). Another potentially important factor, applying to both the East and the West, was the number of rich aristocrats who were eligible for municipal offices. This inherently small number further declined in the course of time. Willingness to bear the heavy financial burden of the magistracies and the decurionate diminished in the second and third centuries AD as the prosperity of the Empire dwindled. A solution to this problem was the lowering of the minimum age. In this way, the honourable offices could remain in the same noble families as before, something deemed preferable to the admission of new men to the city government. Most attestations of young office-holders indeed date from the second and third centuries AD. There were also more positive reasons, such as the desire for hereditary succession. Fathers wanted their sons to succeed them in the honourable offices they held and therefore helped them make a start in politics at as young an age as possible. Admission to the city council at an early age was in itself an extraordinary honour for the child and, even more so, its family. The accumulation of honourable offices by members of a single family greatly enhanced the local prestige of that family. Possibly family strategy played a role too. In extraordinary circumstances it could happen that no adult male was available to carry on the family tradition of participation in local government, owing, for example, to premature death or prolonged absence resulting from appointments to high office in distant provinces. In such cases, a family could put forward a youth for the vacant position and thus perpetuate the prestige of the family. The above-cited epitaph from Barcino specifies that it was the mother who erected the grave for the son, not both parents. Possibly the father had died earlier. The family

[55] *CIL* XI 6053; cf. *AnÉp* (2003) 598, after AD 185.   [56] See p. 174.

context is essential.⁵⁷ Ultimately, though, the example set by the members of the Hellenistic royal houses and the imperial families may also have played a role. Gaius and Lucius, the intended successors to Augustus, were made consuls-designate at the age of fourteen, while Nero was crowned emperor at just sixteen.⁵⁸

9.3 Concluding remarks

Young men belonging to the senatorial order usually started their senatorial careers at around the age of twenty, carrying out junior appointments. It is therefore incorrect to speak of a *Jugendraum* (or 'time to be young') of ten years, i.e. between ages fifteen and twenty-five, as Eyben does. Before their twenty-fifth year and the quaestorship, sons of senators could undertake all kinds of political and religious offices and activities, in Rome, in their native city, or elsewhere; or they could engage in study. Many of them spent their time meaningfully and prepared for an aristocratic career. For many there was no *Jugendraum* at all, no marginal position, no period of crisis. But, of course, we do not know whether they also behaved seriously outside the sphere of their public office, which would not have consumed all their time. For others, who neither prepared seriously for a public career nor aspired to it but preferred a life of freedom or idling (*otium*), a void may have appeared. Even if they are not entirely comparable to modern adolescents, either in status or in behaviour, there may well have been certain similarities in terms of their conduct and mentality. But the senatorial sons formed only a tiny minority in Graeco-Roman society; hence their position is far from representative of that of ancient youth as a whole.⁵⁹

The number of young knights was higher. Most *equites* chose not to pursue an equestrian career or embarked on it only later in life, around the age of thirty-six. They were usually content with the prestige attached to their rank in their native city, often bestowed at an early age. Some young knights held official positions in their native cities, just like the scions of local noble families. The annual parade of knights temporarily extracted the child and adolescent knights from their own environment and briefly put them on a par with adults (if they in fact attended it).⁶⁰ Even if the

---

⁵⁷ Dmitriev 2005: 48–52, 161.
⁵⁸ Wiedemann 1989: 119–31; Laes 2004a: 147–52. But Augustus forbade Gaius and Lucius to hold office before they turned twenty.
⁵⁹ Kleijwegt 1991: 191. ⁶⁰ Kleijwegt 1991: 219.

youngsters acted in a solemn or adult way during such parades, this is not to say that they behaved similarly during the rest of the year.

Kleijwegt argues that adolescents commonly held magistracies and priesthoods in the cities of the Greek East and that they acted as adults in public life from an early age. He emphasises that young men are represented in official documents as if they performed their duties independently, without mediation by their fathers, on a par with adult office-holders. Some offices, such as priesthoods, not only entailed financial contributions but also required that the young men appeared in public in a ceremonial role as if they were adults. Kleijwegt argues on this basis that the Greek cities presented an image of youths with adult characteristics.[61] At the same time, he implies that the young men possessed an adult mentality and not the typical mindset of adolescents, not even outside the realm of their official persona. New research has, however, undermined this view: magistracies and other public offices were only exceptionally bestowed on young men under the age of, say, twenty-five or twenty-two. The second part of Kleijwegt's view is evidently an unfounded interpretation.

In the Latin West, the number of records of young magistrates and councillors is larger than in the East. This may in part be due to the fact that it was more common in the West to indicate the exact age at death in grave inscriptions. Although the number of records is not substantial, Kleijwegt argues that they suffice to conclude that there was no period of non-participation and non-acceptance for the youths in the Latin municipalities of the West. He furthermore suggests on this basis that there was no adolescence comparable to that observed in modern society.[62] But the office of *decurio* was not a position of responsibility, while magistracies were not entrusted to youths under the age of seventeen, but mostly to adolescents of twenty and older. It would therefore appear that, in the cities in the West, there was a waiting period in politics, which as a rule lasted up to the age of twenty (in the cities in the East, it may have lasted to the ages of twenty-two or twenty-five). Apparently the laws setting a minimum age for office-holding were generally respected.

Elite youths were often associated by their fathers with politics and euergetism (the practice of civic philanthropy). This, combined with their public persona, for example as members of a city council in the West (sometimes from a very early age), must have profoundly affected the young men in question. In this manner, the young councillors were

[61] Kleijwegt 1991: 221, 247, 253–4. [62] Kleijwegt 1991: 273.

9.3 Concluding remarks

prepared mentally for their later roles in public life. They made appearances at various kinds of public display, including distributions, public burials, games, sacrifices, and banquets, where they were expected to conduct themselves as much as possible like adults.[63] Later they would have to perform such duties independently. These young people carried on their shoulders the weight of expectations of their families and native cities. But all this did not turn them mentally into adults. It cannot be ruled out – despite a lack of evidence – that those same young men behaved like modern adolescents in their private lives. In the case of young magistrates, their training for the future went one step further. One may assume that adolescents performed their tasks largely independently, quite possibly with the assistance of some aides. Although this experience must have had consequences for the mental development of the small number of young men involved, as a phenomenon it was marginal both to the elite and to society in general. Politics was, in any case, not the only activity open to young men. They could also participate in youth associations, the *ephebeia* or the *iuventus*. Since young men could not compete in office, they focused on sport instead. This is why sport became one of the most important activities practised within the youth associations. Youths from the local elite could also, however, devote themselves to studying for a career as orators, lawyers, or jurists.

[63] Laes 2004a: 182–4.

CHAPTER 10

Occupational training

10.1 Physicians and jurists in East and West

In the Greek East

In the ancient world, the medical profession was not regulated.[1] There were no exams to pass, nor certificates to obtain. Some young men were trained by older physicians as apprentices. The young would-be physician would 'shadow' the experienced mentor and learn from his example. It is unknown how long an apprenticeship took on average. There were no doubt great differences, as the type of medicine and the skills involved could vary too: from general herb doctor to specialist physician. Other youngsters attended a medical school, a centre where teachers delivered lectures. In the imperial period, all these centres were situated in the Greek world: Alexandria in Egypt, Smyrna, Pergamum, Ephesus. The Greeks had a virtual monopoly in the medical field. The schooling started around the age of fourteen or fifteen, as it did in the other branches of higher education, rhetoric, and philosophy. In the treatise *Introductio ad medicinam*, which is transmitted under the name of the Greek physician Soranus, it is recommended that medical training be started at fifteen, 'the age at which people usually turn from child to young man'.[2] We have but scanty and rather unreliable information on the length of time of the schooling. The durations cited vary from six months to six years. The consensus is that training lasted at least two to three years; possibly a full curriculum took longer. If a student began at around the age of fifteen, he could be a practitioner by seventeen or eighteen. In general terms there were two types of physician. On the one hand, there were 'simple' doctors (*iatroi*); a small minority of these

---

[1] On physicians, see Nutton 2004: 248–71; Samama 2003: 19–27 (training), 59–64 (social status), 72–3 (privileges; see now *SEG* LVI (2006) 1219); Kleijwegt 1991: 135–63; for their social position, see also Pleket 1995.
[2] Rose 1870: 244; the text itself probably dates from the fifth or sixth century AD.

belonged to the municipal elite. On the other, there were *archiatroi*, officially recognised city physicians. From the early thirties BC onwards, all doctors in the Roman Empire were exempt from certain taxes. Augustus granted them the privilege of *immunitas* from all taxes. The edict of Vespasian of AD 74 bestowed further privileges on physicians, including exemption from the obligation to provide lodgings for officials and soldiers, and from civic contributions of any kind, as was also granted to teachers (see 6.3). The emperor Hadrian confirmed these privileges and further specified the civic duties concerned. Shortly after AD 140, the emperor Antoninus Pius restricted the number of beneficiaries. Henceforth, the privilege of immunity from municipal offices and liturgies applied only to a small number of physicians (five or seven or ten per city), depending on the size and rank of the town (cf. the case of teachers in 6.3). The title *archiatros* was now reserved for public doctors who enjoyed official immunity. They constituted an elite among physicians.[3] In spite of their immunity, however, many of these physicians remained active in municipal politics, implying that the individuals concerned were of an aristocratic background. The status of Greek physicians was relatively high during the imperial period.

The sources, mostly grave inscriptions dating from the imperial period, mention a few young physicians. Relevant records were initially collected by Marc Kleijwegt. More recently, all epigraphic sources on physicians have been brought together by Évelyne Samama. She has compiled 507 inscriptions from the third century BC to the sixth century AD, including 473 epitaphs, dedications, and honorific inscriptions mentioning individual physicians.[4] Two physicians, the youngest in the collection, died at the age of eighteen. The first, Apollonides from Heracleia on the Salbace (Caria), is described as 'an eminent young man, a good and skilful physician'. The other, Asiaticus from Xanthus (Lycia), is referred to as 'competent'.[5] Four young physicians died aged nineteen, twenty or twenty-two. The short epitaph of a nineteen-year-old informs us that he had left his native city of Tieium in Bithynia (on the south coast of the Black Sea) in order to study medicine at Smyrna, where he subsequently settled:[6]

---

[3] For *archiatroi*, see Dmitriev 2005: 234; Samama 2003: 43–5; Nutton 1977.
[4] Kleijwegt 1991: 158–60; Samama 2003 esp. p. 24 n. 77. Samama's collection contains some texts relating to young physicians that were overlooked by Kleijwegt: nos. 286, 383, 464.
[5] Apollonides: Robert and Robert 1954: 187 no. 88 (*GV* I 1543; *SGO* I 02/13/01; Samama 2003 no. 251), probably from the first century AD (the passage is partly restored). Asiaticus: *GV* I 241 (*GG* 408; Vérilhac 1978–82 no. 88; *SGO* IV 17/10/07; Samama 2003 no. 286), from the imperial period.
[6] Strubbe 1997 no. 29; Samama 2003 no. 196, from the end of the first or the beginning of the second century AD. The place of origin is not absolutely certain. The other certain records are: *MAMA* VIII 404 (*GV* I 692; Samama 2003 no. 335; *SGO* III 16/61/04; cf. *SEG* XLIX (1999) 1856), a twenty-year-old

Nicetes, son of Glyco, citizen of Tieium, physician, dead at nineteen years. Whoever will violate the gravestone, may he not have a grave. (*I. Smyrna* 1 442)

Papyri from Egypt mention two young physicians aged respectively seventeen and twenty.[7] About ten inscriptions mention young physicians, but without an exact indication of age. For example, the grave inscription of the physician Dionysius from Cruni (later Dionysopolis) in Moesia merely speaks of a premature death, which could refer to a young man in his twenties or early thirties. Another doctor, Calestrius from Choma (in Lycia), is called *neanias*, which provides no more than a vague indication of age.[8] Additionally, we also know of just a few young medical students.[9] In short, the number of young physicians was apparently rather small. There is evidence of no more than half a dozen physicians who were definitely younger than twenty-five;[10] these were clearly exceptions.[11] It is striking that many of these young physicians, including Apollonides and Asiaticus, are identified emphatically as competent in their profession. Perhaps this was not obvious given their short training and lack of experience. It should also be noted that none of these young doctors was a public physician exempt from municipal taxes, not even in the smallest cities.[12]

Neither was the profession of jurist regulated in the Greek world.[13] Many jurists received practical training from an older, more experienced lawyer. Nonetheless, a young man who wished to become a lawyer could read law at

---

man who is referred to as 'a wise physician' in the neighbourhood of Antiocheia near Pisidia (fourth century AD); *IG* XIV 2019 (*IGUR* II 299; Samama 2003 no. 464), a physician aged twenty-two at Rome (imperial period); Samama 2003 no. 383, a physician aged nineteen at Gadara (second century AD).

[7] Kleijwegt 1991: 161: *P. Hamb.* 60 from Hermoupolis Magna (AD 90) and *P. Giss.* 43 (*SB* X 10630; *P. Alex. Giss.* 14) from Apollonopolis Heptakomias (AD 119). The nineteen-year-old physician from Hermonthis (Samama 2003 no. 446) lived in late antiquity, possibly in the fourth century.

[8] Dionysius: *GV* I 520 (*SGO* III 14/16/03; Samama 2003 no. 345); Calestrius: Samama 2003 no. 288.

[9] For example *TAM* V, 1, 432 (Samama 2003 no. 237) from near Collyda, AD 214/215: Lucius, student (*mathetes*) of the physician Tatianus, died at the age of eighteen.

[10] Samama 2003: 24 considers it possible that a young man designated *iatros* in an epitaph was in reality still an apprentice or an assistant to a physician. His parents, who established the grave inscription, were very proud of him. This not only happened in epitaphs; see *SEG* XLI (1991) commentary to no. 680.

[11] Of course, many physicians died in their adult years. While this does not rule out the possibility that they concluded their studies at a young age, such a fact is not recorded in their epitaphs.

[12] Samama 2003 no. 149 refers to twenty-one-year-old Cossinius (or Cossutius) Bassus from Cos (*IGR* IV 1067) as an *archiatros*, but the inscription is only partly preserved. We believe that Bassus, a civic physician, was the father of a son whose name is not preserved (and who was not a physician) and who died at the age of twenty-one. Kleijwegt 1991: 160 identifies Calestrius from Choma (in Lycia) – a *neanias* (see above) – as a public physician, even though the damaged text does not substantiate this. The fact that he enjoyed immunity from public service does not imply that he was one of the official *archiatroi*: he had previously rendered many services to his native city; see Samama 2003: 396 n. 43.

[13] For jurists, see Kleijwegt 1991: 165–86; Jones 2007.

a law school. Most of these schools were located in the Greek East: in Athens, in Berytus (Beirut) in Syria from around the middle of the third century AD, and in Constantinople in the fourth century. In Berytus, a full training in law took four or five years.[14] But it appears that students often quit the school after just a couple of years and started practising law at around the age of twenty or even earlier. The occupation consisted of several different levels. In the imperial period in the East, lawyers, referred to as *nomikoi* (or *pragmatikoi*), were often employed permanently or temporarily as legal advisors to the courts of provincial governors. They also provided counsel to other judges and private persons, both at the provincial level and in municipal courts. They were well respected and often belonged to the municipal elite. Some jurists held the office of *ekdikos* or acted as *syndikos*. The latter was entrusted with defending the rights and privileges of his town before the Roman authorities.[15] We possess about ten records of young *nomikoi* from Asia Minor, mostly in grave inscriptions from the imperial period.[16] In seven texts, the exact age at death is recorded: the youngest passed away at the age of only nineteen; three were twenty-four or twenty-five years old. A few *nomikoi* may have been younger than twenty-five, but their precise age is not indicated. For example, Neoptolemus from Pednelissus (in Pisidia), a *neanias* educated in rhetoric and law, may have been younger or older than twenty-five.[17] Rather more unambiguous information is provided by the epitaph of Zeno from Claudiupolis (in Bithynia). It stresses that he was a famous lawyer, as is often the case in these texts:

> Gnaeus, son of Zeno, and Marciane (made this grave) for their son Zeno, who was already a famous jurist when he died abroad at the age of twenty and who was brought over here; and also for themselves, in memory. (Dörner 1952 no. 154, imperial period)

Young *nomikoi* are only sparsely recorded. Often, they were not teenagers but closer to twenty-five in age. None of the young *nomikoi* acted as *ekdikos* or *syndikos* defending the rights or privileges of his home town before the Roman authorities.

---

[14] Jones Hall 2004: 195–220.
[15] Quass 1993: 137–8, 168–9; Dmitriev 2005: 213–16; Fournier 2007. The *ekdikos* developed into an annual magistracy with broader competences.
[16] Collected by Kleijwegt 1991: 185–6 (some of the cases that he adduces are highly dubious). One may add: *SEG* XLIII (1993) 906 from Amastris, in which a twenty-five-year-old is recorded. It cannot be excluded that the term *nomikos* was sometimes used to refer to a student of law. A bilingual epitaph from Antiocheia near Pisidia calls L. Malius Maximus a *nomikos*; the Latin includes the letters IS, which are interpreted as *i(uris) s(tudioso)*: Maximus was not yet *iuris peritus*: *SEG* LII (2002) 1390; *AnÉp* (2002) 1455a.
[17] *SEG* II 715; *Anatolian Studies* 53 (2003) 124 no. 8f; Neoptolemus died at Rome, second century AD.

188   10 Occupational training

In the Latin West

> I was out of sorts; but at once you visited me, Symmachus, accompanied by a hundred pupils. A hundred hands chilled by the north wind touched me. I did not have a fever, Symmachus. Now I do. (Martial, *Epigr.* 5, 9)

This epigram of Martial shows that young men in Rome who chose medicine as a profession could become apprentices to experienced doctors. This is the case too outside Rome and for lower-class youngsters. Wealthy young men could also read medicine in one of the leading schools in the East.[18] Their age was comparable to that of Greek students. The schooling was generally completed at the age of seventeen or eighteen. This we also know from inscriptions, mostly epitaphs, mentioning the age at death of several young physicians. The youngest we know of from Latin municipalities were seventeen years old, including the ocular physician Phasis from Rome[19] and Julius Sabinianus from Pinna in Italy:

> To the Spirits of the Dead. For Caius Julius Sabinianus, physician, who lived seventeen years, ten months, and fourteen days. Caius Julius Sabinus and Sollia Fortunata made (this grave) for their most loving son and for themselves. (*AnÉp* (1968) 159 and (1992) 341, second half of the first century AD)

Others were eighteen, nineteen or twenty years of age, or slightly older. Overall, about ten physicians under twenty-five are recorded, half of whom were teenagers. There are also a few army doctors aged between twenty and twenty-five.[20]

As a rule, physicians did not belong to the elites of Roman society. Many of them bore Greek names, a sign that they were immigrants from the East. There were also many itinerant physicians.[21] The young physicians belonged mainly to the lower classes; among their numbers were not only male citizens, but also (imperial) slaves, free-born women, and freedwomen.[22]

---

[18] *Notizie dei Scavi* (1917) 290 no. 2 from Rome is the epitaph of Glycerus, a physician aged twenty-four, erected by his teacher.
[19] *AnÉp* (1924) 106.
[20] Sources mentioning young Roman physicians have been collected by Kleijwegt 1991: 161–3, with three army physicians on p. 163. But the army physician from Lambaesis was older than twenty (between twenty-three and twenty-seven). A supplement to Kleijwegt: *RIB* 1618 from Vercovicum in Britannia records an army physician aged twenty-five.
[21] Nutton 2004: 258–60.
[22] A supplement to Kleijwegt: a twenty-five-year old physician, slave of a physician, at Carnuntum (Pannonia Superior): *AnÉp* (1929) 215 (*ZaCarnuntum* 106). A newly discovered text: *AnÉp* (2008) 498, possibly from Trebiae in Italy, the epitaph of a slave (?), *medicus chirurgus*, who died at the age of twenty-one.

In Rome, many jurists likewise received training from an older, more experienced lawyer. Such apprenticeships usually started after the donning of the male toga, under a system that was referred to as 'the school of the forum' (*tirocinium fori*). A good example in this respect is none other than Cicero, who asserts that his legal training with the lawyer Scaevola began when he was fifteen. During his apprenticeship, he attended all public meetings and lawsuits at the Forum. We do not know how long this training took. It was only later, at the age of twenty-six, that Cicero made a name for himself as an orator. Others attracted attention much earlier. In fact, youths tried to impress in high-profile lawsuits at as young an age as possible. In 56 BC, when L. Sempronius Atratinus acted as prosecutor against M. Caelius Rufus, represented by Cicero, he was only seventeen years old.[23] Cicero, rather predictably, tried to belittle him right from the beginning of the lawsuit by referring to him in his oration as *puer* (child):

> But I myself pardon Atratinus (sc. for having brought the charge). He is a very distinguished and excellent young man and he is a friend of mine. He has as an excuse either his love for his father, or compulsion, or his age. If he has voluntarily chosen to bring the charge, I attribute this to his love; if he received an order, to compulsion; if he hoped for any advantage, to his childish age (*pueritia*). (Cicero, *Pro Cael*. 1, 2)

Around the middle of the first century AD, a number of law schools were opened in Rome, followed in the second century by similar institutions in the provinces. One famous school was situated in Carthage, but many Roman youths travelled east to study. The Roman students were similar to their Greek counterparts in terms of age.

As in the Greek East, there were several different levels of jurist. The top-level jurists were legal advisors (*iuris consulti*), who studied legal problems and wrote books on them. They provided legal advice and pleaded in the courts. They also offered private tuition in law. For the most part they were prominent senators. Ranked immediately below them were the practising lawyers (*iuris periti*), who pleaded at the bar, in Rome or in other cities, at the provincial and local levels. Lawyers in the cities often belonged to the local municipal elite and were quite often active in politics too. At the bottom of the professional hierarchy were the legal assistants (*apparitores*) to magistrates, who as a rule were of low social status – plebeians and freedmen.

Kleijwegt has collected the records of young jurists from the West.[24] It appears that various terms were used, including *advocatus*, *iuris peritus*,

---

[23] More examples can be found in Eyben 1977: 254–64; 1993: 72–80.
[24] Kleijwegt 1991: 183–5. Some of the sources contain only a very vague indication of age.

causidicus. The term *causidicus* probably referred to a public lawyer whose job it was to plead cases on behalf of his city. Kleijwegt's source material comprises seven texts, three of which mention a *causidicus*. The youngest attested lawyer was just eighteen years old when he died at Ksaret-Sidi-Amara in Tunisia.[25] He was held 'to be able to speak for his town', indicating that he was considered experienced enough to defend the interests of his city in legal disputes. He, too, was thus a *causidicus*. The following epitaph also comes from Tunisia, from the Masculula area:[26]

> To the Spirits of the Dead. Quintus Pomponius Fortunatus, son of Quintus from the tribe Quirina, *aedilis*, was a man praised for his exceptional honesty and modesty. His integrity was firmly established. His moderation was truly renowned. His earnest was extremely great ... He was a young man, just, with an elevated and friendly character, an experienced legal expert (*iuris peritus*). In his earliest youth he complied with the self-restraint common to older people and was considered their equal. He lived twenty-two years and two months. His brothers, Proculus and Festa, took care that he was buried here. (*CIL* VIII 27505; cf. *ILTun* 1675, undated)

Two of the young jurists were teenagers; the five others were in their twenties. All of these individuals had completed at least part of their education. It is quite remarkable that in the Roman world, unlike in that of the Greeks, young lawyers could represent their city.

So what does the source material tell us about young physicians and jurists in the East and West of the Roman Empire? For one thing, it suggests that in the Greek world the number of young physicians and jurists was low. Young jurists were, as a rule, around twenty-five years old. Similarly, in the Roman world young physicians and jurists were uncommon. Again, young jurists were usually around twenty-five. A small number of sources mentions physicians and jurists who were still teenagers. They held positions of responsibility and apparently operated on equal terms with adults. However, there are some lingering afterthoughts. Does the small number of records – approximately ten for each group – not imply that young physicians and jurists were rather exceptional, precocious or highly talented young men, who consequently were much admired by their contemporaries? On the other hand, the parents who established the gravestone for their prematurely deceased son may well have exaggerated his qualities as a source of comfort. Does the fact that jurists in Greek and Roman society were for the most part aged twenty-five or older not indicate that the ancients were

---

[25] *CIL* VIII 12159; cf. *ILTun* 595, undated. [26] Another example in *CIL* V 5894, cited on p. 179.

rather reluctant to entrust positions of such responsibility to young people? And is this not further corroborated by the observation that nowhere in the ancient world were young men appointed as public city physicians, while nowhere in the Greek world did they act as public lawyers? Conversely, is the fact that, in the Roman world, young men could already be physicians in their late teens not related to the lower esteem in which this occupation was held? On the balance of the available evidence, we conclude that young men were rarely entrusted with positions of responsibility and prestige.

10.2 Other occupations

Free-born children from families of the lower classes were put to work at a young age to increase the household income. They worked in all sectors of the economy. Some remained unskilled, others received training, usually of a practical nature. Still others learned a job at home, from their father or from a relative. They were deployed in agriculture and in a variety of occupations, including as shoemakers, cooks, smiths, bakers, entertainers, shopkeepers, and traders, as many texts from literature, Roman law, and sepulchral inscriptions show. Children were initiated in jobs at an early age, so that, by the time they had reached adolescence, they were working alongside or together with adults.[27]

A parent or a relative of the child could conclude an apprenticeship contract with a master for the youngster's training. Forty-two such contracts on papyrus have been passed down to us from Egypt, mostly from the imperial period.[28] They contain all kinds of information on the actual jobs, payment of wages, provision of food and clothing, working hours, holidays, and so on. The crafts mentioned include weaving, construction work, shorthand, wool carding, embroidering, nail making, copper smithing, and embalming. The apprentices were for the most part free-born boys (with the exceptions of at least one free girl and a number of male and female slaves). The exact age of just one child is known: a fourteen-year-old slave girl. It is generally believed that most apprentices were twelve or thirteen years old at the start of the contract. Training took between one and eight years, perhaps three years on average. Therefore, at the onset of adolescence, the apprentices may or may not have completed their training. They would, in any case, have lived and worked among adults. We have no way of telling

---

[27] Laes 2006a: 164–70, 174–93 and 2011: 189–91; Bradley 1991: 112–16.
[28] Laes 2006a: 170–4 and 2011: 191–5 with earlier bibliography, among others Bradley 1991.

what this submersion in the adult world entailed for the adolescents. They may have had little time and occasion for other activities than work: some contracts stipulate that the apprentices had to toil all day long from sunrise to sunset (except on about twenty holidays a year). Most of the aforementioned aspects are covered in the apprenticeship contract of a boy whose name is not preserved, originating in Oxyrhynchus in AD 183:[29]

> Ischyrion son of Heradion and of . . ., of Oxyrhynchus, and Heraclas son of Sarapion also called Leon son of Heraclides and of . . ., of the same city, weaver, make this mutual contract. Ischyrion agrees that he has given as an apprentice to Heraclas the . . . of . . ., Thonis, a minor, to learn the art referred to from the first of next month, Phaophi, for a period of five years. He will deliver him to attend his teacher for the stated period every day from sunrise to sunset. The boy must do everything that he is ordered to by the said teacher, like other apprentices. He will be fed by Ischyrion. And for the first two years and for seven months of the third year Heraclas shall pay no wages for the boy, but in the remaining five months of the said third year Heraclas shall pay as wages to the said apprentice 12 drachmae a month, and in the fourth year likewise as wages 16 drachmae a month, and in the fifth year likewise 24 drachmae a month. And Heraclas shall furnish to the said apprentice in the current twenty-fourth year a tunic worth 16 drachmae, and in the coming twenty-fifth year a second tunic worth 20 drachmae, and in the twenty-sixth year likewise another tunic worth 24 drachmae, and in the twenty-seventh year another tunic worth 28 drachmae, and in the twenty-eighth year likewise another tunic worth 32 drachmae. The boy shall have twenty holidays a year on account of festivals without any deduction from his wages after the payment of wages starts. But if he is idle for longer than this or is absent through illness or insubordination or for any other reason, Ischyrion shall be bound to deliver him to his teacher for an equivalent number of days. The boy must remain then with him and perform all duties as aforesaid without wages. He will be fed by Ischyrion, because the contract has been made on these terms. Heraclas on the other side consents to all these provisions and agrees to instruct the apprentice fully for the period of five years in the aforesaid art as far as he knows it himself and to pay the monthly wages as said before, beginning from the eighth month of the third year. Neither of them shall be permitted to violate any of the aforesaid provisions, and the one who violates them shall pay to the one who observes them a penalty of 100 drachmae and to the treasury the same amount. This agreement is valid. The twenty-fourth year of the emperor Caesar Marcus Aurelius Commodus Antoninus Augustus Armeniacus Medicus Parthicus Sarmaticus Germanicus Maximus, Thoth 25.

[29] *P. Oxy.* IV 725.

10.2 Other occupations

(Signed) I, Heraclas son of Sarapion also called Leon, have made this contract and consent to all the aforesaid provisions. I, Thonis also called Morous son of Harthonis, have written for him, as he does not know to write. (after Hunt and Edgar 1970 I: 40–5 no. 14)

Although similar customs also existed outside Egypt, children were, as a rule, trained informally. When they became adolescents, their life did not change substantially: they continued to work practically every day. Their labour no doubt became harder as they grew older. The documents do not provide information on the private lives of these youngsters, their thoughts, their feelings. The historian of antiquity is not as fortunate as his colleagues specialising in the Early Modern period, who, for example, can rely on lively tales about the world of apprentices in London in the sixteenth century and their relationships with their masters.[30] We can only regretfully conclude that, while the majority of boys and girls in the ancient world were required to work, we possess no insight whatsoever into how they coped mentally with life in the adult world of labour.

Like free-born children from the lower social classes, slaves began to work at an early age, albeit for the benefit of their masters. Under Roman law, a slave child could be put to work from the age of five.[31] Young slaves performed many kinds of jobs, including in agriculture, handicrafts, commerce, and domestic service, and they were presumably trained for this work on the job, sometimes in a large and wealthy household. Female and male slaves were also employed in prostitution. Some slaves were trained as apprentices, just like free-born children. We possess an apprentice contract from Oxyrhynchus for an under-age female slave, Thermouthion, who was apprenticed as a weaver for four years.[32] In the imperial household and in the homes of certain wealthy aristocrats there was a *paedagogium*, a private school for the training of domestic servants. This was also the case in Pliny's house, for example. Imperial *paedagogia* are documented from the reign of the emperor Tiberius. We know of trainees ranging in age from twelve to eighteen.[33] These slaves were trained for domestic service, for personal care (masseurs, cooks, chamberlains) or for administrative functions (secretaries, clerks). Imperial slaves belonged to the *familia Caesaris*. After their training, they would be employed at the imperial palace in Rome, for example as doorkeepers, or in the administrative staff of an imperial office, either in

---

[30] Smith 1973.   [31] *Dig.* 7, 7, 6, 1 (Ulpian); cf. Laes 2000: 6–7; Wieber 2007; Laes 2011: 165–6.
[32] *P. Oxy.* XIV 1647 (second century AD). The Egyptian apprenticeship contracts mention a total of ten slave-girls, all of whom were trained as weavers.
[33] Pliny, *Epist.* 7, 27, 13; cf. Laes 2011: 186–7; for imperial *paedagogia*, see Herrmann-Otto 1994: 319–23.

Rome or in the provinces, or on an imperial domain in the Empire. Faustus was such an imperial slave:[34]

> To the Spirits of the Dead. Faustus, imperial freedman, assistant in the imperial bureau for Latin correspondence, lived nineteen years, four months, and sixteen days. Artemisius, his paedagogue and freedman, set up this grave for this most extraordinary boy (*puer*). (*CIL* VI 8613)

Leaving aside his premature death, Faustus seems to have been very fortunate during his life. Not only was he set free at the unusually young age of nineteen – imperial slaves were generally manumitted at between thirty and forty years of age – but he himself also owned a slave, Artemisius, apparently his former paedagogue, whom he set free. Another female slave in the imperial service was the eighteen-year-old Paezusa. She was employed at the imperial palace in Rome as an *ornatrix* (dresser or hairdresser) to the daughter of the emperor Claudius:

> Paezusa, dresser (?) of Octavia, daughter of Caesar Augustus, lived eighteen years. Philetus, (slave) of Octavia, daughter of Caesar Augustus, made this grave from his own money for his very beloved partner and for himself. (*CIL* VI 5539)

Many slaves in large aristocratic houses and in the imperial household were house-born. Their training began at an early age. But in the Greek and Roman worlds large numbers of slaves were imported from distant regions: they were captured in warfare or purchased by Roman traders from foreign rulers, or kidnapped by marauders in remote areas on the fringes of the civilised world.[35] Not only adults were carried off, but so too were children and adolescents. We possess the sepulchral inscription of such a slave, Mygdonius. He was enslaved in warfare in Parthia in the first century AD. One can easily imagine how greatly such a young man would have been traumatised by being forcefully removed from his home in Parthia or the highlands of Galatia or the forests of Germany to end up in the metropolis of Rome, with its crowded streets and high-rise apartment buildings. He would have been completely alone, without parents and relatives, entirely disoriented, and unable to understand a word of the Latin language. And, above all else, he would have been utterly humiliated by being deprived of his freedom. The new slave was quickly put to work. Eventually, Mygdonius' life took a turn for the better: he was set free and

---

[34] For more records of imperial slaves aged twenty-one or less, and who worked as subordinates within an imperial department or in housekeeping, see Boulvert 1974: 149 n. 259.
[35] McKeown 2007: 124–40 on the supply and replacement of slaves.

reached a respectable age, as he himself recounts (albeit in faulty grammar) in his grave inscription (at Ravenna):[36]

> Caius Julius Mygdonius, Parthian by birth, born in freedom, captured at an early age and transferred to Roman soil. I became a Roman citizen thanks to the help of Fate. I prepared my grave at the age of fifty. I succeeded to grow up from youth to old age. Accept me willingly now, my grave. With you I will be freed from all sorrows. (*CIL* xi 137; *CLE* 1580)

10.3 Excursus: the schooling of the physician Galen

As we have mentioned before, there are few sources documenting the successive phases of the schooling of a young man in antiquity. We do however possess the vast body of medical writings by the imperial court physician Galen, who provides many details about his own training.[37]

Galen was born at Pergamum in AD 129 into a well-to-do family. His father, Aelius Nicon, was a wealthy landowner, a member of the local nobility, and a Roman citizen. He was a man of great culture and learning. It was Galen's father who taught him mathematics, logic, and grammar (of course of the classical Attic dialect) up to the end of his fourteenth year.[38] Then there followed an introduction to dialectic and philosophy by philosophers in the city of Pergamum. The young Galen frequented several philosophers and so became acquainted with the leading philosophical movements of his time: Stoicism, Epicureanism, Platonism, and the Peripatetic school. Galen was sixteen years old when his father had a dream, said to have been sent by Asclepius. It was a dream that would shape his son's future: the boy turned towards the study of medicine. Medical science would become his second field of activity alongside philosophy: not ordinary medicine (for that was connected with manual labour, and hence deeply despised by the aristocrats), but medicine intertwined with philosophy.[39] Galen, still a teenager, probably became a member of the prestigious group of the *therapeutai* of the sanctuary of Asclepius at Pergamum, one of the most important medical and cultic centres at the time; it was composed

---

[36] For more 'success stories' about foreign slaves who ended up doing well, see Bradley 1994: 47. Bradley further mentions on p. 48 the story of a young woman, born in Osrhoene in Mesopotamia, who was sold on the slave market in Tripoli in Phoenicia; she ended up in Oxyrhynchus in Egypt at around the age of seventeen: *P. Oxy.* XLII 3053, from AD 252.

[37] For a biography of Galen, see Schlange-Schöningen 2003. See also Laes 2008.

[38] Galen, *De ord. libr.* 4 (19, 59 Kühn). On the Attic dialect, see Galen, *De diff.* 2, 2 (8, 568 Kühn).

[39] The dream is mentioned in the autobiographic work *De ord. libr.* 4 (19, 59 Kühn). It is in all probability a literary motif, an element of self-representation. On the concept of philosophical medicine in Galen's thought, see Kudlien 1986: 154–60.

of magistrates, men of letters and members of the municipal aristocracy. Father Nicon passed away when Galen was nineteen years of age. Being the only son and heir, he acquired a substantial income. For at least four more years he continued his medical studies at Pergamum. He became acquainted with the leading medical schools or sects of his time: the Pneumatists, who relied chiefly on the doctrines of the Stoic philosophy; the Dogmatists, who appealed exclusively to the Hippocratic doctrine of the four *humores* (humours); and the Empiricists, who were more practically oriented. Thereafter, Galen made several journeys and stayed with renowned philosophers and physicians: in Smyrna, Corinth, and Alexandria in Egypt. In the last of these cities he attended a choice of lectures, especially on anatomy. He came into contact with the fourth medical school, the sect of the Methodists, who followed Epicurus' theory of atoms.[40]

In 157, Galen returned to his native city of Pergamum for a prestigious appointment: as physician to the troupe of gladiators owned by the high priest of Asia. This provided him with a unique opportunity for gaining practical experience in anatomy, in healing wounds and fractures, and in performing surgery. In addition to this demanding position, he continued to study medical theory and philosophy. Possibly a local riot put an end to his career at Pergamum; he may have found himself on the wrong side in one of the local political squabbles. At the age of thirty-two, he left for Rome, where he became a court physician.[41]

---

[40] Galen's training offers no real clues regarding the average length of a physician's schooling, *contra* Kleijwegt 1991: 157. Galen stayed only a short time in Corinth, because Numesianus, the teacher whom he had intended to visit, had already left for Alexandria. In the latter city he did not receive a real training; see Schlange-Schöningen 2003: 85–99.

[41] On the basis of the Suda, it has been claimed that Galen died around AD 199. See however Nutton 1995, who situates his death around the year 216.

CHAPTER 11

Marriage

11.1 Roman marriage as an institution

Legal texts are the main sources for our knowledge about the institution of Roman marriage. As Roman jurists were primarily concerned with antiquarian matters, we are informed about marriage customs that were quite often outmoded or old-fashioned by the imperial era. This 'antiquarian focus' emphatically left its mark on twentieth-century scholarly debate on Roman marriage.[1] Its interest was likewise mainly in older ways of contracting a marriage, such as the *cum manu* marriage, which could take the forms of *confarreatio* (involving the offering of spelt bread), *coemptio* (involving the symbolic sale of the bride), and *usus* (involving a year of cohabitation). Since the 1980s, scholarly attention has turned to the impact of marriage on Roman family life. More recently, there has been a surge in interest in late antiquity, including through a microhistorical approach to individuals and the writing of personal narratives.[2] In this chapter, we intend to take a fresh look at the well-studied subject of Roman marriage, focusing on how it shaped young people's daily lives and experiences.

During the imperial era, almost all marriages were contracted *sine manu*, implying that legally the bride did not become a member of her husband's family. She maintained a degree of economic independence: any inheritance from her parents, for example, remained her own. Among the upper classes there was a strong moral duty to provide a dowry. From a legal point of view, the dowry became the husband's property, and it was his responsibility to look after it. Dissolution of the marriage could imply a duty to return the dowry to the woman for her maintenance. This is an important distinction between Roman society and present-day societies such as India,

---

For an introductory essay on legal and social aspects of Roman marriage, see Eyben, Laes, and Van Houdt 2003b: 178–81. The standard work on Roman marriage is Treggiari 1991.
[1] See Fayer 1994 and 2005 (a study over a thousand pages long!). [2] Evans Grubbs 2009.

where the bride and her family are also commonly required to provide a dowry, but without any possibility of reclaiming it.[3]

At first sight, Roman marriage seems a familiar and easily recognisable institution. It was both monogamous and heterosexual. The desire of the two partners to live together and their willingness to care jointly for their offspring were considered important.

> Marriage is a contract between man and woman and a community for life, a participation in divine and human law. (*Dig.* 23, 2, 1 (Modestinus))

According to Cicero, the nuclear family was the corner-stone of society.[4] But although this notion may sound quite familiar to modern ears, such superficial similarities should not blind us to some of the fundamental differences between the institutions of marriage in ancient Rome and those in today's society. Roman marriage was essentially a private matter. No public official became involved and there was no marriage register. If two persons decided to live together as husband and wife, then husband and wife they were. The state merely imposed social restrictions. A legal marriage could be contracted only by two persons of free status, possessing full Roman citizenship. Only then did marriage ensure that legal offspring fell under the *patria potestas* and were regarded as full Roman citizens. Unlike nowadays, marriage was a question of social status, not morality. Inscriptions from Rome confirm that those who were legally able to contract a marriage generally did so (marriage was not possible, for instance, if one of the partners was a slave).[5] The manner in which a marriage was contracted was also completely free: neither ceremony nor performance was required. According to the same principles, divorce was legally very simple: the marriage came to an end if the partners had lost the will to live together. To enact a divorce, it sufficed for the husband or, from early times, the wife to inform the other partner orally or in writing, personally or through an intermediary, that the union had ended. In the case of divorce, there were certain customs, just as in marriage, but they were not obligatory: the house keys were taken away, formulas such as 'pack your bags' (*res tuas habeto*) were spoken, a messenger or a letter announcing the divorce was dispatched. As marrying was quick and easy, it was difficult in cases of dispute to ascertain whether a marriage had actually been contracted. To be sure, there were couples who opted to live in concubinage (a term that had no

---

[3] It is important to bear this in mind when discussing the problem of female infanticide in Roman society; see Rawson 2005: 7.
[4] Cicero, *De off.* 1, 54.   [5] Rawson 1974.

overtones of moral condemnation) rather than in a legal union. The testimony of friends or neighbours sufficed to affirm that there had been an intention of contracting a marriage. A dowry could also count as a proof.

11.2 Age at first marriage

What was the average age of marriage for Roman boys and girls? This is of course a crucial matter for scholars studying youth in Roman society. The contracting of a marriage is often considered to be the start of a new stage in life, the end of (carefree) youth. As with other aspects of Roman society involving figures and statistics, average age at marriage is difficult to ascertain. Since there are no marriage registers to rely on, the scholar must make do with other sources, which can at best provide a general indication.

Legal texts merely mention minimum ages for marriage. It is unclear, though, whether these corresponded with social reality. Brides were supposed to be sexually mature (*viripotens*), hence twelve years was set as the legal minimum age. Grooms had to have reached adulthood, marked by the donning of the *toga* at approximately fifteen years, as previously discussed.[6] At the same time, the texts hint that the age limits were sometimes ignored: we read about a woman who married before the age of twelve (according to the jurist Pomponius, she became a lawful wife only at the moment she turned twelve years old) and about the adultery of a girl under the age of twelve.[7] For betrothal, which was not a legal obligation, the minimum age of seven is mentioned. But in this case, the fiancées often lived at their parental homes until the wedding day.[8]

In an attempt to gain some insight into the social reality of marital ages, Keith Hopkins (1965) has examined the relatively small sample of inscriptions specifying the duration of a marriage and the ages at death of both husband and wife. On this basis he arrives at a very early average age of marriage for girls of between twelve and fifteen. Though Hopkins' research method seems plausible at first sight, his results are somewhat distorted by the fact that deceased young wives were more likely to be commemorated in such inscriptions, which inevitably pushes down the average age.[9] The analytical approach taken by Brent Shaw (1987) is more sophisticated: it takes due account of the relationship between the commemorator and the commemorated. Up to what age are deceased girls commemorated mainly

---

[6] *Dig.* 24, 1, 65 and 36, 2, 30 (Labeo); 48, 5, 14, 8 (Ulpian).
[7] *Dig.* 23, 2, 4 (Pomponius); 48, 5, 14, 8 (Paul) (adultery). See also n. 14 below on Sparta.
[8] *Dig.* 23, 1, 4 and 9 (Ulpian).   [9] Hopkins 1965.

by their parents, and from what age does the number of commemorating husbands increase? This way, a much larger number of funerary inscriptions can be taken in to account, leading to the conclusion that girls usually married in their late teens while men were generally aged between twenty-five and thirty at first marriage.[10] This hypothesis is confirmed by surviving data from the Egyptian census lists. Papyri preserved in the dry desert sand of Egypt contain data from the censuses that were conducted every fourteen years in this particular province (which does however immediately raise the question of whether Egypt was representative of the other provinces of the Empire). The data from Egypt suggest the following: at the age of fifteen only 12% of girls were married; this proportion increases to over 60% by age twenty, and to 85% by age twenty-five. The average age difference between husband and wife was seven and a half years.[11] Apparently, then, Roman society displayed a pattern of early marriage, with women marrying in their late teens or early twenties and men between the ages of twenty-five and thirty. In 2007 Walter Scheidel convincingly argued that this general hypothesis may be advanced with some certainty, while claims which go into greater detail should be made only with the utmost caution, and with due consideration of the confounding variables revealed by comparative evidence from later periods (e.g. the Tuscan census of 1427 reveals remarkable differences in the marital ages of grooms between the city of Florence and small villages).[12]

So far, there has been no systematic research into the age of marriage specified in Greek inscriptions. It would, however, appear that a pattern of early marriage for girls (with fourteen or fifteen as the average age of first marriage) and somewhat later for men (around thirty on average) comes close to reality.[13] Plutarch thought it worth mentioning that Spartans did not take girls as their brides when they were still immature and not yet fully grown. This made them an exception among the Greeks and the Romans.[14] In an inscription from the Bithynian city of Prusa in Asia Minor, we read about a married girl who died at age twelve. In the same town, a woman died at age twenty after seven years of marriage. She was survived by three children.[15]

Scholars have widely agreed that the so-called Mediterranean marriage pattern, characterised by an average age of marriage of eighteen for girls and

---

[10] Shaw 1987, confirmed by Saller 1987.
[11] See Frier 1999 and 2001. Saller 2001: 99–102 provides an excellent survey with ample methodological observations. Cf. also Laes 2011: 30, 252–4.
[12] See Scheidel 2007a esp. pp. 401–3 on the study by Lelis, Percy, and Verstraete 2003.
[13] Pomeroy 1997: 4–9 and 25–7; Saller 2001: 98–9.   [14] Plutarch, *Numa* 26, 1–3.
[15] *I. Prusa* I 54; I 65.

between twenty-five and thirty for men, comes nearest to the everyday reality of marital life in the Roman world. However, literary sources sometimes suggest a different reality. As mentioned in a previous chapter (see 6.7), Ovid claims to have been still almost a child when he entered into his first marriage. Caesar was betrothed to Cossutia around age fifteen, and married Cornelia soon thereafter. Caligula married Junia Claudilla shortly after the shaving of his first beard and the donning of the *toga* at age eighteen. And Nero was seventeen when he was wed to his stepsister Octavia, aged thirteen.[16] New research by Lelis, Percy, and Verstraete has collected all this literary evidence and on this basis rekindled the argument that the average age at marriage was fifteen years or younger for girls and between seventeen and twenty-two for boys. However, this hypothesis mainly concerns the upper classes, where dynastic motivations may have played an important role. For the middle classes, the Mediterranean marriage pattern seems much more plausible.[17]

Finally, there is the practice of marriage with prepubescent girls, younger than the legally fixed age of twelve. No doubt such marriages did occur and sometimes they were also consummated, possibly even resulting in pregnancy. Sexual intercourse with a young wife was a husband's prerogative, even if the girl had not yet reached puberty. Indeed, ancient physicians connect first intercourse with first menstruation. Literary evidence unambiguously points in the same direction, and legal texts mention the possibility of adultery on the part of girls under the age of twelve. The custom of early marriage also exists in Islamic countries and among the Berber people.[18]

11.3 Wedding ceremonies

In the Latin West

For Roman girls, the ceremony of marriage marked the transition from childhood to adulthood. Unlike boys, they had no rite of passage such as the donning of the *toga virilis*. As a symbolic farewell to childhood, they

---

[16] Ovid, *Tristia* 4, 10, 69–70; Suetonius, *Jul.* 1; *Cal.* 10–12; *Nero* 7.
[17] Lelis, Percy, and Verstraete 2003. Their hypotheses, which went against previous research, were initially well received; see for example McCall 2006. See, however, Scheidel 2007a for a convincing criticism, though he does leave open the possibility of an earlier marital age for the upper classes.
[18] Ancient doctors: Soranus, *Gyn.* 1, 17; 1, 28 (pregnancy before menstruation!) and Rufus of Ephesus, in Oribasius, *Lib. inc.* 2, 1–7; 21–4. Literary testimonies: Quintilian, *Inst. or.* 6, praef.; Pliny, *Epist.* 8, 10, and 11; Plutarch, *Numa* 26, 1–3. Juridical: *Dig.* 48, 5, 14, 8 (Ulpian). The relevant passages are collected in Durry 1955 and 1956. See Eyben, Laes, and Van Houdt 2003a: 186–91; Eyben, Laes, and Van Houdt 2003b: 215–16; Laes 2004b.

sacrificed their toys on the day of their wedding.[19] A passage from the church father Arnobius leads one to suppose that girls too offered their *toga praetexta* of childhood before Fortuna Virginalis (unlike men, adult women never wore a *toga*, unless they were prostitutes). Nothing further is known about the ceremony mentioned by Arnobius.[20] Dressed in her childhood attire, the young girl also made sacrifices before Mutunus Tutunus, a counterpart of the Greek god of copulation and fertility Priapus. Just like boys, girls slept in their *tunica recta* on the night before their wedding.[21]

For the rest, the differences with bridegrooms in terms of ceremonial dressing are striking.[22] On their wedding day, brides wore a yellow–red veil (*flammeum*).[23] Their hair was twined in six tresses, the parting being made by a spearhead that had been dipped in the blood of a dying gladiator,[24] and it was subsequently adorned with ribbons of wool, symbol of virginity. The bridal gown was a long, white garment, which was held together with a special knot by a woollen belt, again as a symbol of virginity.[25] Beneath the veil, the bride wore a wreath of flowers that she had picked herself. The matron of honour (*pronuba*) had to be a woman who had been married only once (*univira*).

The sources provide ample information on the proceedings of a wedding feast. First, the omens were consulted and sacrifices made to the gods. The banquet usually took place in the bride's parental home. Only after darkness had fallen would the bride be carried to her new husband's home in a procession. Friends of the couple would provide torchlight, sing obscene songs about the bridegroom's virility, and throw nuts at the couple as a symbol of fertility or a farewell to childhood. After arriving at the bridegroom's house, the bride would be carried across the threshold. A sacrifice of fire and water would be made to the gods. Some visitors might have accompanied the couple into the house. The bridegroom would then offer his wife fire and water as symbols of her entrance into the new household. Incense would be burnt at the altar of the household gods.

---

[19] Ps.-Acro, *Schol. in Hor. Serm.* 1, 5, 65; Persius Flaccus, *Sat.* 2, 70.
[20] George 2001: 184. See Arnobius, *Adv. nat.* 2, 67. See p. 31, n. 20.
[21] Festus, *De signif. verb.* 342 and 364 (ed. Lindsay).
[22] On wedding ceremonies for girls, see Torelli 1984: 33–42; Treggiari 1991: 161–80; Hopkins 1999: 42–50; Eyben, Laes, and Van Houdt 2003a: 183–6; Olson 2008. La Follette 1994 deals with the finery of the bride. On colours, see Casartelli 1998 and Sebesta 1997.
[23] Important testimonies on the *flammeum*: Suetonius, *Nero* 28; Pliny the Elder, *Nat. hist.* 21, 46; Festus, *De signif. verb.* 79 and 172 (ed. Lindsay); Nonius Marcellus, *De comp. doctr.* 541.
[24] Festus, *De signif. verb.* 55 (ed. Lindsay) offers different explanations, thereby assuming that the Romans themselves no longer understood the significance of these symbolic acts.
[25] On the *cingulum* as a symbol of virginity, see Varro, *Men.* 187 (Bücheler); *De ling. Lat.* 5, 114; Petronius, *Satyr.* 67; Festus, *De signif. verb.* 55 (ed. Lindsay); Nonius Marcellus, *De comp. doctr.* 236.

The marital bed, covered with an immaculate white *toga*, would have been prepared in advance. To the accompaniment of loud laughter, man and wife would be led to the bedroom. The husband would preferably claim his marital privileges during the first wedding night. Two murals in a bedroom of the Roman Villa Farnese show quite explicitly the act of intercourse between a married couple. The first scene shows a man with a timid woman in his bed, while the second scene features a woman fully dedicated to the sexual act. She has obviously mastered the game of love and is able to satisfy her husband's desires. However, sexual performance was not a basic condition for a marriage to be legally valid. In Ulpian's words:

> Not sleeping together, but consent, certifies a marriage. (*Dig.* 50, 17, 30 (Ulpian))

The whole wedding ceremony leaves a modern audience feeling confused. To the bridegroom, particularly if he was over twenty, the contracting of a marriage marked the entry into a new phase of life, though the change would not have been very dramatic. As mentioned above, he had been able to experiment with sex from the time he came of age. For this he had young male or female slaves at his disposal, and a visit to a brothel was rather encouraged. After becoming a husband, the Roman man still enjoyed a certain degree of liberty in sexual matters. Roman marriage was characterised by a double moral standard: other norms applied to men than to women, who were expected to guard their chastity. Despite the admonitions of pagan moralists and Christian authors, this remained the moral standard up into late antiquity. According to the Roman concept of marriage, sexual faithfulness on the part of the male was not indispensable to a happy and harmonious marital life.[26]

But how would a young Roman girl have experienced the initiation rite of marriage? We do not know, for example, whether a girl from the middle classes who married in her late teens would have had any sexual experience. Most probably, she would have been expected not to. Virginity was considered important, although not for religious reasons. One source mentions an examination of virginity carried out by a midwife.[27] In the case of Roman upper-class girls, sexual chastity was required prior to marriage. In fact, this requirement for sexual purity also meant that unmarried girls were not allowed to attend banquets where obscene jokes were told.[28] Ancient

---

[26] Treggiari 1991: 299–309; Nathan 2000: 179–80; Eyben, Laes, and Van Houdt 2003a: 196–8 and 202. Remarkable examples in Suetonius, *Aug.* 69 (letter by the married Antony); Valerius Maximus, *Fact. et dict. mem.* 6, 7, 1 (Scipio's wife values her husband's concubine); Plutarch, *Praec. coniug.* 140b.
[27] Cyprian, *Epist.* 4, 4.   [28] Varro, *Men.* 11 (Bücheler = 9 Cèbe).

lexicographers mention the expression 'married words' (*nupta verba*) – words that only married women were allowed to hear because, as a result of their experience of the bridal bed, they had been initiated into the secrets of sexuality.[29] The sudden confrontation with sexuality and the machismo of the first bridal night must have signalled a dramatic change in the lives of aristocratic girls, who just a day earlier had commemorated their childhood. Unfortunately these girls are not given a voice in the available source material. However, in a brilliant evocation of a fictitious Roman wedding ceremony, one of Keith Hopkins' characters, a time traveller in Pompeii, utters the following words:

> The bride, sitting there demurely (what else could the poor lass do?), figured only briefly as a potential beguilement, who might divert the groom from penetration and victory. What on earth was she thinking? Being there unfortunately didn't help us understand Roman emotions. Her father's house, with its pervasive erect phalli and pictures of violent conflict between men and women, must have had an influence. But how? Perhaps she was used to it all. I felt sympathetic. Only last night, she had dedicated her girlish clothes and childhood toys at the temple of Venus, but what sort of love was this?[30]

In the Greek East

We are equally well informed about wedding ceremonies in ancient Greece, though again no author provides a complete description of the actual proceedings. Our sources belong mostly to the Golden Age of Athens, the fifth century BC, but writings from the imperial era suggest that similar ceremonies continued to exist. Certainly conquest by the Romans did not mean that the inhabitants of the Greek parts of the Empire suddenly gave up their identity to share a Roman way of everyday life.[31]

As popular customs and traditions are usually long-lived, we may imagine wedding ceremonies in the Greek East to have proceeded more or less as follows. The Greeks, too, had a system of betrothal, known as *engue*, whereby a girl could be promised to a man before witnesses. The two parties would also make arrangements regarding a dowry. As in Roman tradition girls could be betrothed at an early age. Subsequently, they would remain at the parental home, but the future husband was expected to foot his fiancée's bill.[32]

---

[29] The expression appears in Festus, *De signif. verb.* 174 (ed. Lindsay); see Lentano 1996.
[30] Hopkins 1999: 37. [31] See Woolf 1994. [32] Garland 1990: 218.

11.3 Wedding ceremonies

On her wedding day, the young girl was expected to perform some ritual acts.[33] Mention is made of the offering of hair and the belt of virginity, the sacrifice of toys as a symbolic farewell to childhood, and a ritual bath.[34] The bride would sit veiled at the wedding table. Most probably, the bridegroom would not have attended the feast, simply showing up at the end of the day to take his bride with him in a wedding chariot. In a nocturnal procession, accompanied by torchlight and a group of friends singing bridal hymns, the couple would make for the bridegroom's house. On the bridal chariot, the groom would be flanked by his wife on one side and by his best friend on the other. The young bride would be welcomed at her new home by her mother-in-law. The entrance into the new house was symbolised by a ceremony at the hearth, at which the young couple would be sprinkled with nuts and dried fruit, while a young boy would distribute the contents of a basket of bread. Only after this ceremony would the bride take off her veil with a ritual gesture.[35] The groom would then lead her to the bedroom where the couple were to spend their first wedding night. Outside, before the closed door, the attendants would sing bridal songs. There was also the strange custom of the doorkeeper, known as the *thuroros*:

> One of the groom's friends is called *thuroros*. He takes his place before the door, and prevents the women from rushing to the bride's assistance when she cries out for help. (Pollux, *Onom.* 3, 42)

The actual wedding feast would take place only the day after. This was when the members of the two families would meet each other and exchange presents.

As in the Roman tradition, sexual initiation and the loss of virginity were crucial components of the first wedding night in the Greek world.[36] And, as with the Romans, not every single wedding ceremony in the Greek tradition followed the same solemn pattern. In fact, no ceremony was obligatory. Marriage was often a private business agreement between two families. In wedding contracts from the Hellenistic and the Roman periods which have been preserved on papyri, one reads about the rights and duties of men and women. A wife had to obey her husband and to administer the household

---

[33] For descriptions of the Athenian bridal ceremony, see Garland 1990: 217–25; Oakley and Sinos 1993; Pomeroy 1997: 79–81.
[34] Pollux, *Onom.* 3, 38 (cutting of the hair); Pausanias, *Perieg.* 2, 33, 1 (belt); *Anth. Pal.* 6, 280 (toys); Euripides, *Ph.* 347 (ritual bath).
[35] See Gherchanoc 2006 on this 'game' of veiling and unveiling.
[36] On marriage and sexual initiation in the papyri, see Triantaphyllopoulos 1988: women gave a present to young men when they had lost their virginity, and men exchanged presents with women for the same reason.

together with him. A man had to respect his wife and was not allowed to have a mistress or illegitimate children.[37] The contracts were signed by the bridegroom on the one hand and the girl's family (sometimes both her mother and father) on the other.

11.4 What did it mean to contract a marriage?

Although that is as far as the concrete information goes, it is possible to surmise more about the ins and outs of the contraction of a marriage. With some imagination and empathy, one can get an idea of the sometimes difficult choices Roman youngsters had to face. For one thing, one may wonder whether marriages were sometimes forced upon the partners. Did women's rights come into consideration? Or should Roman marriage be seen as an institution for the submission and oppression of often young brides in a male-oriented society?

Reciprocal consent was, in any case, an important concept in Roman marriage, as the jurist Paul asserts:

> A marriage cannot exist if all parties have not given their consent: the couple and those who wield *potestas* on them. (*Dig.* 23, 2, 2 (Paul))

In the third century, Ulpian similarly remarked the following:

> A marriage is considered legitimate when both partners have the right to contract a marriage, when both man and woman are sexually mature, when both have given their consent in the case that they are not submitted to paternal power, and when also their parents agree, in the case that they are submitted to paternal power. (*Tit. Ulp.* 5, 2)

The implications of this assertion are quite clear: neither a boy nor a girl could be forced into marriage. As mentioned above, the harsh demographic realities of life in antiquity meant that, more often than not, the fathers of newly weds were no longer alive. The notion of the omnipotent Roman *pater familias* should therefore be qualified to some extent: at the age of twenty-five, only 40% of Roman men had a father who was still alive.[38] On the other hand, it was not possible to contract a marriage without the consent of the fathers or guardians. What is more, until the second century AD a father had the right to disband the marriage of his son or daughter. According to Ulpian, the emperor Antoninus Pius (AD 161–80)

---

[37] For marital contracts, see Yiftach-Firanko 2003.   [38] See the tables in Saller 1994: 48.

11.4 What did it mean to contract a marriage?

was the first to ban this tradition: henceforth fathers did not have the right to break up marriages being conducted on good terms.[39]

Little is known about actual instances of disputes. Sometimes a case or a judgement that has been preserved in legal sources can be informative. On 6 November AD 285 the emperors Diocletian and Maximinian are recorded as having given the following response to a certain Sabinus, who had applied to their jurisdiction:

> The teaching of the laws does not permit even a son in the legal power of his *pater familias* to be forced to take a wife against his will. Therefore you, just as you desire, after the precepts of the law have been preserved, you are not prevented from joining in marriage to yourself a woman whom you wanted, in such a way, however, that you have your father's consent in contracting the marriage. (*Cod. Iust.* 5, 4, 12; transl. J. Evans Grubbs)

It seems Sabinus was unhappy with the partner his father had chosen for him. What is more, he may have found someone else. According to the emperors, he could not be forced to marry the spouse his father preferred. However, if he wanted to marry the girl of his choice, he would nonetheless have to persuade his father. We do not know what happened next, so a whole series of interesting questions remains unanswered. What if his father persisted in his first choice? If Sabinus went ahead and married his preferred partner, his marriage may have been illegitimate. This may in turn have resulted in him losing his right to an inheritance and to financial support from his father. And any children born of the controversial union may have been deemed illegitimate, so that they would have to forfeit the inheritance of their grandfather. The outcome will, of course, have depended largely on the age of Sabinus, his personality, and his financial circumstances. Perhaps he simply broke with his father. Or perhaps he married without suffering the potentially dire consequences: if, ultimately, his father failed to protest loudly or simply resigned himself to his son's stubbornness, a clever jurist might subsequently have argued that he had tacitly consented.[40]

Subtle or less refined manipulations most probably also occurred. As the second-century jurist Celsus puts it:

> If, when his father forces him, the son takes a wife whom he would not marry of his own free will, he has nevertheless contracted marriage, which is not contracted between those who are unwilling. He appears to have preferred this course. (*Dig.* 23, 2, 22 (Celsus); transl. J. Evans Grubbs)

---

[39] *Dig.* 43, 30, 1, 5 (Ulpian); Paulus, *Sent.* 5, 6, 15.
[40] Evans Grubbs 2005a: 103–5. For another case of tacit consent, see *Cod. Iust.* 5, 4, 5.

To be sure, if the son was young and dependent on his father, we can easily imagine him going along with his father's wishes. As for under-age girls, they most likely had little choice but to resign to the will of their father. As Ulpian explains:

> If she doesn't fight against her father's wishes, she is understood to consent. Moreover, the liberty to dissent from her father's decision is only allowed to her, if her father chooses a fiancé who is disgraceful or unworthy in his way of life. (*Dig.* 23, 1, 12 (Ulpian); transl. J. Evans Grubbs)

But the *fait accompli* also worked the other way around: if a father had not protested against his daughter's marriage, he was understood to consent to it.[41]

Things became even more complicated when a guardian had been appointed to an under-age girl. On 8 May AD 199 the emperors Caracalla and Severus responded as follows to a query from a man called Potitus:

> When a girl's marriage is being sought and there is no agreement between her guardian (*tutor*) and her mother and relatives concerning the choice of a future husband, the judgement of the governor of the province is necessary. (*Cod. Iust.* 5, 4, 1; transl. J. Evans Grubbs)

We do not know who Potitus was. A provincial official who did not know how to resolve a particular dispute? A desperate suitor? A relative of the girl? Her guardian? The case seems to revolve around a *tutor impuberum*, a guardian for girls under the age of twelve who had lost their father. Her young age was no obstacle to making marriage plans.[42] If a fatherless girl was older than twelve, her wishes were taken into account:

> Management of the business affairs of the female ward is the *curator*'s duty; but she can marry by her own decision. (*Dig.* 23, 2, 20 (Paul); transl. J. Evans Grubbs)

As previously mentioned, fatherless children who had reached the age of majority (twelve for girls, fourteen for boys) but were under twenty-five were granted a *curator minorum*. On 24 February AD 241 the emperor Gordian III wrote:

> In joining marriage, neither the *curator*, who is responsible only for administering his ward's property, nor the relatives by blood or marriage have any authority to intervene, but the wish of the person whose marriage is being discussed must be considered. (*Cod. Iust.* 5, 4, 8; transl. J. Evans Grubbs)

---

[41] *Dig.* 23, 1, 7, 1 (Paul); see Evans Grubbs 2005a: 101.   [42] Evans Grubbs 2005a: 109–10.

11.5 Marriage as the end of youth for boys?

Although marriage did not mark a drastic change in matters of sexuality for a young Roman groom, it did bring with it new financial responsibilities: the care for a (new) house or property (it was rather rare for families extending to married brothers and sisters and their children to live under the same roof),[43] managing the dowry, taking care of wife and children. In this context, ancient sources do mention the 'bridal yoke' that represents the end of the carefree and untroubled period of youth. This is a particularly popular motif with the comic writers Plautus and Terence:[44] a rake has fallen desperately in love with a girl of lower social status. He wants to enjoy a life of liberty, and certainly does not intend to satisfy his father's wishes for the future. Of course, what the father has in mind is a marriage with a girl of high social standing. In Terence's *Andria*, the son Pamphilus laments that his father Simo is trying to restrain him far too early in life:

> It is you yourself, father, who has prescribed an end to all this. Certainly, the time is near that I'll have to live according to another's way. Meanwhile, let me live my life now for some time in my own way. (Terence, *Andria* 151–3)

The slave Davus tries to persuade father Simo that his son has finally reconciled himself with marriage:

> When it was permitted, when his age allowed it, he had a love affair ... Now he needs a wife. He has set his mind upon a wife. (Terence, *Andria* 443–6)

A legal wife will make things better:

> Let's give him a wife. I expect ... that, tied down by habit and a voluntary marriage, he will easily extricate himself then from his evil habits. (Terence, *Andria* 560–2)

Of course, Terence's comedies for the most part go back to Greek originals, but Roman audiences must have recognised the situations portrayed and appreciated the underlying humour. Besides, the same ideas occur in other contexts. Cicero was confident that marriage with his daughter Tullia would correct the worrying conduct of the aristocrat Dolabella. The poet Statius mentions a young man who was keen to accept the marital yoke in order to come to terms with himself. Pseudo-Plutarch asserts that the marital yoke is the most effective way of taming those who are addicted to joy and pleasure.[45] Tellingly, he goes on to argue that this is the case not so

---

[43] Laes 2006a: 26–7.　[44] Eyben 1977: 90–2.
[45] Cicero, *Ad fam.* 8, 13, 1; Statius, *Silv.* 1, 2, 26–9; Ps.-Plutarch, *De lib. educ.* 13f. For these and other similar texts, see Eyben 1977: 91–2.

much for psychological reasons as for economic ones. He recommends that a man should take a wife who is not much wealthier than himself. Otherwise, one becomes not the husband of one's wife, but the slave of her dowry!

The insistence on contracting a marriage in order to restrain youthful lust is also a popular topos with the church fathers. In the Christian era, marriage and sexuality were evidently viewed in another context, though the church fathers remained deeply rooted in the ancient medical tradition, claiming that female loose morals were due to biological causes.[46]

11.6 Girls and marriage: a history of submission?

In a short essay on the virtue of women, Plutarch serves up a bizarre story. Once upon a time, the city of Miletus was hit by a wave of suicides among young girls. Physicians blamed the peculiar air above the city, arguing that it drove young girls, whose minds were already unstable by nature, to a manic desire to hang themselves. The wave seemed irrepressible, until someone suggested that the naked corpses of the suicide victims should be put on display in the market square. The shame of being exhibited in this way made young girls think twice before taking their own lives, and hence the storm of suicides abated.[47] To the ancient – male – authors, the explanation for the strange female juvenile behaviour was simple. They sought it not in profound psychological causes, but in physiology: bad air or, even more commonly, the accumulation of blood caused by insufficient opening of the vagina for menstruation. In their view, these young girls had to marry as soon as possible and engage in sexual intercourse in order for the moods of manic hysteria, depression, and suicidal thoughts to disappear almost automatically.[48]

Surely, though, there was more to it than that? The prevalence of suicidal thoughts among girls experiencing puberty was a recurrent motif in ancient literature, from mythology to poetry and medical treatises.[49] Apparently it was clear to the ancient authors that this stage of life was fraught with anxieties and emotions. There was the fear of not marrying owing to, for example, one's family being unable to afford a dowry. An unmarried woman was a *femme manquée*; she would stay a girl forever. And if girls

---

[46] Laurence 2005.   [47] Plutarch, *De mul. virt.* 249 b–d.
[48] Hippocrates, *De virg. morb.* 1 (8, 467–70 Littré); Pliny the Elder, *Nat. hist.* 28, 44. See Garland 1990: 168–9.
[49] Van Hooff 1990: 22–6.

11.6 Girls and marriage: a history of submission?

did enter into marriage, there was the fear of the sudden and abrupt initiation into the world of sexuality. An epigram tells of a young bride who was torn apart by guard dogs as she tried to flee the house on her wedding night, out of fear at the prospect of her first act of sexual intercourse. The poem states quite unequivocally that this fear was common among young girls.[50] Various literary texts similarly mention that the life of young married women was not at all enviable because of the implied submission and the perils of pregnancy (see Fig. 11.1).[51] In the first or second

11.1 Mummy mask of Aphrodite, daughter of Didas, from Hawara, Fayum, c. AD 50–70. Instead of a portrait painted on a wooden board, a funeral mask could be attached to the mummy. It was made of stucco or cardboard and was painted realistically. This mask shows the entire bust, with the woman (about twenty years old) holding a bouquet of flowers in her right hand. (British Museum, London.)

[50] *Anth. Pal.* 9, 245.
[51] See for instance Sophocles, *Ter.* (fr. 538 Radt = 524 ed. Nauck²). See also Laes 2004b on young mothers and death in childbed.

century AD, an inscription from Thracian Tomis, in present-day Romania, tells a tragic story:

> My husband Perinthus provided this altar and this stele.
> Dear passer-by, should you wish to know who I am and whose I was:
> When I was thirteen years of age, a child worthy of her family, I fell in love:
> I married and bore three children for this man.
> First a son, then two daughters, spitting images of their mother.
> Then I bore my fourth child. I wish I had never borne it:
> First the baby died, I followed in death somewhat later.
> I was thirty years of age when I was deprived of the sunlight.
> My name is Caecilia Artemisia. Here I lie.
> My support and husband is Perinthus,
> My son is called Priscus, my daughter Hieronis.
> The other is Theodora; she is still a baby and does not know that I have died.
> My husband Perinthus is alive and weeps softly over me,
> And my dear father grieves too because I am not there any more.
> My mother Flavia Theodora also lies buried here,
> As well as my father-in-law Caecilius Priscus.
> So this was my family. Now I have really died.
> Farewell, dear passer-by, you who pass my grave, whoever you are.
>
> (*GV* I 1161)

So perhaps the medical texts focus on physiology while the contemporary literary sources contain hints of a female subculture. Should we imagine girls in antiquity harbouring common fears and holding similar expectations due to their being in close contact with peers and elder women within a female inner circle? Although interesting, such suppositions are hard to prove given the predominantly male origin of ancient literature.[52] Nonetheless, these are questions that every historian with a capacity for empathy should dare to ask.

We should not however be blind to the harsh realities of life as a young girl in the Roman world. Moreover, early marriage and pregnancy, often with fatal consequences for both mother and child, are still a reality in many developing countries in the world today, in Asia, Africa, and South America. In some Islamic countries the legal marital age for girls is strikingly low. Perhaps the stories of these young women, their early initiation into marital life and sexuality, and their place in society as women, can help us draw a picture of what it actually meant to be a young woman in ancient Rome. At the same time, there are clearly differences. In Rome, there was no religious requirement for virginity before marriage, for example. Furthermore, we

---

[52] The rare surviving poems by female authors do not bring us closer to the female experience, since this work is often more about subtle imitations of the male poetic aesthetic. See Hemelrijk 1999: 146–84.

11.6 Girls and marriage: a history of submission?

must guard against rash generalisations or easy prejudices. One cannot simply assume that all marriages involving young brides were unhappy or hotbeds of tension and manifestations of an institution designed for the submission of wives. Cross-cultural research has shown that women often succeed in finding ways of fulfilling more than a merely passive role in their relationships with men, thanks to their contacts in a female inner circle that is inaccessible to those men and where secrets and coping strategies are shared. The Palestinian Muslim scholar of Islam Maysam al-Faruqi argues quite firmly that western feminists have a good deal to learn from the experiences of Muslim women. While fully recognising the excrescences of radicalism and fanaticism, she points to certain benefits of Muslim society: women live in a protected network of family relationships and are not burdened by individualism, marriage and divorce are relatively easy, the extended family supports the combination of work and family care.[53] In antiquity marriage and procreation constituted the very purpose of women's lives. It was towards this ideal that girls were educated, in the same way as they were in the West at least up to the Victorian era. Ideals that differed from present-day notions resulted in different patterns of adult life. An inscription from a Greek community in Rome in the first or second century AD tells the following story of married life:

> Euenus built this grave for his wife Margaris,
> As a tribute to his dear and loving wife.
> He married her when she was still a girl, thirteen years of age.
> They were married for fifty years.
> Then she died at age sixty-three.
> All her life, she made her husband happy.
>
> (*IG* xiv 1831; *GV* i 666)

Indeed, while this text may not correspond to our expectations of marital life, it does not rule out the possibility that this was actually a happy marriage.

Neither a radical feminist approach nor a naively rosy outlook do justice to the reality faced by young girls in Roman society. Moreover, historians of antiquity cannot but concede that many questions concerning Roman marriage remain unanswered. Since there were no official registers of births, and since the implementation of state control was far from absolute, it was by no means inconceivable, for example, for a husband simply to leave his wife and to live out the rest of his life elsewhere.[54] Furthermore, we know hardly anything at all about the marital life of the lower classes, both in the

---

[53] Al-Faruqi 2000. [54] See Sandirocco 2003 on legal aspects.

cities and in the country. What were the lives like of a herdsman and his wife in the countryside, an artisan and his spouse in the city, a veteran and his lady on the small plot of land allotted to them on his retirement from military service? Were their relationships very different? Alas, we can only conclude that a social stratification of the various kinds of marital relations in antiquity is beyond the present possibilities of historical research.

CHAPTER 12

Youth and Christianity: continuity or change?

Youth and Christianity could easily be the subject of a whole book. Such a study, which has yet to be written, would have to take into account a wide variety of aspects: conceptions of power and authority, attitudes towards the body and sexuality, education and Christianity, the new faith and family life, and so on.

Obviously, it is impossible to discuss all these topics at length in a single chapter. We can however focus on aspects where we expect to discern differences, in terms of both conceptions and practice, between paganism and Christianity. Such an approach immediately raises the vexed question of the impact of Christianity on the world of antiquity – a question that has been answered in different ways depending on the ideological background of the scholar concerned. It is also a topical subject in research. The Norwegian scholar Odd Magne Bakke has argued that Christianity was the main factor in the discovery of the child as a person (*When Children Became People*): the church fathers put great emphasis on the soul of the young child and Christian authors spoke out against abortion, exposure, and paedophilia. Great importance was attached to the religious education of the child, which was also implied in liturgy.[1] Other researchers have focused instead on continuity. According to them, Christianity ultimately offered nothing new or revolutionary, but merely perpetuated certain patterns originating in a strict pagan morality from the first and second centuries AD.[2]

May we assume that the first Christians constituted a young church, preaching a drastically new attitude in the relationships between young and old? What do we know about age limits for priests and monks? Is

---

[1] Bakke 2005. For a brief account of the topic of children in early Christianity, see Laes and Strubbe 2006: 125–32. On the changed attitudes of Christians concerning the issue of paedophilia, see Laes 2006a: 241–7 and 2011: 268–73.
[2] Veyne 2007. As in earlier publications, Veyne strongly opposes the view that the Church brought about drastic change, including in matters of sexuality. See Veyne 1978.

Christianity responsible for the emergence of the sexually frustrated adolescent? And do the sources provide any informative stories about young Christians? These are the questions we will try to answer in the present chapter.

12.1 Early Christians: a young church?

According to Celsus, a pagan intellectual of the second century, Christianity was an alarming social phenomenon. He criticised the new faith as a religion for fools, the uneducated, women, and children. In a vivid description of daily life, he provides an account of how woolworkers, cobblers, laundrymen, and other illiterate folk sneakily approach women and children and whisper into their ears that they should no longer obey their schoolmasters and fathers. If the master or any other person with intellectual authority came across them, these clandestine preachers would flee. And they also encouraged the children of the rich to convene with their peers from the lower classes to learn together about the perfect ways of the new faith.[3] By placing Christianity in the context of fools, women, slaves, and children, Celsus situates the religion that he hated so much on the periphery of ancient society. In other words, he treats it as a religion that could not claim the respect or the understanding of fully fledged male aristocrats, people in possession of their full intellectual capacities. Of course, one may ask whether Celsus was not in fact making use of a rhetorical commonplace that fitted into his polemic against Christianity, rather than actually referring to the reality of his era. In all likelihood, both explanations are true to some extent. Celsus thus aptly describes how early Christianity spread informally through extended households, where people of very different social standing lived next to and mixed with each other.[4] We may well imagine how children and young people were introduced to the new religion by slaves and other domestic staff.

But does all this imply that young people also used to administer early Christian communities? And was the traditional pattern, whereby the elder governed the young, ever reversed in such communities?[5] In his epistles, the apostle Peter writes from Rome to the first Christian communities in Asia Minor, telling the elders to govern the flock of the Lord with wisdom.

---

[3] Origen, *Contra Cels.* 3, 40; 3, 44; 3, 50.
[4] See MacDonald 2003 for an excellent synthesis. See Osiek and MacDonald 2005 for a history of these early house churches.
[5] Eyben 1999 cols. 432–3 and Barclay 2007 are excellent on the question of youth in early Christian communities.

12.1 Early Christians: a young church?

The younger members are urged to subject themselves to the older, but the author eagerly adds that every one should be guided by humility in dealing with others.[6] In the Epistle to Titus, Paul addresses the first Christian communities in Crete. In this letter too, just two age categories are mentioned: young and old. The older members are implored to demonstrate their temperance, dignity, self-control, faith, love, and compassion, as well as endurance. Older women are told to behave with dignity in all aspects of life and particularly to give advice to younger women on how to run the household and how to care for their husband and children. The addressee Titus is told to instruct the younger men by good example and by encouraging them always to behave with self-control.[7] The letter to the first Christians of Corinth from the late first century, which according to tradition was written by Pope Clement I, mentions a revolt against the elders. Authority needs to be restored by reinforcing the rule of those 'appointed elders', while younger members must learn to show moderation and respect.[8] The same tenor is found in Polycarp's second-century letter to the Christians of Philippi: in order to avoid deviant moral behaviour (i.e. sexual misconduct), youths must receive guidance from the 'elders and deacons'.[9]

There are only a few dissenting voices when it comes to the authority of the elders. In one example, Paul writes from Macedonian Philippi to his beloved disciple Timothy in Ephesus:

> Let no one look down on you because you are young, but set an example for the believers in your speech, conduct, love, faithfulness, and purity. (*1 Timothy* 4, 12)

At the same time, though, he urges his disciple to treat older men and women respectfully, as if they were his own father and mother.[10] In his epistle to the Christians of Magnesia, Ignatius had to use all his power of persuasion to have young Damas accepted as head of the community. His youthfulness, Ignatius writes, was merely outward appearance, and the elders, who were capable of seeing through it, knew that he possessed wisdom in God.[11]

In all likelihood, the opposition between young and old was used mainly to consolidate positions of power within the first Christian communities. Most probably, the term *presbyteroi* referred to older persons appointed to

---

[6] *1 Peter* 5, 1–5. [7] *Titus* 2, 1–8.
[8] Clement of Rome, *Epist. ad Corinth.* 1, 3; 3, 3; 47, 6; 54, 2. See Barclay 2007: 235–6.
[9] Polycarpus, *Epist. ad Philipp.* 5–6. See Barclay 2007: 237–8.   [10] *1 Timothy* 5, 1–2.
[11] Ignatius, *Epist. ad Magn.* 3, 1–2.

positions of authority.[12] If leaders happened to be younger, the authors took great pains to persuade the members of the community that the individual concerned was worthy and competent. Admittedly, when Paul appointed leaders in Thessalonica, Corinth or Philippi, he never mentioned age as a criterion. Perhaps Paul had an alternative theological point of view in these matters. But other factors may also have played a role: the Christians of the first generation did not have much choice in electing their leaders; they often held negative views of the contemporary world and of their life experiences in that world; they believed the end of time was nigh; and they believed that anyone could be blessed by the Spirit, not just the older members.[13]

From the second generation on, as the early Christian communities grew more stable, old age increasingly became a guarantee of authority. The 'young church' gradually disappeared. In this respect, Christianity was not essentially different from Judaism. The Babylonian Talmud states: when Rabbi Eleazar ben Azariah was appointed as head of the Sanhedrin at the age of eighteen, it was feared that the people would not accept him because of his youthful appearance. But then a miracle happened and overnight his beard turned white.[14]

12.2 Young office-holders within the church

The opposition between the traditional reverence for the wisdom of old age and the belief that every age can be agreeable to God is a recurrent motif in the history of priesthood in the early church.[15] The latter viewpoint, which was certainly more idealistic than the former, was supported by arguments of tradition. The ideal of the *puer senex*, the child with the wisdom of an old man, was a widespread topos in both Greek and Latin pagan literature and popular traditions as well as in theoretical–philosophical works.[16] The Old and the New Testaments also provided various forceful examples of maturity in young people. After all, did not Jesus teach in the synagogue at age twelve?[17] And had not John the Baptist, who was just a few months older than Jesus, announced the coming of the Messiah?[18] Church fathers from

---

[12] Barclay 2007: 234–5 on age as a criterion for holding power.
[13] Barclay 2007: 239–41. On the appointments by Paul, see *1 Thessalonians* 5, 12–13; *1 Corinthians* 16, 15–16; *Philippians* 1, 1. For a negative view on the contemporary world: *Galatians* 1, 4.
[14] *B. Ber.* 28 a. On Christianity, Judaism and old age, see Campbell 1994.
[15] Eyben 1995: 102–3 offers extended bibliography on ages and ordination in the early Church. Gnilka 1972 offers an extensive treatment of the motif of the overcoming of age.
[16] Gnilka 1972: 47–71.   [17] *Luke* 2, 41–52.   [18] Gnilka 1972: 239–45.

late antiquity also cited the cases of Paul's disciple Timothy and young Damas, whom we have dealt with in the previous section. Were these young men not the predecessors of the bishops (cf. the Greek *episkopoi*)? But there were also strong counter-arguments. The risk of jealousy and gossip was always rife when a young priest was appointed, simply because the life experience and wisdom of an older man were traditionally valued more highly. Moreover, an adequate preparation for the priesthood required a considerable amount of time and training. Finally, the Holy Scripture also provided arguments against the appointment of priests at a young age: Jesus was already thirty years old when he entered public life, and the minimum age for Levites to be allowed to read the whole of the Bible was twenty-five.[19]

There are some notable examples of young priests. In the Greek East, John Chrysostom was probably only twenty when he heard that he would be ordained as a priest – his response was to flee.[20] While there are many parallels for this refusal, the question remains whether it should be regarded as a topos illustrating the modesty of the prospective priest or as an account of reality.[21] In the sixth century, Theodosius of Sicyon was ordained at the age of eighteen, first as a reader (*lector*), and two days later as a subdeacon, deacon, and priest. The other bishops protested, but the ordaining bishop maintained that God had assured him that the young man possessed the competence to perform these duties. As an example, he referred to the New Testament case of Timothy.[22]

However, it is equally significant that such early ordinations often aroused strong protest or at least criticism from fellow Christians.[23] In the mid-fourth century, an ecclesiastical career, a *cursus honorum* with a fixed hierarchy of functions and ages, was introduced (see Table 12.1). What was involved here was not so much a canonical rule, universally implemented, but a regulation with local variants. Nonetheless, we may safely assume that these regulations point to widely accepted practice. Our first source is a letter by Pope Siricius from the year 335. The papal decree by Zosimus dates from 418. The secular regulation of the *Novellae* dates from the year 546.

These data show quite clearly that Christians in late antiquity were very reluctant to ordain young candidates. Indeed, the responsibilities of the priesthood and the duties of a bishop no doubt required much skill and experience.[24]

---

[19] Eyben 1995: 104–6; Eyben 1999 col. 436 on the age of thirty.
[20] Eyben 1995: 110. See John Chrysostom, *De sacerd.* 1. 3. [21] Eyben 1995: 109 n. 49; 114 n. 68.
[22] Georgius of Eleusis, *Vita Theod. Sic.* 3, 21 (*Acta Sanctorum apr.* 3, 38).
[23] Gnilka 1972: 170–89 on the discussion between 'idealists' and 'realists' concerning age.
[24] Eyben 1995: 113–20 offers detailed discussion on minimum ages for holding ecclesiastical office.

Table 12.1 *The ecclesiastical career (mid-fourth century)*

Source	Lector[a]	Subdeacon	Deacon	Priest	Bishop
Siricius, *Epist.* 1, 9, 13 (PL 13, 1142)	From first childhood to the age of 14	From the beginning of *adulescentia* (14 or 18 years of age?)	30 yrs	35 yrs	45 yrs
Zosimus, *Epist.* 9, 3, 5 (PL 20, 672–3)	From first childhood	20 yrs	25 yrs	30 yrs	–
Nov. 123, 13	18 yrs	25 yrs	25 yrs	30 yrs	35 yrs[b]

Notes:
[a] On child readers in liturgy, see Peterson 1934; Eyben 1995: 118 n. 113; Laes and Strubbe 2006: 130.
[b] *Nov.* 123, 1, 1.

We do not have the space here to go into monastic life in detail. Circumstances dictated from what age postulants were admitted and whether or not children could live in monasteries (cf. the issue of the oblates).[25] We know for certain that there were children and young people at Egyptian monasteries. They were often young apprentices, contracted to learn a particular kind of labour, or sons who had followed their fathers into monastic life.[26] Often one reads about a vocation for monastic life at the age of eighteen. Anthony, the father of all the monks of the Egyptian desert, is said to have been eighteen when he retreated to the remoteness of the desert.[27] However, this age is to be understood symbolically. The Greek letter combination IH not only stands for the number eighteen, but it also forms the initials of Jesus' name. Both in the Greek East and the Latin West, there was an idealistic tradition that age was of no significance at all in monasteries, as it was a relic of the Old World.

> In a convent, there is no reign of age nor dignity. There is only equality. (Ps.- Cyprian, *De sing. cler.* 14)

In the Latin West, the Benedictine rule is an example of this 'idealistic' conception of age. New life begins on the day of entrance into the monastery: 'age' or rank (or rather seniority) is counted from this day on, so that the younger of two monks in the exterior world may have greater seniority within the realm of the monastery. Important decisions are to be taken by

---

[25] On oblates, see Boswell 1988.
[26] On apprentices, see MacCoull 1979. See also Vuolanto 2005: 125.
[27] Athanasius, *Vita Anton.* 2, 1.

the entire council of monks, where the opinion of the younger brothers carries equal weight, as Benedict states explicitly. In the election of the abbot, the deans or the *cellarius*, age should never be decisive. Only the master of the novices and the doorkeeper need to be slightly older. Should older novices enter the monastery, it would be very difficult for a novice master to train them if he were young himself. A doorkeeper should preferably be a senior so that he be better able to resist the temptation of exploring the outside world.[28]

It would be incorrect to view monasteries as 'revolutionary' institutions where traditional age categories were invalidated and where young people were offered new opportunities and chances. In reality, the average age upon entering a monastery was around twenty; maturity and thus age were certainly taken into account in assigning important duties.[29] In questions of old versus young, it was usually the recklessness of youth that was, somewhat stereotypically, given prominence, not the notion of age restrictions *per se*.

12.3 Young people and sexuality

> I was about fifteen years of age. As my parents could not afford it, I didn't attend school; I lived with my parents. At that time, the weed of sensual desire raged above my head, and there was no hand to pull up the weeds. When my father at the bathhouse saw that my puberty had begun and that I was covered with the signs of restless youth, he joyfully brought the message to my mother, as he was eager to have grandchildren soon. He was drunk with that sort of drunkenness by which the world forgets its Creator and worships the Creation rather than You ... But in my mother's heart, You had already placed Your temple and the foundation of Your holy dwelling. My father was still and only very recently a candidate for baptism. My mother panicked in pious fear and emotion. For me, although I was not yet baptised, she feared the twisted roads on which they walk 'who have turned their backs towards You, not their faces' (Jeremiah 2: 27). (Augustine, *Conf.* 2, 3, 6)

These are the words of Augustine, who in the year 369 had returned from the town of Madaura to his parents in Thagaste, where he was confronted with the onset of puberty. Readers of Augustine's *Confessions* undoubtedly remember the harsh words with which the church father complained

---

[28] *R. Benedicti* 63, 1 (seniority); 3, 3 (council); 64 (election of an abbot); 21, 4 (*decani*); 31, 1 (*cellarius*); 58, 6 (master of the novices); 66 (doorkeeper).
[29] Gnilka 1972: 201–2 on the very careful application of 'idealistic' conceptions of age.

about this period of crisis in his life: 'I wasn't in love at all, but I was in love with love ... What I needed the most, was to love and to be loved, most of all if I could enjoy the body of the one that was in love with me.'[30] As a seventeen-year-old, he had been allowed to study at Carthage: 'all around me, the cauldron of impudent loves bubbled'.[31] During his time there, his chief pleasure had been in going to the theatre: 'full of reflections of my own unhappiness, fuel for my burning desire'.[32] Undoubtedly at his mother's suggestion, he had attended church services in the city. It was possibly at church that he had his first encounter with a member of the opposite sex.[33] Be that as it may, his mother Monica would take care of his alliance with a concubine (whose name we never learn).[34] It was a kind of second-rate marriage, a union involving no legal obligation whatsoever, which was meant to temper his ferocious youth:

> In these years, I had one woman. She wasn't joined up with me in what one calls a legal marriage. In any case, my restlessly wandering passion, deprived of any reason, had found her for me. One woman, I say, and I was sexually faithful towards her. In this way, I could experience for myself the difference between a wise union of marriage, which is contracted in order to procreate, and an agreement based on pleasure and lust, in which children are born against the couple's will. But once they are born, one has to love these children anyway. (Augustine, *Conf.* 4, 2, 2)

Indeed, from the union with his concubine, a son, Adeodatus, was born.[35] At age twenty, Augustine was charged with the care of a wife and a child, in contrast with his peers and other itinerant professors.

The emotional testimonies of Augustine, the tormented searcher for God, and his almost pathetic aversion to sexuality and sin would earn him a particular reputation, as if he were responsible for the subsequent ecclesiastical disapproval of physicality and sexuality.[36] Moreover, the *Confessions* raise the suspicion that we are dealing with a young man suffering from an identity crisis, or a crisis of adolescence. Hence the question arises as to whether Christianity is, in a way, responsible for the emergence of the sexually frustrated adolescent.

---

[30] Augustine, *Conf.* 3, 1, 1.   [31] Augustine, *Conf.* 3, 1, 1.   [32] Augustine, *Conf.* 3, 2, 2.
[33] Augustine, *Conf.* 3, 3, 5.
[34] Brown 2000: 27–8; 50–2 (suggestion regarding Monica's role in the choice of concubine).
[35] See also Augustine, *Conf.* 9, 6, 14 on the death of Adeodatus at the age of sixteen ('I had nothing to do with the boy, except the sin').
[36] Brown 2000: 500–3 rightly stresses the need for a nuanced approach: 'On the issue of sexuality, we must be careful not to "demonize" Augustine' (p. 502).

12.3 Young people and sexuality

The difference between paganism and Christianity in matters of sexuality is especially clear in relation to masturbation. The 'masturbation mania', which manifested itself from the sixteenth century onwards in western thought, resulting in its condemnation for moral and religious reasons, was completely unknown to the ancient world. Only sporadically, and mainly in physiological treatises, is mention made of the dangers of bodily exhaustion through excess. Others maintained that masturbation implied a waste of sperm and thus of human life.[37] The advice given to monks was completely different though. Masturbation was not considered to satisfy even a natural urge. This could only be the case if a nocturnal emission occurred, while the sleeper was unaware of stimulating dreams. In their quest for personal sanctity and asceticism, the desert fathers went so far as to regulate nocturnal ejaculations during sleep.[38]

From ancient medical texts, it is particularly clear how greatly pagan and Christian ideas on sexual asceticism and self-control differed. According to ancient physicians, intercourse was a form of outburst that, in terms of intensity, differed very little from a sudden fit of anger. In the same way as young aristocrats had to learn to measure their steps, to moderate their voice, and to control their posture, so the sexual fire had to be carefully reined in so as to keep it under control. An all too active sex-life indicated a lack of restraint. The most virile man was he who refrained from needlessly spilling his sperm. 'Men who retain their chastity, are stronger and better than others and thus lead a more healthy life', according to the physician Soranus.[39] In this context, Galen believed in the benefits of castrating Olympic athletes, so that they would become stronger while retaining their reserves of bodily heat.[40] There are, however, no texts from Galen's time that point to men's anxiety over sex. The sexual act was just one of the many aspects of life which they were supposed to learn to control through good sense and education, in the same way as they had to learn to become modest in taking in food, and thoughtful about the way they trained their bodies with physical exercise. In some instances, ancient medical authors actually recommended coitus. Young men who wish to take care of their

---

[37] See Schouten 1971–2 for a Neo-Latin poem on the subject (a typical example of the campaigns against masturbation that were staged from the sixteenth century onwards). Ancient doctors opposing masturbation: Hippocrates, *De morb.* 2, 51 (7, 73 Littré); *De affect. int.* (7, 199–200 Littré). It is mentioned mockingly in Varro, *Men.* 235; Martial, *Epigr.* 9, 41. Unlike in these passages, it is not treated as a genuine problem in many other texts. See Krenkel 1979.

[38] Masturbation and nocturnal emissions are considered problematic only in the ascetic life of the early monks. See Foucault 1984: 160–5; Brakke 1995.

[39] Soranus, *Gyn.* 1, 30.   [40] Galen, *De sem.* 1, 15 (4, 571 Kühn).

health, maintains Galen, should make love even when the act does not give them particular pleasure.[41]

It is not hard to imagine how the Christian emphasis on asceticism might have caused anxiety when the proverbial storms of youth broke out.[42] Marriage was sometimes proposed as a way of calming such tempestuous feelings. Around the year 270, the inhabitants of a small village in the Egyptian Fayum saw the young Anthony struggle with the devil as he tried to liberate himself from earthly desires. The devil had appeared to him in his sleep as a beautiful woman. Young Anthony fled into the desert and became the leading example and founding father of numerous desert monks in the Egyptian wilderness.[43]

It is often assumed that, for reasons of chastity and continence, the average age of marriage of Christian boys and girls was lowered. New research, however, has called into question the validity of this hypothesis.[44] Moreover, more extensive evidence points to the existence of continuity, even if the authors are intent on stressing the radical change that Christianity brought about. According to the *Vita Melaniae*, a hagiography that was particularly popular in the Middle Ages, the wedding between Melania and Pinian, descendants of wealthy senatorial families, took place in the year 399.[45] She was fourteen years of age, he was seventeen. From the beginning, Melania opposed the marriage, which had been forced upon her by her family. She begged her husband to forsake the sexual aspects of their union and to agree to live their lives in chastity as a devout couple. But Pinian's motives for the wedding were clear: only after the birth of two children would he agree to renounce sexual intercourse. Melania tried to run away on several occasions from her parents' home (an indication that they stayed at the parental home for a while after their wedding), but ultimately she yielded, not least at the insistence of some respected priests. The couple's first child died in its first few years. The second baby did not survive beyond a few days. Owing to the early pregnancies, Melania's health steadily deteriorated. Only then did Pinian give in to his wife's wish that they should live together in a spiritual union, as 'brother and sister'.

At that time, Melania was twenty years of age, Pinian twenty-three. Despite their relatives' vehement objections, they began to distribute their wealth among the poor. Nothing or nobody could stop their charitable zeal.

---

[41] Galen, *De loc. aff.* 6, 5 (8, 417–18 Kühn).
[42] Eyben 1996 offers an extended survey of Christian passages on the storm of youth.
[43] Athanasius, *Vita Anton.* 5.   [44] Aubin 2000. See Eyben, Laes, and Van Houdt 2003b: 198–203.
[45] For a most readable summary and commentary, see Nathan 2000: 91–7.

Subsequently, they travelled to Egypt and to the East. Pinian eventually died in Jerusalem in the year 431. Melania survived him. This biography suggests that marital customs had changed very little within the Christianised aristocratic elite in late antiquity. Admittedly, Pinian married at a younger age than was usual in preceding centuries, but Melania was in her mid-teens, like many girls in that period. The marriage had been arranged and had nothing to do with romantic love. The power of the *pater familias*, the importance of the family's patrimony, and the desire for male descendants were all factors that continued to come into play.

The question as to whether Christianity brought about substantial change in respect of young people and sexuality can be answered only in a qualified way. Christian sources pay ample attention to the heart-breaking choice the young had to make between 'the desire of the flesh' and the Christian ideal of chastity. Those who opted for an ascetic life or the life of a monk made a radical choice that broke with hopes and expectations that had been cherished for ages. And as religious life was popular in those times, one should not underestimate the impact of Christian thought. On the other hand, marital practice did not change that much in late antiquity. And the Christian ascetic ideals did not appear out of the blue, but had been long foreshadowed in non-Christian philosophical movements.[46]

12.4 Excursus: a real-life case of early Christian youth: the *Vita Severi*

Around 515, Zacharias Scholasticus recorded the life of Severus, the patriarch of Alexandria. Many biographies of saints or great Christians from that period have come down to us, but the text by Zacharias is perhaps the most vivid of such accounts, offering rich information on life as a Christian youngster in the late fifth century, by which time Christianity had defeated paganism quite decisively. Zacharias wrote in Greek, but the only preserved version is a rendering in Syriac.[47]

Severus was born to a noble family in Pisidia. After the death of his father, his mother sent him and his two brothers to Alexandria to learn grammar and rhetoric. At the time, Zacharias, the subsequent author of the biography, was also living as a student in Alexandria. One of their fellow-students

---

[46] Eyben, Laes, and Van Houdt 2003b: 195–8. Standard works on asceticism in pagan philosophy and early Christianity include Foucault 1984 and Brown 1988. See also Wimbush 1990 and Esler 2000.

[47] Zacharias Scholasticus, *Vita Sev.* (ed. Kügener). The authors wish to thank Emiel Eyben for drawing their attention to this exceptional text.

was Paralius, a Christian who had two pagan brothers; they practised sorcery, invoked demons, and performed incantations. A third brother lived as a monk in the nearby monastery of Enaton. Paralius used to pay visits to this brother; he had extended theological discussions with him, and read the works of numerous church fathers. Thus he returned from Enaton, capable of taking part in the debates with his pagan peers, who idolised the grammarian Horapallon. As they were unable to demonstrate with intellectual arguments that they were right and Paralius was wrong, they resorted to citing the miracle of a sterile woman who had purportedly given birth. Paralius mocked their superstition. He sarcastically denounced the worshipping of animals as gods in Egypt (cats, dogs, and apes!): Isis, he asserted, was no more than a glorified prostitute. Horapallon's students could not bear these insults. They waited until their teacher had left and then viciously attacked the zealous Paralius. Badly beaten up, he sought refuge with the club of the *philoponoi*, Christian students who were closely connected with the monastery of Enaton and whose main aim was to win new Christian souls among their peers. They rescued Paralius and fled together to the monastery at Enaton, where the great abbot Salomon gave them shelter. The abbot also informed the patriarch of Alexandria. As a result severe riots broke out. Although the pagans had hidden the statues of their gods, many were destroyed by a crowd of angry Christians. They carried away twenty cartloads of precious statues! One pagan sanctuary was razed to the ground. Also during this great riot, many students were converted to Christianity, as were Paralius' two brothers, who subsequently became monks at Enaton. Zacharias, for his part, fell seriously ill (a punishment from the gods, according to the pagans), but he recovered and gave a fiery speech in which he once again attacked pagan superstition. Young Severus witnessed all this as a friend and fellow-student. Although he was already a believer, he was not yet following the catechism.

Not long afterwards, Severus left for Beirut to study law. He was joined by his friend Zacharias the following year. Here the young men joined a group of Christian students led by Evagrius. Together they read Genesis and texts by various church fathers, and in the evenings they prayed together at church. Meanwhile, it had emerged that numerous books on magic and necromancy were circulating in Beirut. House searches involving students resulted in some grave discoveries: statues of gods and forbidden books were confiscated and destroyed. One student showed great remorse at having turned to paganism. As a former Christian, he had resorted to magic out of love for a woman. He was now prepared to betray his pagan fellow-students. Many of these students had an Egyptian–Alexandrian background. As a consequence, a new (orchestrated?) revolt broke out: many pagans fled the city, while others converted (under coercion?) and were baptised. But Severus was not convinced that this was the right moment to be baptised, since he was living in a city rife with temptations, where brothels were prominent. His friends, however, insisted and brought him to a shrine at Tripolis, where he was finally baptised. After his return to Beirut, Evagrius became his spiritual father. The young Severus was so fanatical in his asceticism that he forsook all earthly desires and became emaciated to such an extent that his flesh seemed to have shrunk.

As the end of his studies was approaching, Severus decided to return to his home town and to embark on a career as a lawyer. On his way back, he paid a visit to his master and godfather Evagrius, who had retired to a monastery near Jerusalem. Only then did Severus discover his true vocation: instead of a lawyer's gown, he would henceforth wear the monastic habit; religious books replaced legal writings; pleading before court made way for the tough regime of monastic life. A whole group of Christians gathered around the pious monk Severus. When, early in the sixth century, the unity of the Egyptian church was threatened by monophysitism, the emperor decided to send Severus to Alexandria as the new patriarch.

CHAPTER 13

Conclusion

Awareness of one's own assumptions and a readiness to question one's own ideological background – these are the basic conditions for conducting an open debate, no matter whether political or ideological. The debate over youth in the Roman Empire can similarly benefit from such an openness of mind. Ultimately, one's position on the whole issue will depend on one's attitude towards the Other, be they from a different culture or another era. In very general terms, one could argue that the Other from the past is so different from us that it is virtually impossible today to imagine his or her world. Alternatively, one can adhere to the belief – as we have done in this book – that people of different cultures and different epochs are nonetheless connected; that we all share certain features and characteristics for the simple reason that we are all human beings. At the same time, one can approach the history of private life from one of several different angles. Those whose interest lies in external aspects will primarily focus on such elements as institutions, images, and customs. Observing a statue of a young man striking the serious pose of an orator, such historians might draw attention to the adult pattern of expectations that ancient society apparently imposed upon young men. Those whose focus lies more on the interior aspects will tend to explore other sources that arguably reveal more about the psyche of the youngsters concerned: youthful poetry, behaviour overstepping the mark of expectations, lamentations by adults that youth is heading in the wrong direction and is not complying with the expectations of proper (adult) behaviour (see Fig. 13.1).

As pointed out in the first chapter of this book, we fully acknowledge the biological basis of being young. This entails that we take into account the possibility of characteristically reckless, irresponsible, and rebellious behaviour by young people, as this is part and parcel of the biological reality of being human. On the other hand, we are no adherents of deterministic sociobiological theory: it has been our intention as historians to highlight

13 Conclusion

13.1 Fresco from Herculaneum (approximately AD 70). A licentious youth paints the town red. The young man, half-naked and seated on a bed, raises a cup in the shape of a horn in his right hand. Before him on the bed sits a prostitute with a translucent robe around her torso. She beckons a nearby servant who carries a box. In front of the bed is a small table on which stand more cups.
(National Archaeological Museum, Naples.)

how Graeco-Roman society and youths in particular coped with this biological fact of life.

First of all, let us consider society, or its outward aspect. One can hardly deny that Roman society was not particularly appreciative of the 'storms of youth'. It was deemed important to proceed as quickly as possible to the adult phase of life, where seriousness reigned. *Il faut que jeunesse se passe* ('Youth must pass') is a proverb that would surely have appealed to the Romans. Indeed, one will search in vain for an appreciation of childhood *per se* among Roman authors. This accounts for the fact that there was no clearly demarcated period of youth and very little in the way of differentiating terminology, as few subdivisions were made in the youth stage of life. Nor was there an elaborate medical and psychological discourse on puberty. Literature primarily assigns negative attributes to youth, such as the stereotypical complaint of the elderly that youngsters lack the serious attitude and self-control of adulthood. In the same way, official inscriptions and iconographical sources depict young people as small adults, as successors to their parents and ancestors. Those same sources admire youths who display early maturity, thereby representing the ideal image of society. On the other hand, parents were generally tolerant of youthful excesses, as they believed they were transitory.

In daily life, this same ambivalent attitude towards young people was reflected in a certain reluctance to entrust them with positions of responsibility. In central government a young man had to wait until the age of twenty-five before being able to enter the *cursus honorum* (though this did not imply that, up to that point, days were spent idling). In the cities of the Roman Empire political offices and priesthoods were for the most part assigned to young people from about the age of twenty. Exceptions did occur, but quite rarely. Moreover, it emerges on closer scrutiny that the political offices held by young people were mainly representative functions. In this manner, a teenager could occupy a seat on the local city council (*curia*) and thus enhance the prestige of his family. Real political office, implying action and decision-making, was rarely assigned to teenagers. Meanwhile, upper-class youngsters were commonly linked with the political work and the euergetism of their fathers and families. As regards the professional responsibilities of young people from the upper class, it is true that the sources speak of some physicians and lawyers who, by modern standards, were very young. Most young jurists, though, entered the profession at around twenty-five. Individuals in their early twenties were never appointed as civic lawyers or physicians. Several years of training were inevitably required in order to fulfil such positions properly. Whether or not these young people from the elite felt excluded from adult society, and whether or not they developed or cultivated a specific sense of youthfulness, is unknown. It is simply the case that our sources neither affirm nor refute this.

As regards the inner self, we note at once that society created a space for experiencing a youth phase of life, at least for the male population within society's small elite. In the city of Rome poets from the upper classes came to express a new sense of vitality at the beginning of the imperial era, evoking a desire to live freely. It is, however, a matter of debate as to what extent this feeling was peculiar to youths. Youngsters from the urban elites often went off to study abroad from around their fifteenth to their twentieth years. Far away from parental supervision, populations of such students in ancient academic towns developed subcultures that approximated in many ways to what we tend to refer to as a youth culture. The majority of the young males from the urban elites, however, studied in their own home towns. Instruction from the rhetor did not occupy these youngsters for whole days, though, so they were left with ample leisure time. Many filled these hours with membership of youth associations, known as *iuventus* in the Latin West and as *ephebeia* in the Greek East. But the activities of these clubs, too, were rather limited and by no means took up the whole day. One can imagine that such associations, with their strong focus on sports and martial arts, could serve as outlets for tensions, aggression, and undisciplined behaviour. And, as such associations were made up predominantly or even exclusively of young people, there was no doubt potential for the emergence of a youth subculture. On the other hand, ephebes and *iuvenes* were kept in check by their magistrates, and the ephebes were, furthermore, educated to exhibit responsible civic behaviour. In the period following puberty, young people, and certainly those from the wealthier walks of life, had sufficient sexual outlets at their disposal, which may have helped avoid certain frustrations. Young men usually married when they were already well into their twenties.

The key question remains: did aristocratic young people seize the opportunity that their freedom offered to develop a specific sense of youthfulness and way of life? Again, different answers present themselves. One could argue that the question itself is hardly to the point, that sociocultural history must deal with the concepts and ideas prevailing in a given society, and that, both from the Roman point of view and from an outside perspective on the structure of Roman society, a youth subculture appears a sheer impossibility (Pleket). Or one could maintain that the majority of young people behaved very much as they were expected to, that the young men depicted in reliefs and inscriptions as earnest aristocrats really did act in this way in their daily lives (Kleijwegt). In our view, both the aforementioned positions are too extreme. Of course, we are faced with the enormous difficulty that Roman young people rarely revealed their inner selves or took centre-stage (an observation that applies *a fortiori* to women, children, slaves, and disabled people in Roman society). But we do have testimonies about young people overstepping the mark in student clubs and local associations. There is evidence of parents struggling with their teenage children, and in some periods of Graeco-Roman history we even come across indications of actual generational conflict. In poetry and oratory, too, we find references to what the ancients themselves considered to be manifestations of youthful recklessness. These are the aspects that Eyben puts forward emphatically as the characteristic features of young Romans. On the other hand, Pleket and Kleijwegt have rightly redressed the balance by rejecting concepts such as adolescence and a crisis of puberty, or terminology such as 'teenager', in the context of Roman society. Such concepts and ideas, as well as the notion of youth as a well-defined age category, were alien to the Roman way of thinking and to their social practice.

13 Conclusion

Historians of antiquity agree that the question of youth was mainly an issue of the male upper class. The majority of girls and boys entered the world of labour after a short period of schooling (if they attended school at all). Their introduction to the labour process was a gradual one, since work was part and parcel of the daily lives of their parents. The question of whether there were associations for young people of the lower classes, be it out in the country (where about 80% of the population lived)[1] or in the cities (similar to the carnival associations or guilds for apprentices in the Middle Ages and Modern period), is bound to remain unresolved, since the available sources provide no information on this matter. How youngsters from the lower classes coped with puberty, how they fitted into the adult world and how the adults viewed them will also remain a mystery. Likewise, the question of girls' experiences within a hypothetical female inner circle remains largely unanswered: comparative data from other cultures and societies suggest that at least the possibility of such circles existed. But the social expectation was that they did not experience a phase of youth. Unfortunately, female subculture has left hardly any traces in a literature dominated almost entirely by males.

So did being young in ancient Greece and Rome involve going through a period of restlessness and upheaval? It did in the sense that it is a biological fact of life that changes occur in the human body during the teenage years. This may have resulted in tension and conflict within some families: there is indeed evidence of rebellion by some young people and even violence; there were sexual and other outbursts. So to an extent youth may indeed, in a general way, be described as a stormy phase in life. However, one should be careful not to oversimplify and to use this notion as a *passe-partout*, a cliché that supposedly demonstrates that people of past eras were 'just like us' and behaved 'just like us'. Indeed, there are important and essential differences between Graeco-Roman society and modern-day society, not only in terms of prevailing notions and concepts, but also in respect of social structures and practice, so that ultimately Greek and Roman youths cannot but have behaved very differently from today's youngsters. In this study, we have tried to do justice both to eternal and universal aspects of human behaviour and to differences determined by culture. In so doing, we hope to have offered the reader an enriching intellectual confrontation with a society that sometimes seems very close and sometimes very far away.

---

[1] Unless one accepts the assumption that urban and rural populations were not as sharply differentiated in classical antiquity as in some later European contexts. In that case, most farmers may have resided in urban settlements, such as the 'agro-towns' of southern Italy or Sicily. For this view, see Hansen 2006 and Scheidel 2006. For a different opinion, see Garnsey 1998: 107–31.

Bibliography

All abbreviations of journals in the bibliography and the text are those used in *L'Année Philologique*: http://www.annee-philologique.com/files/sigles_fr.pdf

Al-Faruqi, M. (2000) 'Women's self-identity in the Qur'an and Islamic law', in *Widows of Faith: Muslim Women Scholar-Activists in North America*, ed. G. Webb. Syracuse: 72–101.

Amedick, R. (1991) *Die Sarkophage mit Darstellungen aus dem Menschenleben: Teil 4, Vita Privata*. Berlin.

Ameling, W. (2004) 'Wohltäter im hellenistischen Gymnasion', in Kah and Scholz (2004): 129–61.

Ariès, Ph. (1973) *L'enfant et la vie familiale sous l'Ancien Régime*, 3rd edn. Paris.

Armisen-Marchetti, M. (2004) 'L'enseignement de la philosophie à Rome', in Pailler and Payen (2004): 201–10.

Atherton, C. (1998) 'Children, animals, slaves and grammar', in *Pedagogy and Power. Rhetorics of Classical Learning*, eds. N. Livingstone and Y. L. Too, *Pedagogy and Power. Rhetorics of Classical Learning*. Cambridge: 214–44.

Aubin, M. M. (2000) 'More apparent than real? Questioning the difference in marital age between Christian and non-Christian women of Rome during the third and fourth century', *AHB* 14: 1–13.

Ausbüttel, F. M. (1982) *Untersuchungen zu den Vereinen im Westen des römischen Reiches*. Kallmünz.

Austin, M. M. (ed.) (1981) *The Hellenistic World from Alexander to the Roman Conquest: a Selection of Ancient Sources in Translation*. Cambridge and New York.

Babamova, S. (2005) *Epigrafski spomenici od Republika Makedonija datirani spored Makedonskata provinciska era (Epigraphic Monuments of the Republic of Macedonia Dated according to the Macedonian Provincial Era)*. Skopje.

Bagnall, R. S. and Derow, P. (eds.) (2004) *The Hellenistic Period*. Malden, Mass.

Bakke, O. M. (2005) *When Children Became People. The Birth of Childhood in Early Christianity*. Minneapolis.

Baldwin, B. (1984) *Studies on Late Roman and Byzantine History, Literature and Language*. Amsterdam.

Bancalari Molina, A. (1998) 'La problemática de la juventud en la sociedad Romana: propuesta de enfoques para su estudio', *FlorIlib* 9: 41–68.

Banchich, Th. M. (1993) 'Julian's school laws: *Cod. Theod.* 13.5.5. and *Ep.* 42', *AncW* 24: 5–14.
Barclay, J. M. (2007) 'There is neither old nor young? Early Christianity and ancient ideologies of age', *NTS* 53: 225–41.
Baroin, C. (2010) 'Remembering one's ancestors, following in their footsteps, being like them: the role and forms of family memory in the building of identity', in Dasen and Späth (2010): 19–48.
Barton, C. A. (1999) 'The Roman blush: the delicate matter of self-control', in *Constructions of the Classical Body*, ed. J. I. Porter. Ann Arbor: 212–34.
    (2001) *Roman Honor. The Fire in the Bones*. Berkeley, Los Angeles, and London.
Beard, M. (2008) *Pompeii. The Life of a Roman Town*. London.
Becchi, E. and Julia, D. (eds.) (1998) *Histoire de l'enfance en Occident* 1 *(de l'Antiquité au* XVII *siècle)*. Paris.
Berger, A. (1932) art. 'Minores', in *RE* 15, 2: cols. 1860–89.
Berger, S. (2008) 'De Spartaanse *krypteia*. Een rondgang langs Parnon en Taygetos', *Lampas* 41: 149–63.
Birley, A. R. (1997) *Hadrian. The Restless Emperor*. London and New York.
Boll, F. (1913) 'Die Lebensalter. Ein Beitrag zur antiken Ethologie und zur Geschichte der Zahlen', *NJA* 16: 89–145.
Bonner, S. (1977) *Education in Ancient Rome*. London.
Bormann, D. (2006) 'Jugend. Rom – Republik und Kaiserzeit', in Christes, Klein, and Lüth (2006): 72–8.
Boscolo, F. (2003) '*Iuvenes* a Mediolanium e dintorni', in *Miscellanea in onore di Franco Sartori per l'80° compleanno*, Trento: 257–68.
Boswell, J. (1988) *The Kindness of Strangers. The Abandonment of Children in Western Europe from Late Antiquity to the Renaissance*. New York.
Boulvert, G. (1974) *Domestique et fonctionnaire sous le Haut-Empire romain. La condition de l'affranchi et de l'esclave du prince*. Paris.
Bouley, E. (2003) 'L'éducation éphébique et la formation de la "*juuentus*" d'après quelques documents des provinces balkaniques et danubiennes', in *Histoire, espaces et marges de l'Antiquité: hommages à Monique Clavel-Lévêque*, eds. M. Garrido-Hory and A. Gonzalès. Besançon: 195–207.
Boymel Kampen, N. (2007) 'What could Hadrian feel for Antinoos? Emotional possibilities in a story of sexual passion', in *Geschlechterdefinitionen und Geschlechtergrenzen in der Antike*, eds. E. Hartmann, U. Hartmann, and K. Pietzner. Stuttgart: 199–209.
Bradley, K. (1985) 'Child labour in the Roman world', *Historical Reflections* 12, 2: 311–30, reprinted in Bradley (1991), 103–25.
    (1991) *Discovering the Roman Family. Studies in Roman Social History*. Oxford.
    (1994) *Slavery and Society at Rome*. Cambridge.
Brakke, D. (1995) 'The problematization of nocturnal emissions in early Christian Syria, Egypt and Gaul', *JECS* 3: 419–60.
Brélaz, C. (2005) *La sécurité publique en Asie Mineure sous le Principat (Ier –IIIème s. ap. J.-C.). Institutions municipales et institutions impériales dans l'Orient romain*. Basel.

Brind'Amour, L. and Brind'Amour, P. (1971) 'La deuxième satire de Perse', *Latomus* 30: 999–1024.
Brown, P. (1988) *The Body and Society: Men, Women and Sexual Renunciation in Early Christianity*. New York.
  (2000) *Augustine of Hippo. A Biography*, 2nd edn. Berkeley and Los Angeles.
Burckhardt, L. (2004) 'Die attische Ephebie in hellenistischer Zeit', in Kah and Scholz (2004): 193–206.
Burkert, W. (2004) art. 'Initiation', in *Thesaurus Cultus et Rituum Antiquorum* II. Los Angeles: 91–124.
Burrow, J. A. (1986) *The Ages of Man: a Study in Medieval Writing and Thought*. Oxford.
Campbell, R. A. (1994) *The Elders. Seniority within Early Christianity*. Edinburgh.
Carey, C. (1997) *Trials from Classical Athens*. London and New York.
Casartelli, A. (1998) 'La funzione del colore nell'abbigliamento romano della prima età imperiale', *Aevum* 72, 1: 109–25.
Champlin, E. (1987) 'The testament of the piglet', *Phoenix* 41: 174–83.
Chankowski, A. S. (2004a) 'L'entraînement militaire des éphèbes dans les cités grecques d'Asie Mineure à l'époque hellénistique: nécessité pratique ou tradition atrophée?', in *Les cités grecques et la guerre en Asie Mineure à l'époque hellénistique. Actes de la journée d'études de Lyon 10 octobre 2003*, eds. J.-C. Couvenhes and H.-L. Fernoux. Tours: 55–76.
  (2004b) 'L'éphébie, une institution d'éducation civique', in Pailler and Payen (2004): 271–9.
Christes, J. (1998) 'Jugend im antiken Rom – "*absence of adolescence*" oder "*restless youth*"?', in Horn (1998a): 141–66.
Christes, J., Klein, R. and Lüth, Chr. (eds.) (2006) *Handbuch der Erziehung und Bildung in der Antike*. Darmstadt.
Christien, J. and Ruzé, F. (2007) *Sparte. Géographie, mythes et histoire*. Paris.
Claassen, J.-M. (2008) *Ovid Revisited. The Poet in Exile*. London.
Cole, S. G. (1984) 'The social function of rituals of maturation: the *Koureion* and the *Arkteia*', *ZPE* 55: 233–44.
Cootjans, G. (2000) 'Le pubis, les poils pubiens et l'épilation', *RBPh* 78, 1: 53–60.
Corbeill, A. (2001) 'Education in the Roman republic: creating traditions', in Too (2001): 261–88.
Corbier, M. (2006) *Donner à voir, donner à lire. Mémoire et communication dans la Rome ancienne*. Paris.
Corvisier, J.-N. (2001) 'L'adolescence en Grèce antique d'après les sources médicales grecques', in *Entre dépendance et indépendance, de l'enfance à l'âge adulte. Colloque international organisé par l'Université de Paris IV Sorbonne, l'Université de St. Quentin en Yvelines et la Société de Démographie Historique, 22–24 septembre 2000*. Paris: 55–67.
Cribiore, R. (2001) *Gymnastics of the Mind. Greek Education in Hellenistic and Roman Egypt*. Princeton and Oxford.
  (2007) *The School of Libanius in Late Antique Antioch*. Oxford and Princeton.

Crone, E. (2008) *Het puberende brein. Over de ontwikkeling van de hersenen in de unieke periode van de adolescentie*. Amsterdam.

Crone, E. A. and Dahl, R. E. (2012) 'Understanding adolescence as a period of social-affective engagement and goal flexibility', *Nature Reviews Neuroscience* 13: 636–50.

Crowther, N. B. (1991) '*Euexia, eutaxia, philoponia*: three contests of the Greek gymnasium', *ZPE* 85: 301–4, reprinted in Crowther (2004): 341–4.

  (2004) *Athletika. Studies on the Olympic Games and Greek Athletics*. Hildesheim.

D'Amore, L. (2007) 'Ginnasio e difesa civica nelle *poleis* d'Asia Minore (IV–I sec. a.C.)', *REA* 109: 147–73.

Dasen, V. and Späth, Th. (eds.) (2010) *Children, Memory, and Family Identity in Roman Culture*. Oxford.

De Bruyn, T. S. (1999) 'Flogging a son: the emergence of the *pater flagellans* in Latin Christian discourse', *JECS* 7, 2: 249–90.

De Ligt, L. (2001) '*D*. 47, 22, 1, pr.-1 and the formation of semi-public *collegia*', *Latomus* 60: 345–58.

Demos, J. and Demos, V. (1969) 'Adolescence in historical perspective', *Journal of Marriage and the Family* 31: 632–8.

Derks, T. (2009) 'Van toga tot terracotta: het veelkleurige palet van volwassenwordingsrituelen in het Romeinse rijk' *Lampas* 42: 204–28.

Devijver, H. (1974) 'De leeftijd van de ridderofficieren tijdens het vroeg-Romeinse keizerrijk', *Handelingen der Koninklijke Zuidnederlandse Maatschappij voor Taal- en Letterkunde en Geschiedenis* 28: 83–146.

  (1976) *Prosopographia militiarum equestrium quae fuerunt ab Augusto ad Gallienum* I. *Litterae A–I*. Louvain.

  (1977) *Prosopographia militiarum equestrium quae fuerunt ab Augusto ad Gallienum* II. *Litterae L–V*. Louvain.

  (1987) *Prosopographia militiarum equestrium quae fuerunt ab Augusto ad Gallienum. Supplementum* I. Louvain.

  (1993) *Prosopographia militiarum equestrium quae fuerunt ab Augusto ad Gallienum. Supplementum* II. Louvain.

Dillon, M. (2002) *Girls and Women in Classical Greek Religion*. London and New York.

Dixon, S. (1988) *The Roman Mother*. London and Sydney.

  (1992) *The Roman Family*. Baltimore and London.

  (1997) 'Conflict in the Roman family', in *The Roman Family in Italy. Status, Sentiment, Space*, eds. B. Rawson and P. Weaver. Canberra and Oxford: 149–67.

  (2007) *Cornelia. Mother of the Gracchi*. London and New York.

Dmitriev, S. (2005) *City Government in Hellenistic and Roman Asia Minor*. Oxford.

Dodd, D. B. and Faraone, C. A. (eds.) (2003) *Initiation in Ancient Greek Rituals and Narratives. New Critical Perspectives*. London and New York.

Dolansky, F. (2008) '*Togam virilem sumere*: coming of age in the Roman world', in Edmondson and Keith (2008): 47–70.

Dörner, F. K. (1952) *Bericht über eine Reise in Bithynien, Österr. Akad. der Wiss., Phil.-hist. Kl. Denkschr.* LXXV, *1*. Vienna.

Dreyer, B. (2004) 'Die *Neoi* im hellenistischen Gymnasion', in Kah and Scholz (2004): 211–36.
Duncan-Jones, R. P. (1977) 'Age-rounding, illiteracy and social differentiation in the Roman empire', *Chiron* 7: 333–53.
Durry, M. (1955) 'Le mariage des filles impubères dans la Rome antique', *RIDA* 2: 263–73.
  (1956) 'Sur le mariage romain. Autocritique et mise au point', *RIDA* 3: 227–43.
Edmondson, J. and Keith, A. (eds.) (2008) *Roman Dress and the Fabrics of Roman Culture*. Toronto, Buffalo, and London.
Esler, P. F. (ed.) (2000) *The Early Christian World* 1. London and New York.
Evans, J. K. (1991) *War, Women and Children in Ancient Rome*. London and New York.
Evans Grubbs, J. (2005a) 'Parent–child conflict in the Roman family: the evidence of the Code of Justinian', in *The Roman Family in the Empire. Rome, Italy and Beyond*, ed. M. George. Oxford: 93–128.
  (2005b) 'Children and divorce in Roman law', in Mustakallio, Hanska, Sainio, and Vuolanto (2005): 33–47.
  (2009) 'Marriage and family relationships in the late Roman West', in *A Companion to Late Antiquity*, ed. Ph. Rousseau. Malden, Mass. and Oxford: 201–19.
Evans, R. J. and Kleijwegt, M. (1992) 'Did the Romans like young men? A study of the *Lex Villia annalis*: causes and effects', *ZPE* 92: 181–95.
Evenepoel, W. and Van Houdt, T. (1997) 'Strategische zelfrepresentatie? Een denkoefening naar aanleiding van Plinius Minor, *Epist.* 7, 5', *Kleio* 27, 1: 29–42.
Eyben, E. (1968) 'Les parents soucieux de l'instruction scolaire de leur fils', in *Antidorum W. Peremans sexagenario ab alumnis oblatum*. Leuven: 39–60.
  (1972) 'Antiquity's views of puberty', *Latomus* 31: 677–97.
  (1973a) 'Die Einteilung des menschlichen Lebens im römischen Altertum', *RhM* 116: 150–90.
  (1973b) 'Roman notes on the course of life', *AncSoc* 4: 230–55.
  (1977) *De jonge Romein volgens de literaire bronnen der periode c. 200 v. Chr. tot c. 500 n. Chr.* Brussels.
  (1981a) 'Was the Roman "youth" an "adult" socially?', *AC* 50: 328–50.
  (1981b) 'Bestond er dan echt geen Romeinse jeugd?', *Lampas* 14: 133–9.
  (1985) 'Geschlechtsreife und Ehe im griechisch-römischen Altertum und im frühen Christentum', in *Geschlechtsreife und Legitimation zur Zeugung*, ed. E. W. Müller. Munich: 403–78.
  (1987) *De onstuimigen. Jeugd en (on)deugd in het oude Rome*. Kapellen.
  (1991) 'Fathers and sons', in *Marriage, Divorce and Children in Ancient Rome*, ed. B. Rawson. Canberra and Oxford: 114–43.
  (1993) *Restless Youth in Ancient Rome*. London.
  (1995) 'Young priests in early Christianity', in Panchaia. *Festschrift für Klaus Thraede*. Münster: 102–20.
  (1996) 'The early Christian view of youth', in Klodt (1996): 239–55.
  (1999) art. 'Jugend', in *RLAC* 19: cols. 388–442.

Eyben, E., Laes, Chr. and Van Houdt, T. (eds.) (2003a) *Amor-Roma. Liefde en erotiek in Rome.* Leuven.
  (2003b) 'Huwelijk en gezin: praktijken, normen en idealen', in Eyben, Laes, and Van Houdt (2003a): 175–203.
Faraone, C. A. (2003) 'Playing the bear and fawn for Artemis. Female initiation or substitute sacrifice?', in Dodd and Faraone (2003): 43–68.
Faraone, C. A. and McClure, L. K. (eds.) (2006) *Prostitutes and Courtesans in the Ancient World.* Madison.
Fayer, C. (1994) *La familia romana* I. *Aspetti giuridici ed antiquari.* Rome.
  (2005) *La familia romana* II. *Aspetti giuridici ed antiquari. Sponsalia. Matrimonio. Dote.* Rome.
Fear, A. T. (1995) 'A Latin master from Roman Spain', *G&R* 42, 1: 57–69.
Firestone, S. (1970) *The Dialectic of Sex: the Case for Feminist Revolution.* New York.
Flandrin, J. L. (1964) 'Enfance et société', *Annales (ESC)* 19: 322–9.
Forbes, C. A. (1933) Neoi. *A Contribution to the Study of Greek Associations.* Middletown.
Foubert, L. (2006) *Agrippina. Keizerin van Rome.* Leuven.
Foucault, M. (1984) *Le souci de soi. Histoire de la sexualité* III. Paris.
Fournier, J. (2007) 'Les "*syndikoi*", représentants juridiques des cités grecques sous le Haut-Empire romain', *CCG* 18: 7–36.
Freeman, D. (1983) *Margaret Mead and Samoa: the Making and Unmaking of an Anthropological Myth.* Cambridge.
Frier, B. W. (1999) 'Roman demography', in *Life, Death and Entertainment in the Roman Empire*, eds. D. J. Mattingly and D. S. Potter. Ann Arbor: 85–109.
  (2001) 'More is worse: some observations on the population of the Roman empire', in *Debating Roman Demography*, ed. W. Scheidel. Leiden, Boston, and Cologne: 139–59.
Frier, B. W. and McGinn, Th. (2004) *A Casebook on Roman Family Law.* Oxford.
Garland, R. (1990) *The Greek Way of Life: from Conception to Death.* Cornell.
  (1993) rev. of Kleijwegt (1991), *JHS* 113: 204–5.
Garnsey, P. (1998) *Cities, Peasants and Food in Classical Antiquity.* Cambridge.
Garrido Bozic, I. M. (1951) 'Quintus filius', *G&R* 20: 11–25.
Gauthier, Ph. and Hatzopoulos, M. B. (1993) *La loi gymnasiarchique de Beroia.* Athens.
Gehrke, H.-J. (2003) 'Bürgerliches Selbstverständnis und Polisidentität im Hellenismus', in *Sinn (in) der Antike. Orientierungssysteme, Leitbilder und Wertkonzepte im Altertum*, eds. K.-J. Hölkeskamp, J. Rüsen, E. Stein-Hölkeskamp, and H. Th. Grütter. Mainz am Rhein: 225–54.
  (2004) 'Eine Bilanz: Die Entwicklung des Gymnasions zur Institution der Sozialisierung in der *Polis*', in Kah and Scholz (2004): 413–19.
George, M. (2001) 'A Roman funerary monument with a mother and a daughter', in *Reading Roman Women. Sources, Genres and Real Life*, ed. S. Dixon. London: 178–89.
Geraci, G. (2001) 'La dichiarazione di nascita e di morte a Roma e nelle provincie', *MEFRA* 113.2: 675–711.

Gherchanoc, F. (2006) 'Le(s) voile(s) de mariage dans le monde grec: se voiler, se dévoiler: la question particulière des *"anakalupteria"'*, *Metis* 4: 239–67.
Gillis, J. R. (1974) *Youth and History. Tradition and Change in European Age Relations 1770–Present.* New York.
Ginestet, P. (1991) *Les organisations de la jeunesse dans l'Occident romain.* Brussels.
Girone, M. (2003) 'Una particolare offerta di chiome', *EA* 35: 21–42.
Gnilka, Chr. (1972) Aetas Spiritalis. *Die Überwindung der natürlichen Altersstufen als Ideal frühchristlichen Lebens.* Cologne and Bonn.
Goette, H. R. (1989) 'Römische Kinderbildnisse mit Jugend-Locken', *MDAI(A)* 104: 203–17.
Gourevitch, D. (2001) *Il giovani pazienti di Galeno. Per una patocenosi dell'impero romano.* Bari.
Haake, M. (2006) *Der Philosoph in der Stadt. Untersuchungen zur öffentlichen Rede über Philosophen und Philosophie in den hellenistischen* Poleis. Munich.
Habermann, W. (2004) 'Gymnasien im ptolemäischen Ägypten – eine Skizze', in Kah and Scholz (2004): 335–48.
Hankinson, R. J. (ed.) (2008a) *The Cambridge Companion to Galen.* Cambridge.
  (2008b) 'The man and his work', in Hankinson (2008a): 1–33.
Hansen, M. H. (2006) *The Shotgun Method: the Demography of the Ancient Greek City-State Culture.* Columbia, Mo. and London.
Harders, A.-C. (2010) 'Roman patchwork strategies: surrogate parenting, socialization, and the shaping of tradition', in Dasen and Späth (2010): 49–72.
Harlow, M. and Laurence, R. (2002) *Growing Up and Growing Old in Ancient Rome. A Life Course Approach.* London and New York.
  (eds.) (2007) *Age and Ageing in the Roman Empire.* Portsmouth.
Harris, W. V. (1986) 'The Roman father's power of life and death', in *Studies in Roman Law in Memory of A. Arthur Schiller*, eds. R. S. Bagnall and W. V. Harris. Leiden: 81–95.
  (1989) *Ancient Literacy.* Cambridge and London.
Hemelrijk, E. (1999) Matrona Docta. *Educated Women in the Roman Elite from Cornelia to Julia Domna.* London and New York.
Hermans, L. (1995) *Bewust van andere lusten. Homoseksualiteit in het Romeinse keizerrijk.* Amsterdam.
Herrmann-Otto, E. (1994) Ex ancilla natus. *Untersuchungen zu den 'hausgeborenen' Sklaven und Sklavinnen im Westen des römischen Kaiserreiches.* Stuttgart.
Herzog, R. (1935), 'Urkunden zur Hochschulpolitik der römischen Kaiser', *Sitz. ber. d. Preuss. Ak. d. Wiss.*: 967–101c.
Hin, S. (2007) 'Class and society in the cities of the Greek East: education during the *ephebeia*', *AncSoc* 37: 141–66.
Hinard, F. (ed.) (1987) *La mort, les morts et l'au-delà dans le monde romain. Actes du colloque de Caen 20–22 nov. 1985.* Caen.
Höhn, G. (1911–12) *Die Einteilungsarten der Lebens- und Weltalter bei Griechen und Römern.* Würzburg.
Hofmeister, A. (1926) '"Puer, iuvenis, senex". Zum Verständnis der mittelalterlichen Altersbezeichnungen', in *Papsttum und Kaisertum*, ed. A. Brackmann. Munich: 287–316.

Hopkins, K. (1965) 'The age of Roman girls at marriage', *Population Studies* 18: 309–27.
  (1999) *A World Full of Gods: Pagans, Jews and Christians in the Roman Empire*. London.
Horn, K.-P. (ed.) (1998a) *Jugend in der Vormoderne*. Cologne.
  (1998b) 'Was ist denn eigentlich die Jugend? Moderne Fragen und vormoderne Antworten', in Horn (1998a): 1–20.
Horster, M. (1996) 'Kinderkarrieren?', in Klodt (1996): 223–38.
Horstmanshoff, H. F. J. (1999) 'Vier-humores-schema volgens Hippocrates, *De natura hominis*', *Hermeneus* 71.2: 65.
  (2006) *Patiënten zien. Patiënten in de antieke geneeskunde*. Leiden.
Huebner, S. and Ratzan, D. (eds.) (2009) *Growing Up Fatherless in Antiquity*. Cambridge.
Hummel, Chr. (1999) *Das Kind und seine Krankheiten in der griechischen Medizin. Von Aretaios bis Johannes Aktuarios (1. bis 14. Jahrhundert)*. Frankfurt am Main, Berlin, etc.
Hunt, A. S. and Edgar, C. C. (1970) *Select Papyri* I. The Loeb Classical Library 266. Cambridge, Mass. and London.
Imber, M. (2008) 'Life without father: declamation and the construction of paternity in the Roman Empire', in *Role Models in the Roman World. Identity and Assimilation*, eds. S. Bell and I. L. Hansen. Ann Arbor: 161–9.
Isayev, E. (2007) 'Unruly youth? The myth of generation conflict in late republican Rome', *Historia* 56: 1–13.
Iskandar, A. Z. (1988) *Galen. On Examinations by which the Best Physicians are Recognized. Edition of the Arabic Version with English Translation and Commentary. Corpus Medicorum Graecorum, supplementum orientale*, IV. Berlin.
Jaczynowska, M. (1978) *Les associations de la jeunesse romaine sous le Haut-Empire*. Wroclaw.
Johnson, M. and Ryan, T. (2005) *Sexuality in Greek and Roman Society. A Sourcebook*. London.
Jones, C. P. (2007) 'Juristes romains dans l'Orient grec', *CRAI* 151: 1331–59.
Jones Hall, L. (2004) *Roman Berytus. Beirut in Late Antiquity*. London.
Joyal, M., McDougall, I. and Yardley, J. C. (2009) *Greek and Roman Education. A Sourcebook*. London.
Kah, D. (2004) 'Militärische Ausbildung im hellenistischen Gymnasion', in Kah and Scholz (2004): 47–90.
Kah, D. and Scholz, P. (eds.) (2004) *Das hellenistische Gymnasion*. Berlin and New York.
Kaser, M. (1971–5) *Das römisches Privatrecht* I–II. Munich.
Kaster, R. A. (1988) *Guardians of Language: the Grammarian and Society in Late Antiquity*. Berkeley and Los Angeles.
Kennell, N. M. (2000) 'The status of the ephebarch', *Tyche* 15: 103–8.
  (2006) *Ephebeia: a Register of Greek Cities with Citizen Training Systems in the Hellenistic and Roman Periods*. Hildesheim.
  (2009) 'The Greek ephebate in the Roman period', *The International Journal of the History of Sport* 26: 323–42.

Kirbihler, F. (1994) 'Les femmes magistrats et liturges en Asie Mineure', *Ktema* 19: 51–75.
Kleijwegt, M. (1991) *Ancient Youth. The Ambiguity of Youth and the Absence of Adolescence in Greco-Roman Society*. Amsterdam.
  (1994) '*Iuvenes* and Roman imperial society', *AClass* 37: 79–102.
  (2004) art. 'Kind', in *RLAC* 20: cols. 865–947.
Klodt, C. (ed.) (1996) *Satura Lanx. Festschrift für Werner A. Krenkel zum 70. Geburtstag*. Hildesheim, Zurich, and New York.
Knight, M. (2001) 'Curing cut or ritual mutilation? Some remarks on the practice of female and male circumcision in Graeco-Roman Egypt', *Isis* 92: 317–38.
Knothe, H.-G. (1982) 'Zur 7-Jahresgrenze der *infantia* im antiken römischen Recht', *SDHI* 48: 239–56.
Kokkinia, C. (2007) 'Junge Honoratioren in Lykien und eine neue Ehreninschrift aus Bubon', in *Griechische Epigraphik in Lykien. Eine Zwischenbilanz*, ed. C. Schuler. Vienna: 165–74.
Kolb, F. (1995) *Rom. Die Geschichte der Stadt in der Antike*. Munich.
Krausman Ben-Amos, I. (2004) 'Inleiding. Trends en thema's in de historiografie van de jeugd', in *Losbandige jeugd. Jongeren en moraal in de Nederlanden tijdens de late Middeleeuwen en de vroegmoderne tijd*, eds. L. F. Groenendijk and B. J. Roberts. Hilversum: 9–22.
Krenkel, W. (1979) 'Masturbation', *WZRostock* 28: 159–72.
Kudlien, F. (1986) *Die Stellung des Arztes in der römischen Gesellschaft. Freigeborene Römer, Eingebürgerte, Peregrine, Sklaven, Freigelassene als Ärzte*. Stuttgart.
Kunst, Chr. (2006) 'Jugend. Spätantike', in Christes, Klein, and Lüth (2006): 79–88.
Kyle, D. G. (1998) *Spectacles of Death in Ancient Rome*. London and New York.
Ladage, D. (1979) '*Collegia iuvenum* – Ausbildung einer municipalen Elite?', *Chiron* 9: 319–46.
Laes, Chr. (2000) 'Kinderarbeid in de Romeinse oudheid. Een vergeten dossier?', *Kleio* 30: 2–20.
  (2004a) 'Children and office holding in the Roman empire', *Epigraphica* 66: 145–84.
  (2004b) 'Jonge moeders, miskramen en dood in het kraambed', *Kleio* 33, 4: 163–85.
  (2005) 'Childbeating in Roman antiquity. Some reconsiderations', in Mustakallio, Hanska, Sainio, and Vuolanto (2005): 75–90.
  (2006a) *Kinderen bij de Romeinen. Zes eeuwen dagelijks leven*. Leuven.
  (2006b) 'Galen on the division of childhood. Some reconsiderations', *RSA* 36: 229–40.
  (2007) 'Inscriptions from Rome and the history of childhood', in Harlow and Laurence (2007): 25–36.
  (2008) 'Goed in je vel. Galenus over gezonde kinderen en fitte tieners', *Kleio* 37: 79–96.
  (2011) *Children in the Roman Empire. Outsiders Within*. Cambridge.

Laes, Chr. and Strubbe, J. (2006) *Kleine Romeinen. Jonge kinderen in het antieke Rome*. Amsterdam.
  (2008) *Jeugd in het Romeinse rijk. Jonge jaren, wilde haren?* Leuven.
La Follette, L. (1994) 'The costume of the Roman bride', in *The World of Roman Costume*, eds. L. Bonfante and J. L. Sebesta. Madison: 54–64.
Laslett, P. (1987) rev. of Burrow (1986), *Ageing and Society* 7: 103–5.
Laurence, P. (2005) 'La faiblesse féminine chez les Pères de l'Eglise', in *Les Pères de l'Eglise face à la science médicale de leur temps*, eds. V. Boudon-Milhot and B. Pouderon. Paris: 351–77.
Le Bohec, Y. (1987) 'Peut-on "compter la mort" des soldats de la IIIième légion Auguste?', in Hinard (1987): 53–64.
Legras, B. (1993) '*Mallokouria* et mallocourètes. Un rite de passage dans l'Egypte romaine', *CCG* 4: 113–27.
  (1999) *Néotês. Recherches sur les jeunes grecs dans l'Egypte ptolémaïque et romaine*. Geneva.
Leitao, D. D. (2003) 'Adolescent hair-growing and hair-cutting rituals in ancient Greece. A sociological approach', in Dodd and Faraone (2003): 109–29.
Lelis, A. A., Percy, W. A. and Verstraete, B. C. (2003) *The Age of Marriage in Ancient Rome*. Lewiston, Queenston, and Lampeter.
Lentano, M. (1996) '"*Noscere amoris iter*": l'iniziazione alla vita sessuale nella cultura romana', *Euphrosyne* 24: 271–82.
Levi, G. and Schmitt, J.-C. (eds.) (1996) *Histoire des jeunes en occident 1. De l'Antiquité à l'époque moderne*. Paris.
Lewis, N. (1983) *Life in Egypt under Roman Rule*. Oxford.
Lloyd, G. E. R. (1964) 'The hot and the cold, the dry and the wet in Greek philosophy', *JHS* 84: 92–106.
  (2008) 'Galen and his contemporaries', in Hankinson (2008a): 34–48.
MacCoull, L. S. B. (1979) 'Child donations and child saints in Coptic Egypt', *East European Quarterly* 13: 409–15.
MacDonald, M. (2003) 'Was Celsus right? The role of women in the expansion of early Christianity', in *Early Christian Families in Context. An Interdisciplinary Dialogue*, eds. D. Balch and C. Osiek. Grand Rapids: 157–84.
Macfarlane, A. (1979) rev. of Stone (1977), *H&T* 18: 103–26.
Marrou, H.-I. (1964) *Histoire de l'éducation dans l'Antiquité*, 6th edn. Paris.
McCall, W. (2006) rev. of Lelis, Percy, and Verstraete (2003), *BMCRev* 2006.05.29. [bmcr.brynmawr.edu/2006/2006-05-29.html]
McGinn, Th. A. J. (2004) *The Economy of Prostitution in the Roman World. A Study of Social History and the Brothel*. Ann Arbor.
McKeown, N. (2007) *The Invention of Ancient Slavery?* London.
Mead, M. (1928) *Coming of Age in Samoa*. New York.
Meadows, D. (1993) rev. of Eyben (1993), *BMCRev* 1993.4.5.24. [bmcr.brynmawr.edu/1993/04.05.24.html]
Melfi, M. (2002) 'Il complesso del "Pythion-Asklepieion" a Paro', *ASAA* 80: 327–60.
Minten, E. (2002) *Roman Attitudes towards Children and Childhood. Private Funerary Evidence (c. 50 BC – c. AD 300)*. Stockholm.

Mitchell, S. and French, D. (2012) *The Greek and Latin Inscriptions of Ankara (Ancyra)* 1. Munich.
Modrzejewski, M. (1955) 'Le droit de famille dans les lettres privées grecques d'Egypte', *JJP* 9: 339–63.
Montserrat, D. (1990) 'P. Lond. Inv. 3078 reappraised', *JEA* 76: 206–7.
  (1991) '*Mallocouria* and *therapeuteria*: rituals of transition in a mixed society?', *BASP* 28: 43–9.
  (1996) *Sex and Society in Graeco-Roman Egypt*. London and New York.
Musgrove, F. (1964) *Youth and the Social Order*. Bloomington.
Mustakallio, K., Hanska, J., Sainio H. L., and Vuolanto V. (eds.) (2005) *Hoping for Continuity. Childhood, Education and Death in Antiquity and the Middle Ages*. Rome.
Nathan, G. (2000) *The Family in Late Antiquity. The Rise of Christianity and the Endurance of Tradition*. London and New York.
Néraudau, J.-P. (1984) *Être enfant à Rome*. Paris.
Nigdelis, P. M. and Souris, G. A. (2005) *Anthupatos legei. Ena diatagma tôn autokratorikôn chronôn gia to gumnasio tês Beroias*. Thessaloniki.
Nilsson, M. P. (1955) *Die hellenistische Schule*. Munich.
Nutton, V. (1977) 'Archiatri and the medical profession in antiquity', *PBSR* 45: 191–226.
  (1979) De praecognitione. On Prognosis, with tr. and comm., *Corpus Medicorum Graecorum* v, 8, 1. Berlin.
  (1995) 'Galen ad multos annos', *Dynamis* 15: 25–39.
  (2004) *Ancient Medicine*. London.
Oakley, J. H. and Sinos, R. H. (1993) *The Wedding in Ancient Athens*. London and Madison.
Olson, K. (2008) 'The appearance of the young Roman girl', in Edmondson and Keith (2008): 139–57.
Orme, N. (2001) *Medieval Children*. New Haven and London.
Osiek, C. and MacDonald, M. (2005) *A Women's Place: House Churches in Early Christianity*. Minneapolis.
Pailler, J.-M. and Payen, P. (eds.) (2004) *Que reste-t-il de l'éducation classique? Relire 'Le Marrou' (Histoire de l'éducation dans l'Antiquité)*. Toulouse.
Parkin, T. (2003) *Old Age in the Roman World. A Cultural and Social History*. Baltimore.
Parkin, T. and Pomeroy, A. J. (2007) *Roman Social History. A Sourcebook*. London and New York.
Pernot, L. (2008) *A l'école des anciens. Professeurs, élèves et étudiants*. Paris.
Perrin-Saminadayar, E. (2007) *Education, culture et société à Athènes. Les acteurs de la vie culturelle athénienne (229–88). Un tout petit monde*. Paris.
Peterson, E. (1934) 'Das jugendliche Alter der Lectoren', *Ephemerides Liturgicae* 48: 437–42.
Petit, P. (1956) *Les étudiants de Libanius: un professeur de faculté et ses élèves au Bas-Empire*. Paris.
Puech, B. (2002) *Orateurs et sophistes grecs dans les inscriptions d'époque impériale*. Paris.

Pleket, H. W. (1979) 'Licht uit Leuven over de Romeinse jeugd?', *Lampas* 12: 173–92.
  (1981a) 'Repliek', *Lampas* 14: 140–3.
  (1981b) 'Stadstaat en onderwijs in de Griekse wereld', *Lampas* 14: 155–78.
  (1990) 'Wirtschaft', in *Handbuch der europäischen Wirtschafts- und Sozialgeschichte*, ed. W. Fischer. Frankfurt: 25–160.
  (1995) 'The social status of physicians in the Graeco-Roman world', in *Ancient Medicine in its Socio-Cultural Context* 1, eds. Ph. J. van der Eijk, H. F. J. Horstmanshoff, and P. H. Schrijvers. Amsterdam: 27–34.
Pollock, L. A. (1983) *Forgotten Children. Parent–Child Relations 1500–1900*. Cambridge.
Pomeroy, S. B. (1997) *Families in Classical and Hellenistic Greece*. Oxford.
Prag, J. R. W. (2007) '*Auxilia* and *gymnasia*: a Sicilian model of Roman imperialism', *JRS* 97: 68–100.
Prescendi, F. (2010) 'Children and the transmission of religious knowledge', in Dasen and Späth (2010): 73–94.
Quass, F. (1993) *Die Honoratiorenschicht in den Städten des griechischen Ostens*. Stuttgart.
Rawson, B. (1974) 'Roman concubinage and other "*de facto*" marriages', *TAPhA* 104: 279–305.
  (2003) *Children and Childhood in Roman Italy*. Oxford.
  (2005) 'The future of childhood studies in classics and ancient history', in Mustakallio, Hanska, Sainio, and Vuolanto (2005): 1–11.
Robert, J. and Robert, L. (1954) *La Carie. Histoire et géographie historique avec le recueil des inscriptions antiques* II. *Le plateau de Tabai et ses environs*. Paris.
  (1989) *Claros* I. *Décrets hellénistiques*. Paris.
Robert, L. (1937) *Etudes anatoliennes. Recherches sur les inscriptions grecques de l'Asie Mineure*. Paris.
Rogers, G. M. (1991) *The Sacred Identity of Ephesos. Foundation Myths of a Roman City*. London and New York.
Roller, M. B. (2006) *Dining Posture in Ancient Rome. Bodies, Values and Status*. Princeton and Oxford.
Rose, V. (1870) *Anecdota Graeca et Graecolatina* II. Berlin.
Rumscheid, F. (2004) 'Inschriften aus Milas im Museum Bodrum', *EA* 37: 42–61.
Saavedra-Guerrero, M. D. (1996) '*Iuvenae* en los *collegia* del occidente romano', *A&R* ser. 9, 41: 24–31.
Saller, R. P. (1987) 'Men's age at marriage and its consequences in the Roman family', *CPh* 82: 21–34.
  (1994) *Patriarchy, Property and Death in the Roman Family*. Cambridge.
  (2001) 'The family and society', in *Epigraphic Evidence. Ancient History from Inscriptions*, ed. J. Bodel. London and New York: 97–117.
  (2012) 'Human Capital and Growth', in *The Cambridge Companion to the Roman Economy*, ed. W. Scheidel. Cambridge: 71–86.
Salmon, P. (1987) 'Les insuffisances du matériel épigraphique sur la mortalité dans l'Antiquité romaine', in Hinard (1987): 99–112.

Samama, E. (2003) *Les médecins dans le monde grec. Sources épigraphiques sur la naissance d'un corps médical*. Geneva.
Sandirocco, L. (2003) 'Binae nuptiae et bina sponsalia', *SDHI* 69: 165–216.
Scheidel, W. (1996) 'Digit preference in age records from Roman Egypt', in *Measuring Sex, Age and Death in the Roman Empire. Explorations in Ancient Demography*, ed. W. Scheidel. Ann Arbor: 53–91.
  (2006) 'Stratification, deprivation and quality of life', in *Poverty in the Ancient World*, eds. M. Atkins and R. Osborne. Cambridge: 40–59.
  (2007a) 'Roman funerary commemoration and the age of first marriage', *CPh* 102: 389–402.
  (2007b) 'Demography', in *The Cambridge Economic History of the Greco-Roman World*, eds. W. Scheidel, I. Morris, and R. Saller. Cambridge: 38–86.
Schlange-Schöningen, H. (2003) *Die römische Gesellschaft bei Galen*. Berlin and New York.
Scholz, K. (2007) 'Mädchenerziehung in Rom', *AU* 50, 1: 35–45.
Scholz, P. (2004) 'Elementarunterricht und intellektuelle Bildung im hellenistischen Gymnasion', in Kah and Scholz (2004): 103–28.
Schouten, C. A. J. (1971–2) 'Een Franeker student trekt tegen de zelfbevrediging ten strijde', *Hermeneus* 43: 259–66.
Schuler, C. (2004) 'Die Gymnasiarchie in hellenistischer Zeit', in Kah and Scholz (2004): 163–92.
Schwarz, A. B. (1952) 'Die justinianische Reform des Pubertätsbeginns und die Beilegung juristischer Kontroversen', *ZRG* 69: 345–87.
Sebesta, J. L. (1997) 'Women's costume and feminine civic morality in Augustan Rome', *Gender and History* 9, 3: 529–41.
Shackelton Bailey, D. R. (2001) *Cicero. Letters to Friends* III. The Loeb Classical Library 230. Cambridge, Mass. and London.
Shaw, B. D. (1987) 'The age of Roman girls at marriage: some reconsiderations', *JRS* 77: 30–46.
  (2001) 'Raising and killing children: two Roman myths', *Mnemosyne* 54: 31–77.
Sherk, R. K. (1988) *The Roman Empire: Augustus to Hadrian*. Cambridge.
Shorter, E. (1975) *The Making of the Modern Family*. New York.
Singor, H. W. (2008) 'De klassieke Spartaanse opvoeding', *Lampas* 41: 131–48.
Smith, S. R. (1973) 'The London apprentices as seventeenth-century adolescents', *P&P* 61: 149–61.
Stone, L. (1977) *The Family, Sex and Marriage in England (1500–1800)*. London.
Strubbe, J. H. M. (1982) 'Het jonge kind in de oudheid', *Kleio* 12: 49–77.
  (1997) *Arai Epitymbioi. Imprecations against Desecrators of the Grave in the Greek Epitaphs of Asia Minor. A Catalogue*. Bonn.
  (1998) 'Epigrams and consolation decrees for deceased youths', *AC* 67: 45–75.
  (2005) 'Young magistrates in the Greek East', *Mnemosyne* 58: 88–111.
Taubenschlag, R. (1944) *The Law of Greco-Roman Egypt in the Light of the Papyri (332 BC–AD 640)*. Warsaw.
Timmer, J. (2008) *Altersgrenzen politischer Partizipation in antiken Gesellschaften*. Berlin.

Tissot, S.-A. (1760) *L'onanisme: dissertation sur les maladies produites par la masturbation*. Lausanne.
Too, Y. L. (ed.) (2001) *Education in Greek and Roman Antiquity*. Leiden.
Torelli, M. (1984) *Lavinio e Roma. Riti iniziatici e matrimonio tra archeologia e storia*. Rome.
Treggiari, S. (1991) *Roman Marriage. 'Iusti Coniuges' from the Time of Cicero to the Time of Ulpian*. Oxford.
Triantaphyllopoulos, J. (1988) 'Virginité et défloration masculines', in *Proceedings of the XVIIIth International Congress of Papyrology. Athens 25–31 May 1986* II, ed. B. G. Mandilaras. Athens: 327–33.
Van Belzen, J. A. (ed.) (1997) *Metabletica en wetenschap. Kritische bestandsopname van het werk van J. H. van den Berg*. Rotterdam.
Van Bremen, R. (1996) *The Limits of Participation. Women and Civic Life in the Greek East in the Hellenistic and Roman Periods*. Amsterdam.
Van den Berg, J. H. (1957) *Metabletica of leer der veranderingen*. Nijkerken.
Van Hooff, A. J. L. (1990) *From Autothanasia to Suicide: Self-Killing in Classical Antiquity*. London.
Van Houdt, T. (1990) 'Strategische zelfpresentatie bij Plinius Minor. *Ep.* 7,5 als mentaliteitshistorische bron', *Kleio* 19, 4: 201–13.
  (2003) 'Liefde, seks en sekserollen: genre en gender in het oude Rome', in Eyben, Laes, and Van Houdt (2003a): 99–134.
  (2009) 'Emiel Eyben als mentaliteitshistoricus van de oudheid', in *Kleio* 38: 64–77.
Van Nijf, O. (1999–2000) 'Athletics, festivals and identity in the Roman East', *PCPhS* 45: 176–200.
  (2001) 'Local heroes: athletics, festivals and elite self-fashioning in the Roman East', in *Being Greek under Rome. Cultural Identity, the Second Sophistic and the Development of Empire*, ed. S. Goldhill. Cambridge: 306–34.
  (2003) 'Athletics, *andreia* and the *askêsis*-culture in the Roman East', in *Andreia. Studies in Manliness and Courage in Classical Antiquity*, eds. R. M. Rosen and I. Sluiter. Leiden and Boston: 263–86.
  (2004) 'Athletics and *paideia*: festivals and physical education in the world of the Second Sophistic', in *Paideia: the World of the Second Sophistic*, ed. B. E. Borg. Berlin and New York: 203–27.
Vatai, F. L. (2004) 'Rhetoric, youth and dissidence in Rome', *AHB* 18: 145–9.
Vérilhac, A.-M. (1978–82) *Paides aoroi. Poésie funéraire* I–II. Athens.
Verstraete, B. (2008) rev. of Laes and Strubbe (2008), *BMCRev* 2008.12.21. [bmcr.brynmawr.edu/2008/2008-12-21.html]
Vesley, M. E. (1998) 'Gladiatorial training for girls in the *collegia iuvenum* of the Roman empire', *EMC* 42 (n.s. 17): 85–93.
  (2003) 'Father–son relations in Roman declamation', *AHB* 17: 159–80.
Veyne, P. (1960) 'Iconographie de la *transvectio equitum* et des Lupercales', *REA* 62: 100–13.
  (1978) 'La famille et l'amour sous le Haut-Empire romain', *Annales (ESC)* 33: 35–63.
  (2001) *La société romaine*. Paris.

(2007) *Quand notre monde est devenu chrétien (312–394)*. Paris.
Ville, G. (1981) *La gladiature en Occident des origines à la mort de Domitien*. Paris and Rome.
Volk, K. (2010) *Ovid. Blackwell Introductions to the Classical World*. Chichester and Malden, Mass.
Vössing, K. (1997) *Schule und Bildung im Nordafrika der römischen Kaiserzeit*. Brussels.
  (2002) 'Staat und Schule in der Spätantike', *AncSoc* 32: 243–62.
  (2003) 'Die Geschichte der römischen Schule – ein Abriss vor dem Hintergrund der neueren Forschung', *Gymnasium* 110: 455–97.
  (2004a) 'Koedukation und öffentliche Kommunikation – warum Mädchen vom höheren Schulunterricht Roms ausgeschlossen waren', *Klio* 86, 1: 126–40.
  (2004b) 'L'état et l'école dans l'Antiquité tardive', in Pailler and Payen (2004): 281–95.
Vout, C. (2005) 'Antinous, archaeology and history', *JRS* 95: 80–96.
Vuolanto, V. (2005) 'Children and asceticism. Strategies of continuity in the late fourth and early fifth century', in Mustakallio, Hanska, Sainio, and Vuolanto (2005): 119–32.
Walsh, P. G. (1961) *Livy: His Historical Aims and Methods*. Cambridge.
Watts, E. (2004) 'Travel to school. What was the attraction?', in *Travel, Communication and Geography in Late Antiquity*, eds. L. Ellis and F. Kidner. Burlington: 11–21.
  (2005) 'The student self in late antiquity', in *Religion and the Self in Antiquity*, eds. D. Brakke, M. L. Satlow, and S. Weitzman. Bloomington: 234–51.
  (2006) *City and School in Late Antique Athens and Alexandria*. Berkeley, London, and Los Angeles.
Wes, M. A. (1981) 'De klas en de kanselarij: onderwijs en overheid in Rome', *Lampas* 14: 192–209.
Westenberg, P. M. (2008) *De jeugd van tegenwoordig!* (Diesoratie uitgesproken tijdens de 433ᵉ dies natalis van de Universiteit Leiden) / *The Youth of Today!* (Commemoration day lecture during the 433rd anniversary celebrations of Leiden University). Leiden.
Wieber, A. (2007) '*Liberi sunt – immo servi sunt*. Vom Leben der Sklavenkinder', *AU* 50: 67–70.
Wiedemann, Th. (1989) *Adults and Children in the Roman Empire*. London.
  (1994) rev. of Kleijwegt (1991), *CR* 44: 370–2.
Wilkinson, P. (1969) 'English youth movements 1908–30', *Journal of Contemporary History* 4.2: 3–23.
Williams, C. A. (1999) *Roman Homosexuality. Ideologies of Masculinity in Classical Antiquity*. New York and Oxford.
Wilson, A. (1980) 'The infancy of the history of childhood', *H&T* 19: 132–54.
Wimbush, V. L. (1990) *Ascetic Behavior in Graeco-Roman Antiquity. A Sourcebook*. Minneapolis.
Woolf, G. (1994) 'Becoming Roman, staying Greek: culture, identity and the civilizing process in the Roman East', *PCPhS* 40: 116–43.

Wörrle, M. (1995) 'Vom tugendsamen Jüngling zum "gestressten" Euergeten. Überlegungen zum Bürgerbild hellenistischer Ehrendekrete', in *Stadtbild und Bürgerbild im Hellenismus*, eds. M. Wörrle and P. Zanker. Munich: 241–50.

(2007) 'Zu Rang und Bedeutung von Gymnasion und Gymnasiarchie im hellenistischen Pergamon', *Chiron* 37: 501–16.

Yiftach-Firanko, U. (2003) *Marriage and Marital Arrangements: a History of the Greek Marriage Documents in Egypt 4th Century BCE – 4th Century CE*. Munich.

Younger, J. G. (2005) *Sex in the Ancient World from A to Z*. London.

Zoumbaki, S. (2004) 'Zur Funktion des Neaniskarchen in den Städten des östlichen Teils des römischen Kaiserreiches', in *Histoire, espaces et marges de l'Antiquité: hommages à Monique Clavel-Lévêque* III, eds. M. Garrido-Hory and A. Gonzalès. Besançon: 193–211.

Zwart, H. (2002) *Boude bewoordingen. De historische fenomenologie ('metabletica') van Jan Hendrik van den Berg*. Kampen and Kapellen.

Index

adulescens, 17, 26, 28–9, 42, 47, 48, 62
adulescentia, 15, 22, 25, 26, 28–9, 34, 43, 165, 220
age
  consciousness, 22, 38–40
  rounding, 38–9
  segregation in school, 74 n. 14
allowance, given by the father: *see peculium*
amulet worn by a child: *see bulla*
anthropology, 6; *see also* Mead, M.
Antinous, 142–3
Antoninus Pius
  marriage law, 206
  privileges for teachers and physicians, 83, 185
apparitor (assistant to municipal magistrate), 189
archiatros (civic physician enjoying immunity), 185, 191
Ariès, Ph., 7–10
Aristotle
  characteristics of youths, 24, 44–6
  puberty, 62–3
arkteia (rite of passage (?) of Athenian girls 'acting the bear'), 52
army, 55
  and *iuvenes*, 129, 134
  and *neoi, neaniskoi*, 73 n. 9
  officers, 165, 167–8
  physicians, 188
Artemis, 50, 52
  Brauronia, 52
  Lysizonos, 52
  Orthia, 50
assistant to municipal magistrate: *see apparitor*
astrology, 28, 43, 140
Augustine, 96, 161
  mother Monica, 222
  puberty and sexuality, 63, 221–2
Augustus
  education of his female kin, 101–2
  Forum of Augustus in Rome, 30, 56–7
  iuventus in Rome, 123
  marriage law, 152

minimum age
  for minor offices in Bithynia, 171
  for quaestorship, 165
  opening hours of brothels, 141 n. 17
  privileges for physicians, 185
  see also Octavian

Baden-Powell, R., 117 n. 40
beard, 138, 218
  depositing of: *see depositio barbae*
  first, 27, 63, 69, 201
  full, 27, 58, 143
  shaving, 58
benefactions
  for education, 74, 85, 114
  to youth groups, 72, 110, 120, 126
  see also gymnasiarch: generosity
benefactor, 75, 78, 106, 112, 133, 150, 166, 175, 176, 178, 180, 230
  public honours, 75, 106, 107, 118, 119, 130
betrothal, 36, 199, 201, 204
bodily harmony: *see euexia*
brain development, 1–2, 15, 136
bulla (amulet worn by a child), 30, 55, 57, 59, 146

Catiline, 48, 151
Cato, 81, 141
Catullus, *see poetae novi*
causidicus (lawyer in the service of a city), 190
characteristics of youth(s), 48
  restlessness, 1, 15–18, 33, 34, 48, 134, 135, 136–49, 221, 232
  see also Aristotle; Cicero; *ferocitas*; Horace; Ptolemy
charivari, 135 n. 92, 139 n. 7
child(ren), 149
  approaching puberty: *see pubertati proximus*
  as knights, 167, 169, 181
  as office holders, 107, 119 n. 48, 119, 171, 173, 178
  as priests, 174, 179

249

child(ren) (cont.)
  associated with the city government, 175
  bodily characteristics, 62, 63, 68
  Christian view, 215
  corporal punishments, 159
  in monasteries, 220
  purity, 63, 174
  schooling, 70–1
  weakness (*infirmitas*), 46
  work, 191, 193
  see also infans; *pais*; *puer*
childhood
  appreciation by Romans, 229
  end, for boys, 55–6
  end, for girls, 59–60, 201–2, 205
  in the division of the life cycle, 23–30
  see also infantia; *pueritia*
choros (group of students around a teacher): *see under* students' lives
Christes, J., 19–20, 24–5, 146 n. 29, 146–7
Cicero, 46, 86, 87, 139, 141, 157, 189, 198, 209
  characteristics of youth(s), 43, 46, 165
  inter-generational conflict, 151 n. 40, 155–6
  misconduct of youths, 158–9
  parental power, 154, 158
circumcision (boys and girls), 53, 54
conflict of generations, 145, 149–62, 231, 232
  in Christian society, 217
  see also Cicero; Quintilian
controversiae (declamations in schools of rhetoric), 86, 87, 157
curator, 33, 208
  lusus iuvenalis, 129
  of the *iuvenes*, 132

declamations in schools of rhetoric: *see controversiae*; *suasoriae*
declaration (written) concerning the status of a boy in Egypt: *see epikrisis*
depositio barbae (depositing the beard), 58
discipline: *see eutaxia*
disorderly behaviour, 75 n. 17, 149
  of ephebes, 118
  of *iuvenes*, 131
  of *neoi*, 75
  of students, 99; *see also* Cicero; Marcus Cicero; students' lives
  see also Nero
divorce, 152, 197, 198, 206–7
dowry, 197–8, 199, 204, 209, 210

education
  higher, *see* higher education
  privileges for teachers, 82–3
  state intervention, 81, 82, 86
  state subsidies, 84–5
  see also paideia
ekdikos (jurist), 187
emancipatio, 153
emperor cult, 106, 118, 130, 131
ephebarch, 109, 119 n. 48, 119–120, 121, 135, 173
  child-ephebarch, 119 n. 48
ephebeia (organisation of ephebes)
  as means of socialisation, 111
  duration, 107, 109–10
  in Athens, 50, 104
  in Egypt, 53, 104
  organisation, 119–20
  see also ephebes
ephebes, 104–20, 133–5, 230–1
  activities and training, 107
    civil virtues, 75, 117–18
    cult ceremonies, 118
    intellectual education, 73–4, 114–16
    military skills, 111–13
    participation in public life, 119
    sports, 113
  age, 107, 109
  behaving as 'social adults'?, 119
  of the first/second/third year, 109 n. 14
  organisation: *see ephebeia*
  overseer: *see ephebophylax*
  social background, 107, 110
  socialisation, 118
  see also ephebarch; gymnasiarch; gymnasium
ephebophylax (overseer of ephebes), 120
epigraphic evidence
  age at first marriage, 199–200
  age rounding in funerary inscriptions, 38–9
  album of *decuriones* of Canusium, 178–9
  consolation decrees, 175–6
  disorderly conduct of youths, 75 n. 17, 75, 149
  female rhetor, 100
  gymnasiarchical law of Beroea, 117
  harmony between generations, 150
  import of slaves, 194–5
  married life, 211–12, 213
  offering of hair, 51–2
  public lectures, 73–4
  shaving of the beard, 58
  teachers from abroad, 83
  young councillors, 173
    in the West, 177–8
  young knights, 167–9
  young lawyers
    in the East, 186–7
    in the West, 189–90

young magistrates
    in the East, 171–3
    in the West, 176–7
young philosophers, 79
young physicians
    in the East, 185–6
    in the West, 188
young priests
    in the East, 173–4
    in the West, 178
young slaves at work, 194
young students abroad, 76–7
youths associated with the city government, 175, 178
youths of the senatorial order, 165–7
see also *ephebeia*; ephebes; gymnasiarch; gymnasium; *iuvenes*; *iuventus*
epikrisis (or *eiskrisis*) (written declaration concerning the status of a boy in Egypt), 53–4
euandria (fitness), 121
euergetes: see benefactor
euexia (bodily harmony, fitness), 75, 117, 121
eukosmia (orderly conduct), 75, 107, 120
    of girls, 120 n. 49
eutaxia (good discipline), 75, 76, 117, 118, 120, 121
Eyben, E., 47
    central theses on youth, 14–16
    on behaviour of youths, 136–8, 144–5, 231
    on inter-generational conflicts, 155
    on young senators, 165–6, 181

ferocitas (restlessness), 15, 46, 135, 136
festival for a daughter at the onset of puberty: see *therapeuteria*
fitness: see *euandria*; *euexia*
fond of
    making an effort, training hard: see *philoponos*
    learning: see *philomathes*
fondness for making an effort, training hard: see *philoponia*
Fortuna Virginalis, 31 n. 20, 202
freed slave(s), 130, 167, 178, 194
    employment
        legal assistant, 189
        physician, 188
        staff of magistrates, 178
        teacher of oratory, 82
    magister of the *iuvenes*, 133
    members of
        associations, 127
        iuventus, 125
    office holders in associations, 133
    sex with freedmen, freedwomen, 140, 143

Galen, 223
    division of the life cycle, 24
    healing sick youngsters, 65–7
    puberty, 61, 64
    schooling, 196
Gallus, Plotius, 81–2
Gillis, J.R., 14
girl(s)
    apprenticeship, 191, 193
    dress, 31, 59, 202
    education, 70, 99–102
    guardian for under-age girls, 208
    marriage before twelve years of age, 199, 201
    marriageable at twelve years of age, 31, 32, 37, 55, 59
    members of *iuventus*, 124, 128, 134; see also *iuvenae*
    terms, 41, 59
    trained as gladiators?, 128
    see also betrothal; marriage; menstruation; puberty; rites of passage; virginity
grammatica, 100 n. 127
grammaticus, 70, 83, 84, 86, 93, 100, 101; see also *grammatikos*
grammatikos, 114
gravitas, 46, 47
groups
    of students around a teacher: see *choros*
    of wandering men: see *vagantes*
    of young girls: see *iuvenae*; *neai*
    of young men: see *iuvenes*; *iuventus*; *neoi*; *neoteroi*
guardian: see tutor
gymnasiarch, 171 n. 27
    and *paideia*, 116, 121; see also in this entry generosity
    ephebes serving as gymnasiarchs, 172–3
    'eternal', 107
    generosity, 72, 74, 106–7, 108–9, 110, 114, 120, 121
    in Egypt, 53
    tasks, 75, 107, 117, 119
    unwillingness to serve as gymnasiarch, 106 n. 5
gymnasiarchical law of Beroea, 75 n. 17, 117
gymnasium, 93, 105–22, 133
    activities of the ephebes, 111–19
    activities of the *neoi*, 72–6
    financing, 106–7
    in Egypt, 53, 106 n. 4
    place of socialisation of youth, 117–18
    'second agora', 106

Hadrian
    love for Antinous, 142–3
    privileges for physicians, 185

hair, 139, 202
  lock of Horus, 54 n. 18
  offering, 50
    boys, 50–2, 54, 58
    girls, 52
    see also Koureotis; mallokouria
  pubic, 61, 63, 64, 68
  see also beard
Heracles, 118, 121
Hercules, 129, 130
Hermaea, 117, 118
Hermes, 115, 117, 118, 121
higher education
  Libanius' school of rhetoric, 89–92
  rhetoric, philosophy in the West, 79–85
  rhetoric, philosophy, law, medicine in the East, 76–9
  see also students' lives
homosexuality, 142–3
Horace, 46
  characteristics of youth, 24
humours of the body, 24, 43, 196
hypephebarchos (under-ephebarch), 119 n. 48
hypogymnasiarch, 173

identity
  civic, 112, 118
  Greek, 112, 116
  Roman, 129, 134
infans: in Roman law, 34–6
infantia, 25, 26, 35
inter-generational conflict: *see* conflict of generations
Isidore of Seville
  division of the life cycle, 23, 28
  puberty, 61
Isis, 51 n. 9
iuris consultus (jurist who gives legal advice), 189
iuris peritus (experienced advocate), 189, 190
iuris studiosus (student of law), 187 n. 16
ius vitae necisque (right over life and death), 151
iuvenae (group of young girls), 124
Iuvenalia (festival), 129
  at Rome, 58
iuvenes (group of young men), 122–33, 134–5, 230–1
  activities and training, 127–31
    combat sports, 127–9
    participation in public life, 130
    religious worship, 129–30
  age, 124–5
  disorderly behaviour, 131
  gender, 123–4
  social background, 125–6
  see also iuvenae; iuventus

iuvenis (young man), 26
  term, 17, 42
iuventa (youth, stage of life), 26
iuventus (association of *iuvenes*, young men)
  as means of socialisation, 132–3
  in Rome, 123
  organisation, 131–2
  see also iuvenes
iuventus (youth, stage of life), 15, 22, 25, 28–9, 47, 139

Jugendraum (time to be young), 15, 17, 20, 108, 146, 147, 165, 166, 181
Juno, 59
Jupiter, 56, 130
jurist: *see* ekdikos; nomikos; pragmatikos; syndikos
  experienced advocate: *see* iuris peritus
  in the service of a city: *see* causidicus
  practical training of a young jurist: *see* tirocinium fori
  who gives legal advice: *see* iuris consultus

Kleijwegt, M., 145, 231
  central theses on youth, 18–19
  on *ephebeia*, 107–8, 111, 118
  on inter-generational conflicts, 150
  on *iuvenes*, 125, 128, 129
  on young *equites*, 167
  on young jurists, 189
  on young office holders, 169–70, 172, 177, 182
  on young physicians, 185
Komyrion (festival), 51
Koureotis (third day of the *Apatouria* festival), 50
kourosyna (hair-cutting ritual), 52
krypteia (rite of passage in Sparta), 49

legal evidence
  age of transition to adulthood, 31–2
  divorce, 198
  maximum age for students, 92, 97
  minimum age
    for office holders, 170–1
    for the work of a slave, 193
  minores and criminal law, 34–6
  paternal power, 159
  privileges for teachers and physicians, 82–3
  protection of *minores*, 32–4
  Roman marriage, 199, 203
    minimum ages, 199
    need for reciprocal consent, 206–8
  see also Lex Laetoria; Lex Villia annalis
Lex Laetoria, 15, 32, 57
Lex Villia annalis, 15, 57, 164–5
Libanius, 78
  school of rhetoric, 89–92
  students' lives and behaviour, 92–3, 96–9

Liber, 56
  Pater, 56
Liberalia (festival), 30, 56; *see also* Ovid
library, 75, 76, 106
literacy, 39, 85, 99, 115
lover of letters: *see philologos*
ludimagister (school teacher), 70, 99
lusus iuvenum (or *iuvenalis*) (local games of *iuvenes*, young men), 129, 132

magister iuvenum (director of the *iuvenes*, young men), 124, 131 n. 81, 132, 133
mallokouria (rite of cutting the lock of hair), 54
Marcus Cicero, 85, 166
  letter to Tiro, 162–3
  misbehaviour as a student, 94, 155–6
marriage, 57, 86, 143–4, 146, 152
  age at first marriage, 199–201
  ceremony, 205
  choice of partner, 153, 155, 156, 158, 207–8
  contract, 206
  end of youth?, 22, 209–10
  girl's experience on her wedding day, 203–4, 210–12
  in Christian society
    age at first marriage, 224
    Augustine, 222
    sexual ethics, 224–5
  legal aspects
    Augustan law, 152
    cum manu, sine manu, confarreatio, coemptio, usus, 197
  parental consent, 57, 152, 206–8
  reciprocal consent, 203, 206–8
  rites on the eve of wedding, 52, 59
  sexual ethics, 203
  transition to womanhood, 30, 52, 59
  see also divorce; dowry
masturbation, 68, 140, 223 n. 37
  Christian attitude, 223
  in 18th cent., 140 n. 11
  on Samoa, 3
matrona, 60, 100, 101
Mead, M., 3–7
Melania, 224–5
menarche, 59, 64, 68, 144, 201
menstruation, 69, 201 n. 18, 210; *see also* menarche
monks
  age, 220–1
  sexuality, 223, 224, 225
  see also Severus, patriarch of Alexandria
mother, 153, 160, 206, 208, 212, 225
  authority over children, 160, 161
  conflict with children, 154, 158, 161 n. 80, 161–2

motherhood as a girl's ideal, 59, 213
  see also Augustine; Seneca
Mutunus Tutunus, 59, 202

neai (group of young girls), 72 n. 3
neaniskarchos (leader of the *neaniskoi*, young men), 73 n. 6
neaniskoi (young men), 72, 111, 149
  leader of: *see neaniskarchos*
neaniskos (young man): term, 26, 41
neoi (group of young men), 50, 148
  age group at the gymnasium, 72, 105, 109
  as ephebarchs, 119
  characterisation by Aristotle, 44–6
  (dis)orderly conduct, 75, 119–20
  military role, 73, 111–12
  participation in public life, 75, 119
  studying abroad
    law, medicine, 79
    oratory, 76–8
    philosophy, 78–9
  training and education at the gymnasium, 72–5, 114, 116
  training in civil virtues, 75, 117
neos (young man): term, 41, 72
neoteroi (group of young men), 72, 149 n. 35; *see also neoi*
Nero, 161, 181, 201
  depositio barbae and *Iuvenalia*, 58
  misconduct in his youth, 138
nomikos (lawyer), 186–7, 187 n. 16
numerology, 23, 29, 30, 36, 61

Octavian, 55, 56, 58, 150, 160
  and his mother Atia, 160
  see also Augustus
older person appointed to a position of authority in the church: *see presbyteros*
orderly conduct: *see eukosmia*
Oribasius: breaking of the voice in puberty, 62–3
Ovid, 144, 147, 201
  Liberalia, 56
  life and education, 102–3

paedagogium, 193
paedagogue, 24, 94
paideia (education), 113, 116
  as a social ideal, 75–6, 115
  see also gymnasiarch; *philologos*; *philomathes*
pais, paides (child, children)
  at the gymnasium, 72, 74, 105, 109, 114, 121
  participation in public life, 75, 119
  term, 41
  training in civil virtues, 117

papyrological evidence, 33
　age at first marriage in census lists, 200
　apprenticeship contract, 192–3
　family relations, 162
　import of slaves, 195 n. 36
　reporting one's age, 39
　students' lives, 89, 94–5
　transaction by a minor, 33
　wedding contracts, 205
　young physicians, 186
　see also *epikrisis*; *mallokouria*; *therapeuteria*
pardon because of (young) age: see *venia aetatis*
parental power: see Cicero; *patria potestas*; Pliny; Plutarch; Ps.-Quintilian; Quintilian; Seneca
patria potestas (parental power), 57, 151–5, 159, 198, 206; see also *ius vitae necisque*; parental power
patricide: see Seneca
patroboulos ((young) man designated from youth to succeed to his father's seat in the city council), 175
patron, 126, 127, 133, 166, 169, 180
Paul (apostle), 217
peculium (allowance, given by the father), 152, 157
Persius, 145
　donning the toga virilis, 57
　youthful sense of life, 20, 146
Peter (apostle), 216
philologos (student; lover of letters), 71
　Homeric philologist, 74, 114
philomathes (fond of learning), 116
philoponia (fondness for making an effort, training hard), 75, 117, 121
philoponos (fond of making an effort, training hard), 76, 226
physician (civic) enjoying immunity: see *archiatros*
Pleket, H.W., 145, 165, 231
　central theses on youth, 16–18, 74 n. 14, 98, 231
　on *ephebeia*, 107–8
　on young office holders, 169–70, 172
Pliny, 84, 87, 166, 193
　behaviour of youths, 47
　on donning the *toga virilis* in Bithynia, 57
　parental power, 154, 157, 158
Plutarch, 200
　marriage, beneficial to young girls, 210
　parental power, 158
poetae novi, 16, 18, 144–8, 230
　youthful sense of life, 20
praefectus iuvenum (prefect of the *iuvenes*, young men), 132
praetextati (sons of councillors waiting to take their fathers' seats in the council)
　municipal, 178–9
　senatorial, 166
pragmatikos (lawyer), 187
presbyteros (older person appointed to a position of authority in the church), 217
Prohaeresius, 95, 96
prostitution, 57, 140–2, 148, 157 n. 64, 193, 202
Ps.-Plutarch
　education, 85
　marriage, 209–10
　vices of youths, 149
Ps.-Quintilian: parental power, 154
Ptolemy
　characteristics of youth, 28
　division of the life cycle, 28
pubertati proximus (child approaching puberty), 35, 36
puberty, 21, 43, 52, 136, 232
　age of boys and girls, 55, 59, 61
　development of sexual desire in boys and girls, 59, 140, 144
　lack of a Greek term, 41
　mental or physical problems of girls, 59, 144, 210
　period of crisis?, 64–5, 231
　physiological changes in boys and girls, 61–4, 68–9
　see also Aristotle; Augustine; Galen; Isidore of Seville; Oribasius; rites of passage; Rufus of Ephesus; Soranus
puer, 189
puer senex, 218
　term, 42
pueritia (childhood), 26, 34, 189

Quintilian, 88
　inter-generational conflicts, 157
　parental power, 159 n. 73
　training in rhetoric, 87, 93
Quintus Cicero, 157, 166
　conflict with his uncle Cicero, 156

restlessness: see *ferocitas*
right over life and death: see *ius vitae necisque*
rite of cutting the hair: see *kourosyna*; *mallokouria*
rites of passage, 49
　for boys
　　in the East and Egypt, 49–52, 54
　　in the West, 55–7, 58
　for girls
　　(?) in Athens of girls 'acting the bear': see *arkteia*

in the East and Egypt, 54–5
in the West (absence of), 59–60
in Sparta: see *krypteia*
see also circumcision; hair: offering
Rufus, M. Caelius, 48, 158–9
Rufus of Ephesus: puberty of girls, 64, 144

school teacher: see *ludimagister*
Scipio Africanus, 146–7, 147 n. 31
scouting, 117 n. 40
self-control, 11, 28, 34, 43–4, 136, 140, 143, 159–60, 229
   female lack of, 59, 144, 161
   in Christian society, 217
   in medical texts, 223
Seneca, 46
   behaviour of youths, 138
   eulogy of his mother, 161
   parental power, 152 n. 45, 159 n. 73
   patricide, 153, 155
Seneca the Elder, 87, 141
   behaviour of youths, 139
Severus, patriarch of Alexandria, 225–7
shame, 64
Shorter, E., 10–11
slave(s), 36, 52, 140, 142, 143, 198, 209
   employment, 193
      domestic service, 193
      paedagogue, 94
      physician, 188
   execution of criminal slaves, 153
   imperial, 188, 194
   importation, 194–5
   members of associations, 127
   iuventus?, 125
   public, 173, 178
   senatus consultum Silanianum, 36
   sex with, 140, 143, 148, 203
   spreading Christianity, 216
   violence against, 159
   see also *paedagogium*
socialisation of youths: see *ephebeia*; ephebes; gymnasium; *iuventus*
sociobiology, 2, 229
Soranus, 184, 223
   puberty of girls, 144
sperm, 28, 64, 69, 223
   canals, 62
   nocturnal emission, 62, 223
   see also masturbation
Stone, L., 10, 11
student: see *philologos*
   of law: see *iuris studiosus*
students' lives

ages, 92
edict of Valentinian I, 97–8
groups around teachers, 93, 95
initiation, 95
tumultuous behaviour, 93–9
suasoriae (declamations in schools of rhetoric), 86, 87
subculture
   female, 212, 232
   of students, 71, 88, 98, 230
   of youths, 17, 19, 231
syndikos (jurist), 187

Testamentum Porcelli, 88
therapeuteria (festival for a daughter at the onset of puberty), 54–5
tirocinium fori (practical training of a young jurist), 80, 189
toga, 202, 203
   praetexta, 30, 55, 57, 59, 146, 202
   virilis, 30, 37, 55–6, 56 n. 26, 57–8, 103, 124, 160, 166, 170–1, 199, 201
tutor (guardian), 35–6, 208
   impuberum, 208

under-ephebarch: see *hypephebarchos*
'university', 77, 84
   'town(s)', 71, 76, 77–8, 93, 98, 221

vagantes (group of wandering men), 140
Van den Berg, J.H., 12–13
Varro: division of the life cycle, 26
venia aetatis (pardon because of (young) age), 33
Venus, 28, 59, 204
virgin, 59, 140; see also virginity
virginity, 59, 144, 202, 203, 205 n. 36, 205, 212
Vulcan, 179

women, 86, 204, 205, 231
   and Christianity, 216, 217
   as physicians, 188
   as priestesses, 174
   associations, 127
   chastity, 203
   dress, 202
   education after marriage, 101
   female inner circle, 213; see also subculture: female
   gymnasium, 106
   holding public office, 107, 161, 172
   life of a young married woman, 214
   literary talents, 100
   philosopher, 101 n. 136
   rhetorical skills, 100–1
   see also *matrona*; *grammatica*

young man: *see adulescens; iuvenis; neaniskos; neos; neoteros*
  designated from youth to succeed to his father's seat in the city council: *see patroboulos*
young men: *see iuvenes; neaniskoi; neoi; neoteroi*
  association of *iuvenes*: *see iuventus*
  director of the *iuvenes*: *see magister iuvenum*
  games of *iuvenes*: *see lusus iuvenum*
  prefect of the *iuvenes*: *see praefectus iuvenum*
  sons of councillors waiting to take their fathers' seats in the council: *see praetextati*
youth (stage of life): *see adulescentia; iuventa; iuventus*
youthful sense of life, 20, 146–8; *see also* Persius; *poetae novi*

Zeus
  Chrysaoreios Propator, 173
  Panamaros, 173
  Panemer(i)os, 51, 52